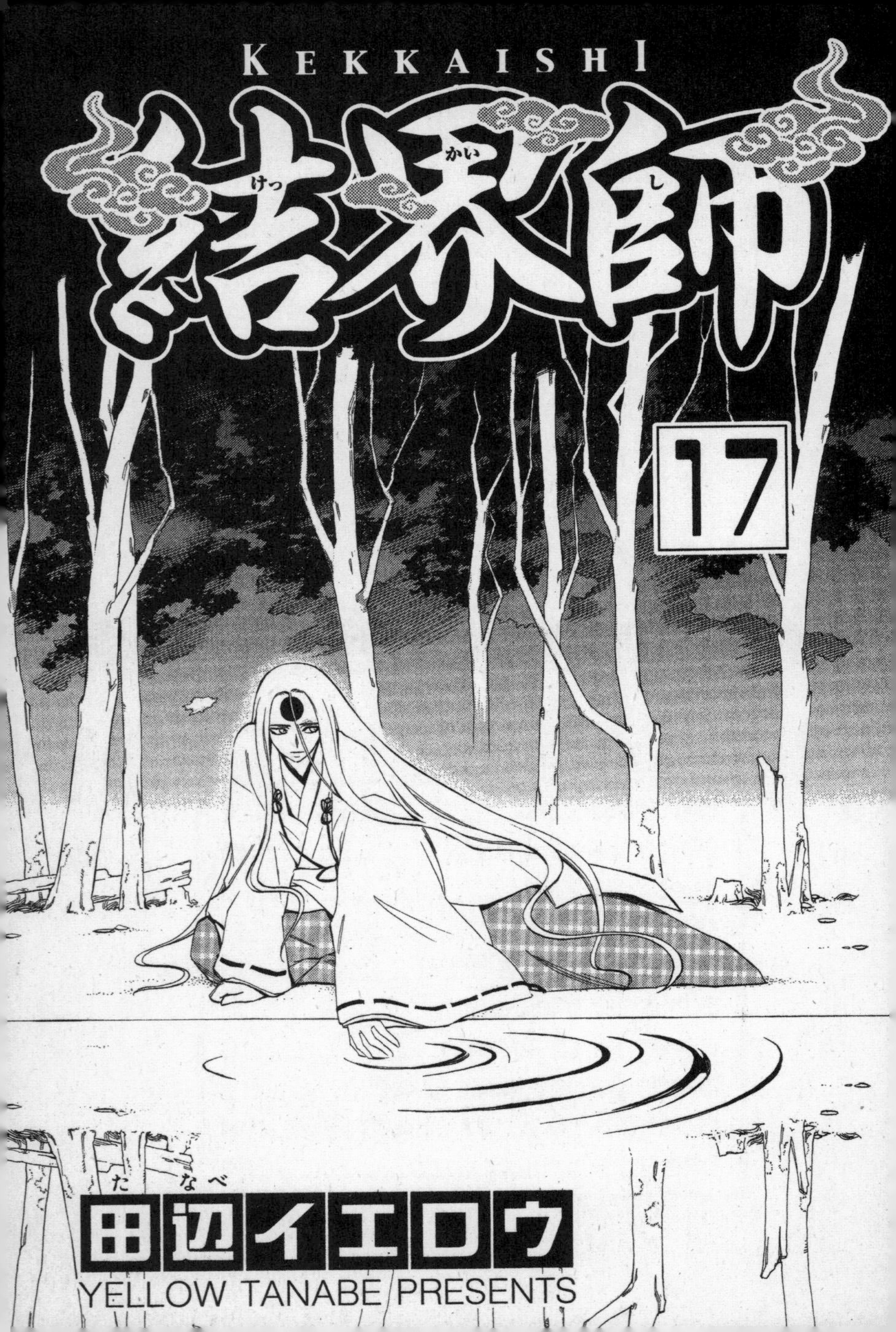
KEKKAISHI
結界師
17
田辺イエロウ
YELLOW TANABE PRESENTS

THE Story THUS Far

Yoshimori Sumimura and Tokine Yukimura have an ancestral duty to protect the Karasumori Forest from supernatural beings called ayakashi. People with their gift for terminating ayakashi are called kekkaishi, or "barrier masters."

Lately the ayakashi have been relentlessly attacking the Karasumori site. This has caused the shadow organization to assert more and more control over the site. As they struggle to deal with these situations, Yoshimori and Tokine gradually perfect their kekkaishi skills.

With school out for spring break Yoshimori is feeling very happy - that is until he receives a phone call from his brother Masamori asking for help. Yoshimori reluctantly agrees to assist Masamori and travels with him to a holy site that is a gateway to the other world. The reason Masamori has for bringing his brother to this site is still unclear.

KEKKAISHI   VOL. 17
TABLE OF CONTENTS

CHapter 155: ABYSS 5

CHapter 156: Deity TAN-YU 23

CHapter 157: MUDO 41

CHapter 158: OLD ALLY 59

CHapter 159: GENUINE ZeKKai 77

CHapter 160: IMMOrtaLitY 95

CHapter 161: IMPERFECTION 113

CHapter 162: MASAMORI'S CHoice 131

CHapter 163: THE GUARDIAN Deity'S Power 147

CHapter 164: JeaLOUSY 165

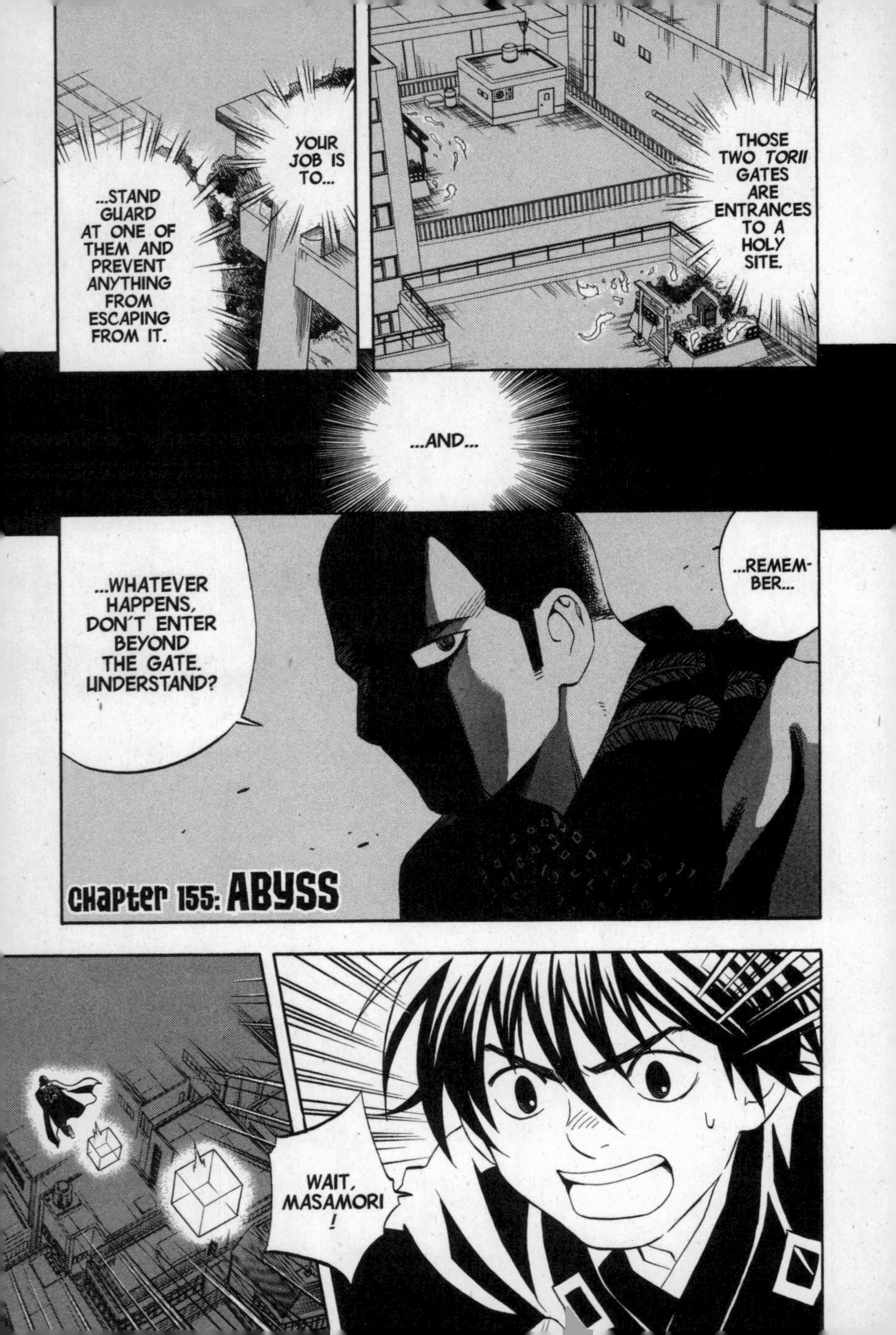
THOSE TWO TORII GATES ARE ENTRANCES TO A HOLY SITE.
YOUR JOB IS TO...
...STAND GUARD AT ONE OF THEM AND PREVENT ANYTHING FROM ESCAPING FROM IT.
...AND...
...REMEMBER...
...WHATEVER HAPPENS, DON'T ENTER BEYOND THE GATE. UNDERSTAND?
Chapter 155: ABYSS
WAIT, MASAMORI!

Chapter 155: Abyss

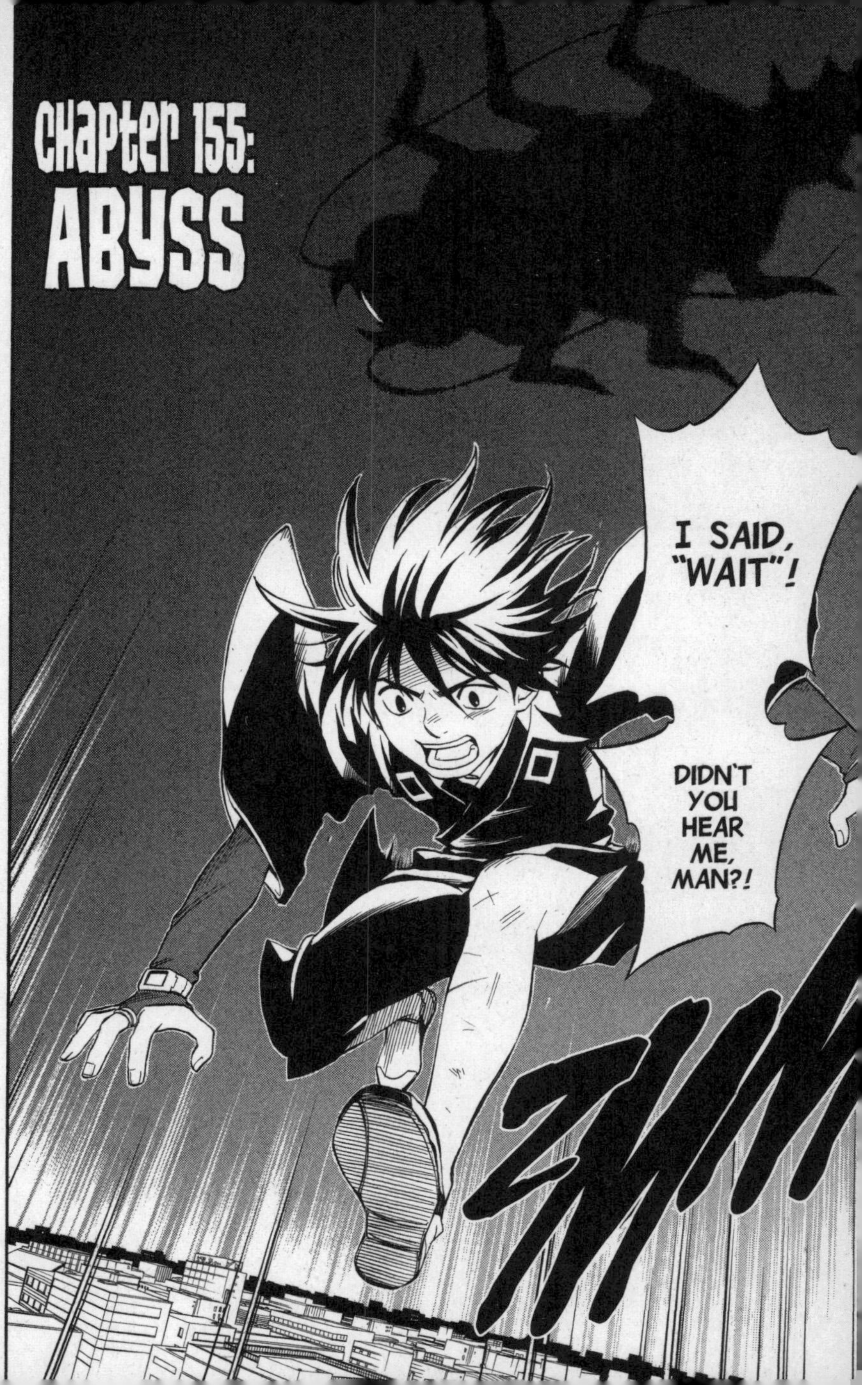
I SAID, "WAIT"!
DIDN'T YOU HEAR ME, MAN?!

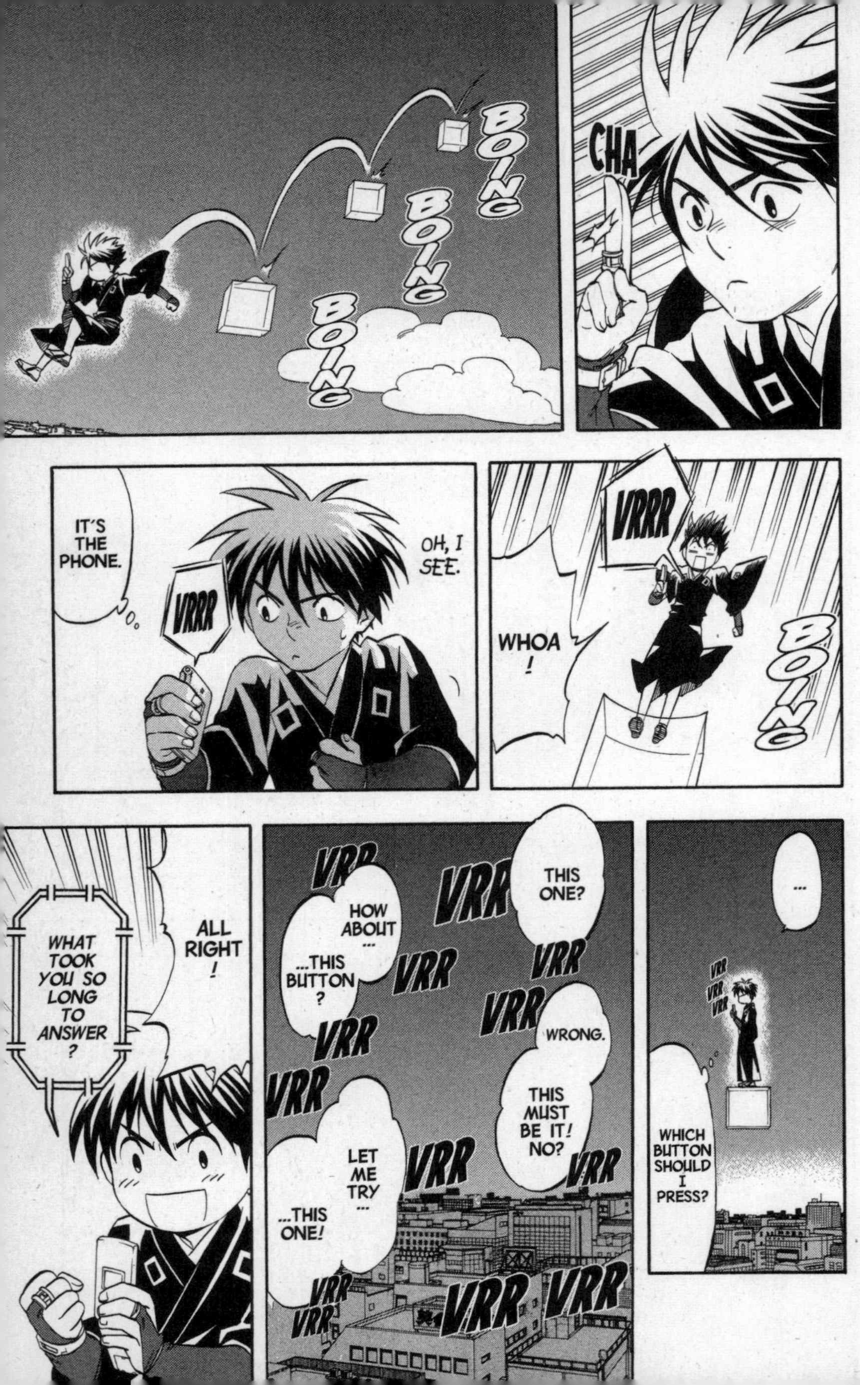
CHA
BOING
BOING
BOING
VRRR
WHOA!
BOING
OH, I SEE.
IT'S THE PHONE.
VRRR
...
VRR
VRR
VRR
WHICH BUTTON SHOULD I PRESS?
THIS ONE?
VRR
HOW ABOUT...
...THIS BUTTON?
VRR
WRONG.
THIS MUST BE IT! NO?
VRR
LET ME TRY...
...THIS ONE!
VRR
ALL RIGHT!
WHAT TOOK YOU SO LONG TO ANSWER?

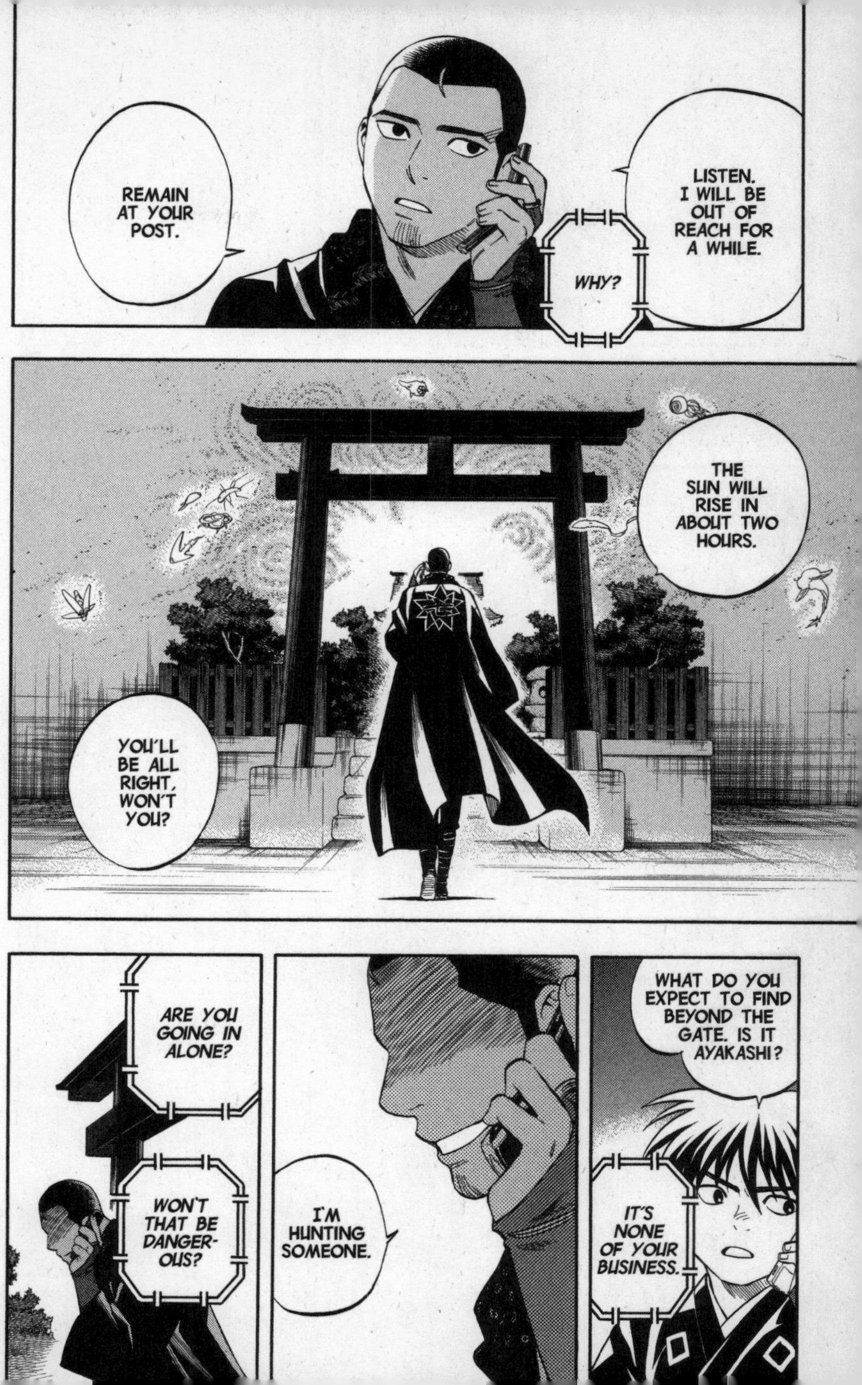
LISTEN. I WILL BE OUT OF REACH FOR A WHILE.
WHY?
REMAIN AT YOUR POST.
THE SUN WILL RISE IN ABOUT TWO HOURS.
YOU'LL BE ALL RIGHT, WON'T YOU?
WHAT DO YOU EXPECT TO FIND BEYOND THE GATE. IS IT AYAKASHI?
IT'S NONE OF YOUR BUSINESS.
I'M HUNTING SOMEONE.
ARE YOU GOING IN ALONE?
WON'T THAT BE DANGER-OUS?

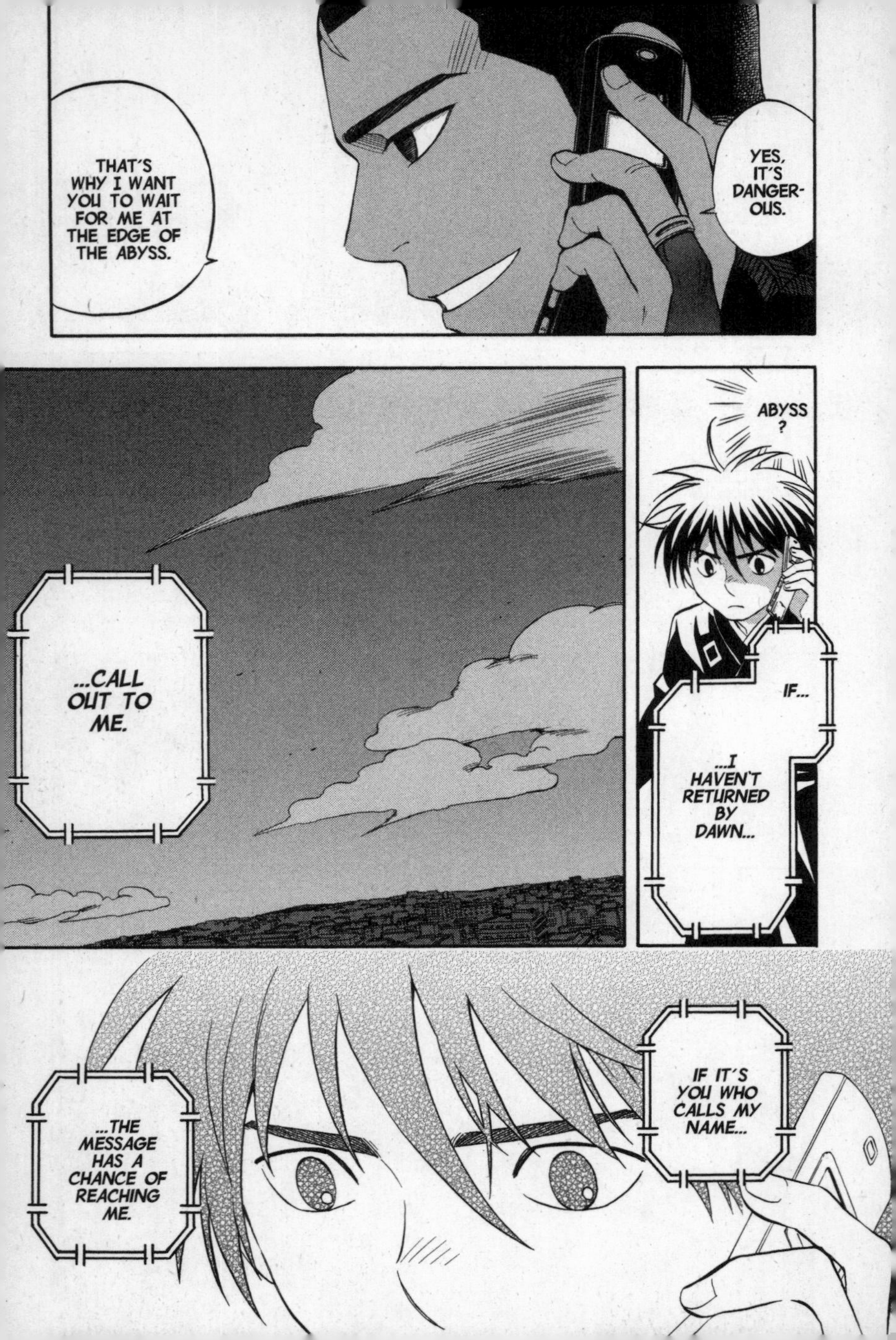
YES, IT'S DANGER-OUS.
THAT'S WHY I WANT YOU TO WAIT FOR ME AT THE EDGE OF THE ABYSS.
ABYSS?
IF...
...I HAVEN'T RETURNED BY DAWN...
...CALL OUT TO ME.
IF IT'S YOU WHO CALLS MY NAME...
...THE MESSAGE HAS A CHANCE OF REACHING ME.

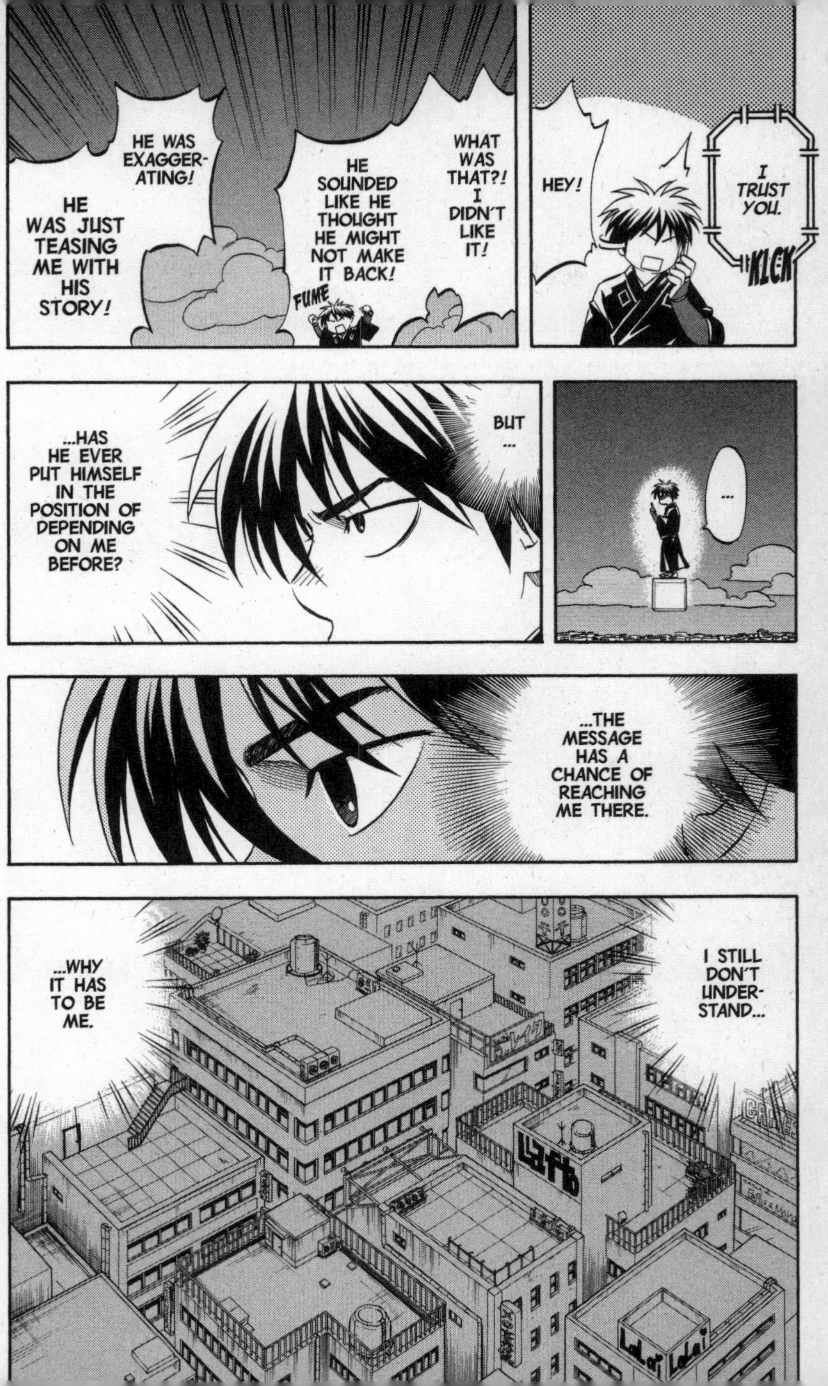
I TRUST YOU.
HEY!
KICK
WHAT WAS THAT?! I DIDN'T LIKE IT!
HE SOUNDED LIKE HE THOUGHT HE MIGHT NOT MAKE IT BACK!
HE WAS EXAGGER-ATING!
HE WAS JUST TEASING ME WITH HIS STORY!
FUME
...
BUT ...
...HAS HE EVER PUT HIMSELF IN THE POSITION OF DEPENDING ON ME BEFORE?
...THE MESSAGE HAS A CHANCE OF REACHING ME THERE.
I STILL DON'T UNDER-STAND...
...WHY IT HAS TO BE ME.

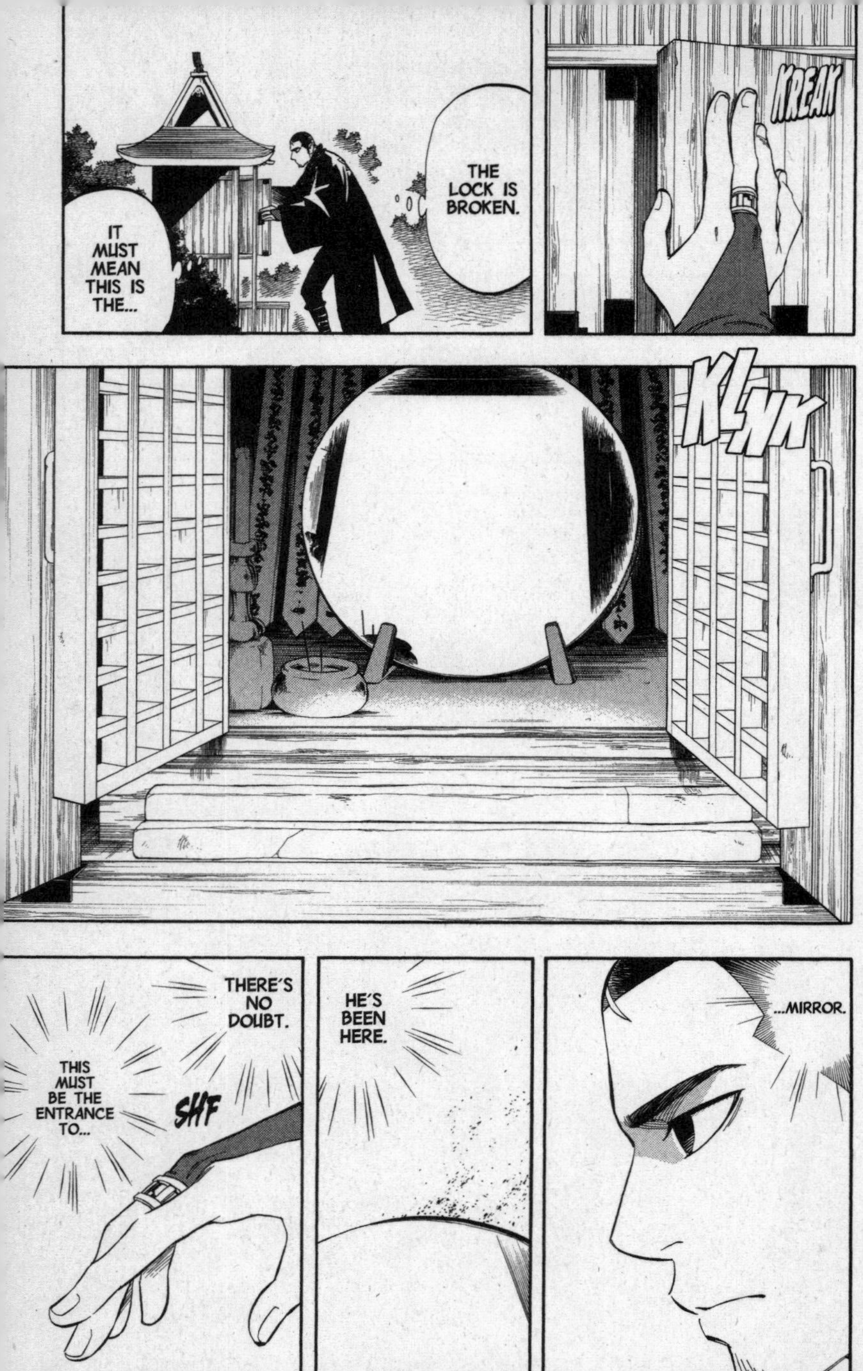
KREAK
THE LOCK IS BROKEN.
IT MUST MEAN THIS IS THE...
KLNK
...MIRROR.
HE'S BEEN HERE.
THERE'S NO DOUBT.
THIS MUST BE THE ENTRANCE TO...
SHF

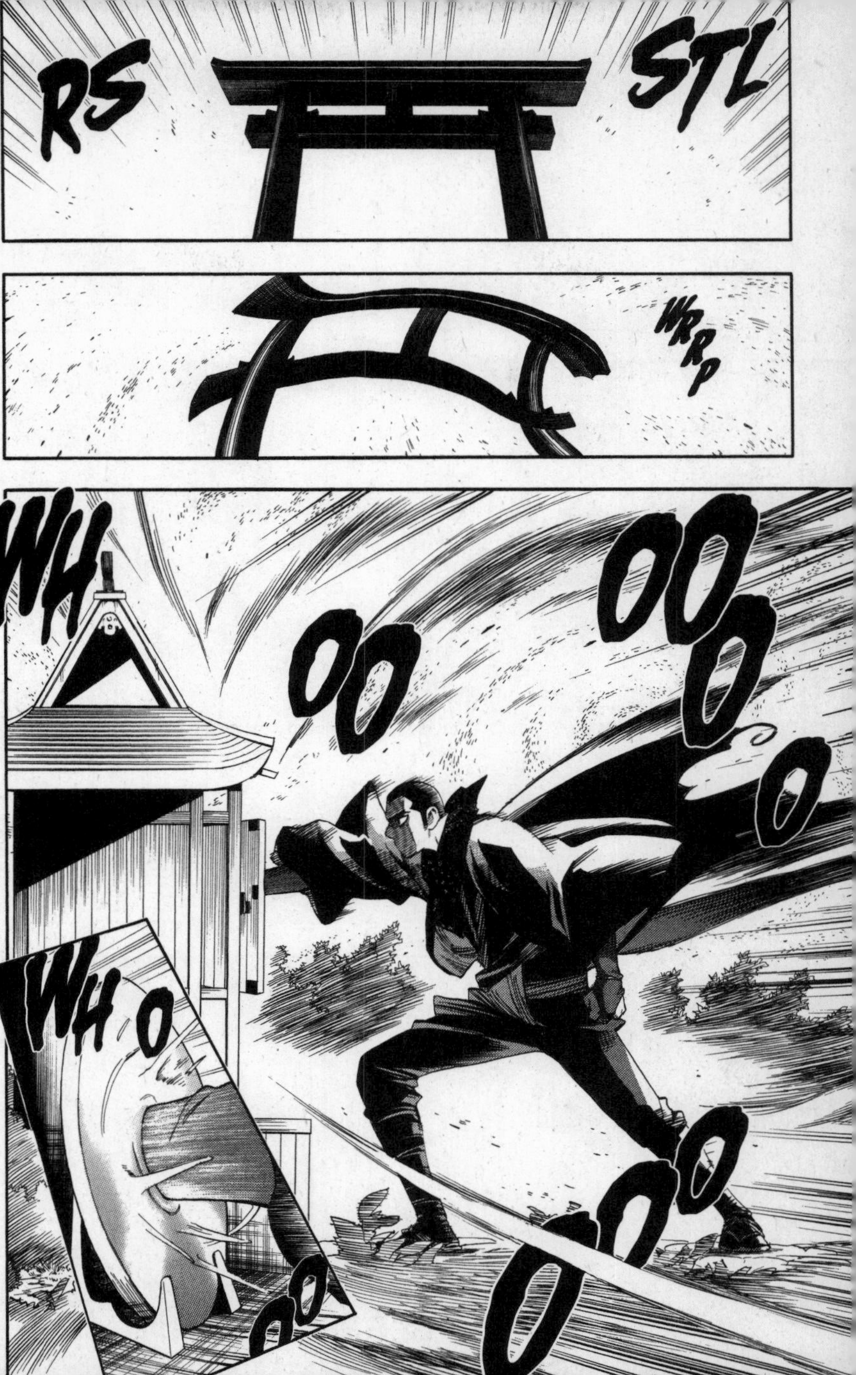
RS
STL
WRRP
WHOOOOOOO
WHOOOO

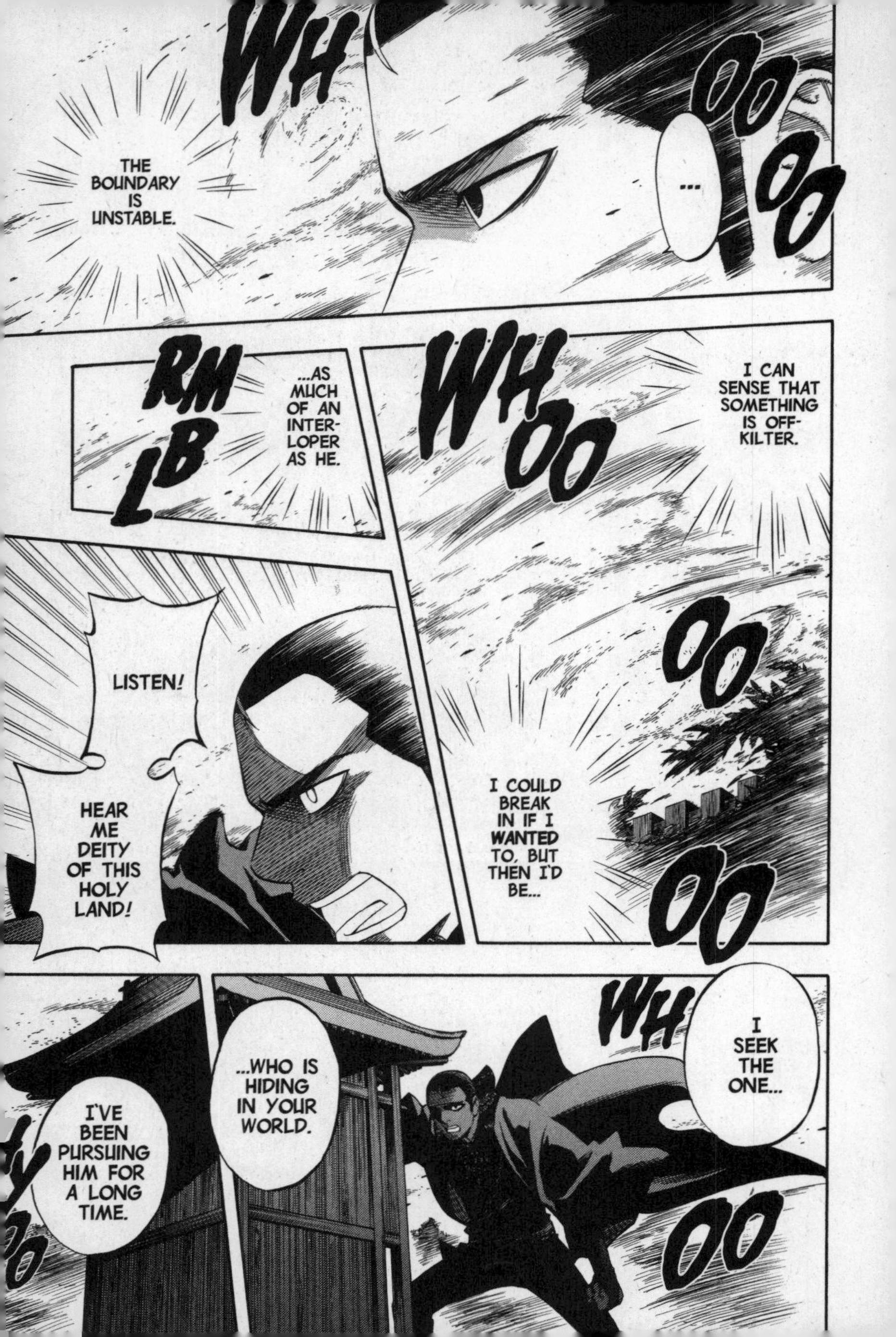
WHOOOOOO
...
THE BOUNDARY IS UNSTABLE.
WHOO
I CAN SENSE THAT SOMETHING IS OFF-KILTER.
OOOO
I COULD BREAK IN IF I WANTED TO, BUT THEN I'D BE...
RMBL
...AS MUCH OF AN INTER-LOPER AS HE.
LISTEN!
HEAR ME DEITY OF THIS HOLY LAND!
WH
I SEEK THE ONE...
OO
...WHO IS HIDING IN YOUR WORLD.
I'VE BEEN PURSUING HIM FOR A LONG TIME.

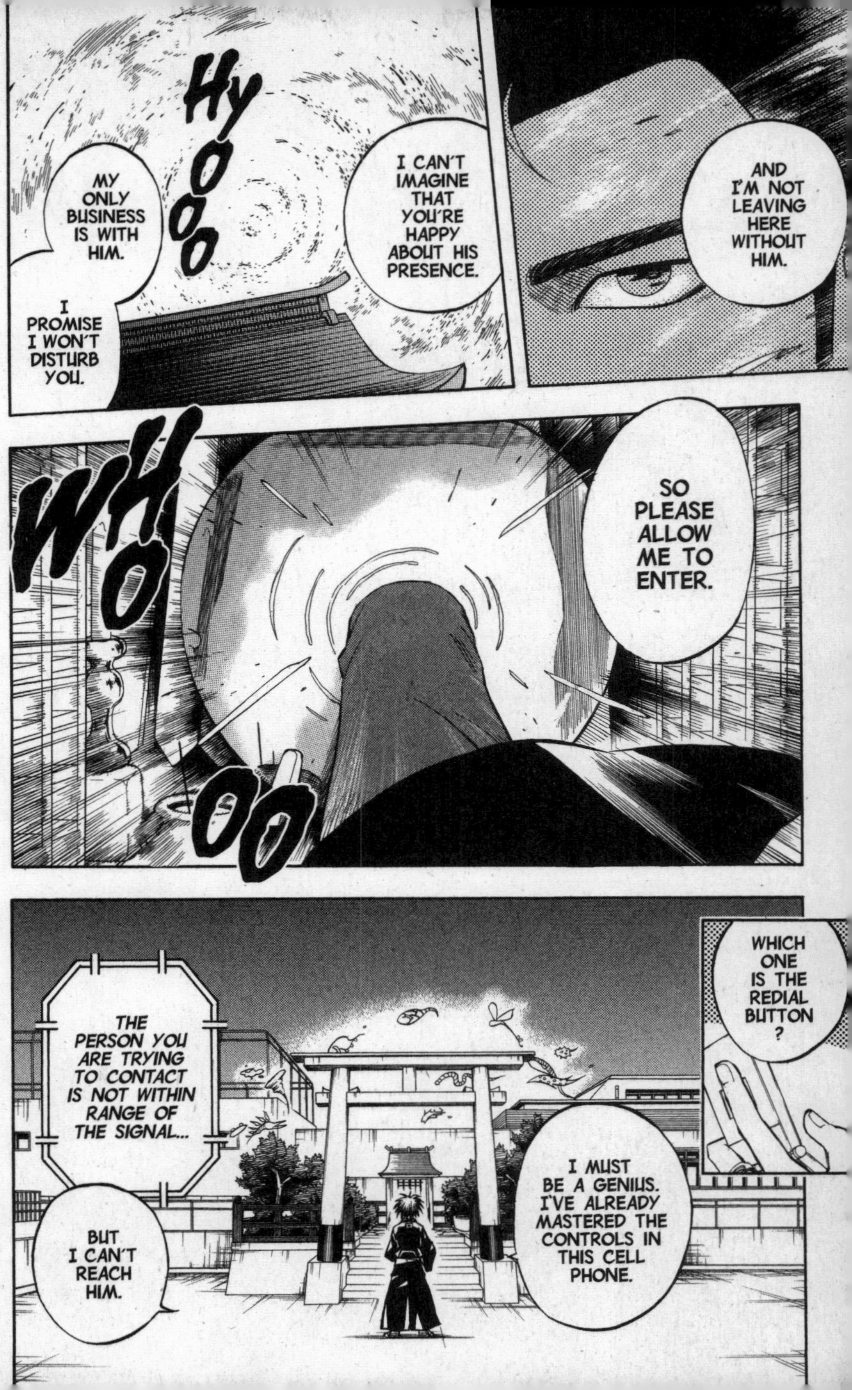
AND I'M NOT LEAVING HERE WITHOUT HIM.
I CAN'T IMAGINE THAT YOU'RE HAPPY ABOUT HIS PRESENCE.
HYOOOO
MY ONLY BUSINESS IS WITH HIM.
I PROMISE I WON'T DISTURB YOU.
SO PLEASE ALLOW ME TO ENTER.
WHOOOO
WHICH ONE IS THE REDIAL BUTTON ?
I MUST BE A GENIUS. I'VE ALREADY MASTERED THE CONTROLS IN THIS CELL PHONE.
THE PERSON YOU ARE TRYING TO CONTACT IS NOT WITHIN RANGE OF THE SIGNAL...
BUT I CAN'T REACH HIM.

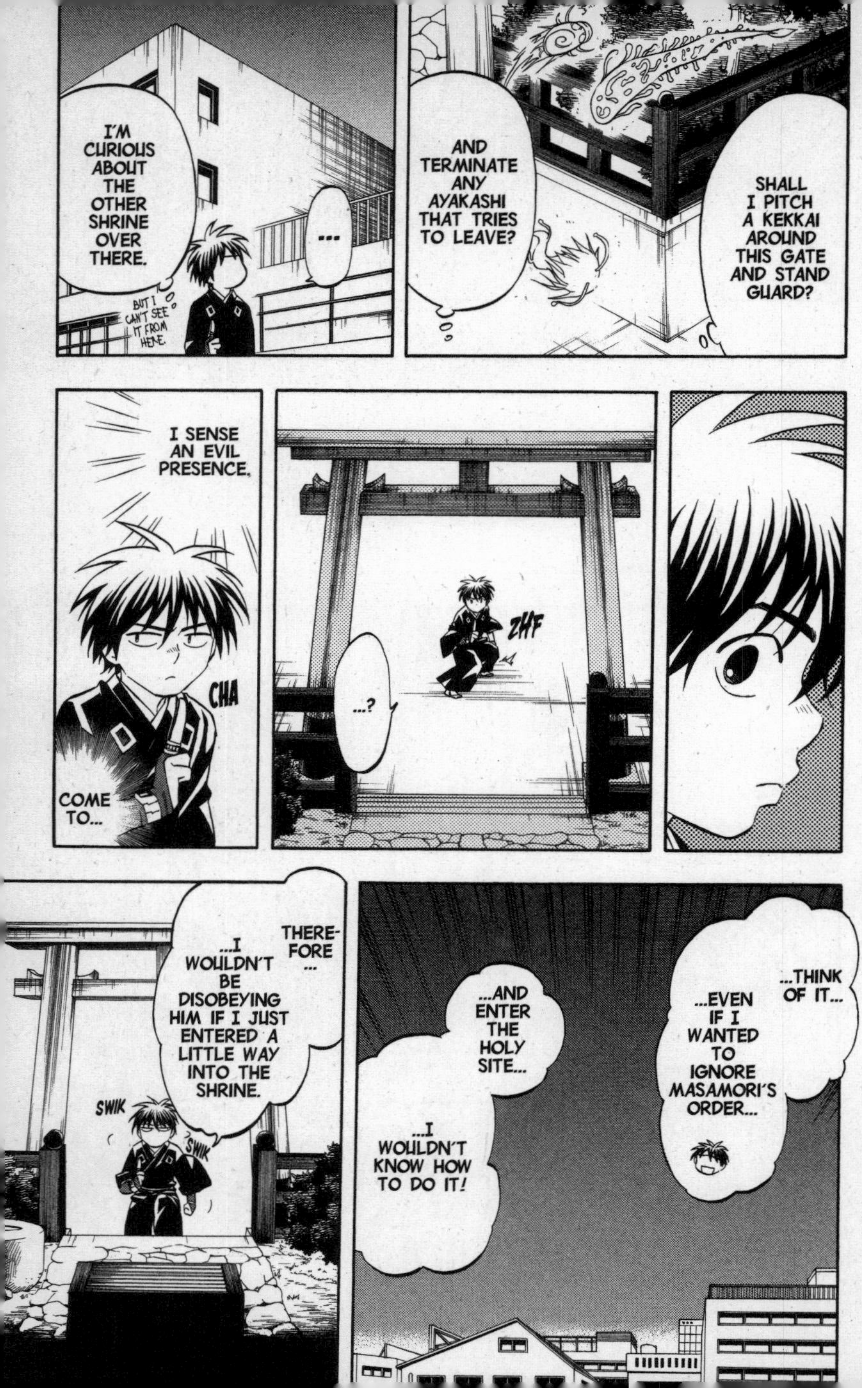
SHALL I PITCH A KEKKAI AROUND THIS GATE AND STAND GUARD?
AND TERMINATE ANY AYAKASHI THAT TRIES TO LEAVE?
I'M CURIOUS ABOUT THE OTHER SHRINE OVER THERE.
...
BUT I CAN'T SEE IT FROM HERE.
ZHF
...?
I SENSE AN EVIL PRESENCE.
CHA
COME TO...
...THINK OF IT...
...EVEN IF I WANTED TO IGNORE MASAMORI'S ORDER...
...AND ENTER THE HOLY SITE...
...I WOULDN'T KNOW HOW TO DO IT!
THEREFORE...
...I WOULDN'T BE DISOBEYING HIM IF I JUST ENTERED A LITTLE WAY INTO THE SHRINE.
SWIK
SWIK

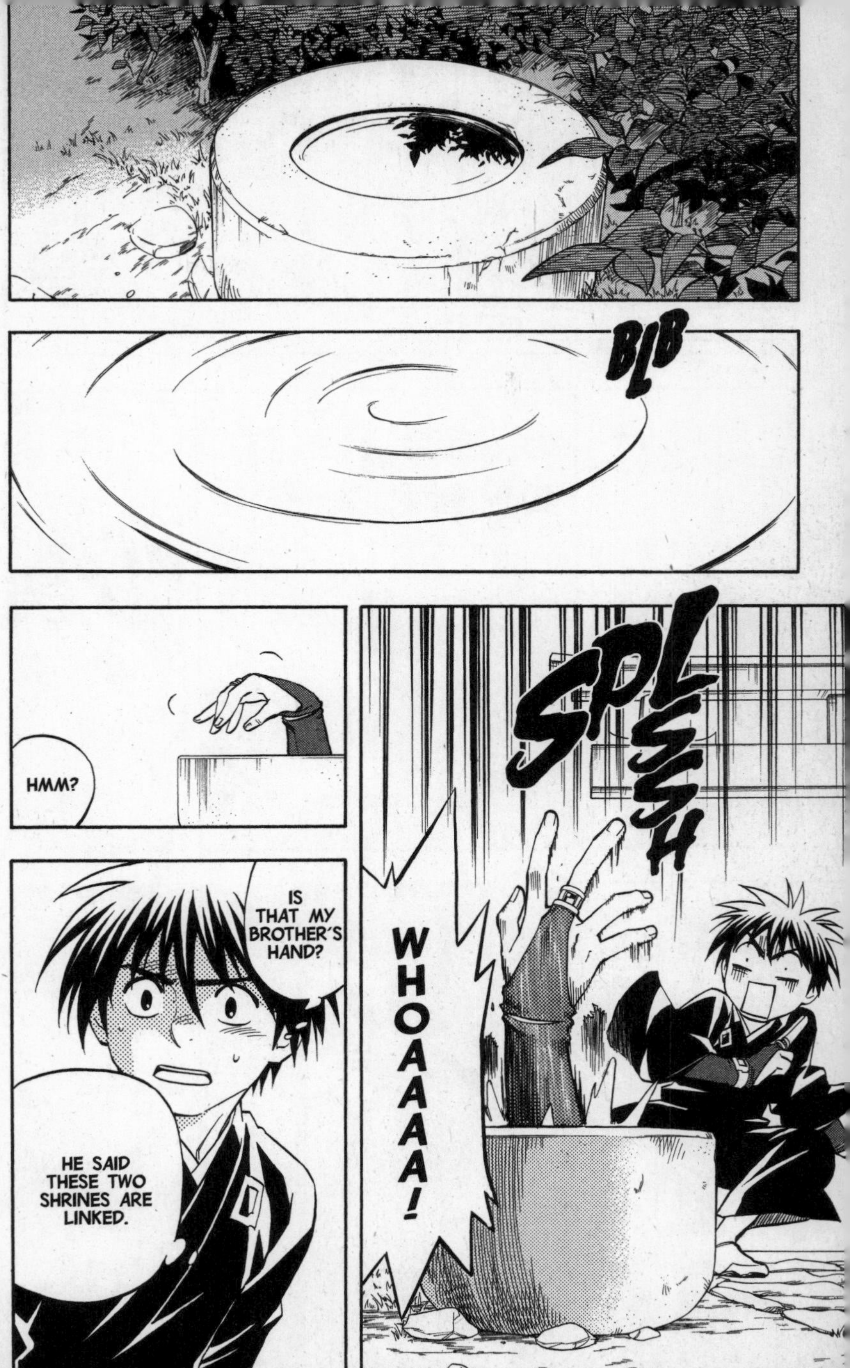
BLB
SPLSH
WHOAAAAA!
HMM?
IS THAT MY BROTHER'S HAND?
HE SAID THESE TWO SHRINES ARE LINKED.

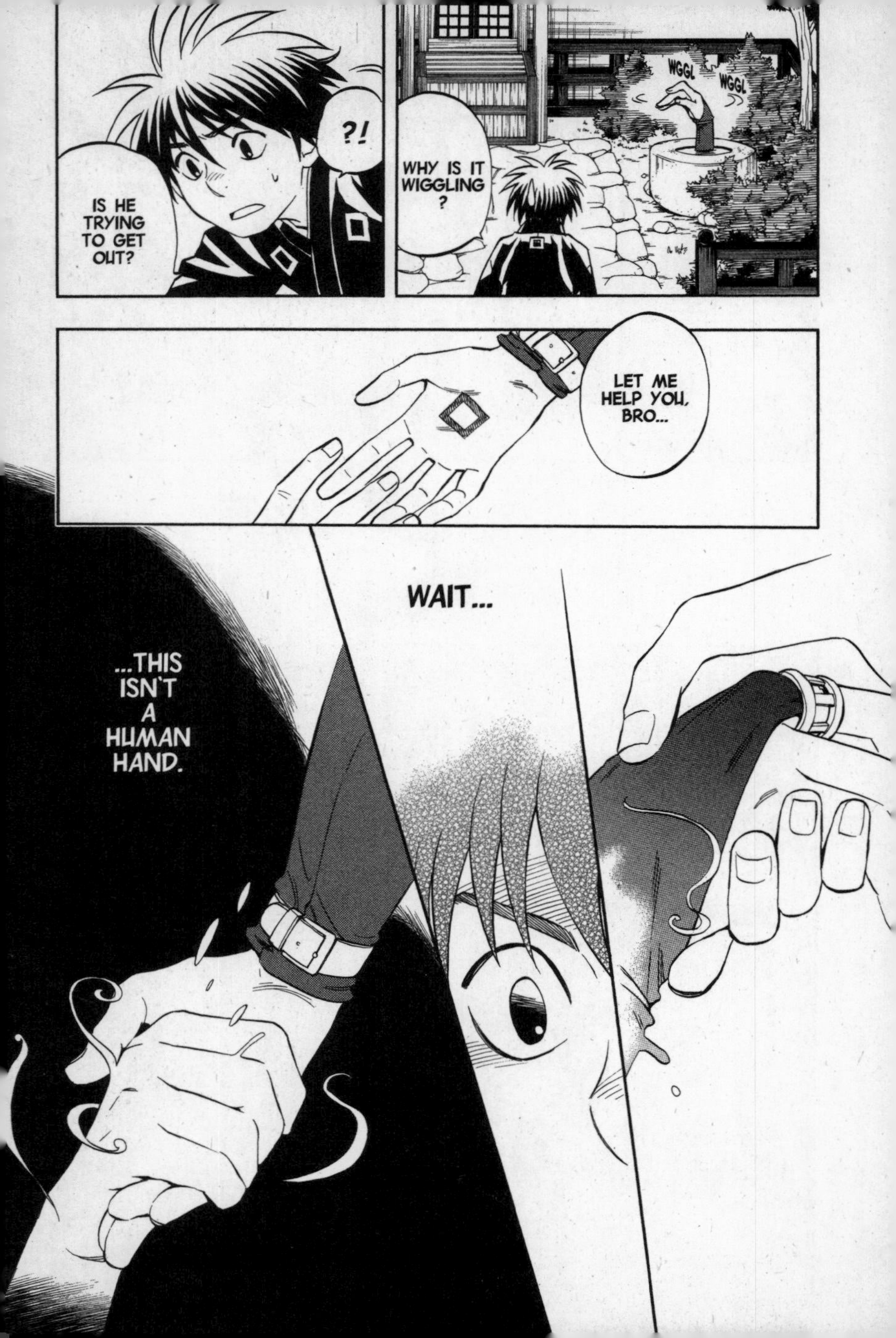
WGGL
WGGL
WHY IS IT WIGGLING?
?!
IS HE TRYING TO GET OUT?
LET ME HELP YOU, BRO...
WAIT...
...THIS ISN'T A HUMAN HAND.

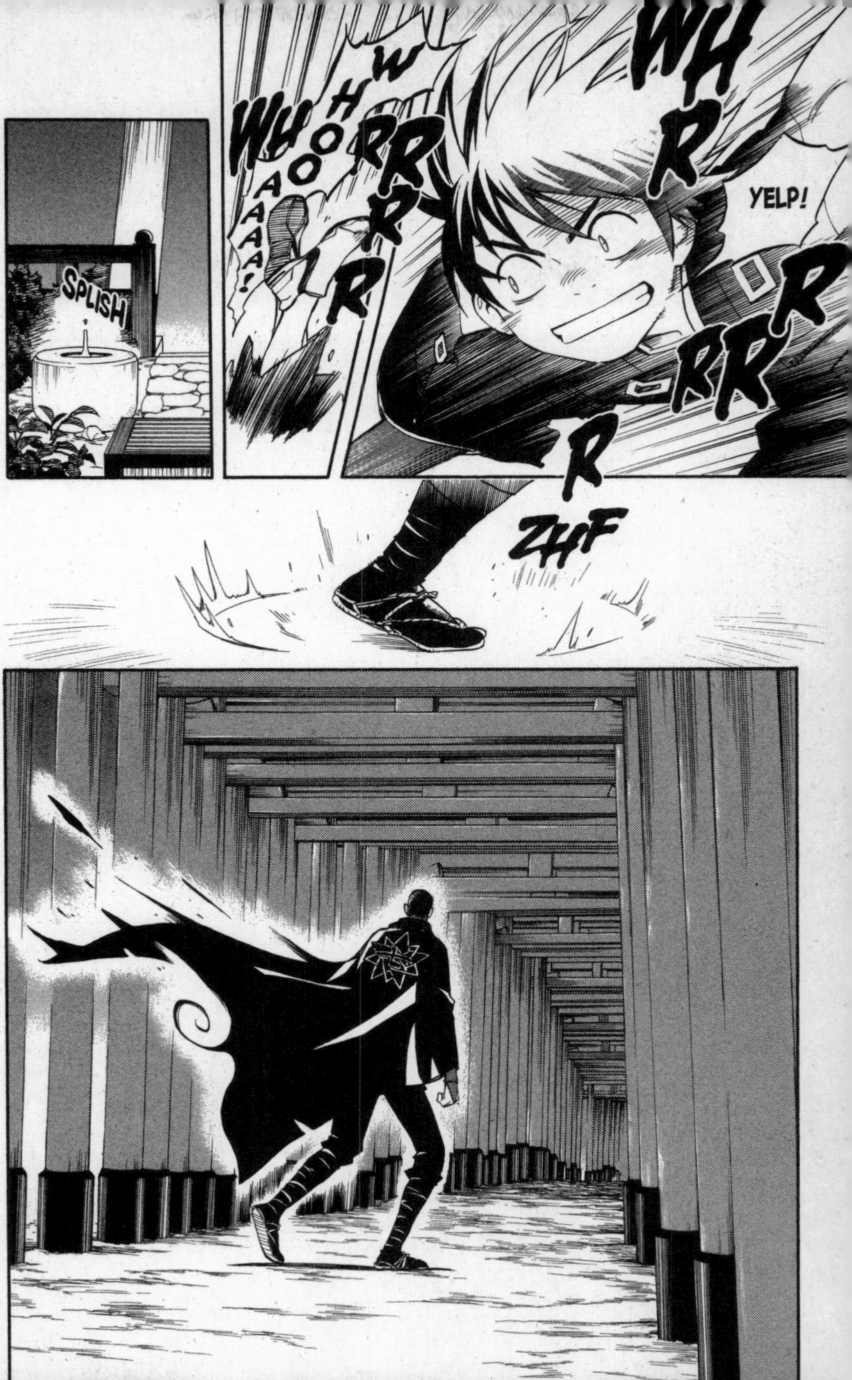
WHRRRRR
YELP!
WHOOOAAAA!
WHRRRR
SPLISH
ZHF

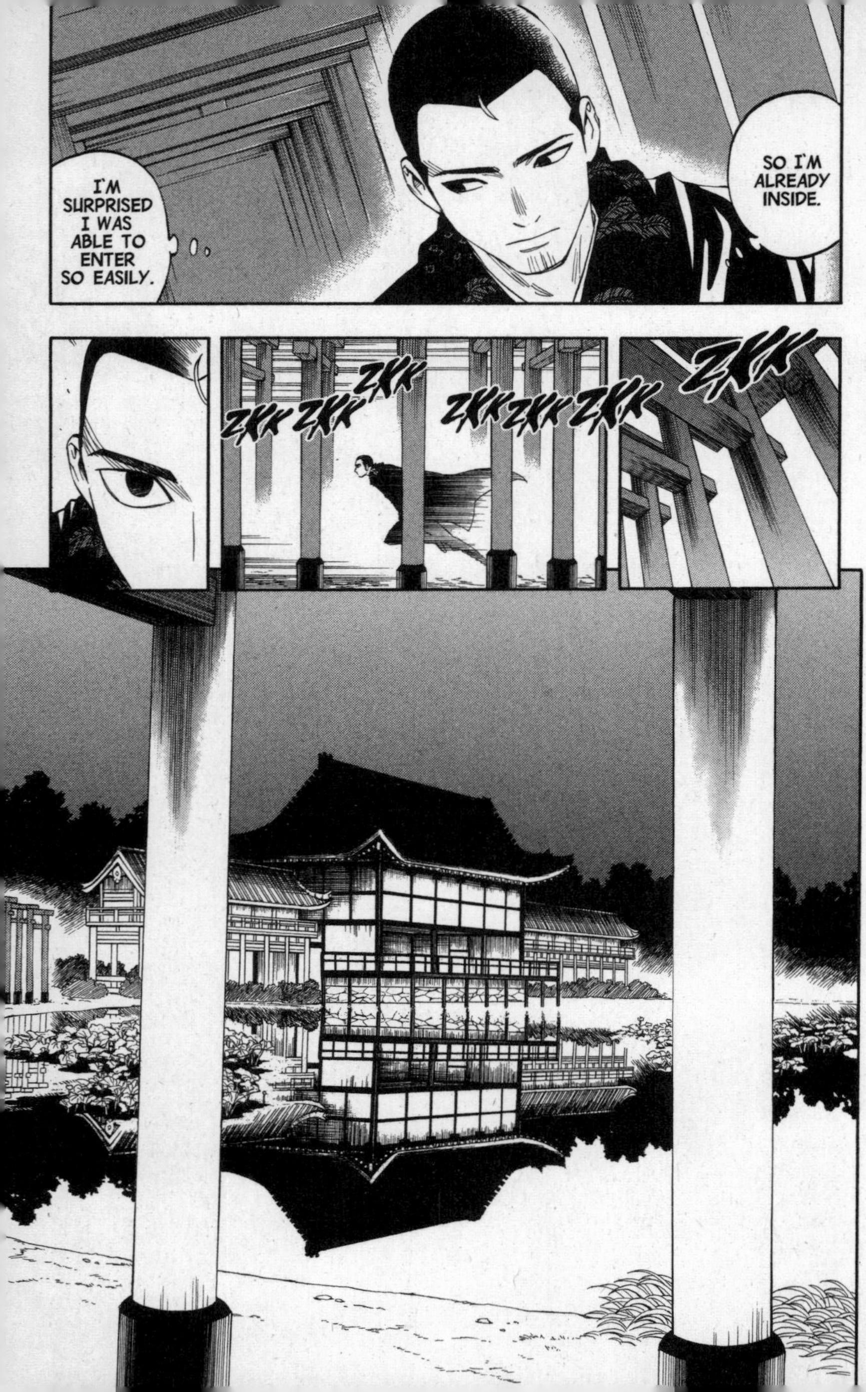
SO I'M ALREADY INSIDE.
I'M SURPRISED I WAS ABLE TO ENTER SO EASILY.
ZKK
ZKK ZKK ZKK
ZKK ZKK ZKK ZKK

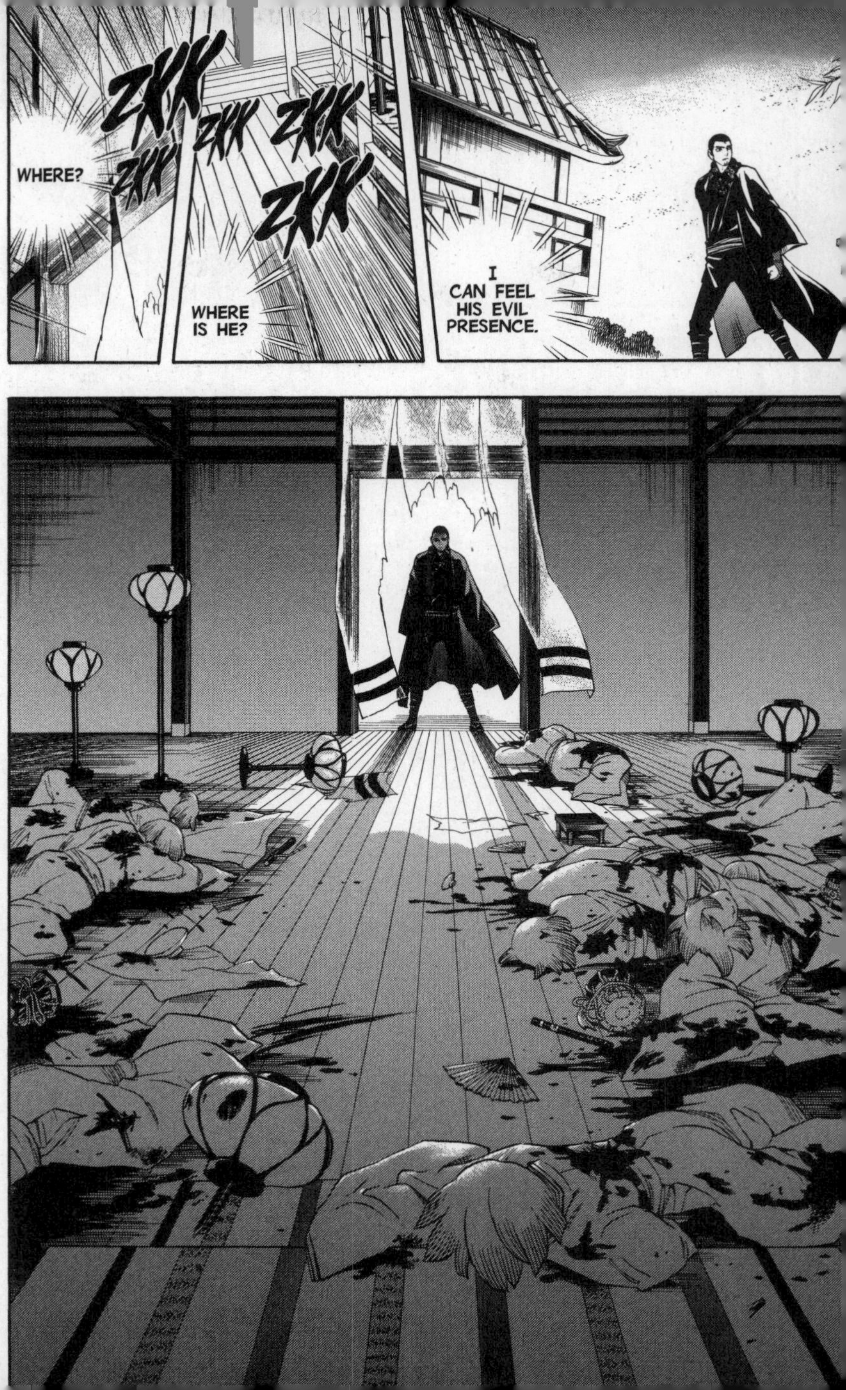

I CAN FEEL HIS EVIL PRESENCE.
ZKK
ZKK
WHERE IS HE?
ZKK
WHERE?
ZKK
ZKK

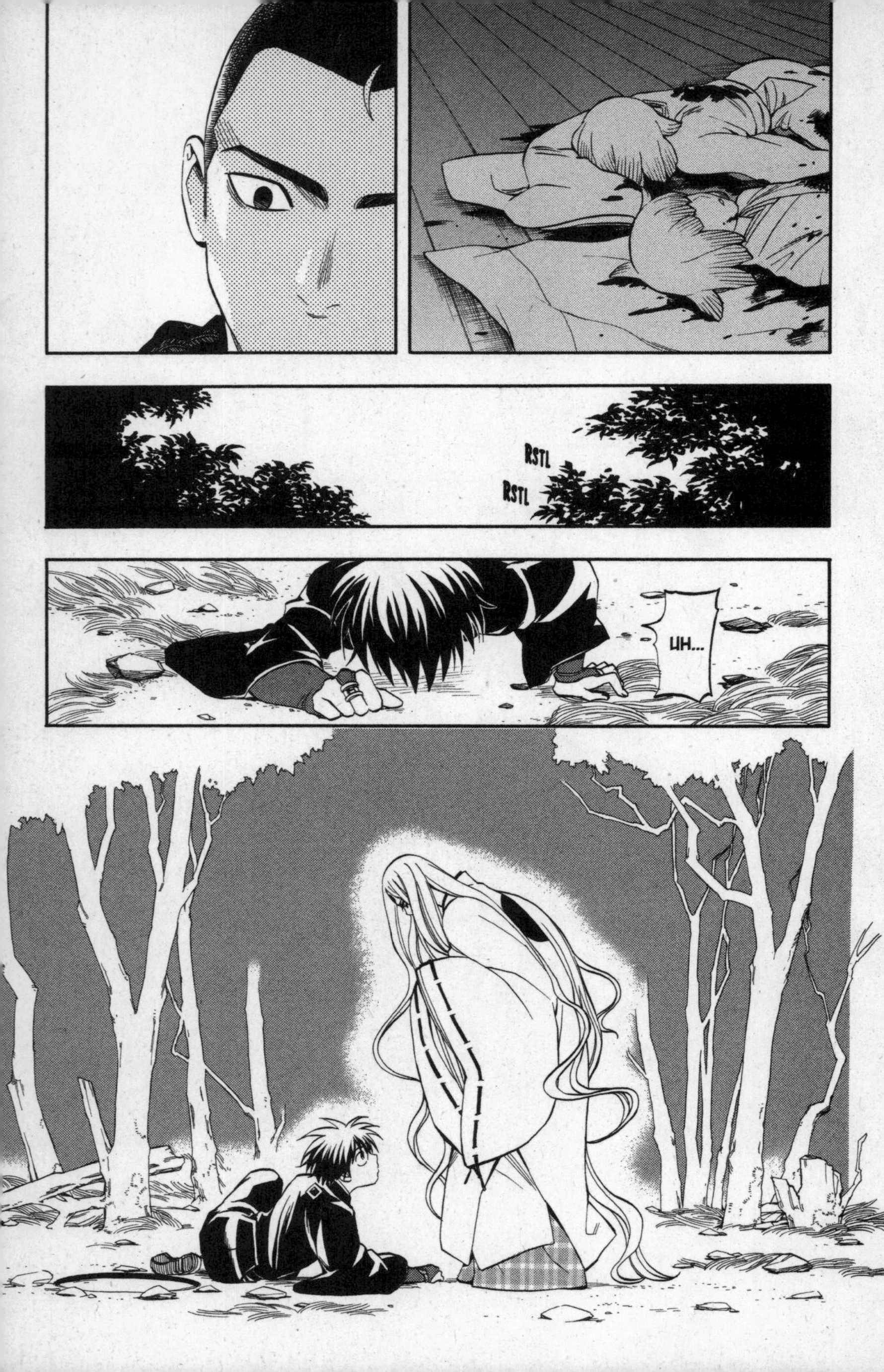
RSTL
RSTL
UH...

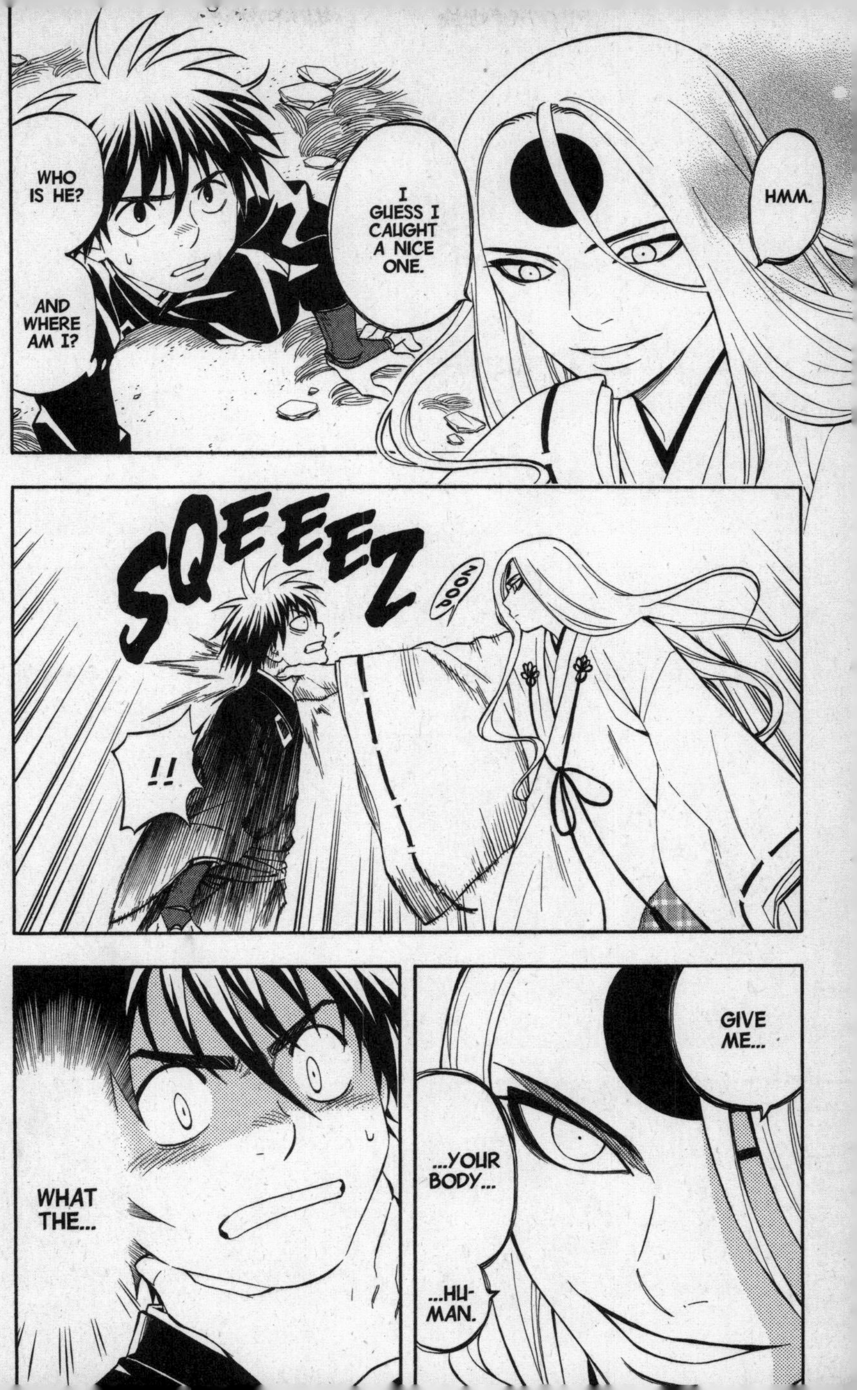
HMM.
I GUESS I CAUGHT A NICE ONE.
WHO IS HE?
AND WHERE AM I?
DOOP
SQEEEZ
!!
GIVE ME...
...YOUR BODY...
...HU-MAN.
WHAT THE...

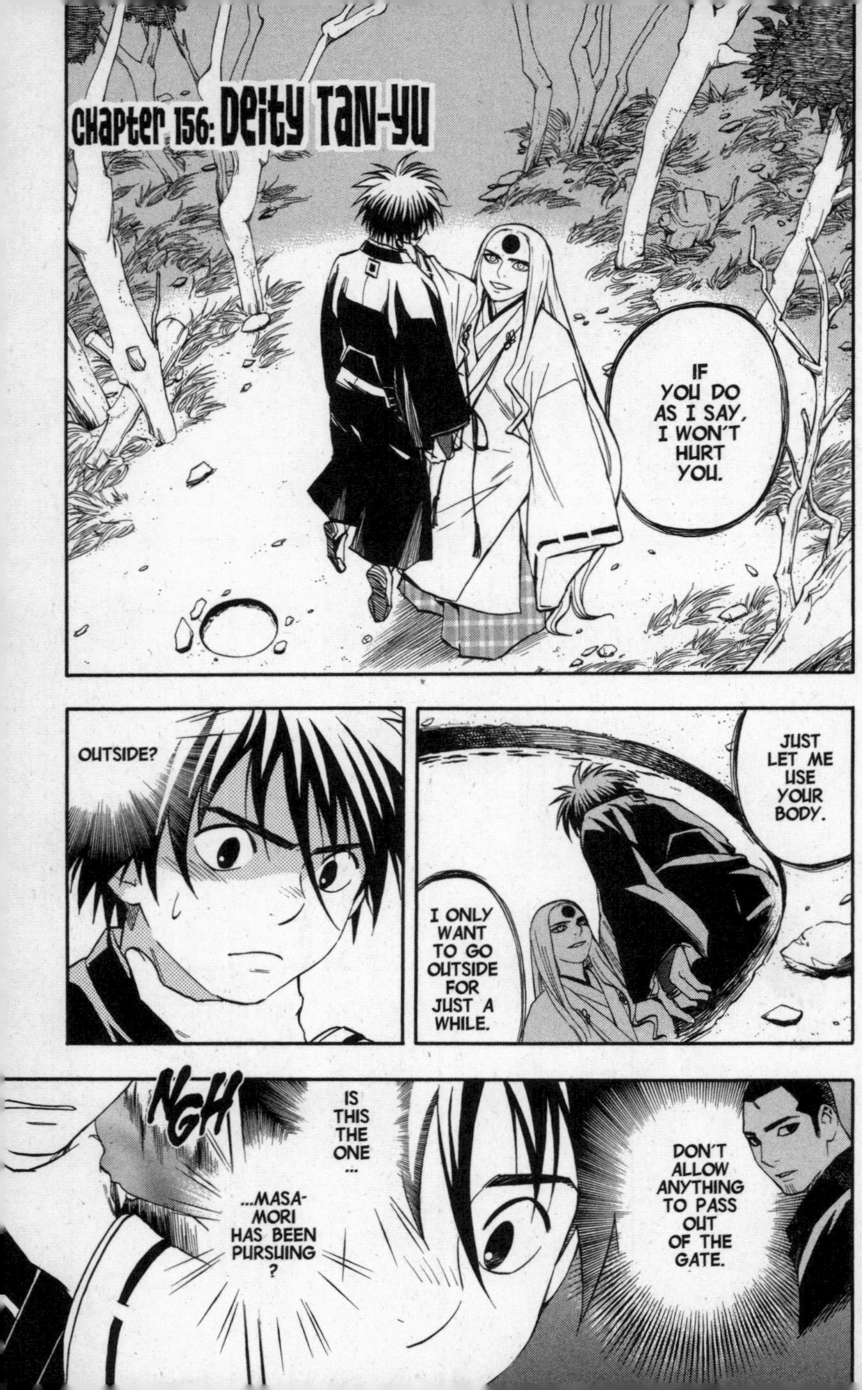
Chapter 156: Deity Tan-yu
IF YOU DO AS I SAY, I WON'T HURT YOU.
JUST LET ME USE YOUR BODY.
I ONLY WANT TO GO OUTSIDE FOR JUST A WHILE.
OUTSIDE?
DON'T ALLOW ANYTHING TO PASS OUT OF THE GATE.
IS THIS THE ONE...
...MASA-MORI HAS BEEN PURSUING?
NGH

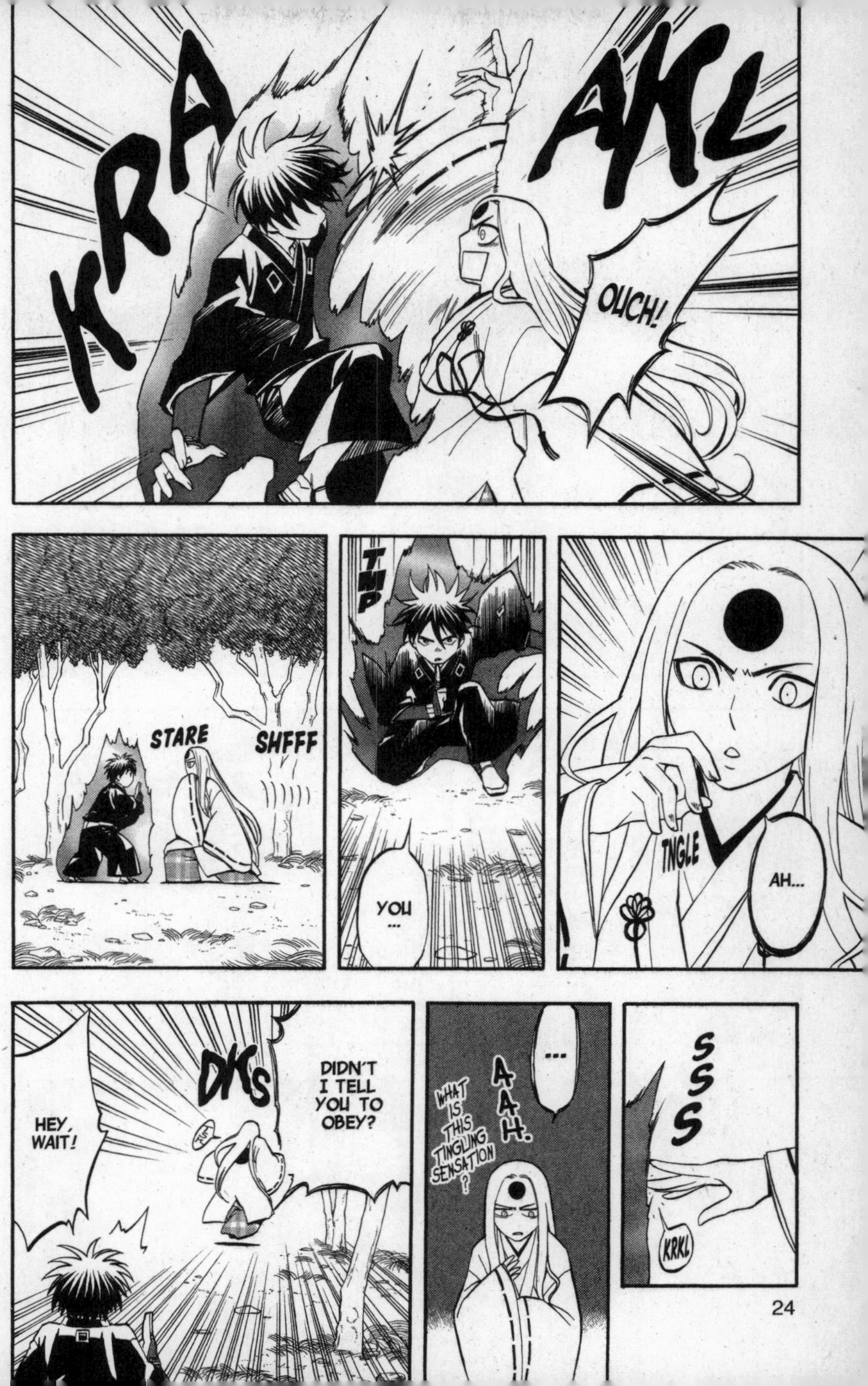
KRA
AKL
OUCH!
TNGLE
AH...
TMP
YOU ...
STARE
SHFFF
SSS
KRKL
...
AAH.
WHAT IS THIS TINGLING SENSATION?
DIDN'T I TELL YOU TO OBEY?
DKS
HEY, WAIT!

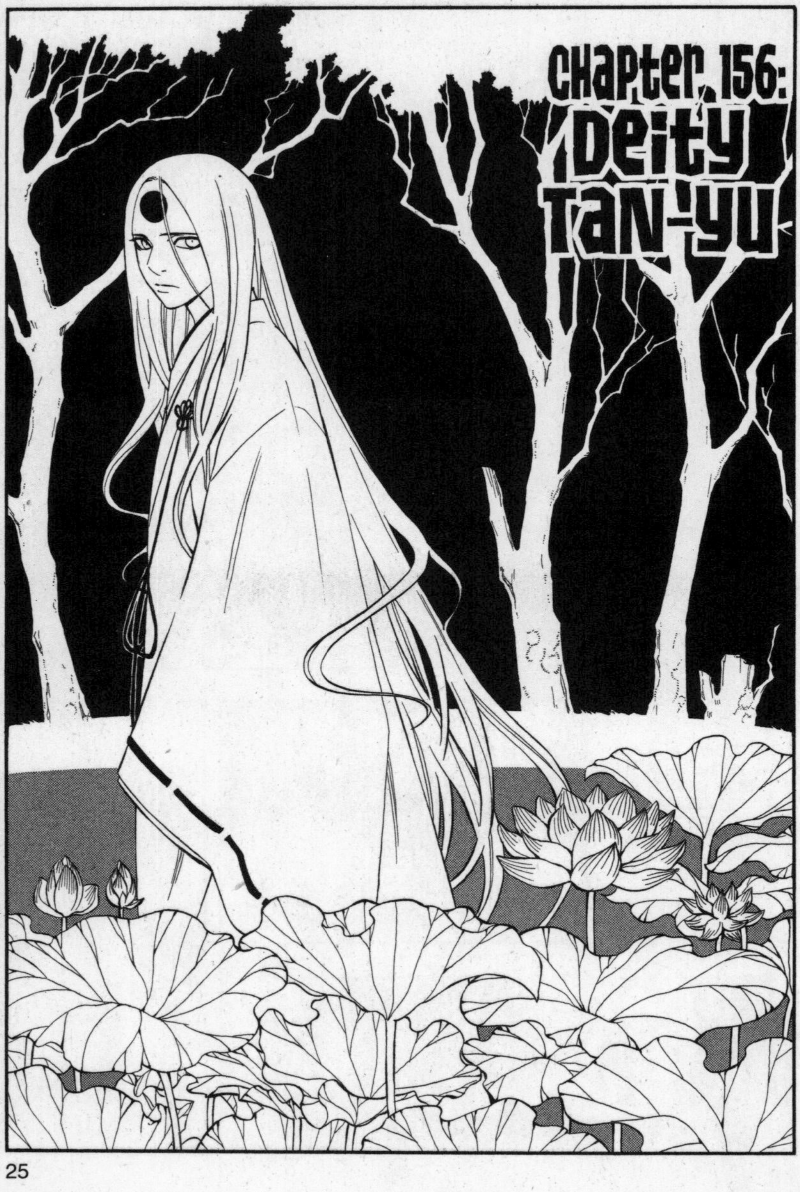
CHAPTER 156:
DEITY TAN-'YU

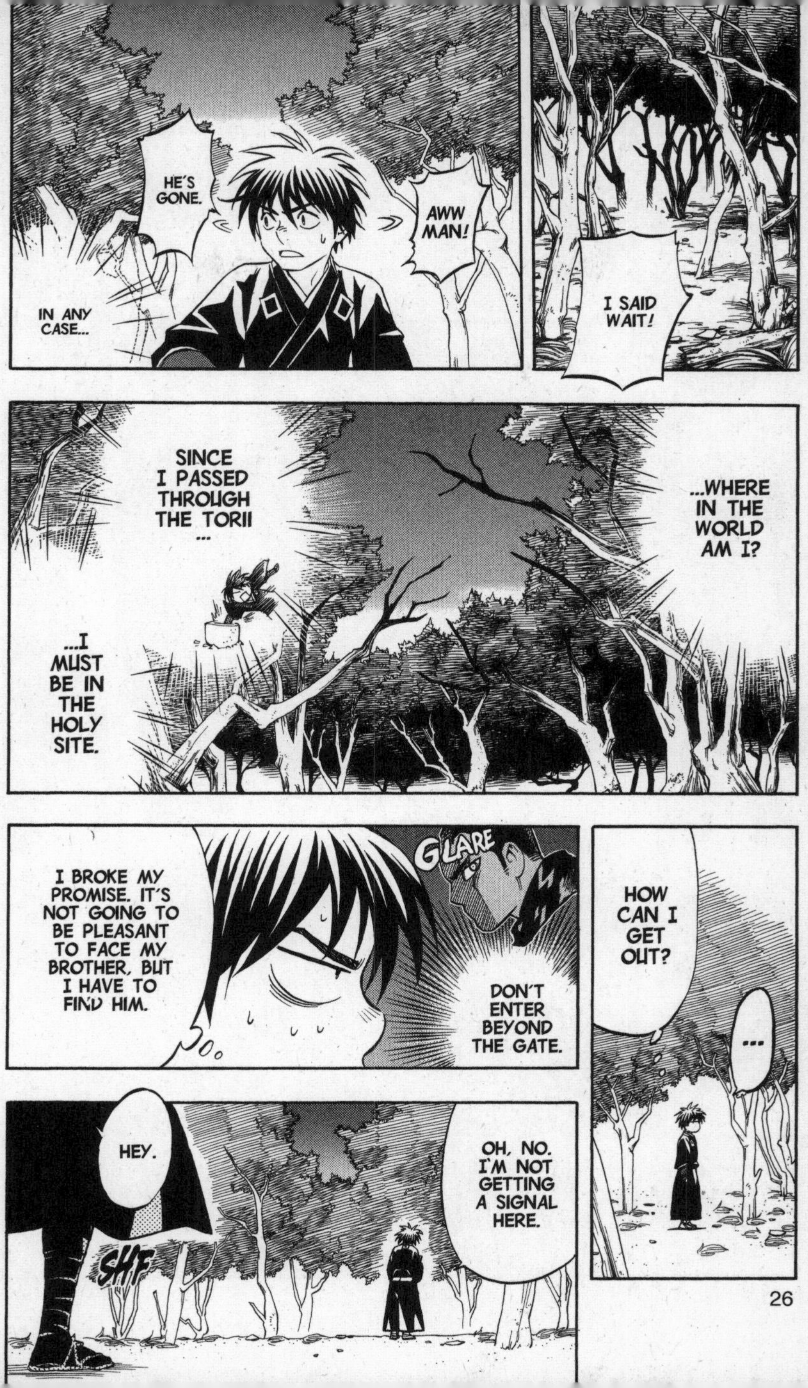
I SAID WAIT!
HE'S GONE.
AWW MAN!
IN ANY CASE...
SINCE I PASSED THROUGH THE TORII ...
...I MUST BE IN THE HOLY SITE.
...WHERE IN THE WORLD AM I?
HOW CAN I GET OUT?
...
GLARE
DON'T ENTER BEYOND THE GATE.
I BROKE MY PROMISE. IT'S NOT GOING TO BE PLEASANT TO FACE MY BROTHER, BUT I HAVE TO FIND HIM.
OH, NO. I'M NOT GETTING A SIGNAL HERE.
HEY.
SHF

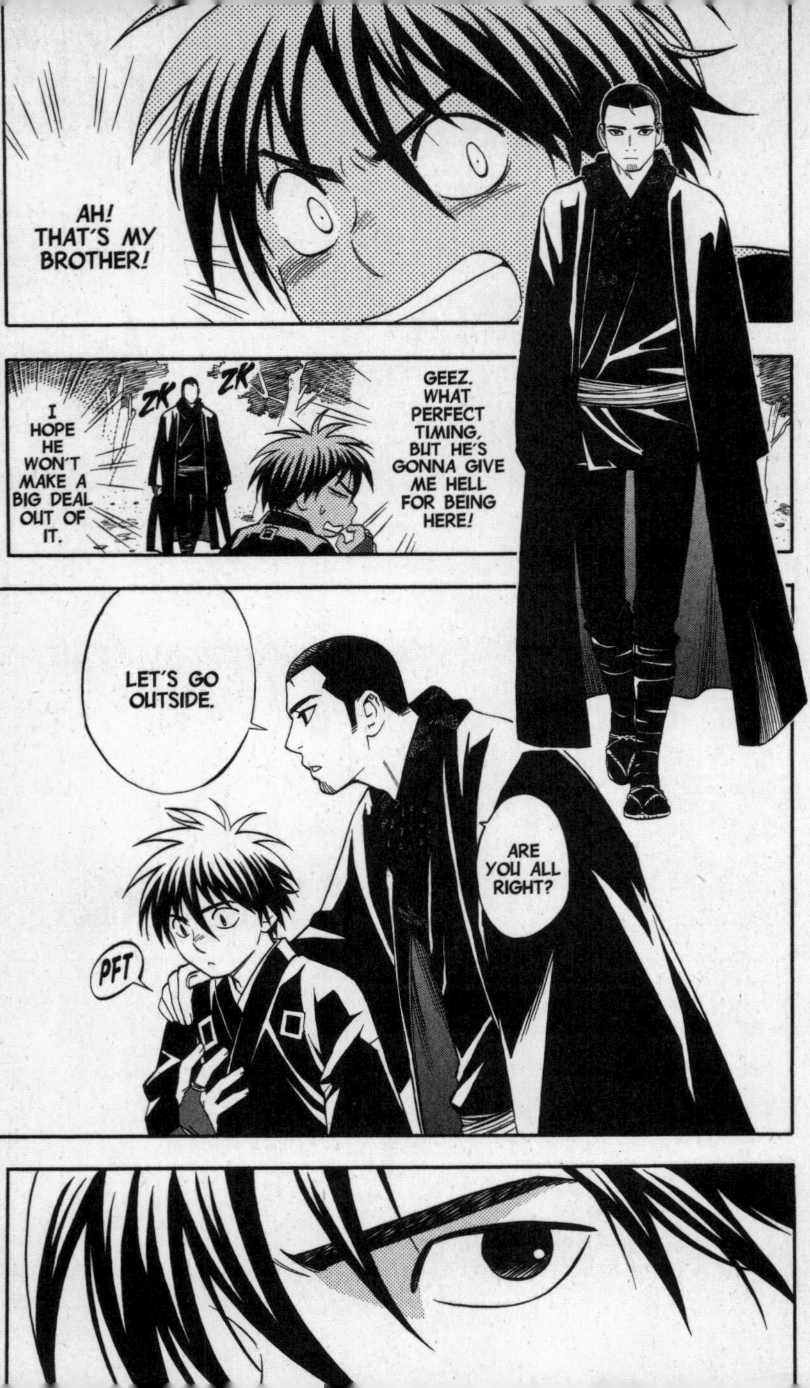
AH! THAT'S MY BROTHER!
ZK
ZK
GEEZ. WHAT PERFECT TIMING, BUT HE'S GONNA GIVE ME HELL FOR BEING HERE!
I HOPE HE WON'T MAKE A BIG DEAL OUT OF IT.
ARE YOU ALL RIGHT?
LET'S GO OUTSIDE.
PFT

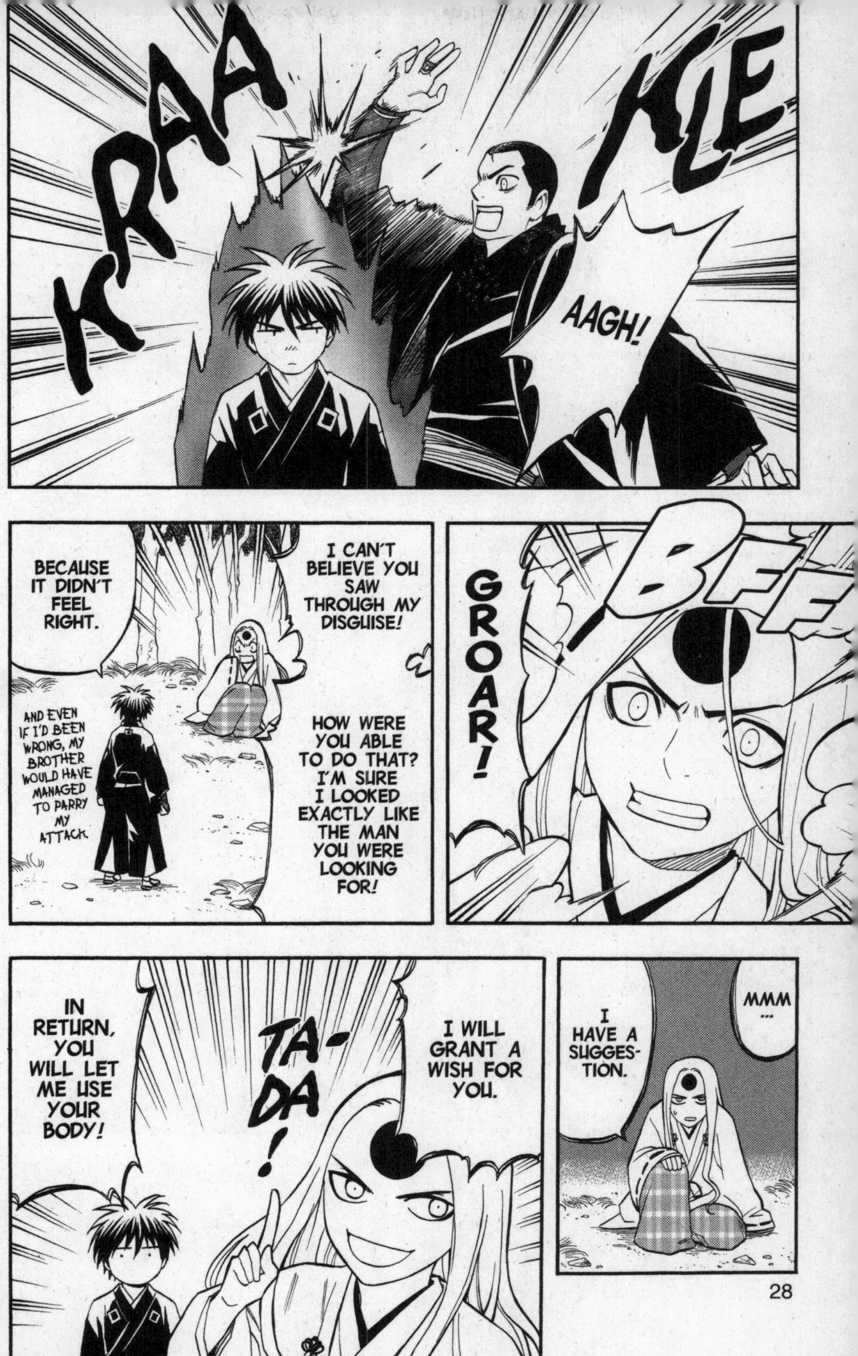
KRAAKLE
AAGH!
BFF
GROAR!
I CAN'T BELIEVE YOU SAW THROUGH MY DISGUISE!
BECAUSE IT DIDN'T FEEL RIGHT.
HOW WERE YOU ABLE TO DO THAT? I'M SURE I LOOKED EXACTLY LIKE THE MAN YOU WERE LOOKING FOR!
AND EVEN IF I'D BEEN WRONG, MY BROTHER WOULD HAVE MANAGED TO PARRY MY ATTACK.
MMM...
I HAVE A SUGGES-TION.
I WILL GRANT A WISH FOR YOU.
TA-DA!
IN RETURN, YOU WILL LET ME USE YOUR BODY!

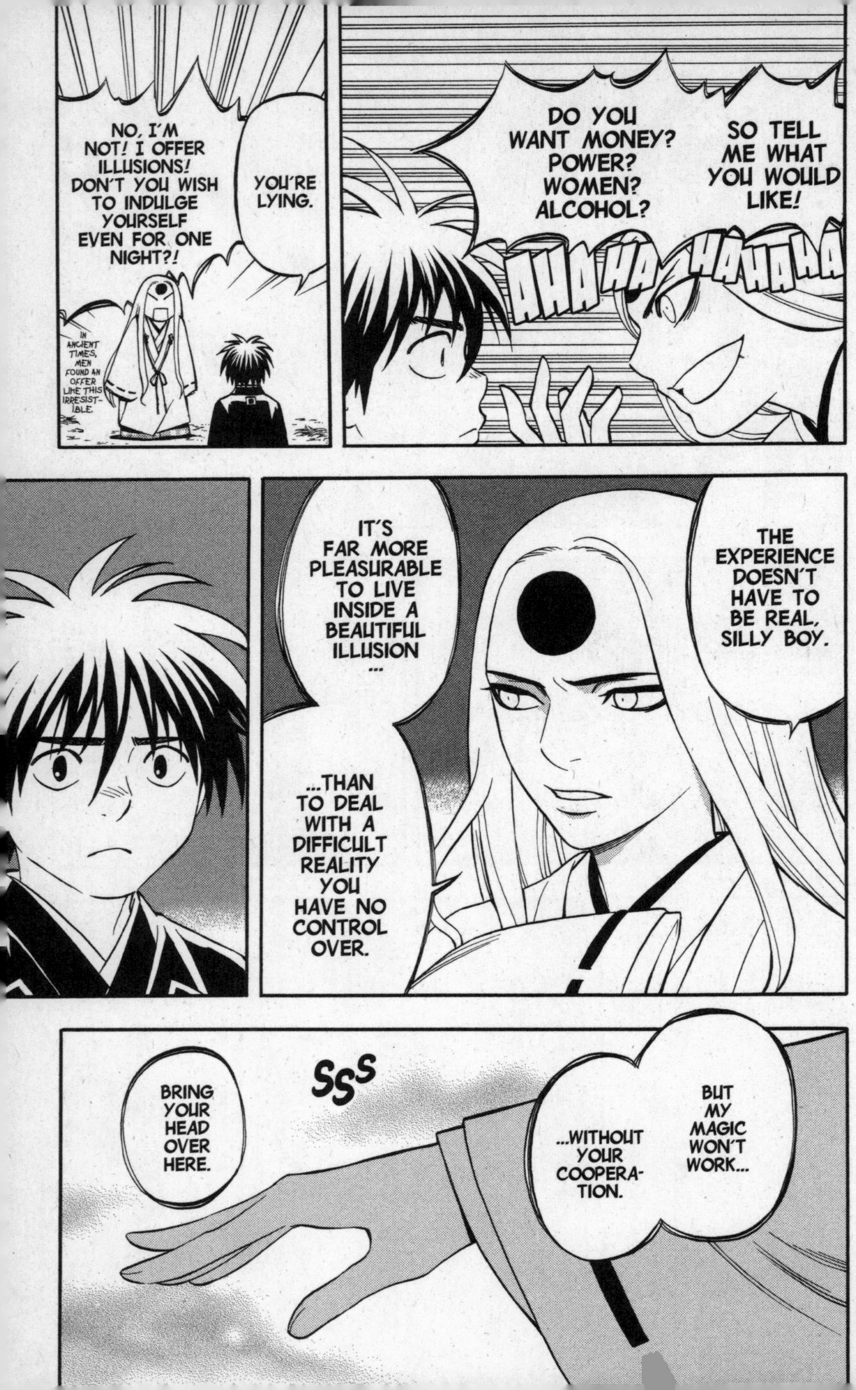
SO TELL ME WHAT YOU WOULD LIKE!
DO YOU WANT MONEY? POWER? WOMEN? ALCOHOL?
HAHAHA HAHAHA
YOU'RE LYING.
NO, I'M NOT! I OFFER ILLUSIONS! DON'T YOU WISH TO INDULGE YOURSELF EVEN FOR ONE NIGHT?!
IN ANCIENT TIMES, MEN FOUND AN OFFER LIKE THIS IRRESISTIBLE.
THE EXPERIENCE DOESN'T HAVE TO BE REAL, SILLY BOY.
IT'S FAR MORE PLEASURABLE TO LIVE INSIDE A BEAUTIFUL ILLUSION...
...THAN TO DEAL WITH A DIFFICULT REALITY YOU HAVE NO CONTROL OVER.
BUT MY MAGIC WON'T WORK...
...WITHOUT YOUR COOPERATION.
SSS
BRING YOUR HEAD OVER HERE.

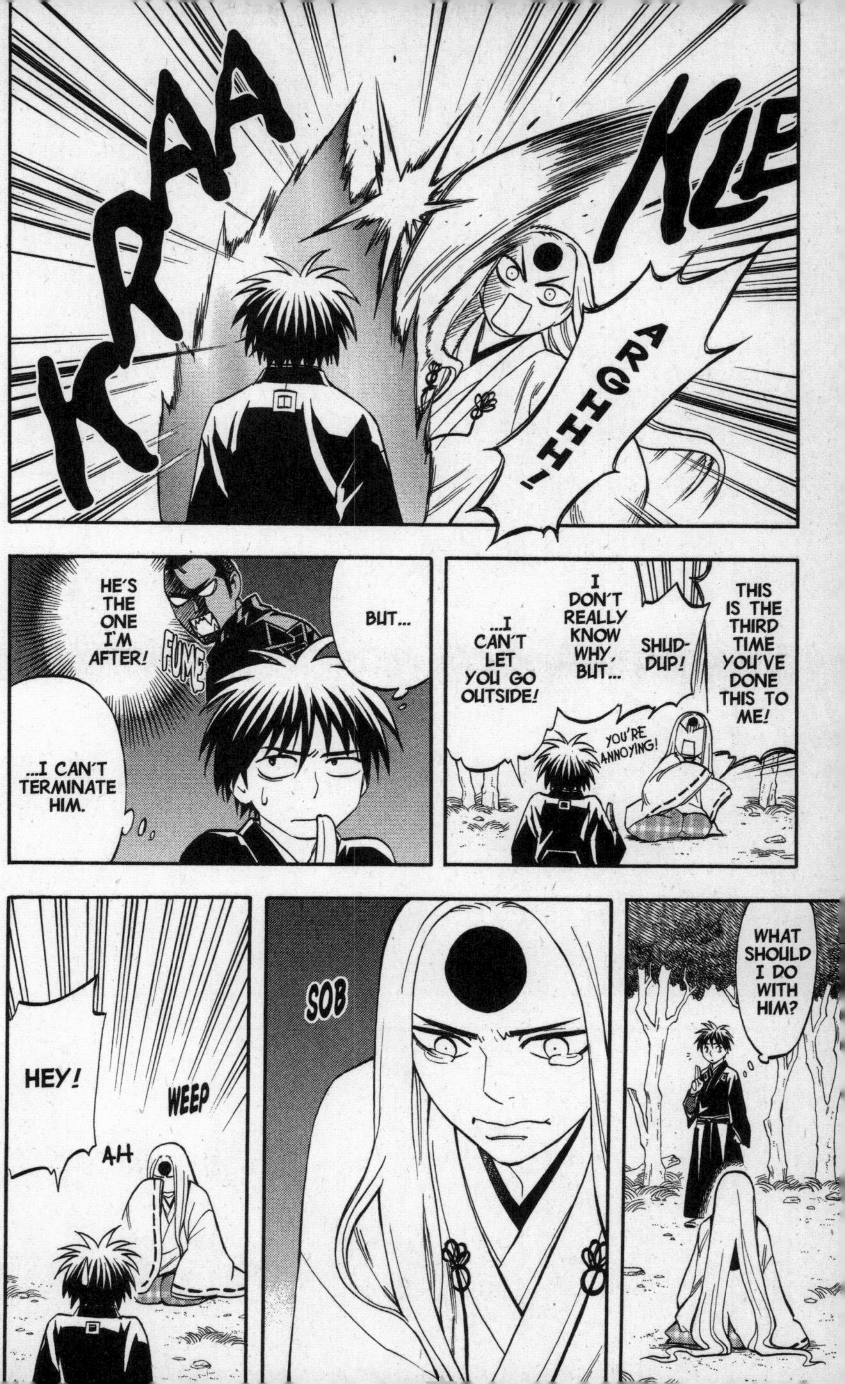
KRAAKLE
ARGHHH!
THIS IS THE THIRD TIME YOU'VE DONE THIS TO ME!
SHUD-DUP!
YOU'RE ANNOYING!
I DON'T REALLY KNOW WHY, BUT...
...I CAN'T LET YOU GO OUTSIDE!
BUT...
HE'S THE ONE I'M AFTER!
FUME
...I CAN'T TERMINATE HIM.
WHAT SHOULD I DO WITH HIM?
SOB
WEEP
HEY!
AH

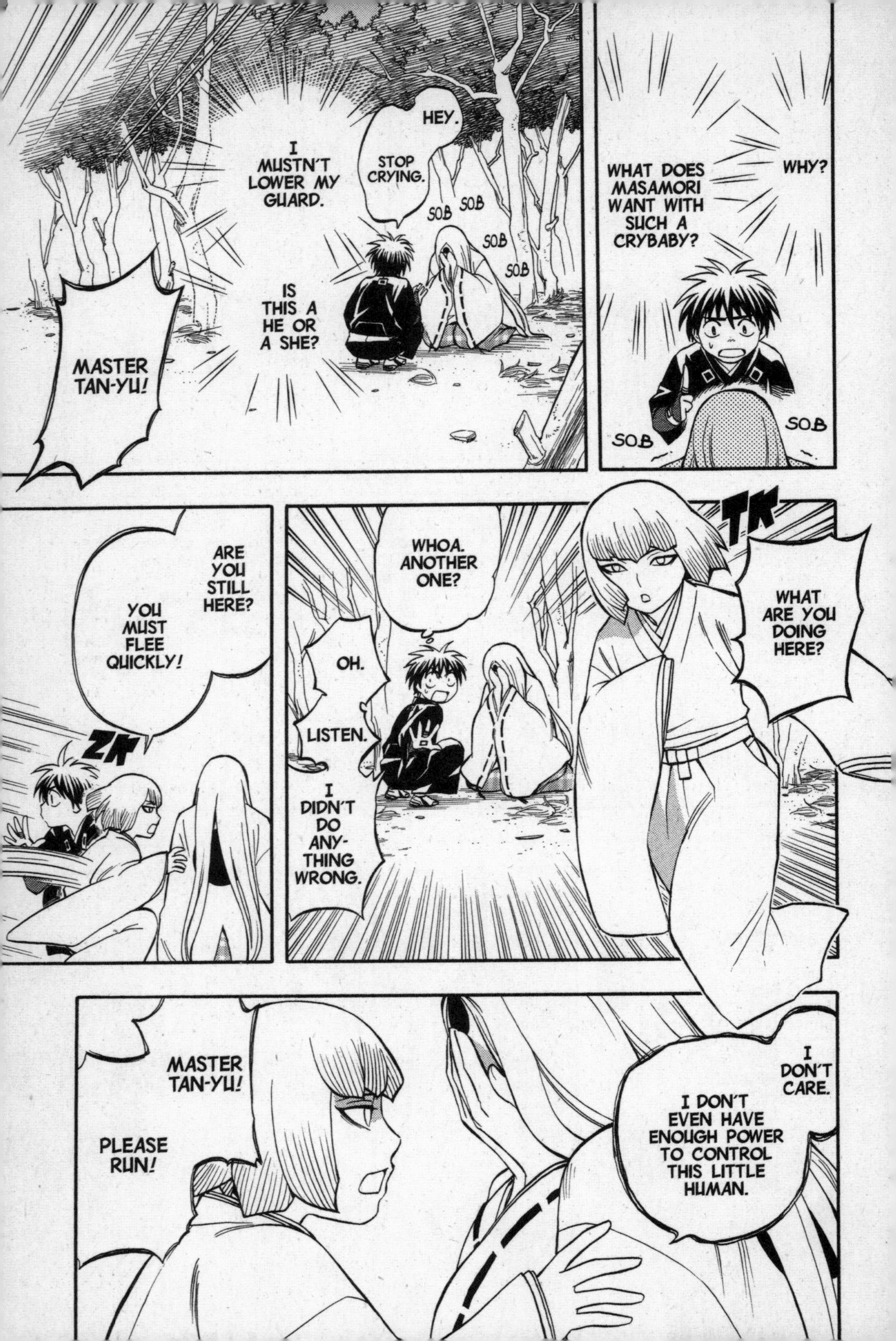
WHY?
WHAT DOES MASAMORI WANT WITH SUCH A CRYBABY?
SOB
SOB
HEY.
STOP CRYING.
SOB
SOB
SOB
SOB
I MUSTN'T LOWER MY GUARD.
IS THIS A HE OR A SHE?
MASTER TAN-YU!
TK
WHAT ARE YOU DOING HERE?
WHOA. ANOTHER ONE?
OH.
LISTEN.
I DIDN'T DO ANY-THING WRONG.
ARE YOU STILL HERE?
YOU MUST FLEE QUICKLY!
ZK
I DON'T CARE.
I DON'T EVEN HAVE ENOUGH POWER TO CONTROL THIS LITTLE HUMAN.
MASTER TAN-YU!
PLEASE RUN!

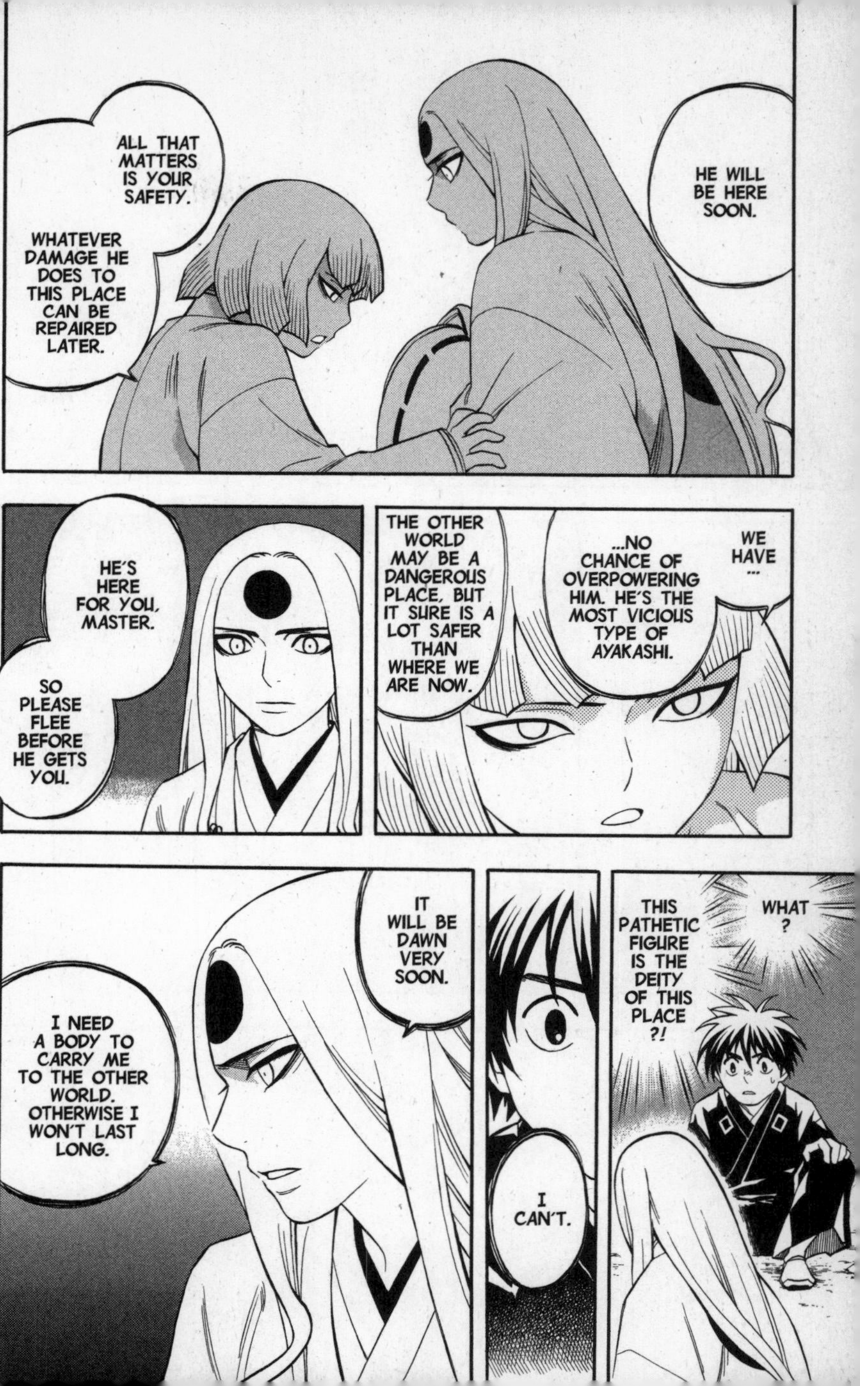
HE WILL BE HERE SOON.
ALL THAT MATTERS IS YOUR SAFETY.
WHATEVER DAMAGE HE DOES TO THIS PLACE CAN BE REPAIRED LATER.
WE HAVE...
...NO CHANCE OF OVERPOWERING HIM. HE'S THE MOST VICIOUS TYPE OF AYAKASHI.
THE OTHER WORLD MAY BE A DANGEROUS PLACE, BUT IT SURE IS A LOT SAFER THAN WHERE WE ARE NOW.
HE'S HERE FOR YOU, MASTER.
SO PLEASE FLEE BEFORE HE GETS YOU.
WHAT?
THIS PATHETIC FIGURE IS THE DEITY OF THIS PLACE?!
I CAN'T.
IT WILL BE DAWN VERY SOON.
I NEED A BODY TO CARRY ME TO THE OTHER WORLD. OTHERWISE I WON'T LAST LONG.

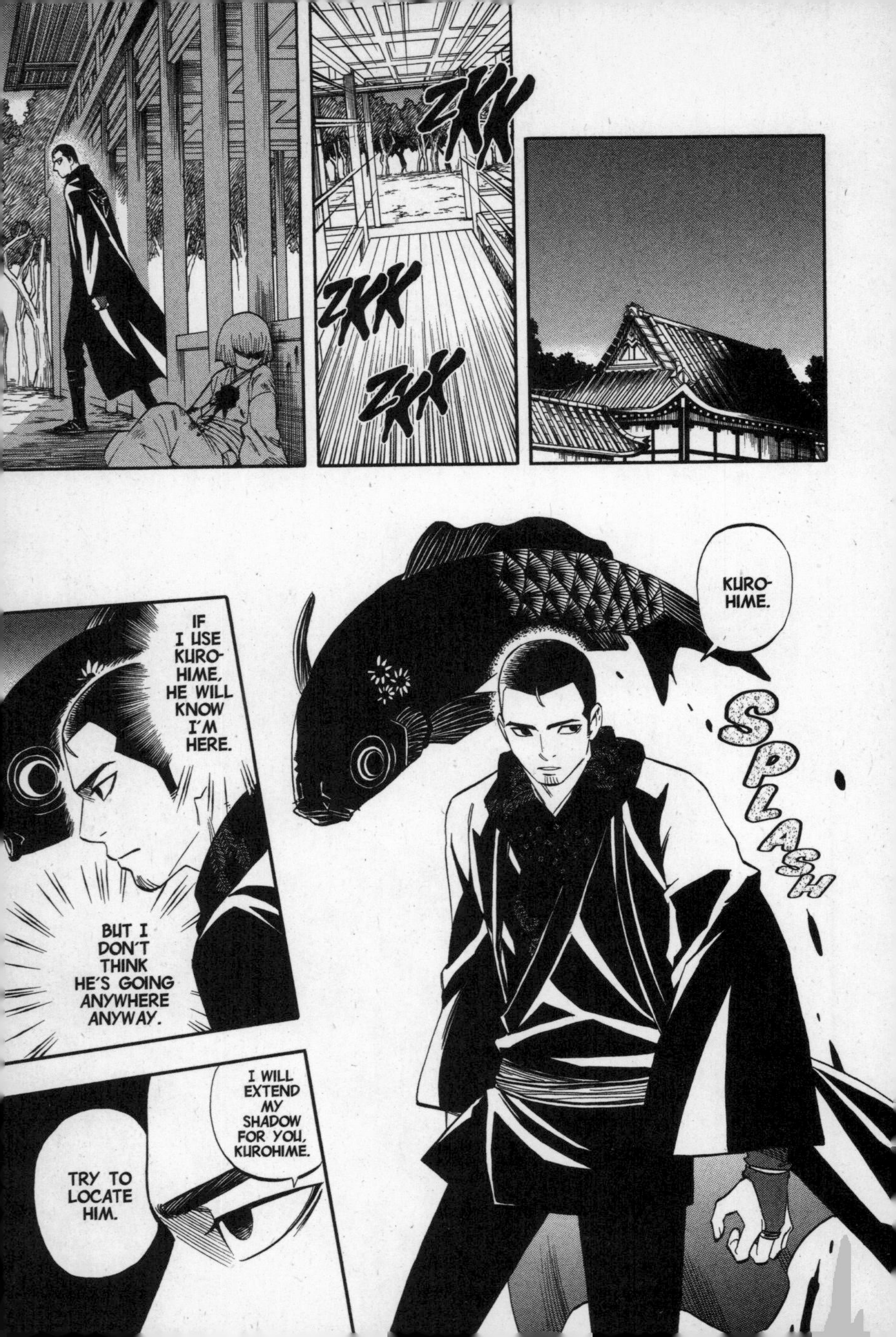
ZKK
ZKK
ZKK
KURO-HIME.
SPLASH
IF I USE KURO-HIME, HE WILL KNOW I'M HERE.
BUT I DON'T THINK HE'S GOING ANYWHERE ANYWAY.
I WILL EXTEND MY SHADOW FOR YOU, KUROHIME.
TRY TO LOCATE HIM.

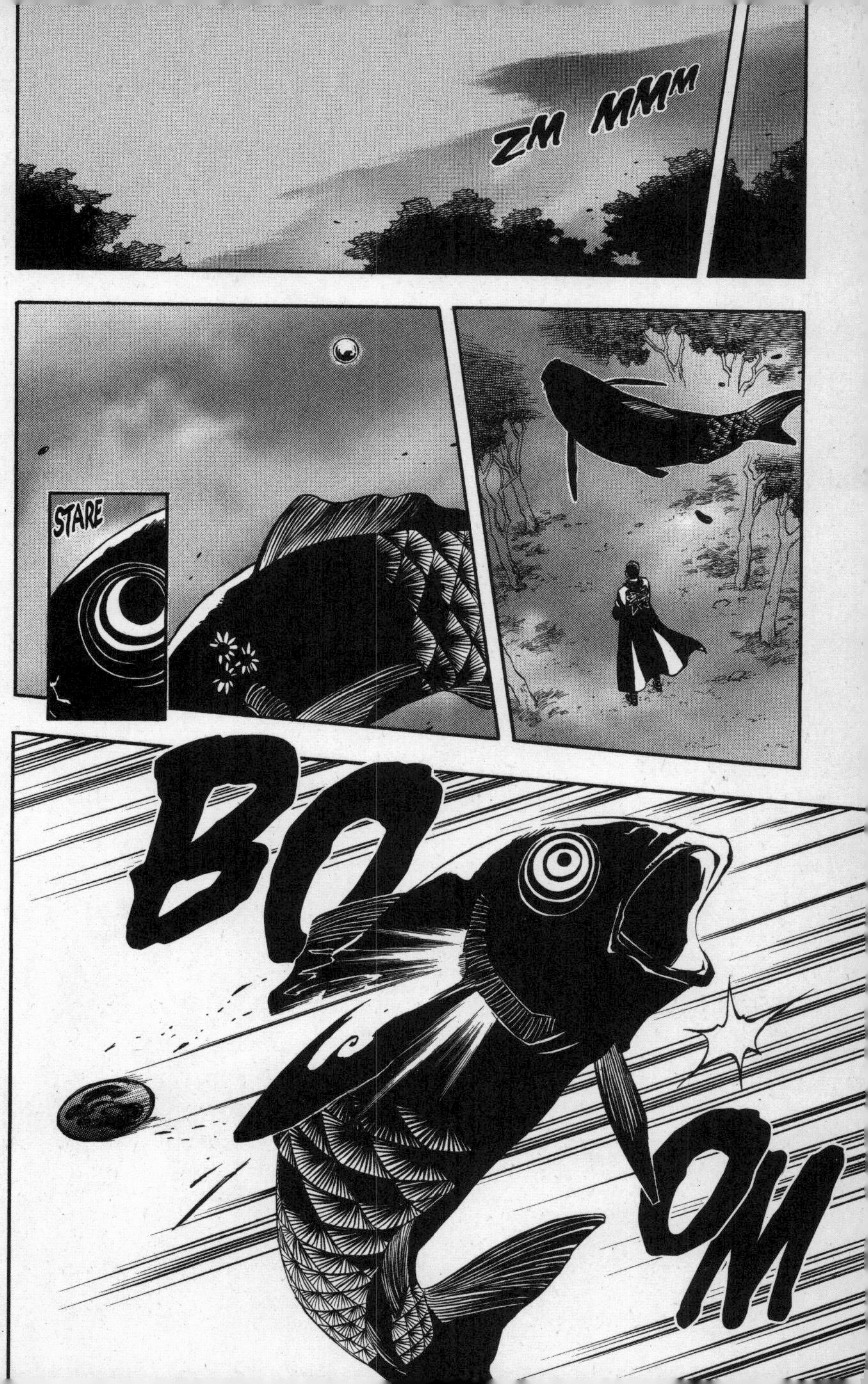
ZM MMM
STARE
BOOM

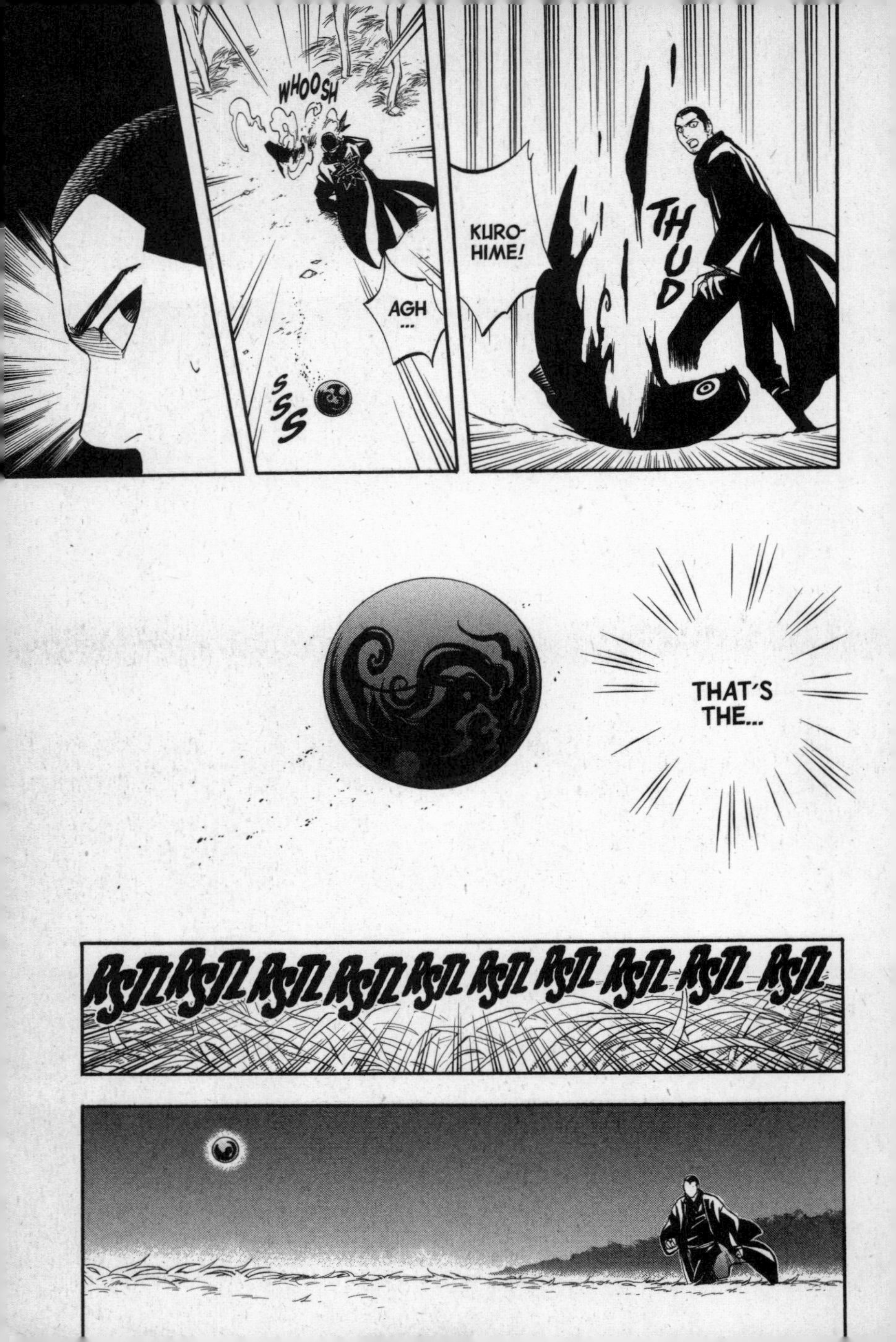

KURO-HIME!
THUD
WHOOSH
AGH ...
SSS
THAT'S THE...
RSTL RSTL RSTL RSTL RSTL RSTL RSTL RSTL RSTL RSTL

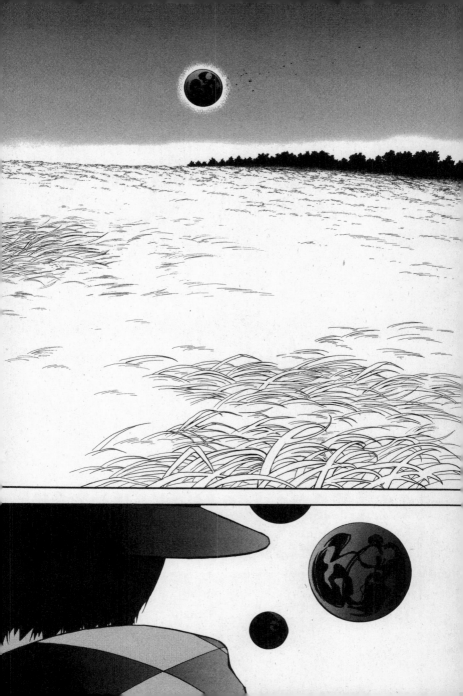

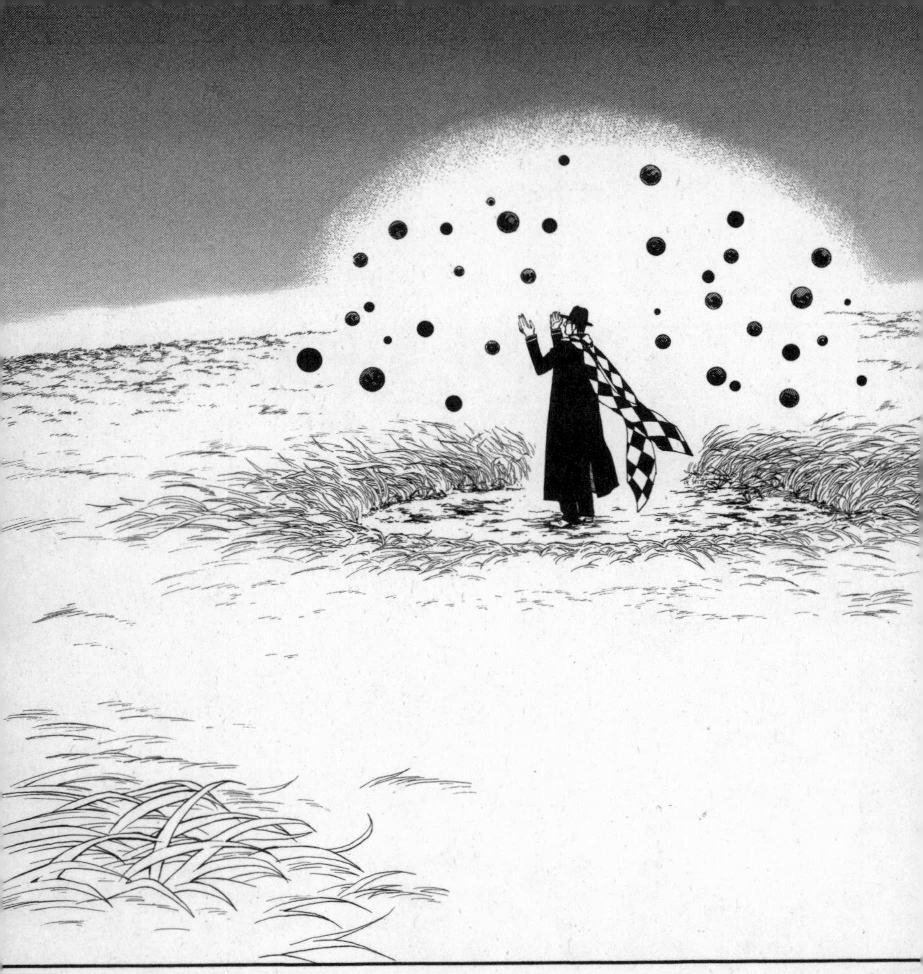
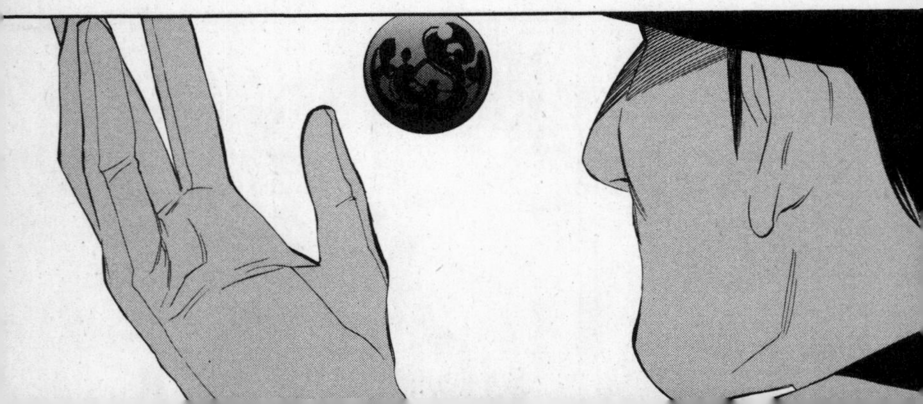

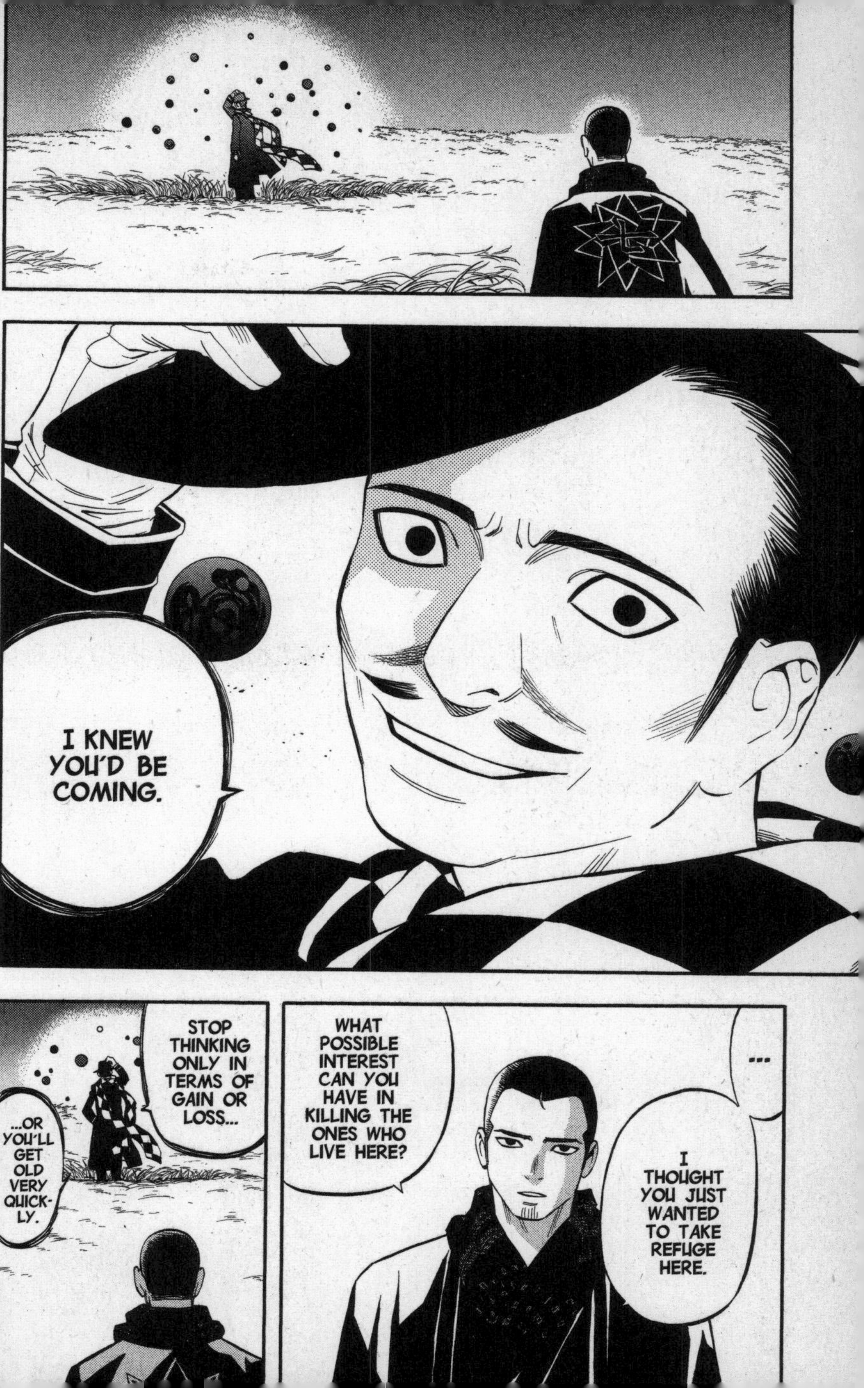
I KNEW YOU'D BE COMING.
...
WHAT POSSIBLE INTEREST CAN YOU HAVE IN KILLING THE ONES WHO LIVE HERE?
I THOUGHT YOU JUST WANTED TO TAKE REFUGE HERE.
STOP THINKING ONLY IN TERMS OF GAIN OR LOSS...
...OR YOU'LL GET OLD VERY QUICK-LY.

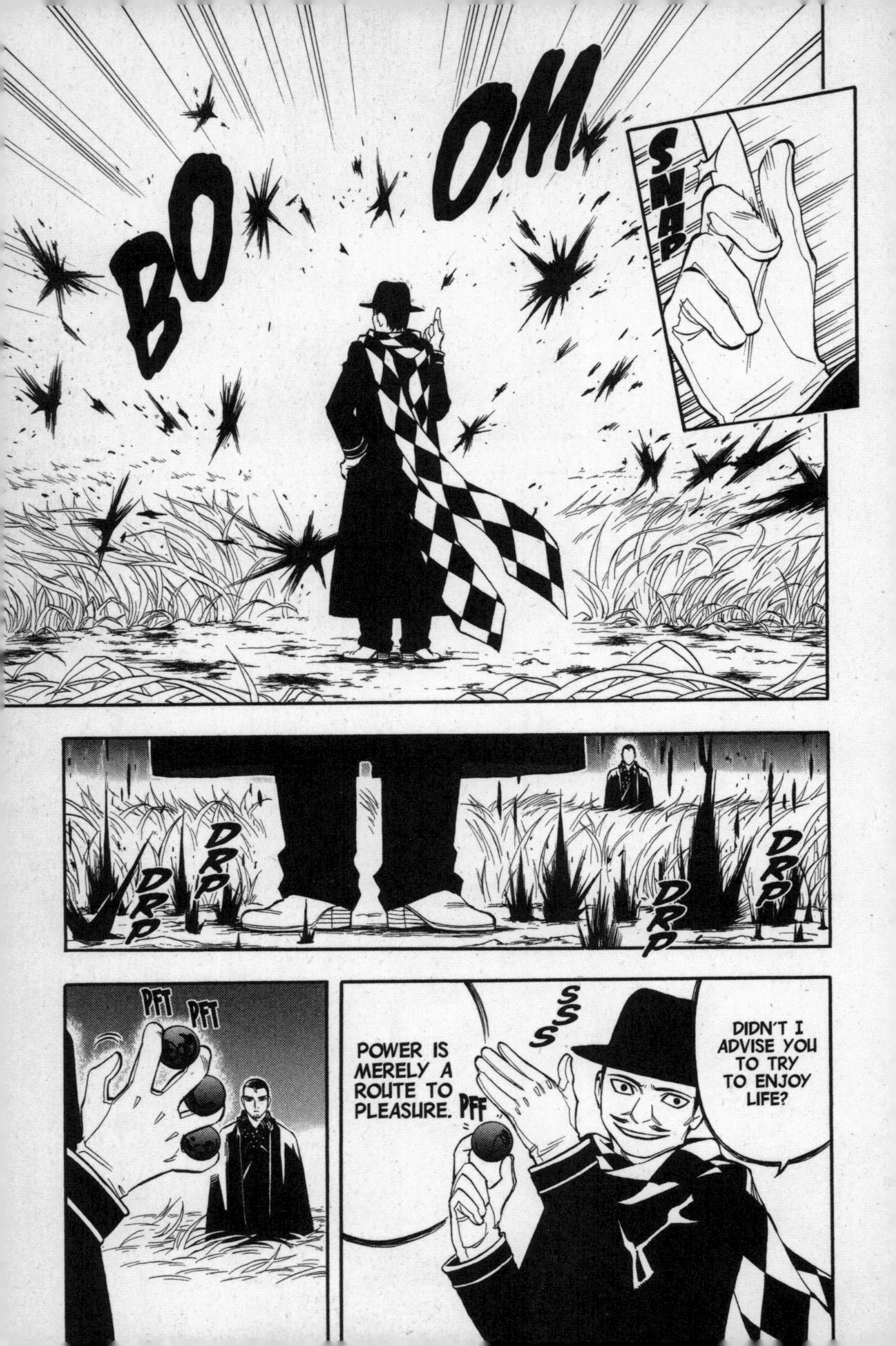
SNAP
BOOM
DRP DRP
DRP DRP
DRP DRP
DIDN'T I ADVISE YOU TO TRY TO ENJOY LIFE?
SSS
POWER IS MERELY A ROUTE TO PLEASURE.
PFF
PFT PFT

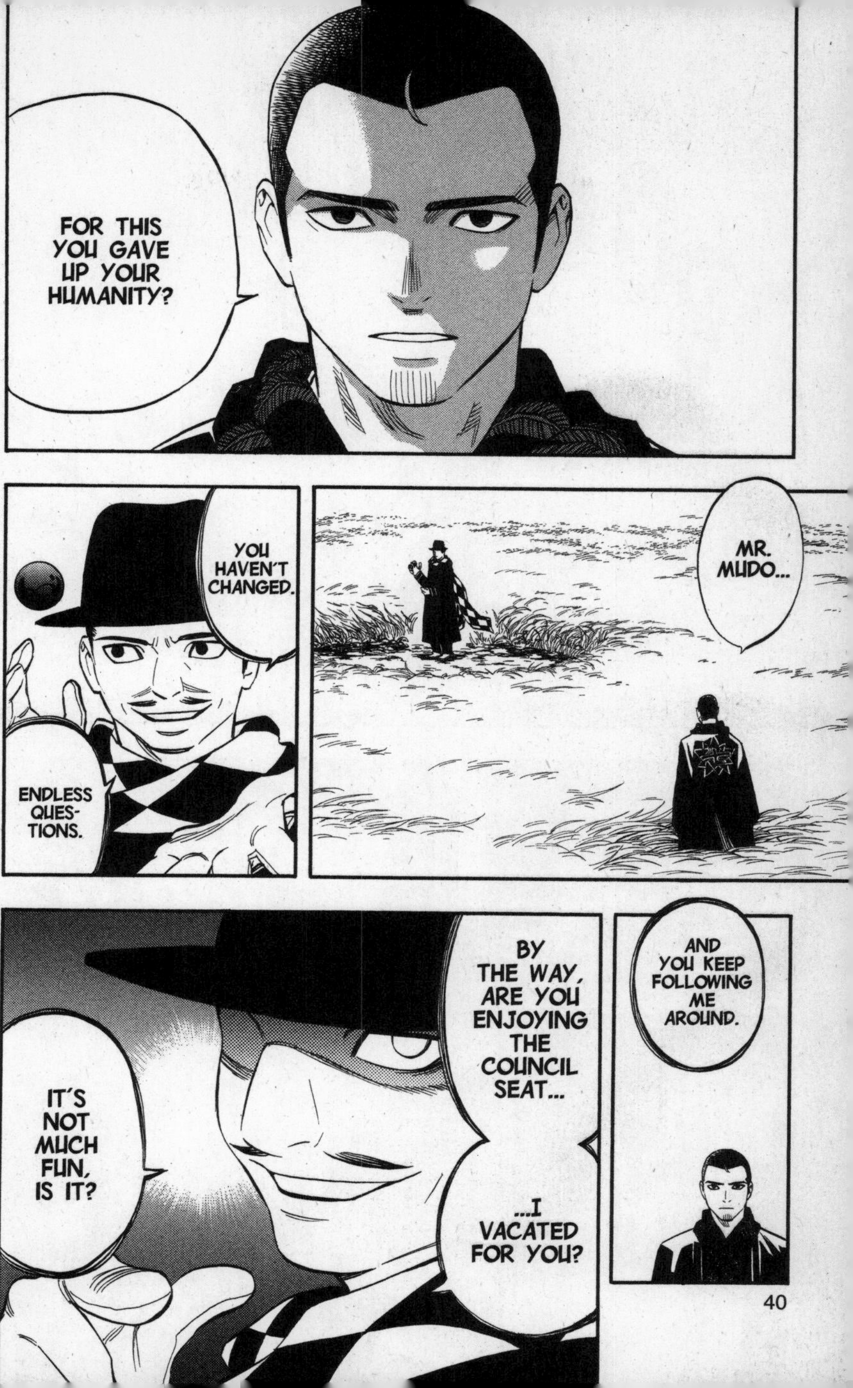
FOR THIS YOU GAVE UP YOUR HUMANITY?
MR. MUDO...
YOU HAVEN'T CHANGED.
ENDLESS QUES-TIONS.
AND YOU KEEP FOLLOWING ME AROUND.
BY THE WAY, ARE YOU ENJOYING THE COUNCIL SEAT...
...I VACATED FOR YOU?
IT'S NOT MUCH FUN, IS IT?

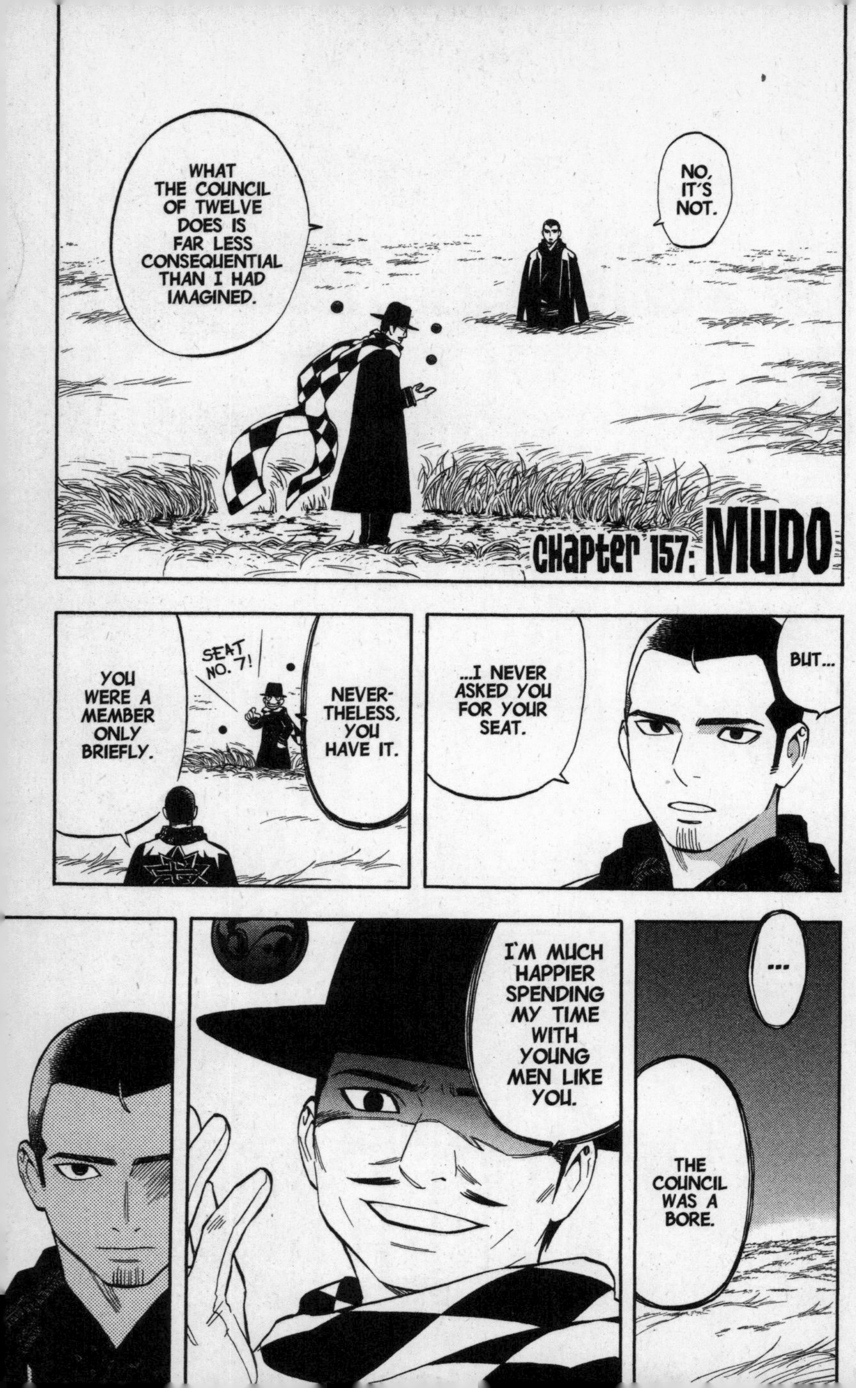
NO, IT'S NOT.
WHAT THE COUNCIL OF TWELVE DOES IS FAR LESS CONSEQUENTIAL THAN I HAD IMAGINED.
Chapter 157: MUDO
BUT...
...I NEVER ASKED YOU FOR YOUR SEAT.
NEVER-THELESS, YOU HAVE IT.
SEAT NO. 7!
YOU WERE A MEMBER ONLY BRIEFLY.
...
THE COUNCIL WAS A BORE.
I'M MUCH HAPPIER SPENDING MY TIME WITH YOUNG MEN LIKE YOU.

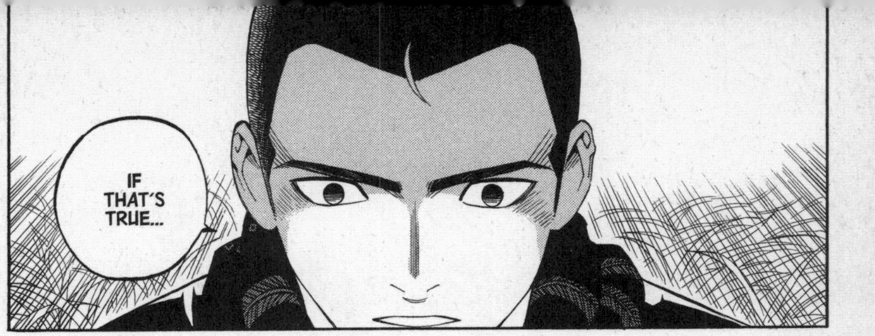
IF THAT'S TRUE...

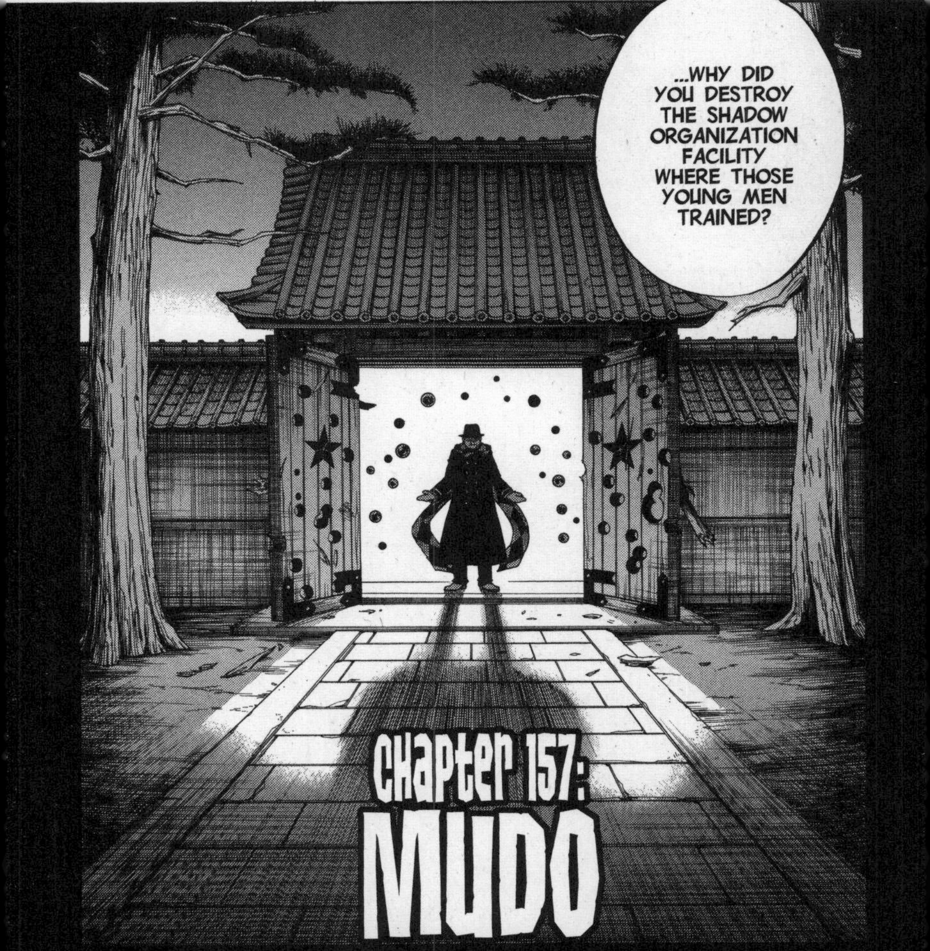
...WHY DID YOU DESTROY THE SHADOW ORGANIZATION FACILITY WHERE THOSE YOUNG MEN TRAINED?
CHAPTER 157:
MUDO

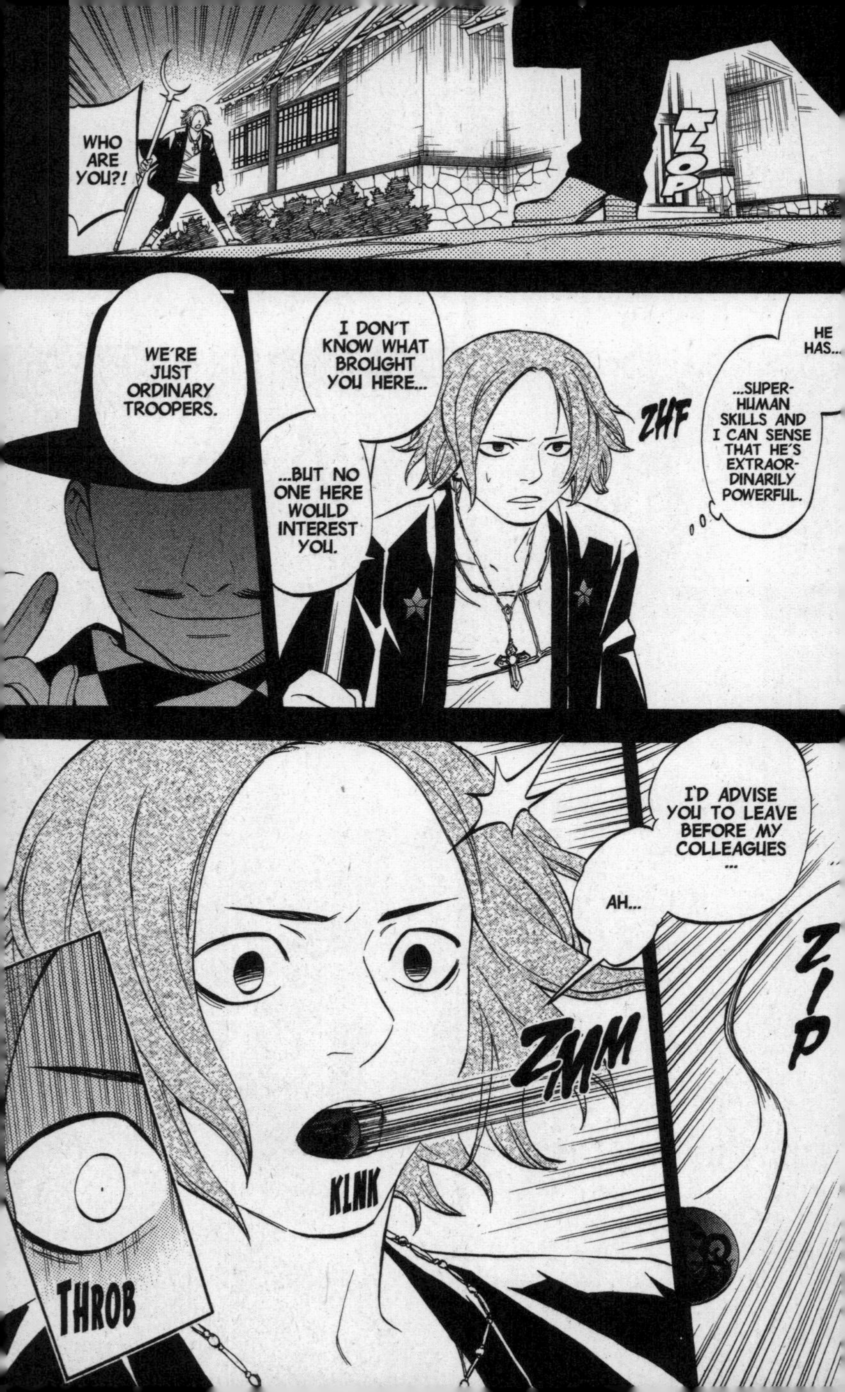

KLOP
WHO ARE YOU?!
HE HAS...
...SUPER-HUMAN SKILLS AND I CAN SENSE THAT HE'S EXTRAOR-DINARILY POWERFUL.
ZHF
I DON'T KNOW WHAT BROUGHT YOU HERE...
...BUT NO ONE HERE WOULD INTEREST YOU.
WE'RE JUST ORDINARY TROOPERS.
I'D ADVISE YOU TO LEAVE BEFORE MY COLLEAGUES ...
AH...
ZIP
ZMM
KLNK
THROB

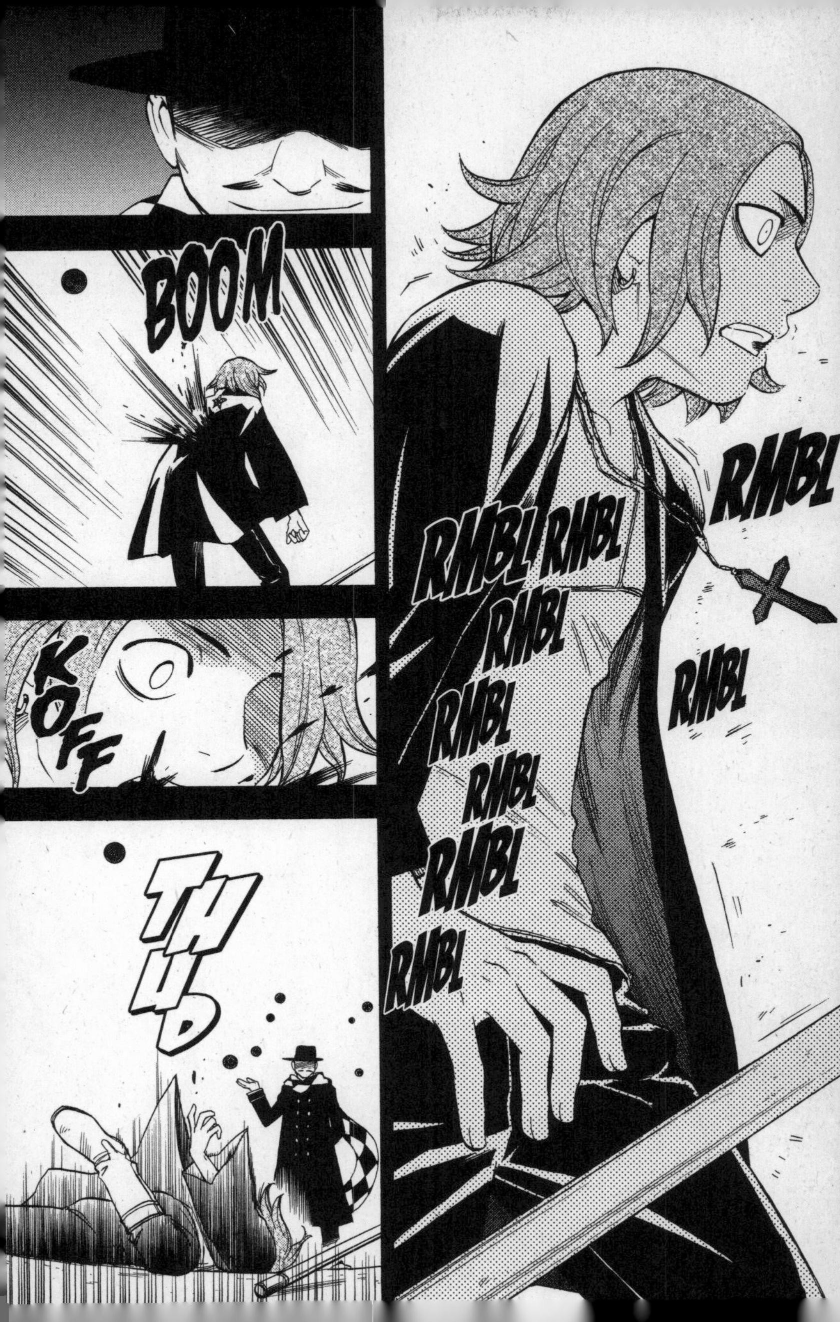

RMBL
RMBL
RMBL
RMBL
RMBL
RMBL
RMBL
RMBL
RMBL
BOOM
KOFF
THUD

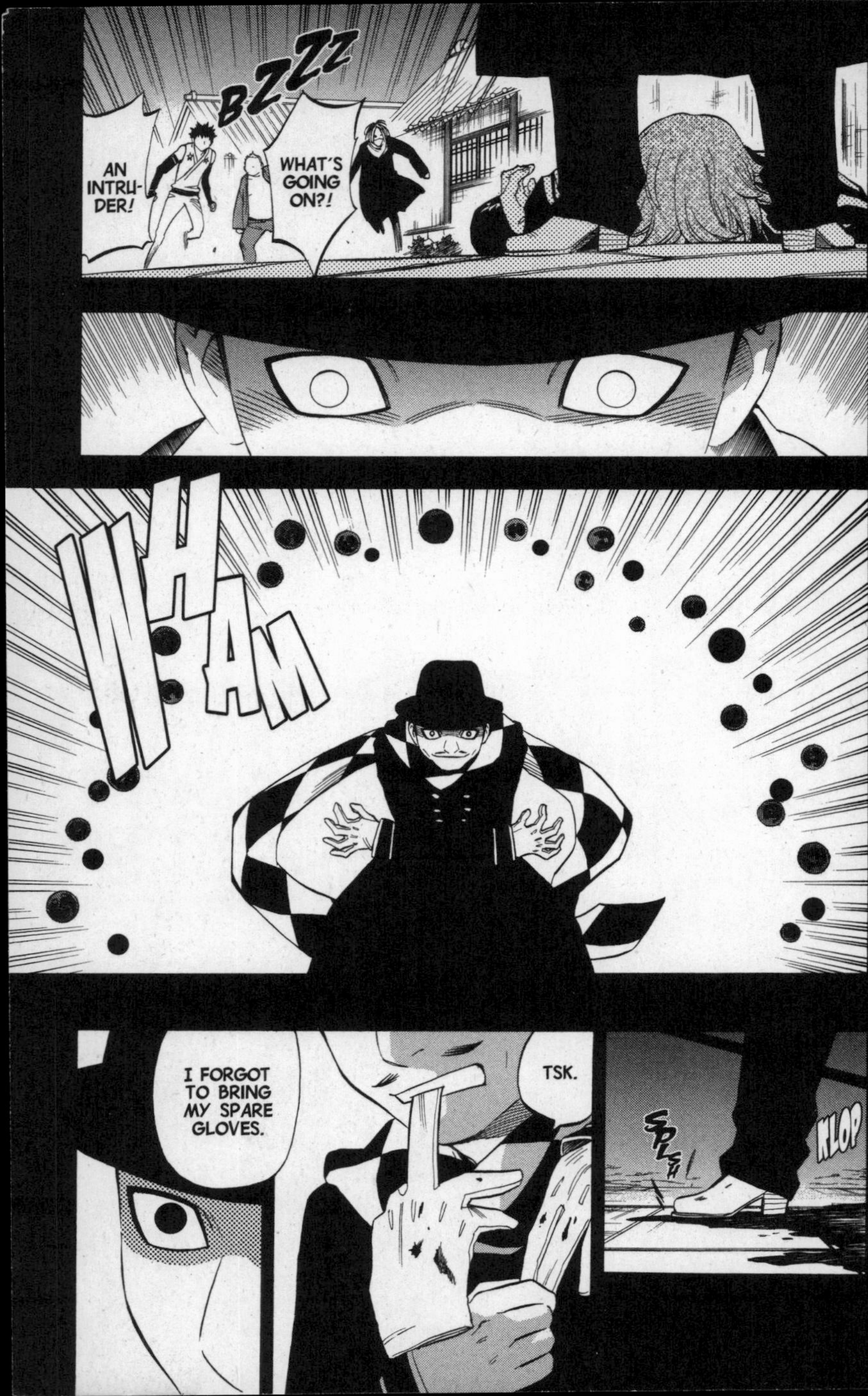
BZZZZ
WHAT'S GOING ON?!
AN INTRU-DER!
WHAM
TSK.
I FORGOT TO BRING MY SPARE GLOVES.
KLOP
SPLSH

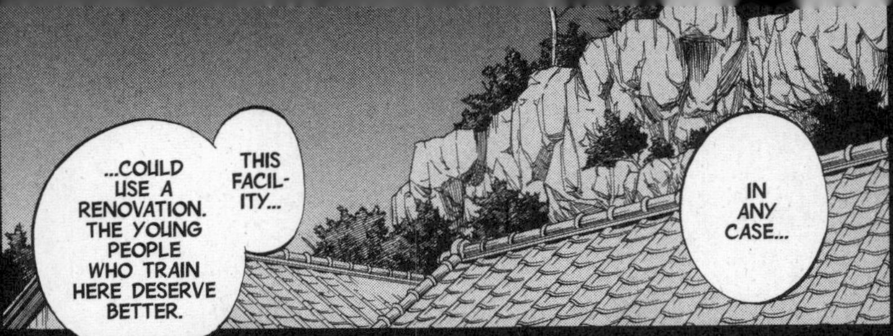
IN ANY CASE...
THIS FACIL-ITY...
...COULD USE A RENOVATION. THE YOUNG PEOPLE WHO TRAIN HERE DESERVE BETTER.
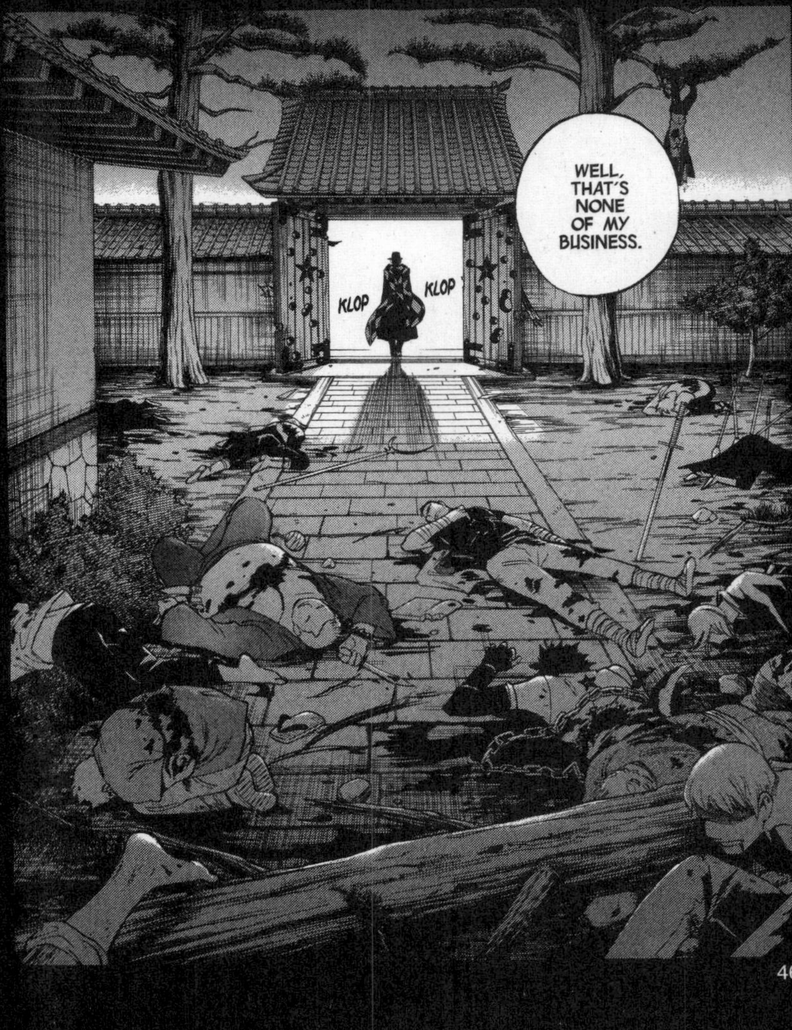
WELL, THAT'S NONE OF MY BUSINESS.
KLOP
KLOP

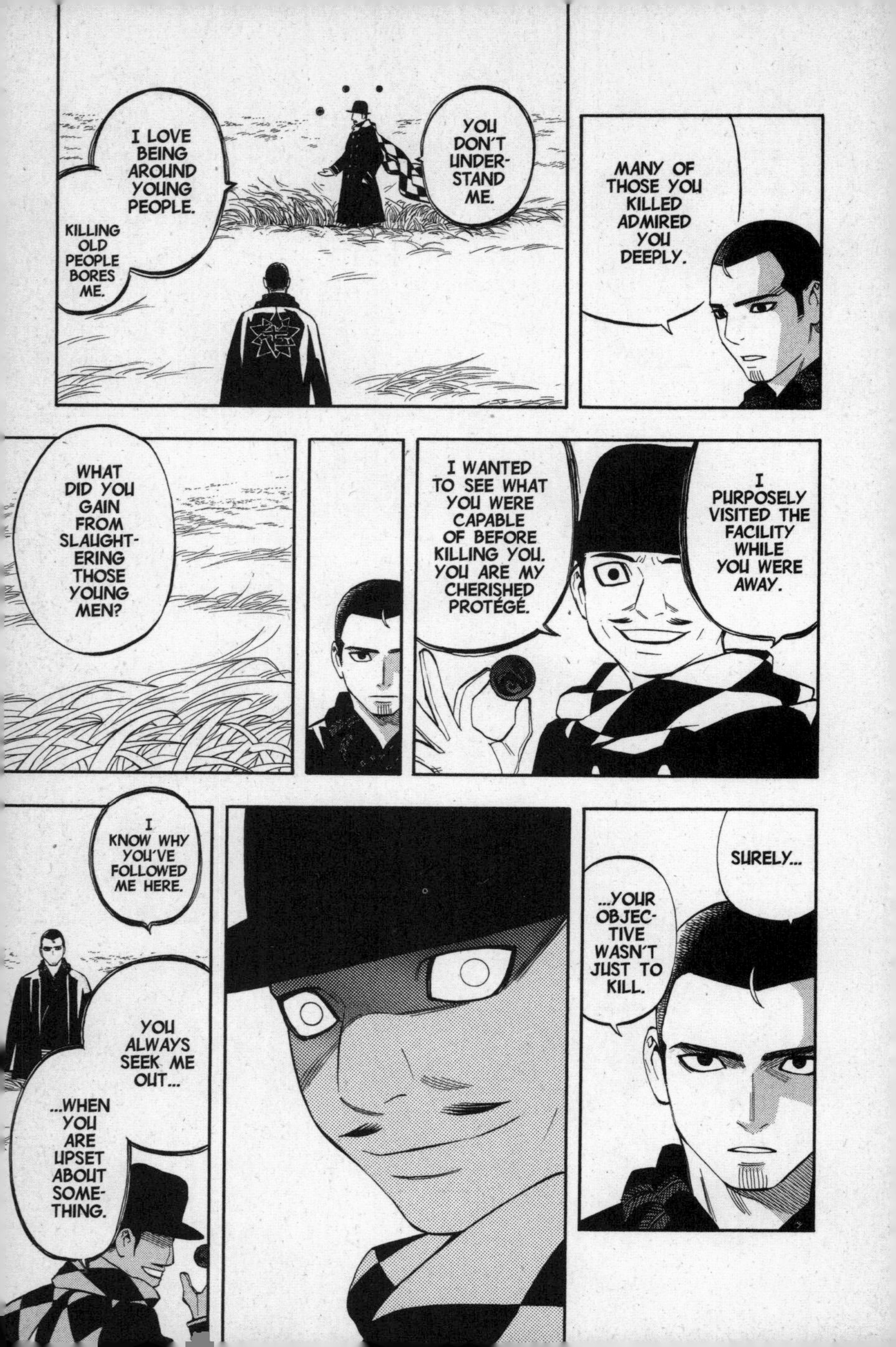
MANY OF THOSE YOU KILLED ADMIRED YOU DEEPLY.
YOU DON'T UNDER-STAND ME.
I LOVE BEING AROUND YOUNG PEOPLE.
KILLING OLD PEOPLE BORES ME.
I PURPOSELY VISITED THE FACILITY WHILE YOU WERE AWAY.
I WANTED TO SEE WHAT YOU WERE CAPABLE OF BEFORE KILLING YOU. YOU ARE MY CHERISHED PROTÉGÉ.
WHAT DID YOU GAIN FROM SLAUGHT-ERING THOSE YOUNG MEN?
SURELY...
...YOUR OBJEC-TIVE WASN'T JUST TO KILL.
I KNOW WHY YOU'VE FOLLOWED ME HERE.
YOU ALWAYS SEEK ME OUT...
...WHEN YOU ARE UPSET ABOUT SOME-THING.

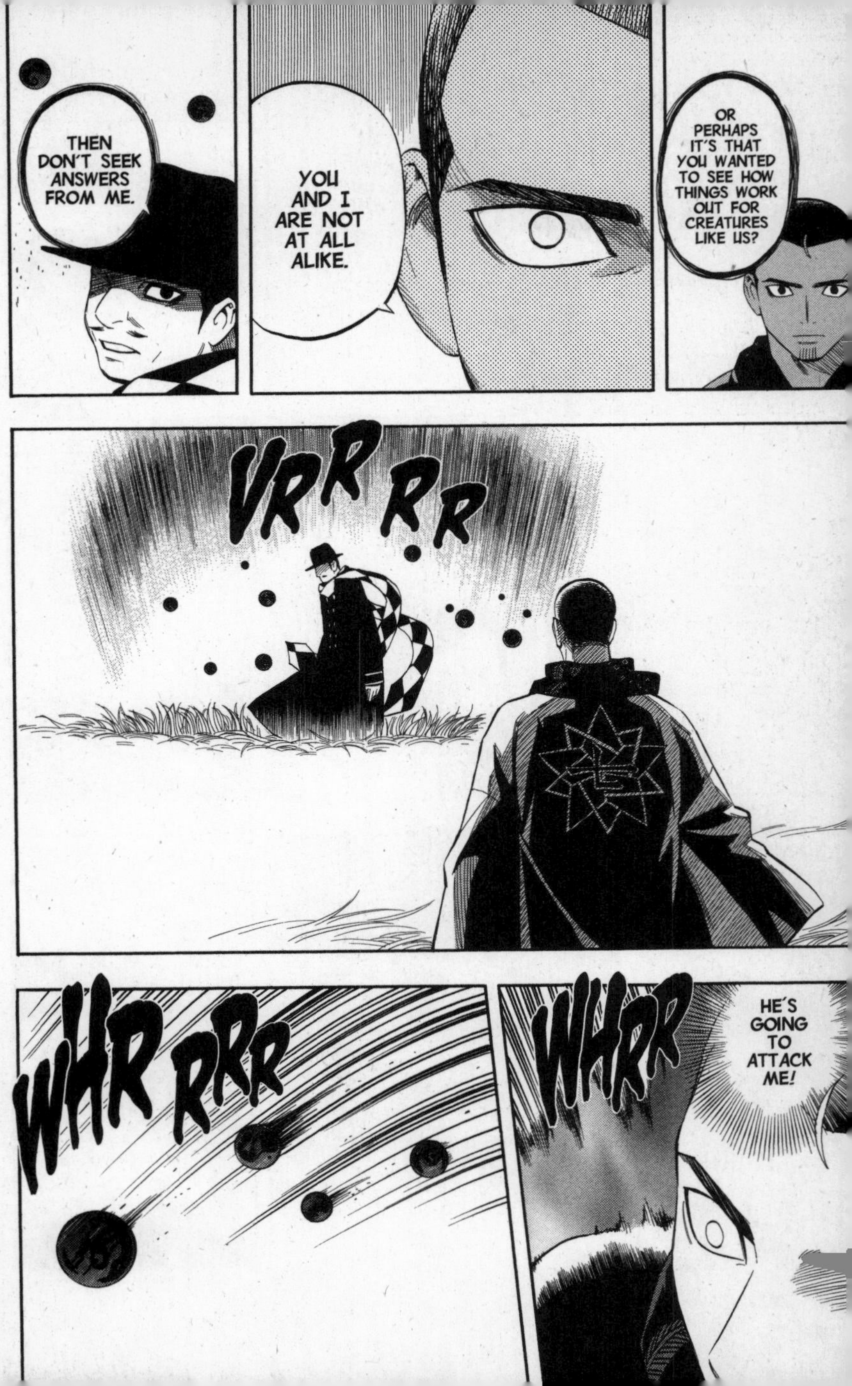
OR PERHAPS IT'S THAT YOU WANTED TO SEE HOW THINGS WORK OUT FOR CREATURES LIKE US?
YOU AND I ARE NOT AT ALL ALIKE.
THEN DON'T SEEK ANSWERS FROM ME.
VRRRR
WHRR
HE'S GOING TO ATTACK ME!
WHR RRR

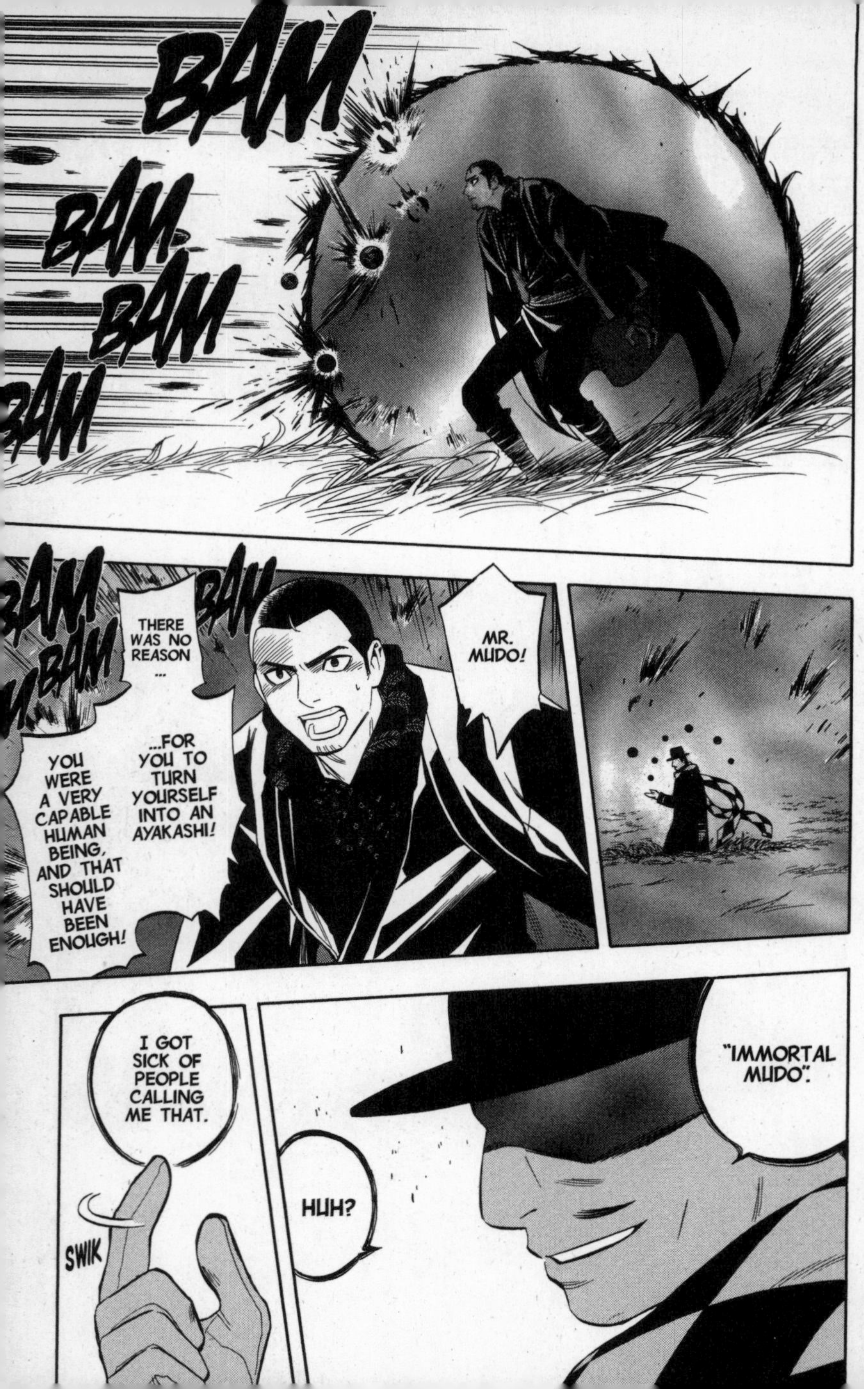
BAM
BAM
BAM
BAM
BAM
BAM
BAM
BAM
MR. MUDO!
THERE WAS NO REASON ...
...FOR YOU TO TURN YOURSELF INTO AN AYAKASHI!
YOU WERE A VERY CAPABLE HUMAN BEING, AND THAT SHOULD HAVE BEEN ENOUGH!
"IMMORTAL MUDO".
HUH?
I GOT SICK OF PEOPLE CALLING ME THAT.
SWIK

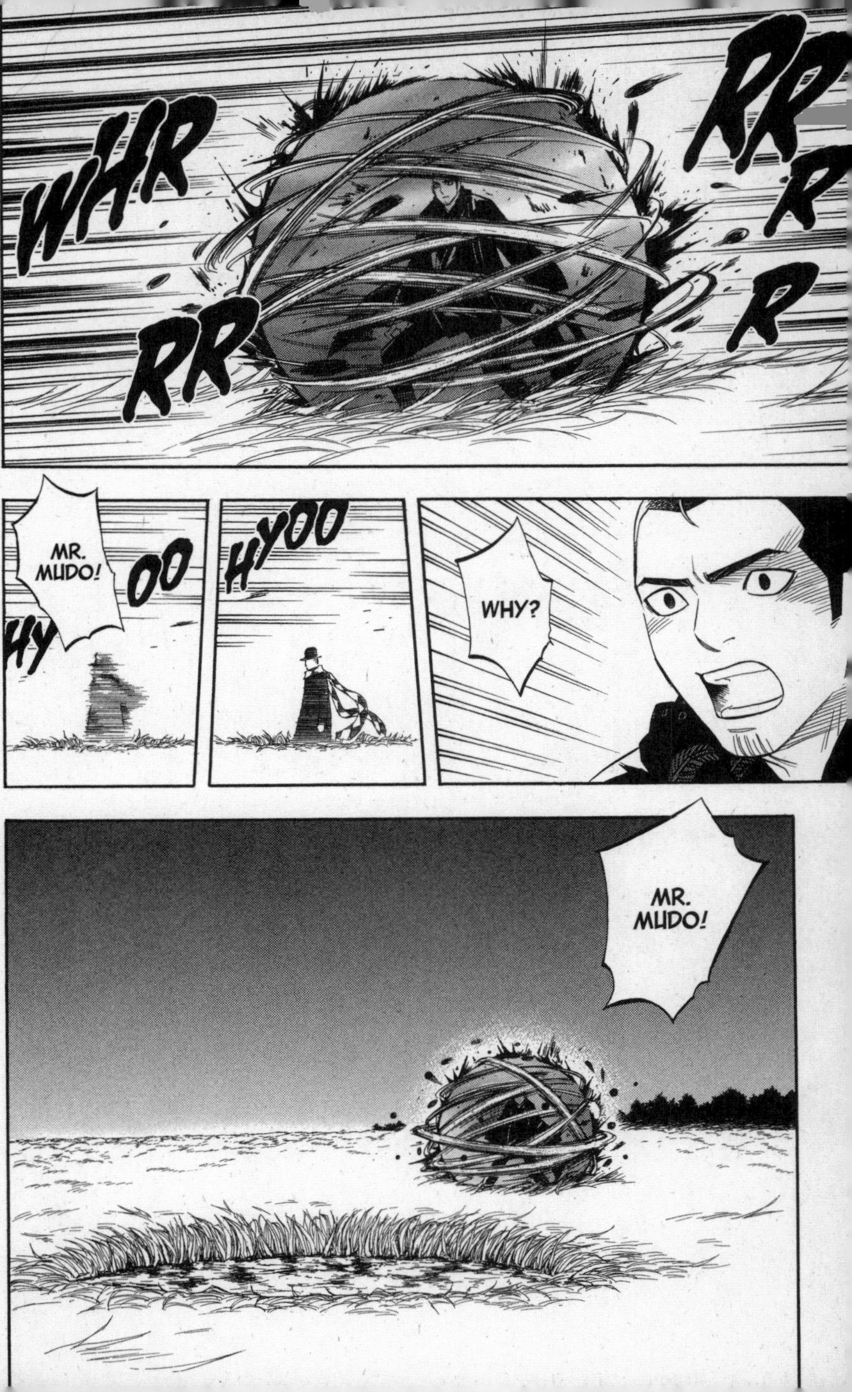
RRRR
WHR
RR
WHY?
HYOO
MR. MUDO!
OO
HY
MR. MUDO!

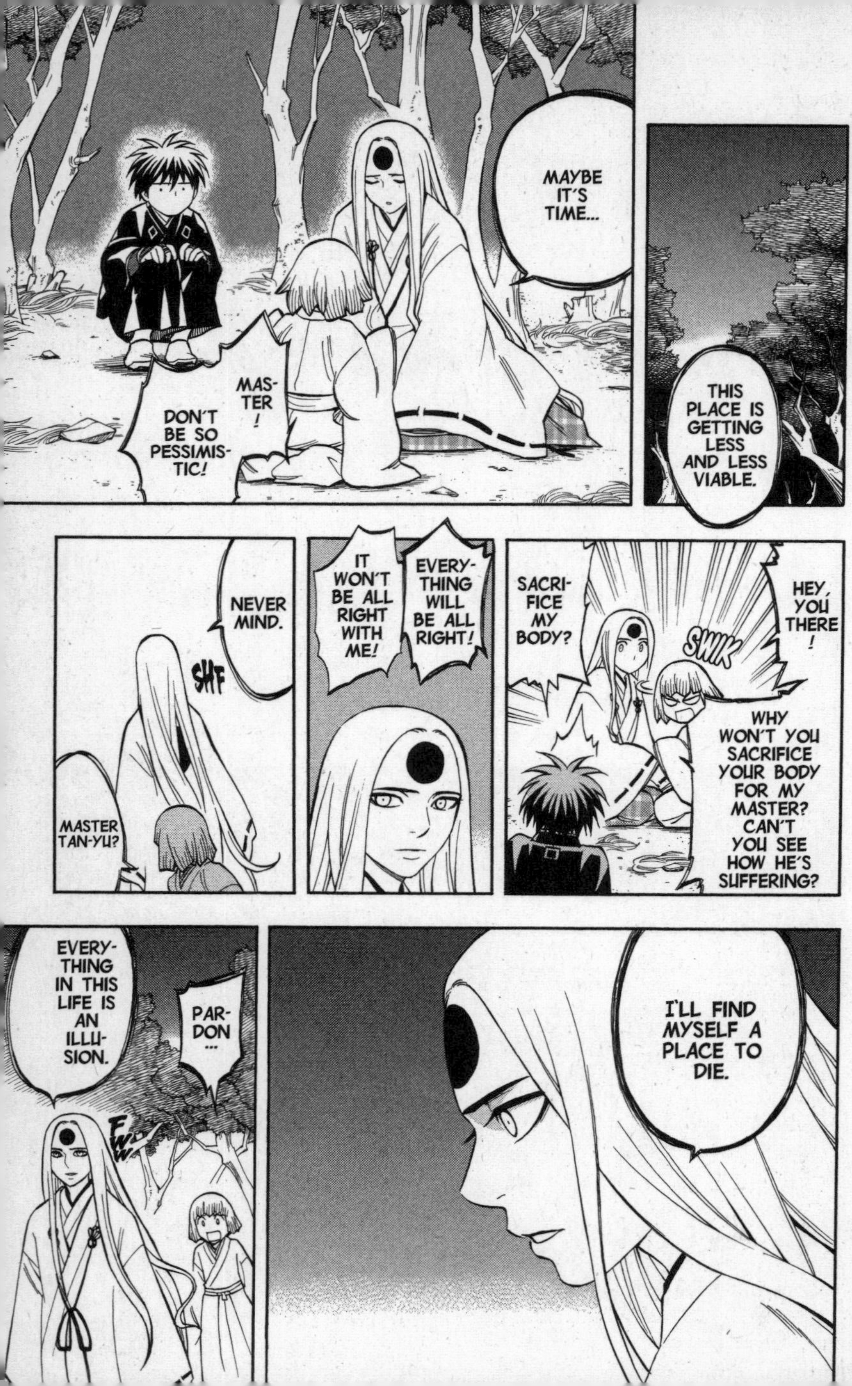
THIS PLACE IS GETTING LESS AND LESS VIABLE.
MAYBE IT'S TIME...
MASTER!
DON'T BE SO PESSIMISTIC!
HEY, YOU THERE!
SWIK
WHY WON'T YOU SACRIFICE YOUR BODY FOR MY MASTER? CAN'T YOU SEE HOW HE'S SUFFERING?
SACRIFICE MY BODY?
EVERYTHING WILL BE ALL RIGHT!
IT WON'T BE ALL RIGHT WITH ME!
NEVER MIND.
SHF
MASTER TAN-YU?
I'LL FIND MYSELF A PLACE TO DIE.
PARDON...
EVERYTHING IN THIS LIFE IS AN ILLUSION.
FWW

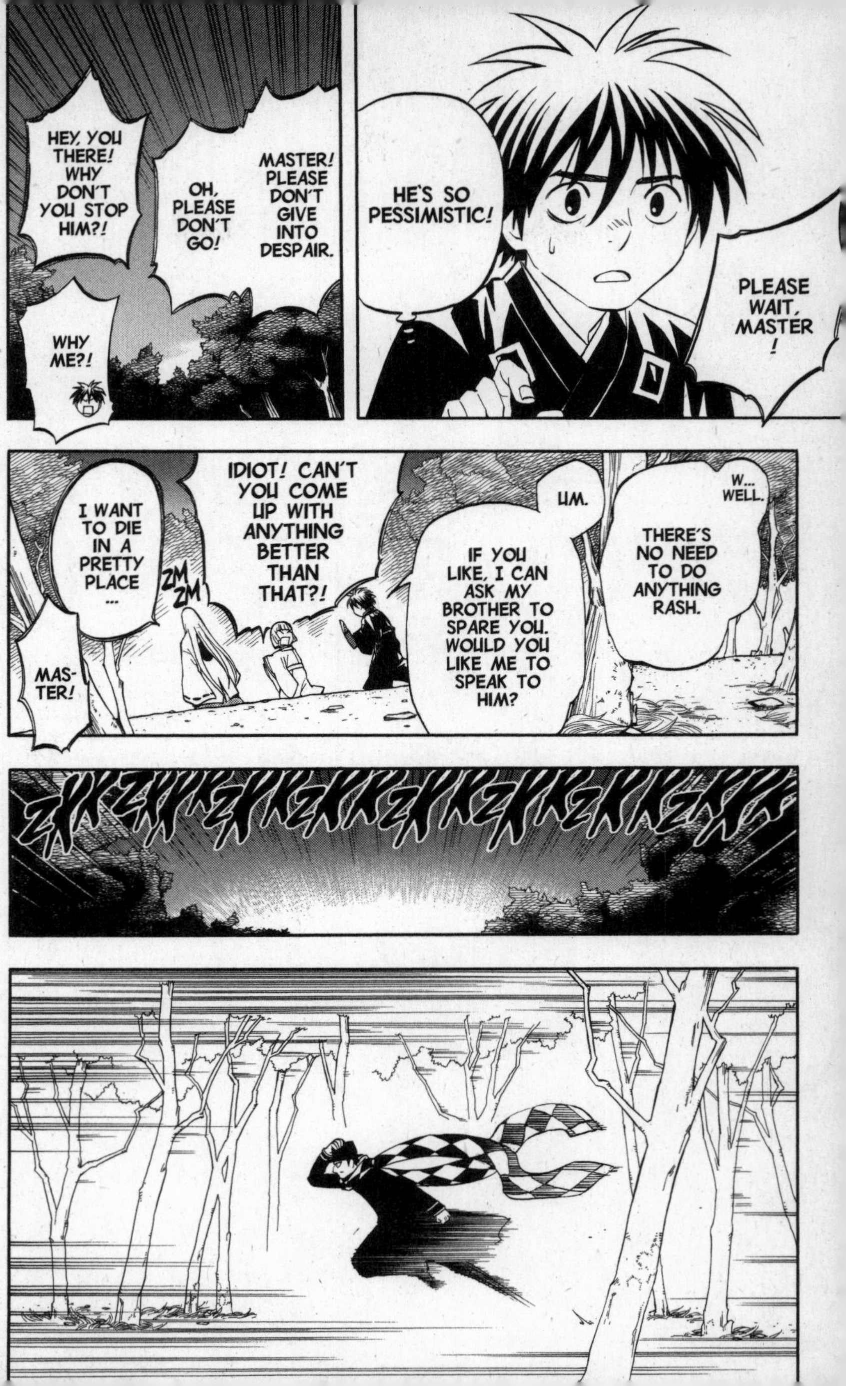
PLEASE WAIT, MASTER!
HE'S SO PESSIMISTIC!
MASTER! PLEASE DON'T GIVE INTO DESPAIR.
OH, PLEASE DON'T GO!
HEY, YOU THERE! WHY DON'T YOU STOP HIM?!
WHY ME?!
W... WELL.
THERE'S NO NEED TO DO ANYTHING RASH.
UM.
IF YOU LIKE, I CAN ASK MY BROTHER TO SPARE YOU. WOULD YOU LIKE ME TO SPEAK TO HIM?
IDIOT! CAN'T YOU COME UP WITH ANYTHING BETTER THAN THAT?!
ZM ZM
I WANT TO DIE IN A PRETTY PLACE ...
MAS-TER!

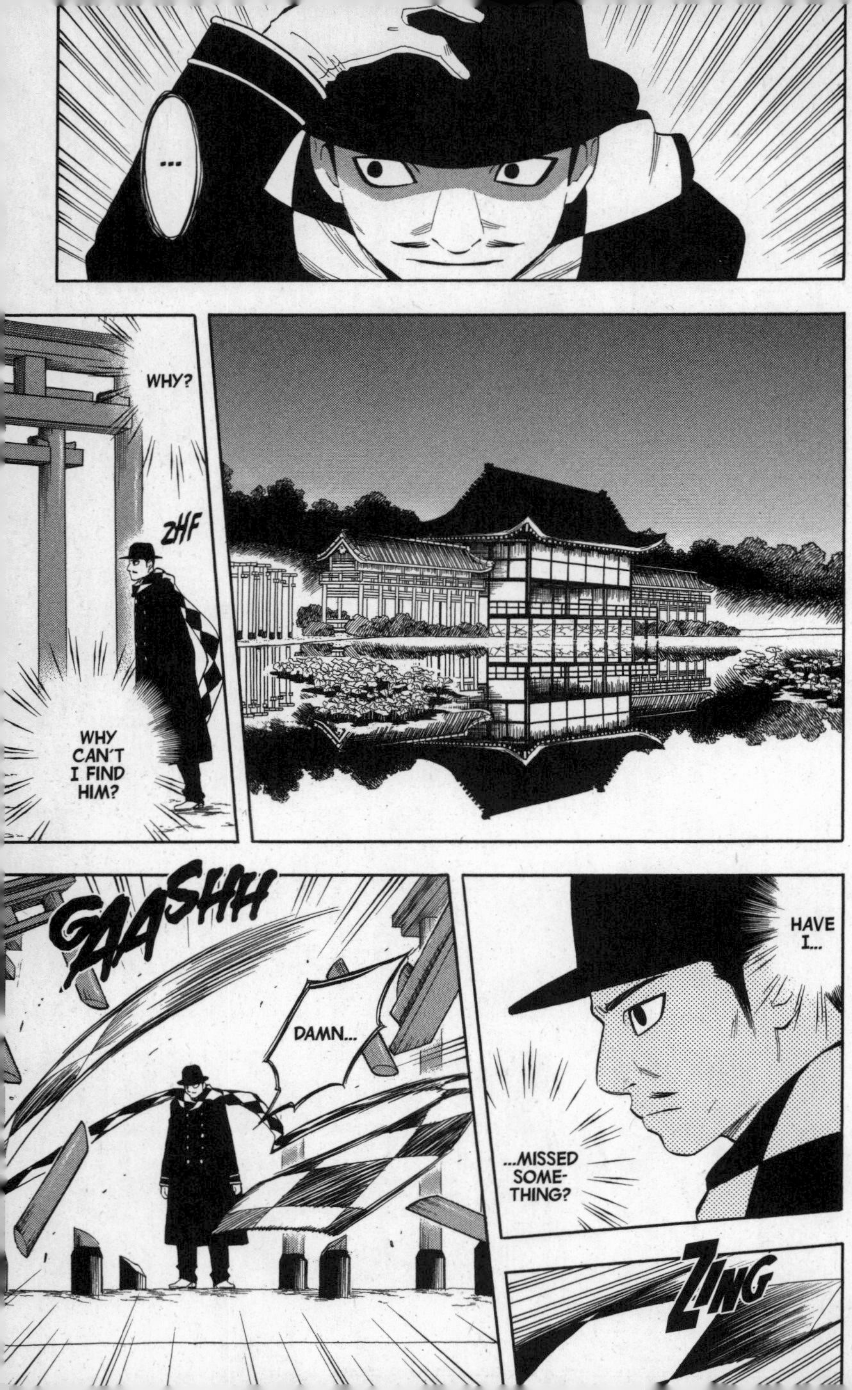
...
WHY?
ZHF
WHY CAN'T I FIND HIM?
HAVE I...
...MISSED SOME-THING?
ZING
GAASHH
DAMN...

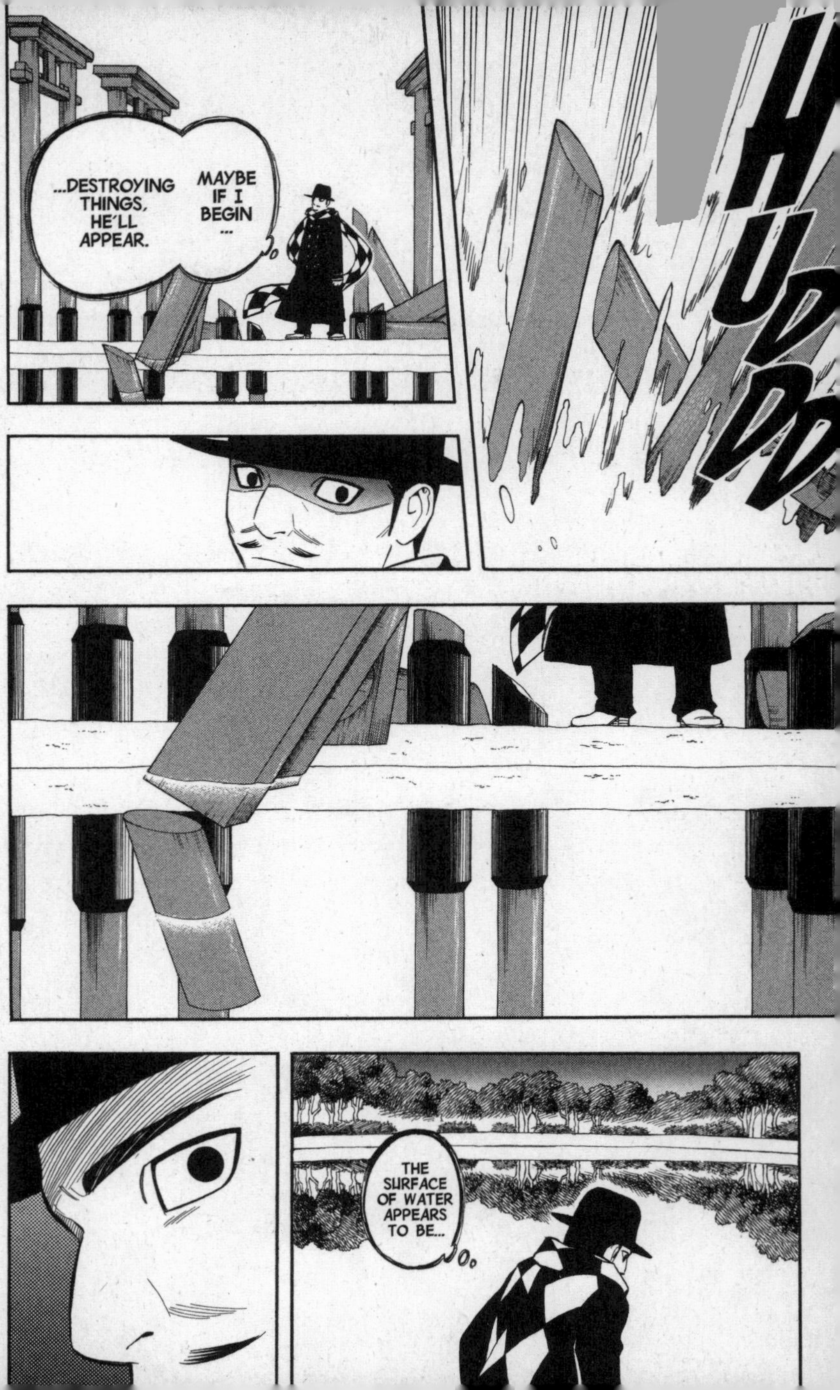
MAYBE IF I BEGIN ...
...DESTROYING THINGS, HE'LL APPEAR.
THE SURFACE OF WATER APPEARS TO BE...

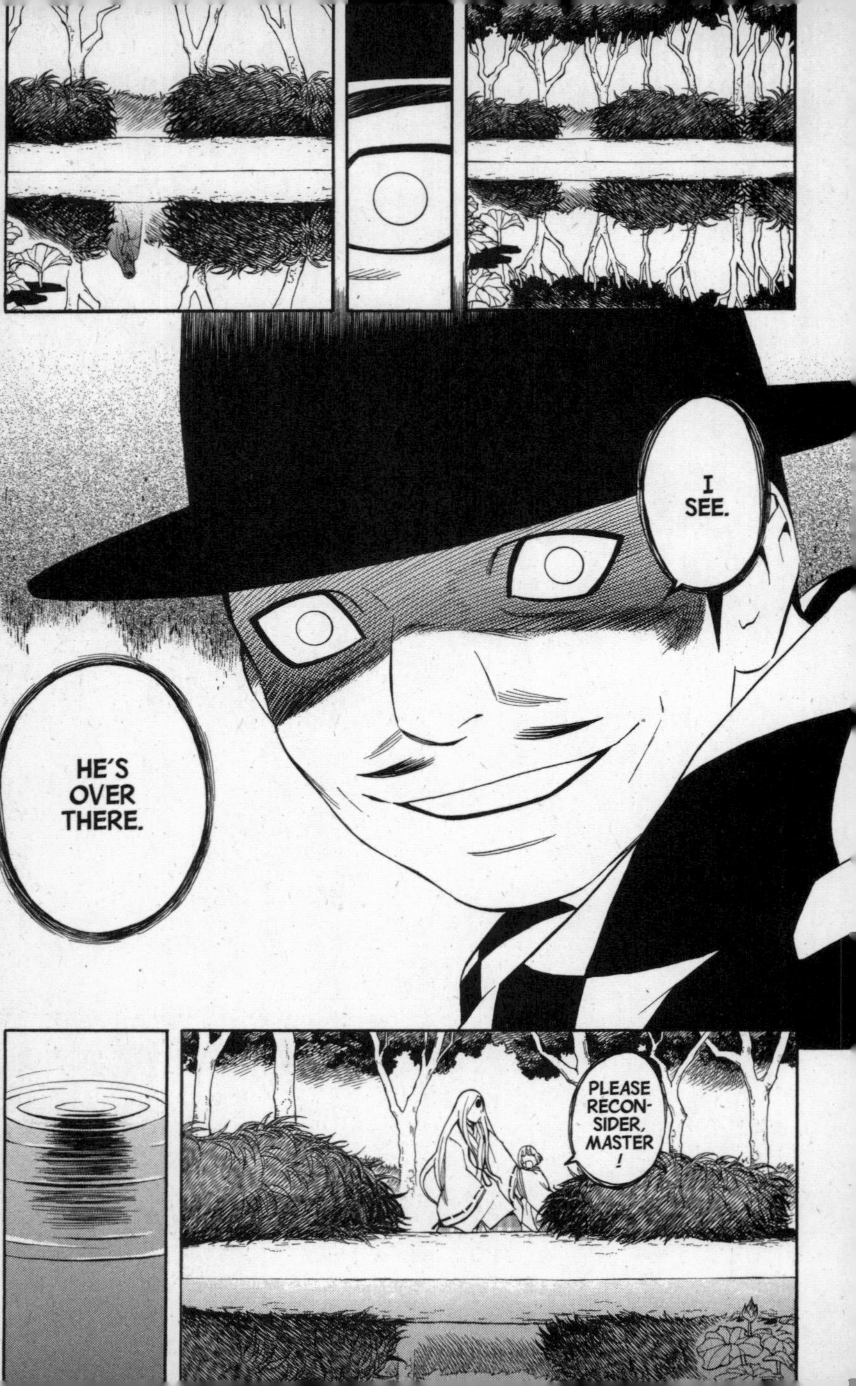
I SEE.
HE'S OVER THERE.
PLEASE RECON-SIDER, MASTER!

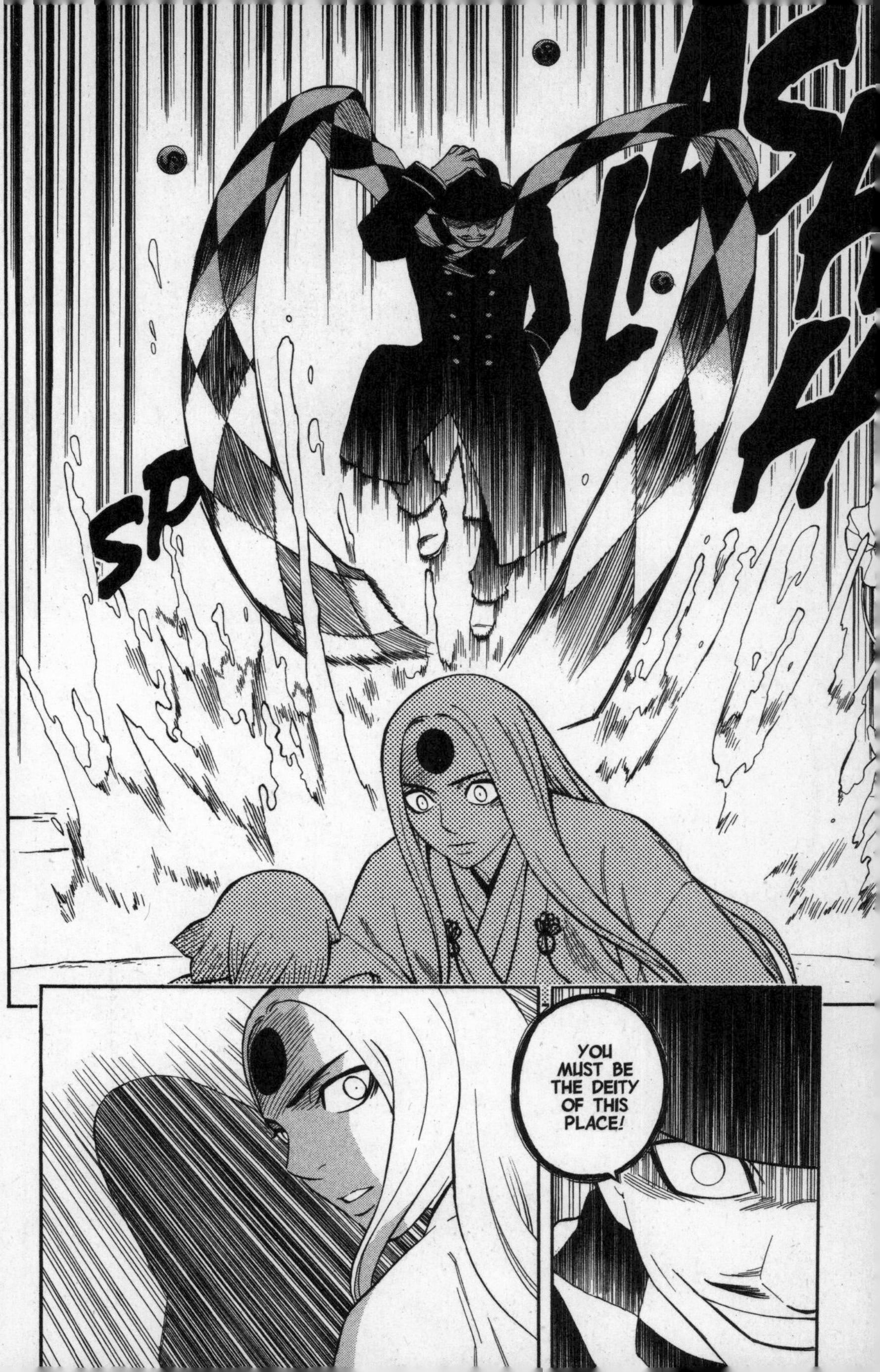
YOU MUST BE THE DEITY OF THIS PLACE!

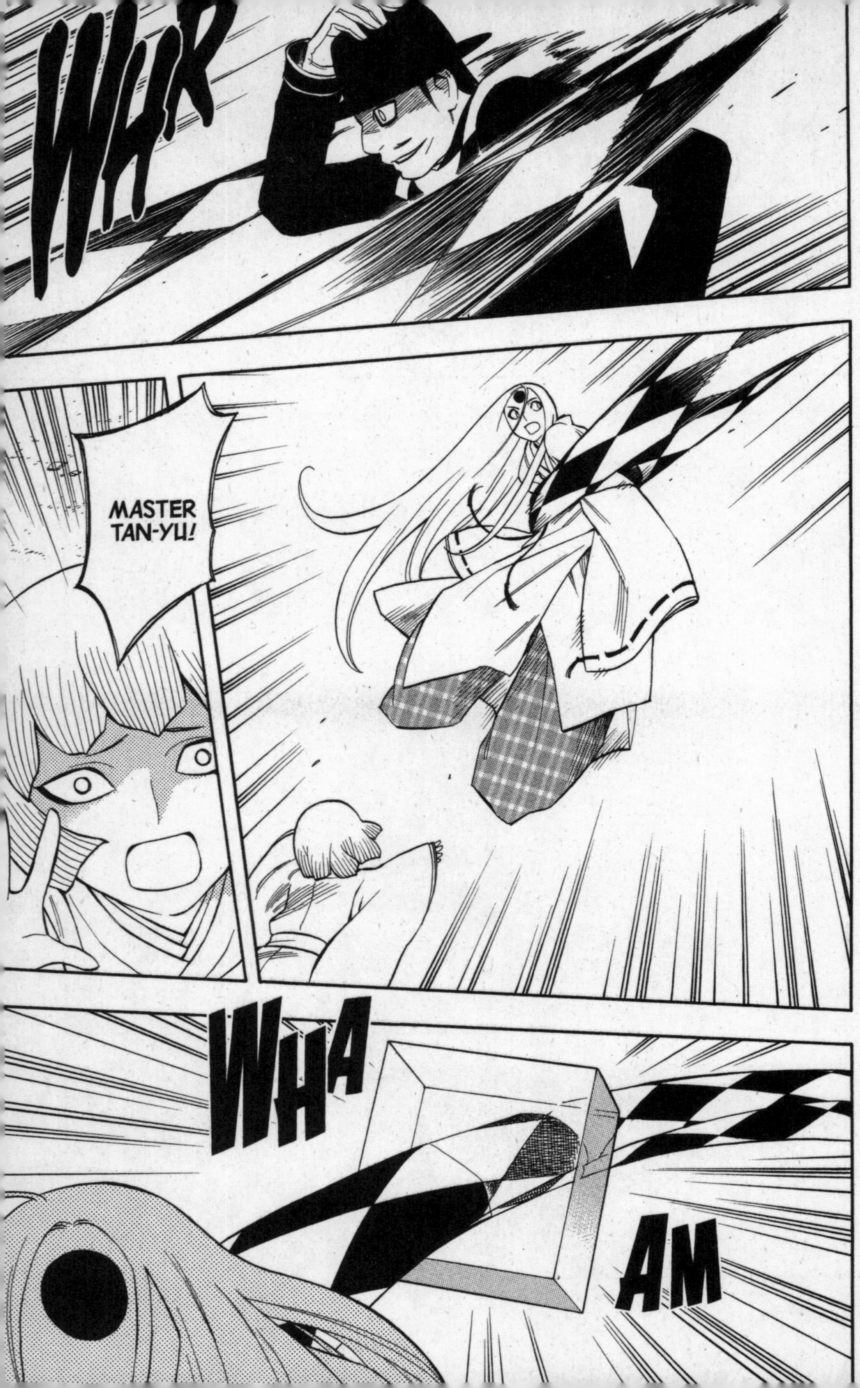
WHIR
MASTER TAN-YU!
WHA
AM

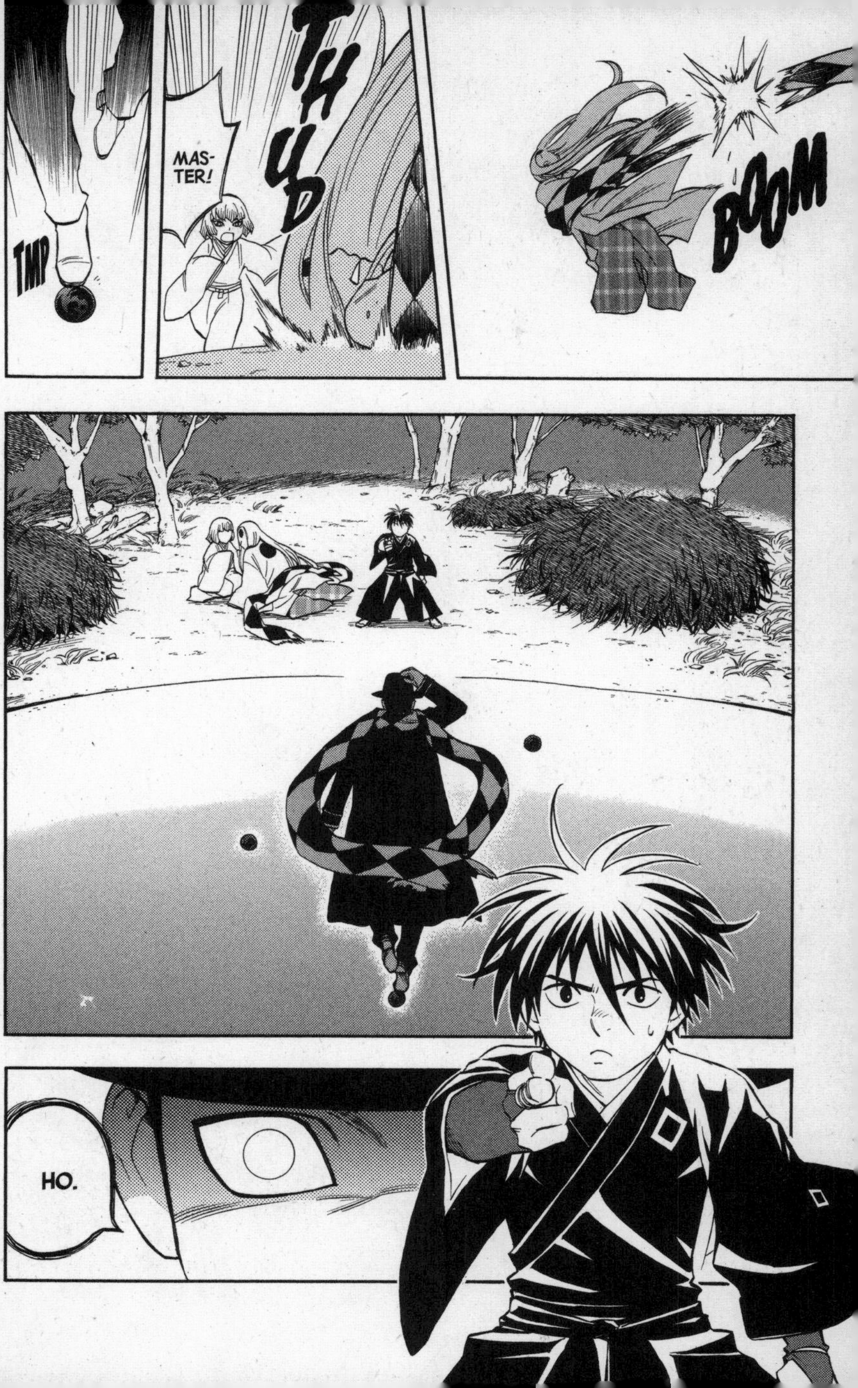
BOOM
THUD
MAS-
TER!
TMP
HO.

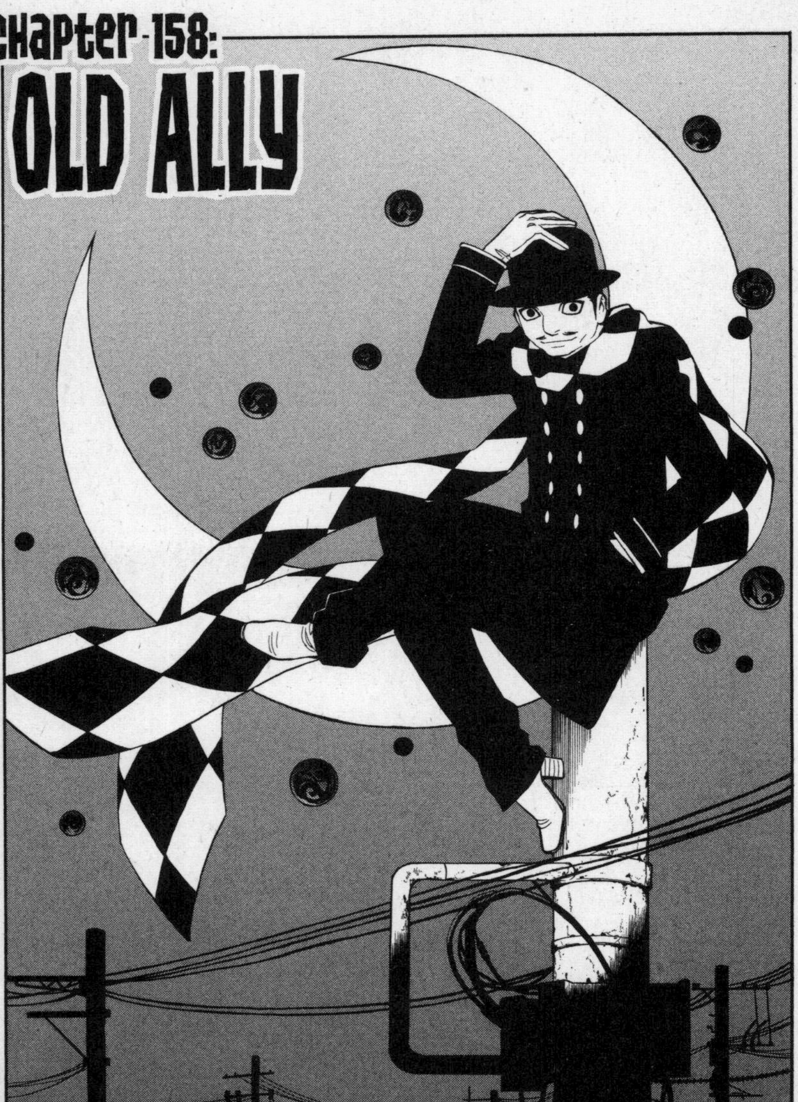
Chapter 158:
OLD ALLY

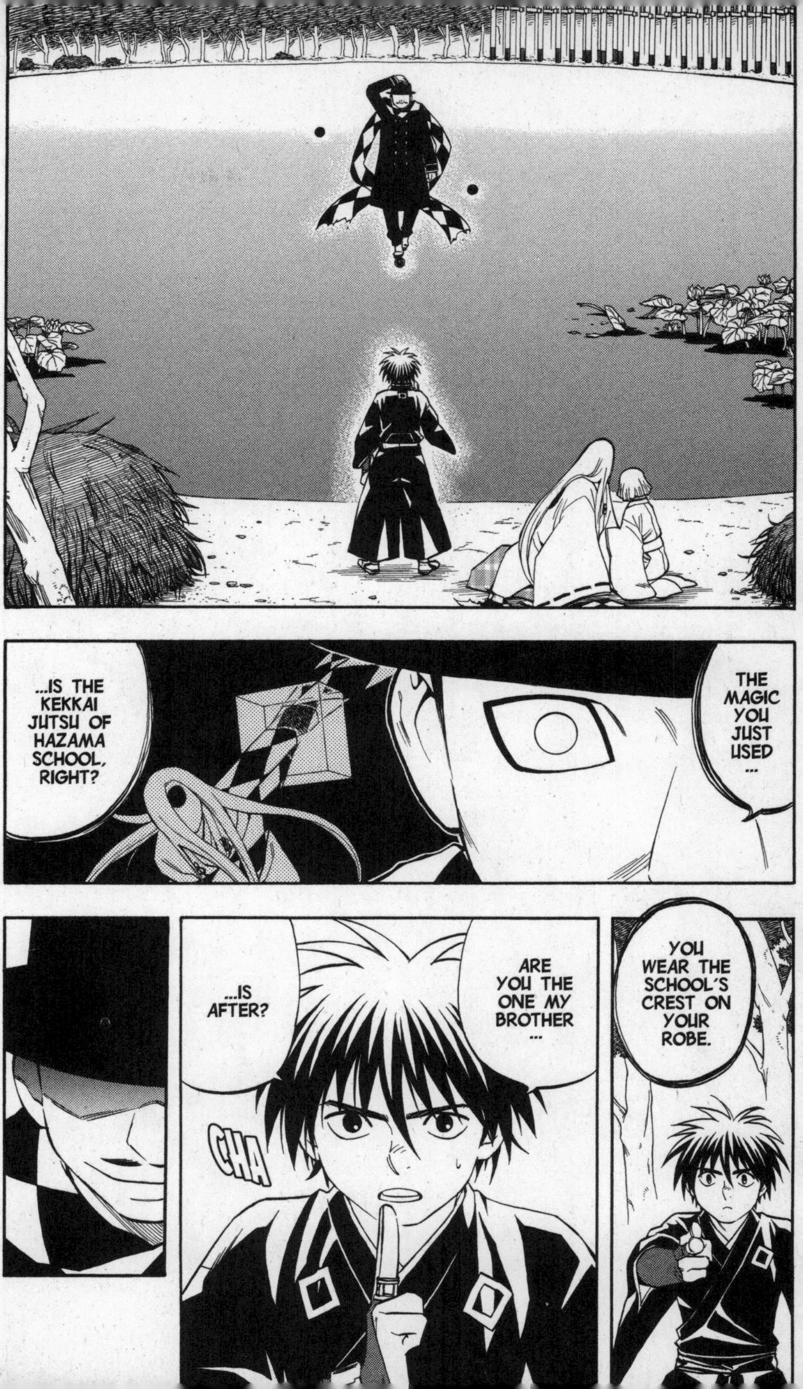
THE MAGIC YOU JUST USED ...
...IS THE KEKKAI JUTSU OF HAZAMA SCHOOL, RIGHT?
YOU WEAR THE SCHOOL'S CREST ON YOUR ROBE.
ARE YOU THE ONE MY BROTHER ...
...IS AFTER?
CHA

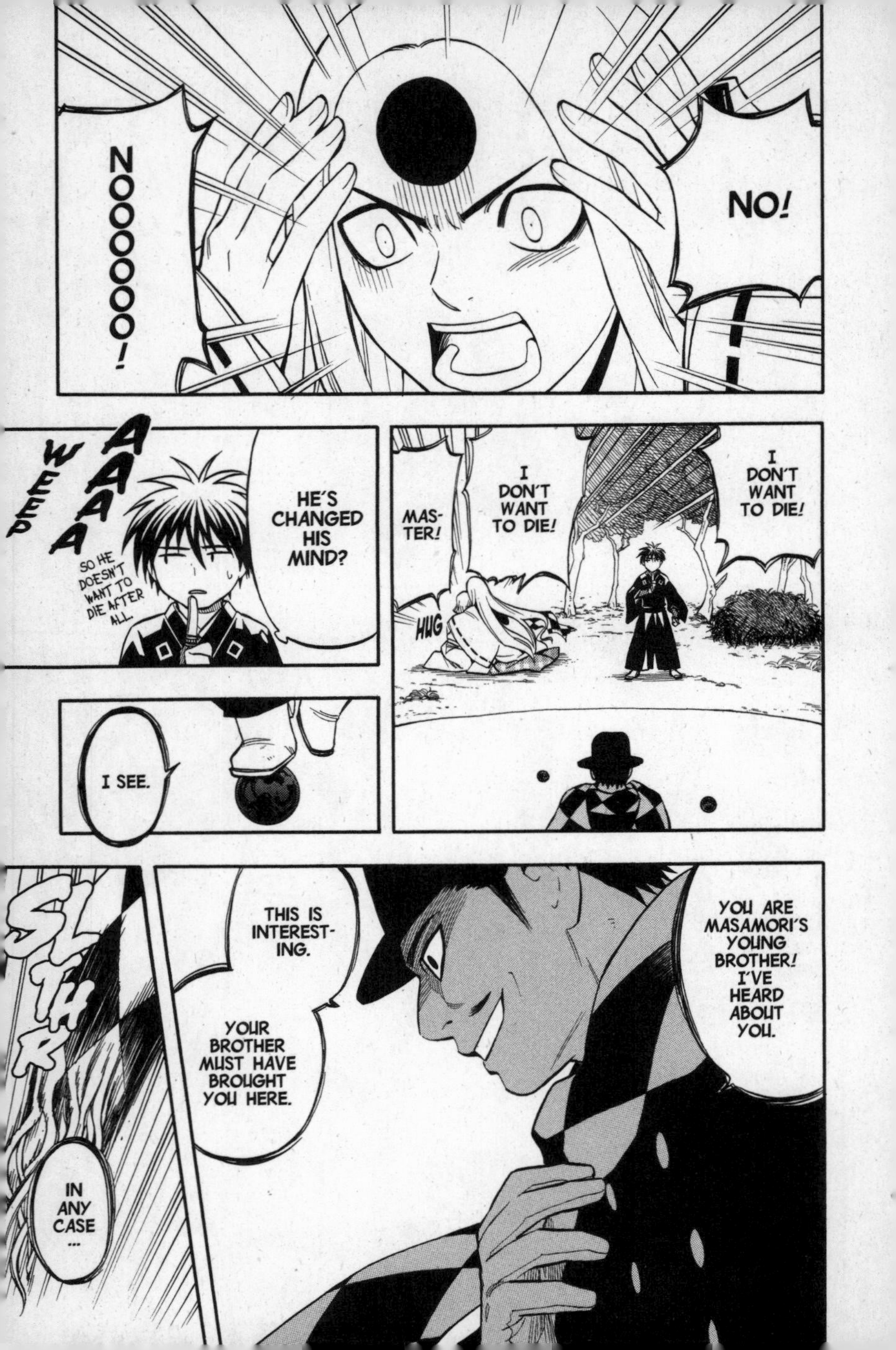
NO!
NOOOOOOO!
I DON'T WANT TO DIE!
I DON'T WANT TO DIE!
MAS-TER!
HUG
HE'S CHANGED HIS MIND?
AAAAA
WEEP
SO HE DOESN'T WANT TO DIE AFTER ALL.
I SEE.
YOU ARE MASAMORI'S YOUNG BROTHER! I'VE HEARD ABOUT YOU.
THIS IS INTEREST-ING.
YOUR BROTHER MUST HAVE BROUGHT YOU HERE.
SLTHR
IN ANY CASE...

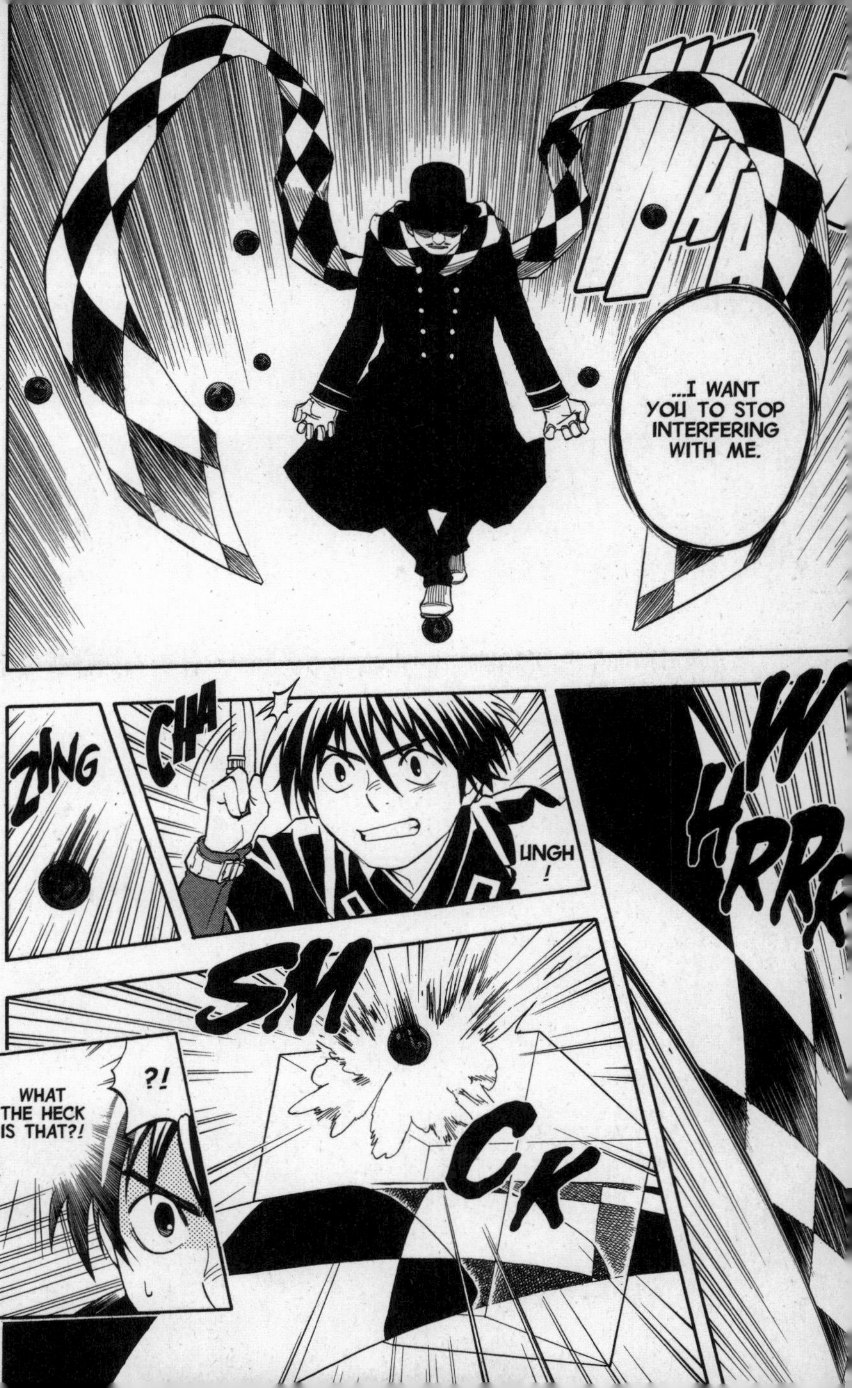
PHA
...I WANT YOU TO STOP INTERFERING WITH ME.
WHRRR
CHA
UNGH!
ZING
SM
CK
?!
WHAT THE HECK IS THAT?!

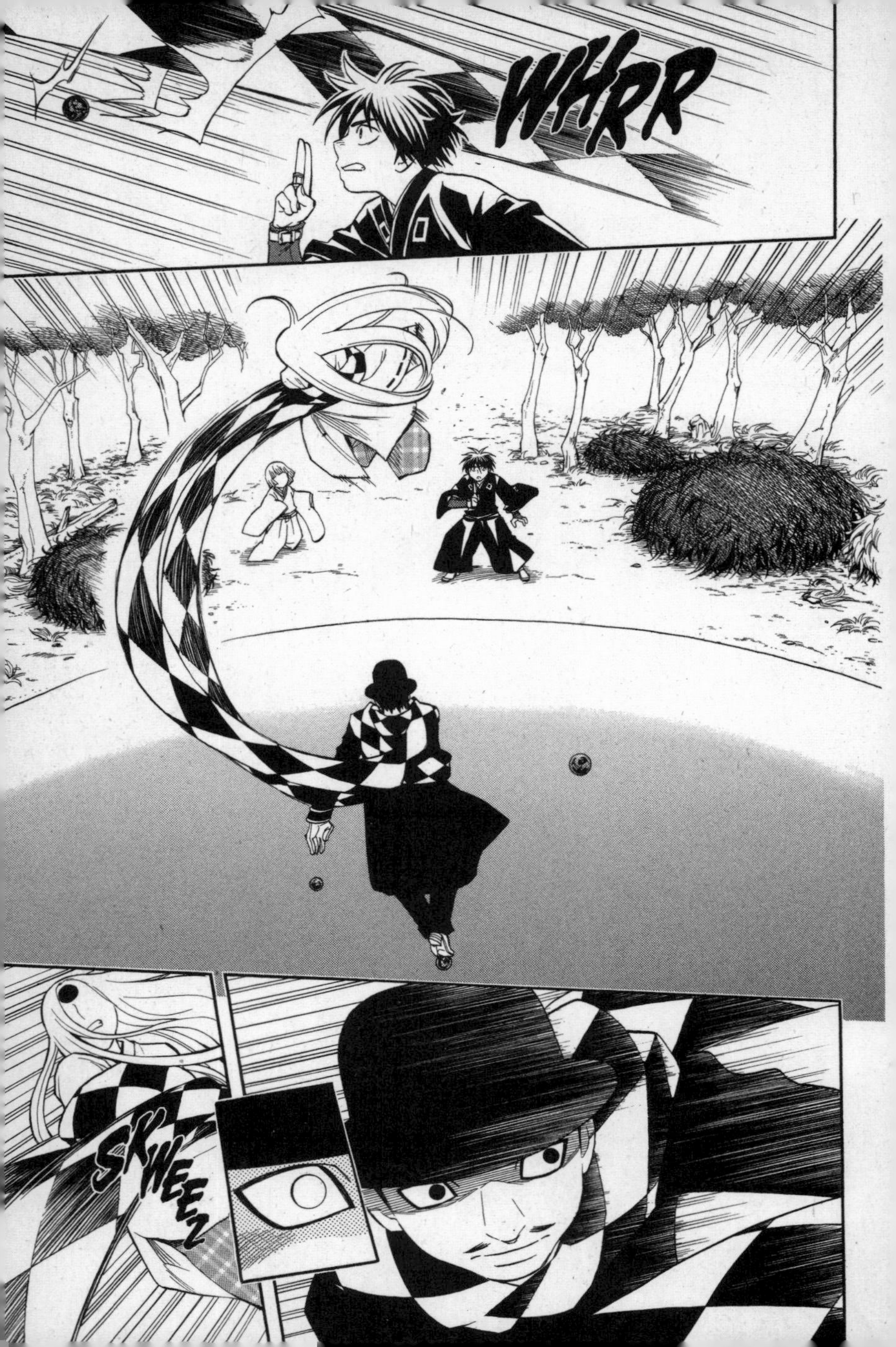
WHRR
SKWEEZ

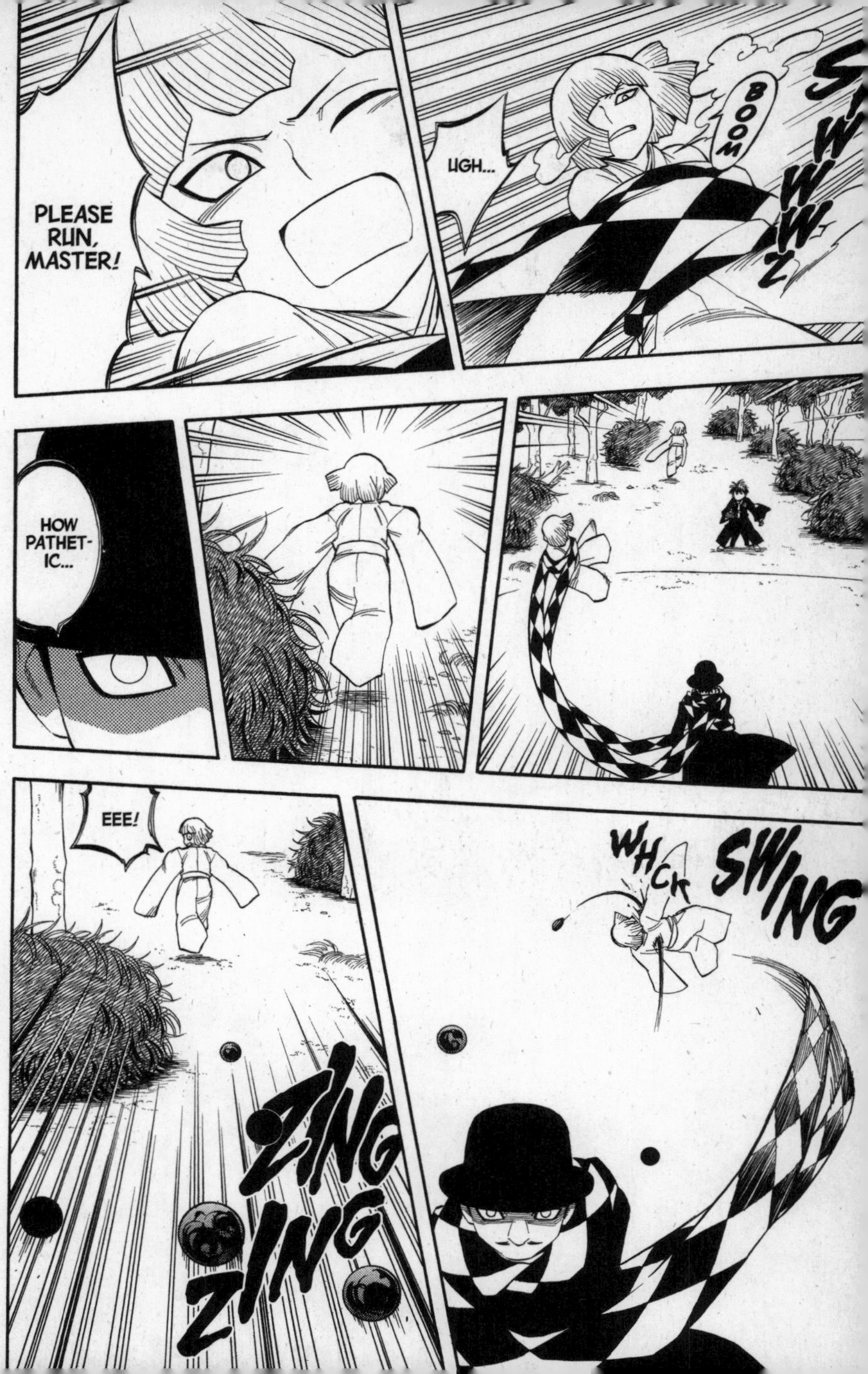
BOOM
SWWWWZ
UGH...
PLEASE RUN, MASTER!
HOW PATHETIC...
WHCK
SWING
ZING ZING
EEE!

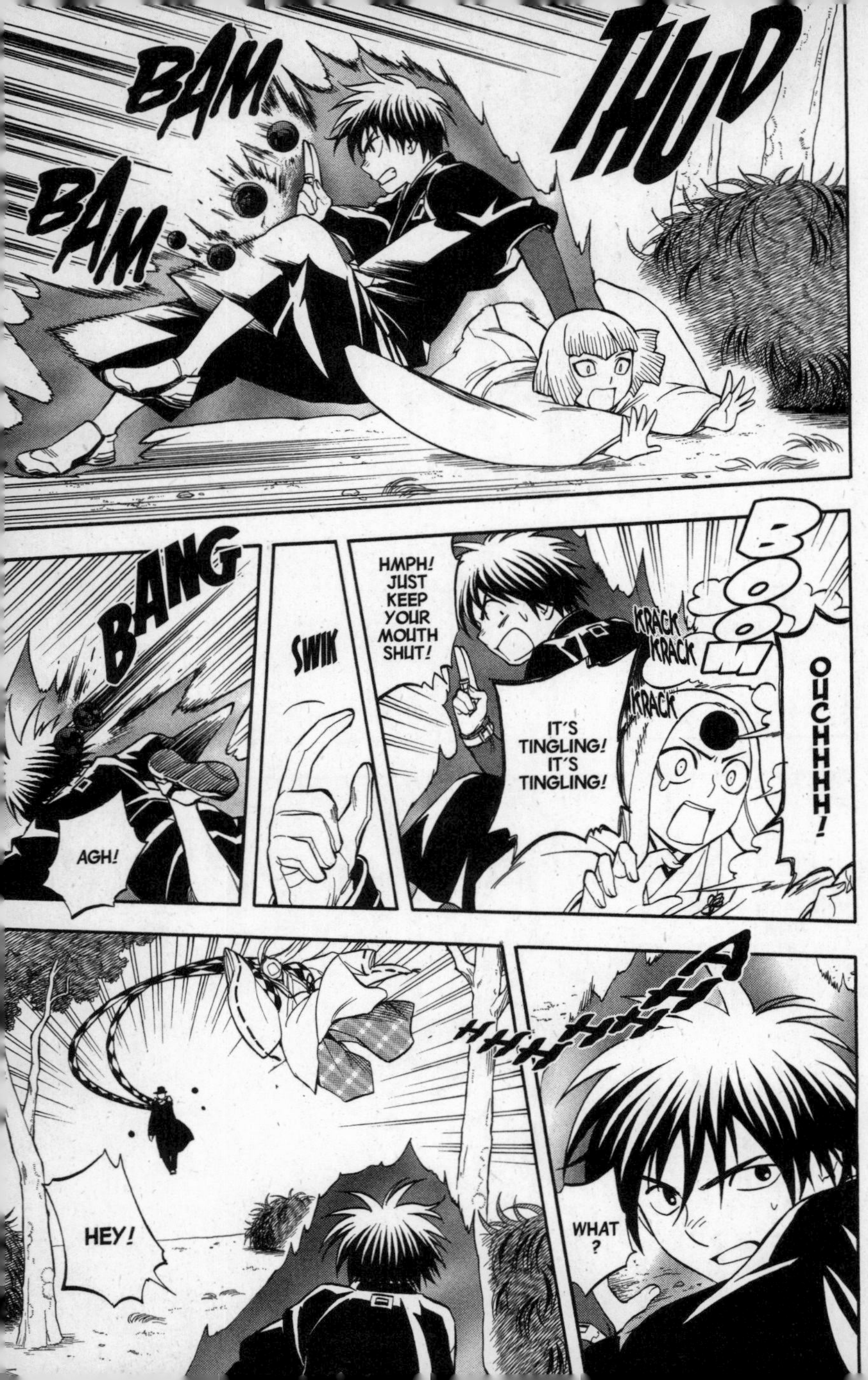
THUD
BAM
BAM
BAM
BOOM
OUCHHHH!
KRACK
KRACK
KRACK
HMPH! JUST KEEP YOUR MOUTH SHUT!
IT'S TINGLING! IT'S TINGLING!
SWIK
BANG
AGH!
HHHHHHHHA
WHAT?
HEY!

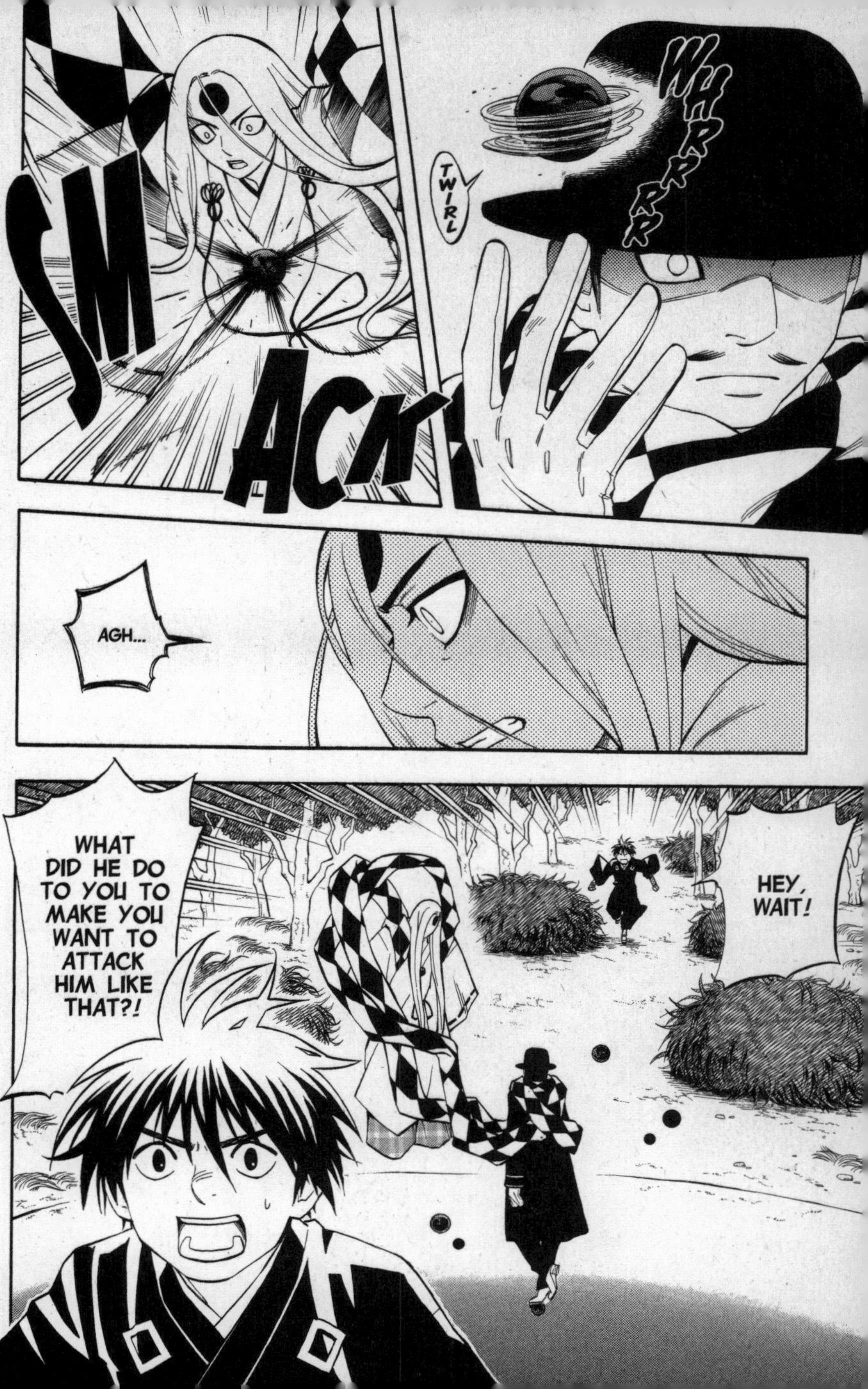
WHRRRRR
TWIRL
SMACK
AGH...
HEY, WAIT!
WHAT DID HE DO TO YOU TO MAKE YOU WANT TO ATTACK HIM LIKE THAT?!

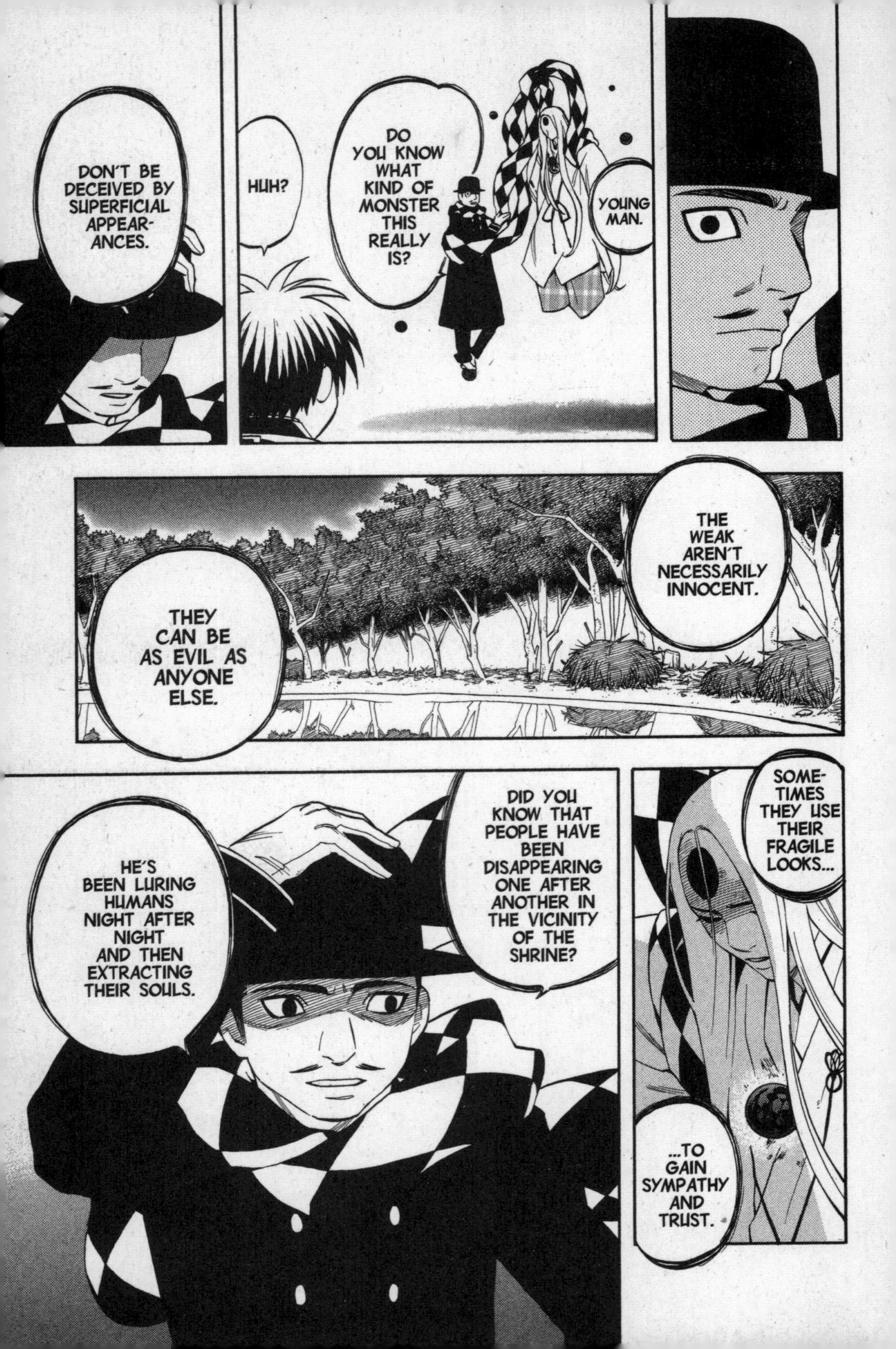
YOUNG MAN.
DO YOU KNOW WHAT KIND OF MONSTER THIS REALLY IS?
HUH?
DON'T BE DECEIVED BY SUPERFICIAL APPEAR-ANCES.
THE WEAK AREN'T NECESSARILY INNOCENT.
THEY CAN BE AS EVIL AS ANYONE ELSE.
SOME-TIMES THEY USE THEIR FRAGILE LOOKS...
...TO GAIN SYMPATHY AND TRUST.
DID YOU KNOW THAT PEOPLE HAVE BEEN DISAPPEARING ONE AFTER ANOTHER IN THE VICINITY OF THE SHRINE?
HE'S BEEN LURING HUMANS NIGHT AFTER NIGHT AND THEN EXTRACTING THEIR SOULS.

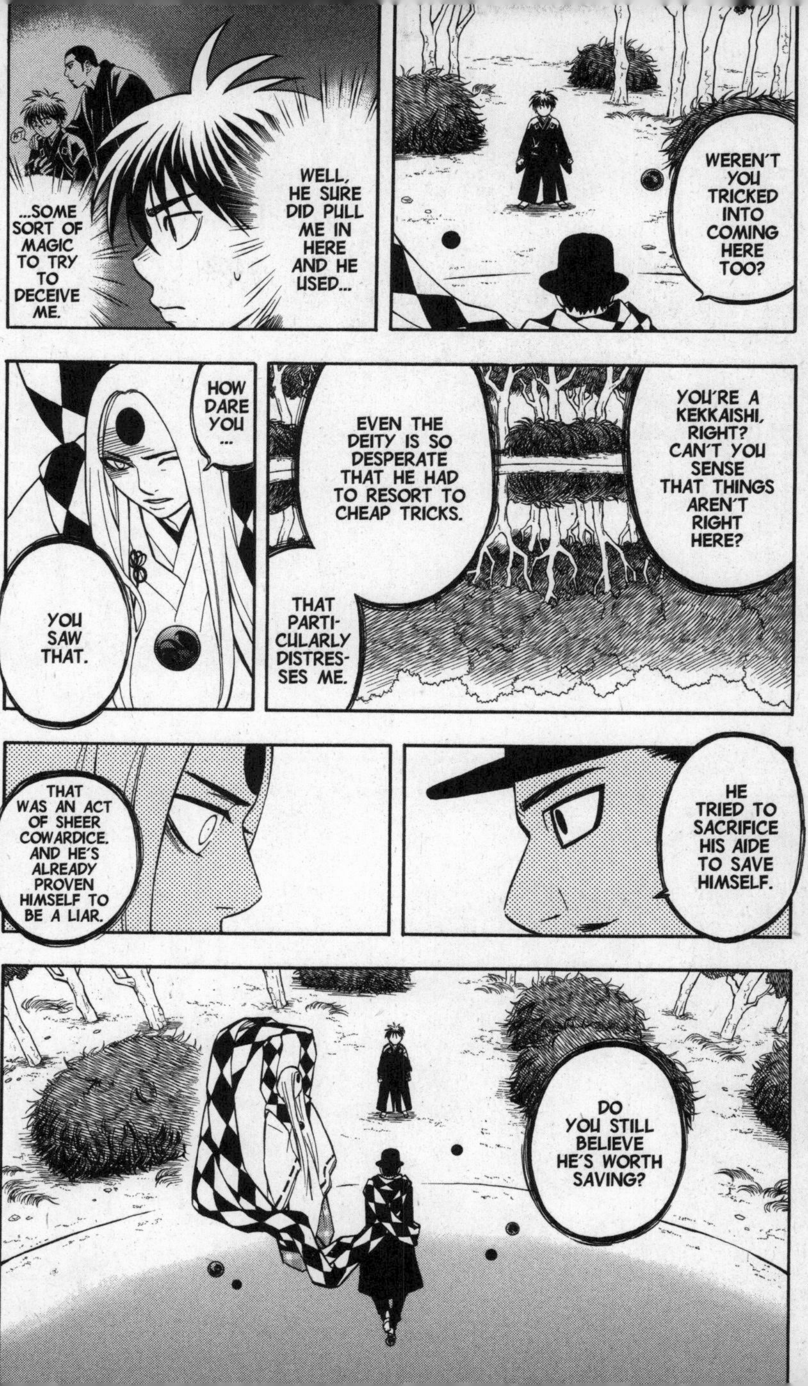
WEREN'T YOU TRICKED INTO COMING HERE TOO?
WELL, HE SURE DID PULL ME IN HERE AND HE USED...
...SOME SORT OF MAGIC TO TRY TO DECEIVE ME.
YOU'RE A KEKKAISHI, RIGHT? CAN'T YOU SENSE THAT THINGS AREN'T RIGHT HERE?
EVEN THE DEITY IS SO DESPERATE THAT HE HAD TO RESORT TO CHEAP TRICKS.
THAT PARTICULARLY DISTRESSES ME.
HOW DARE YOU...
YOU SAW THAT.
HE TRIED TO SACRIFICE HIS AIDE TO SAVE HIMSELF.
THAT WAS AN ACT OF SHEER COWARDICE. AND HE'S ALREADY PROVEN HIMSELF TO BE A LIAR.
DO YOU STILL BELIEVE HE'S WORTH SAVING?

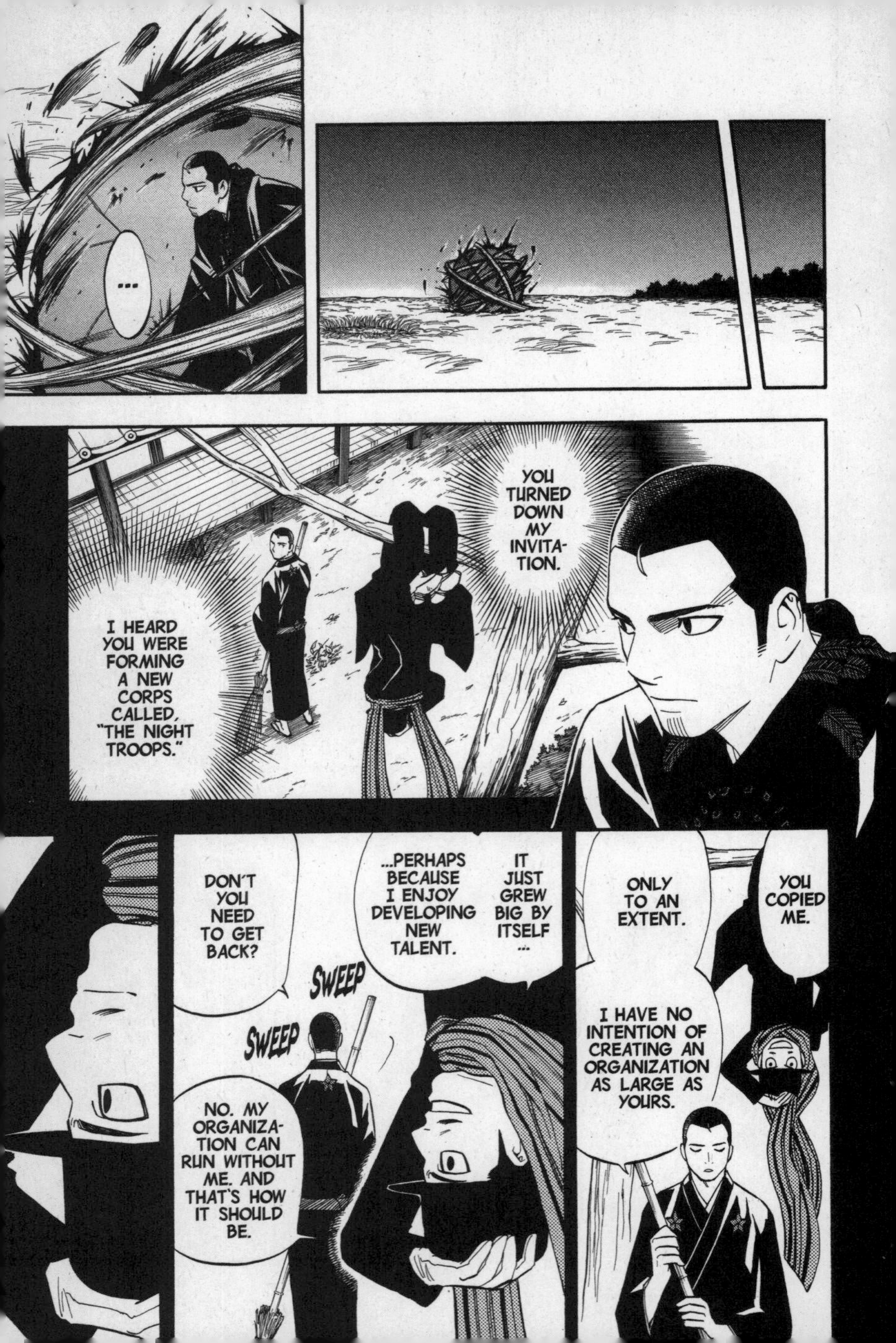
...
YOU TURNED DOWN MY INVITATION.
I HEARD YOU WERE FORMING A NEW CORPS CALLED, "THE NIGHT TROOPS."
YOU COPIED ME.
ONLY TO AN EXTENT.
I HAVE NO INTENTION OF CREATING AN ORGANIZATION AS LARGE AS YOURS.
IT JUST GREW BIG BY ITSELF ...
...PERHAPS BECAUSE I ENJOY DEVELOPING NEW TALENT.
DON'T YOU NEED TO GET BACK?
SWEEP
SWEEP
NO. MY ORGANIZATION CAN RUN WITHOUT ME. AND THAT'S HOW IT SHOULD BE.

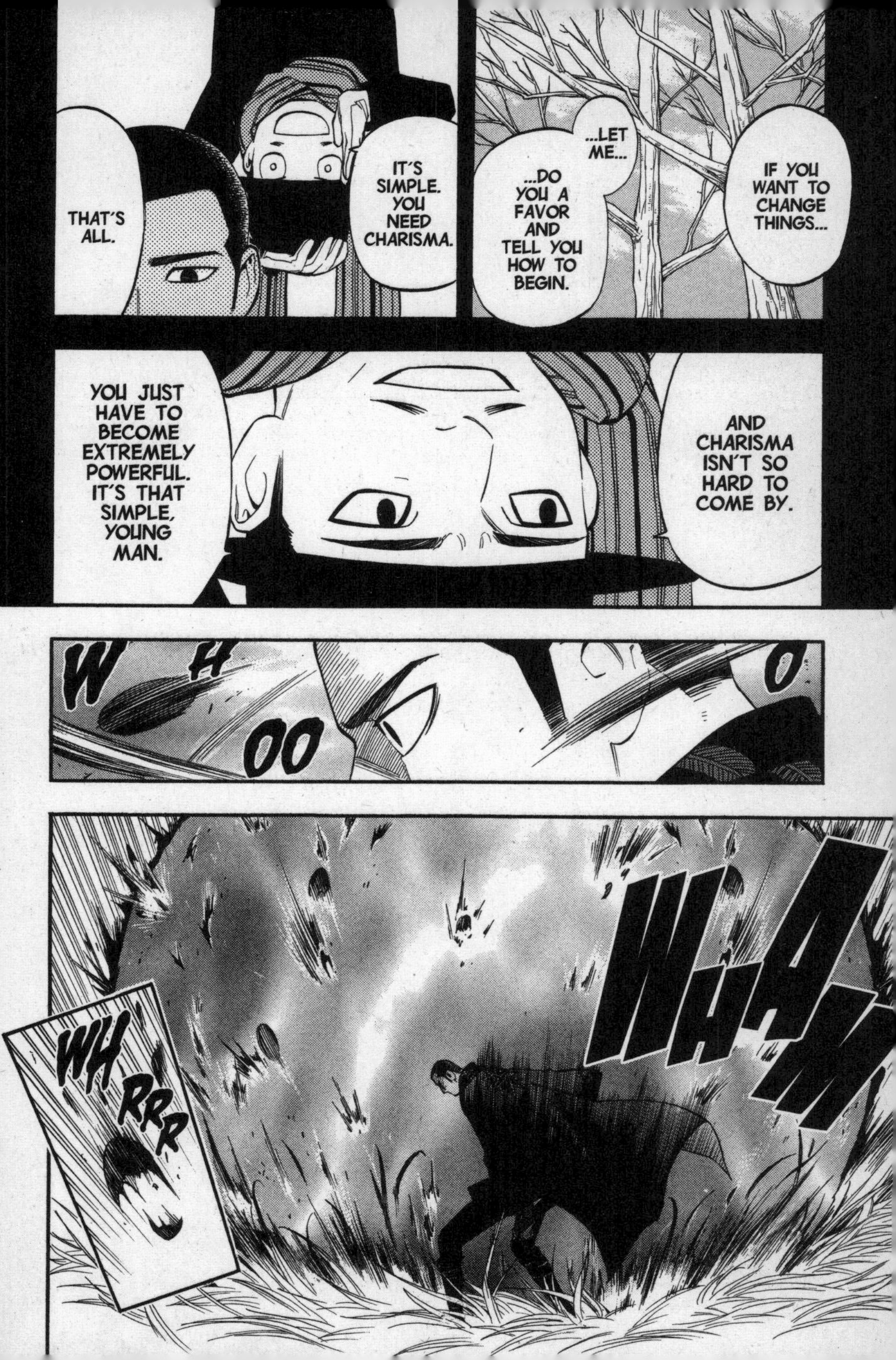
IF YOU WANT TO CHANGE THINGS...
...LET ME...
...DO YOU A FAVOR AND TELL YOU HOW TO BEGIN.
IT'S SIMPLE. YOU NEED CHARISMA.
THAT'S ALL.
AND CHARISMA ISN'T SO HARD TO COME BY.
YOU JUST HAVE TO BECOME EXTREMELY POWERFUL. IT'S THAT SIMPLE, YOUNG MAN.
WHOOO
WHAM
WHRRR

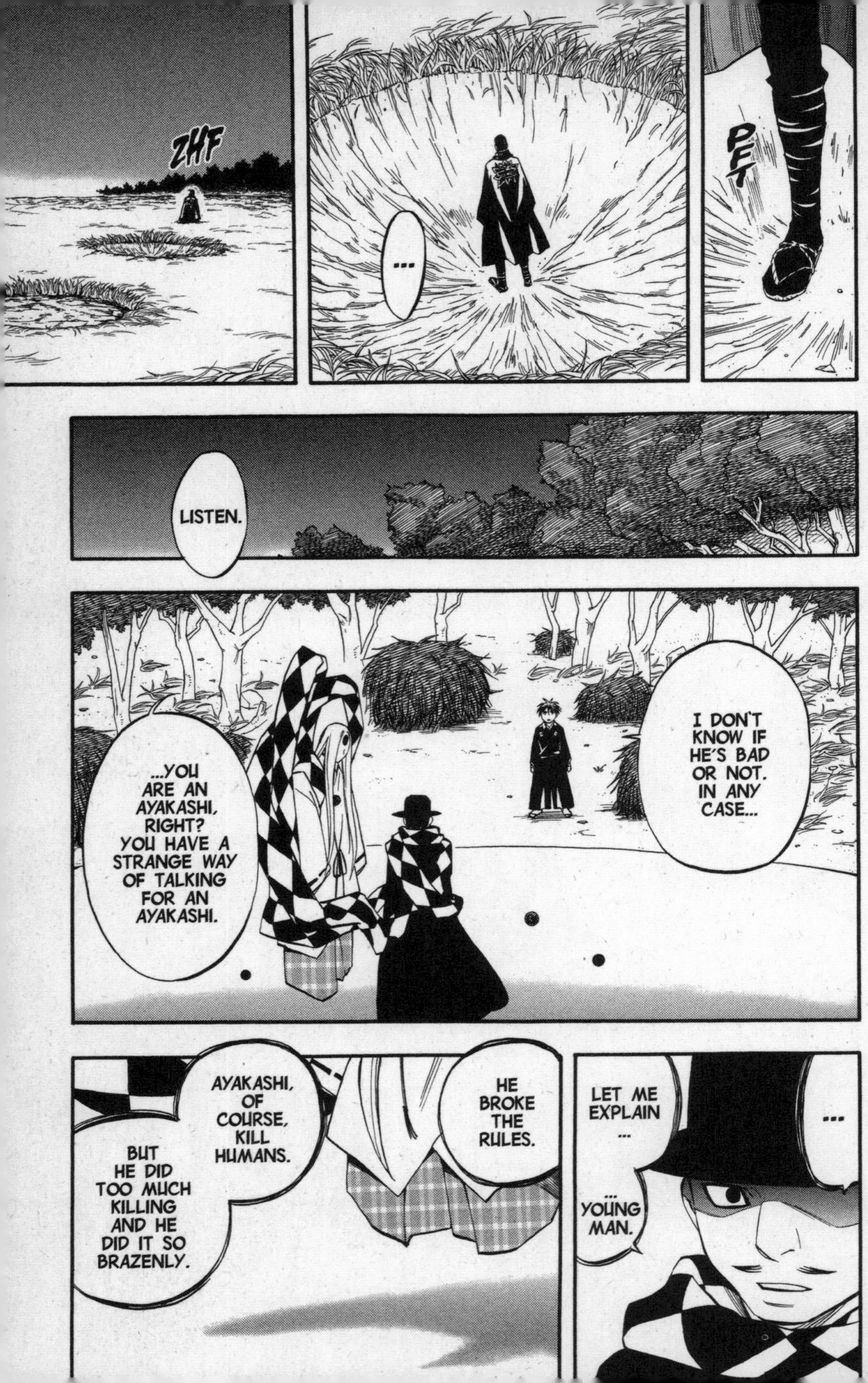
PFT
...
ZHF
LISTEN.
I DON'T KNOW IF HE'S BAD OR NOT. IN ANY CASE...
...YOU ARE AN AYAKASHI, RIGHT? YOU HAVE A STRANGE WAY OF TALKING FOR AN AYAKASHI.
...
LET ME EXPLAIN ... ... YOUNG MAN.
HE BROKE THE RULES.
AYAKASHI, OF COURSE, KILL HUMANS.
BUT HE DID TOO MUCH KILLING AND HE DID IT SO BRAZENLY.

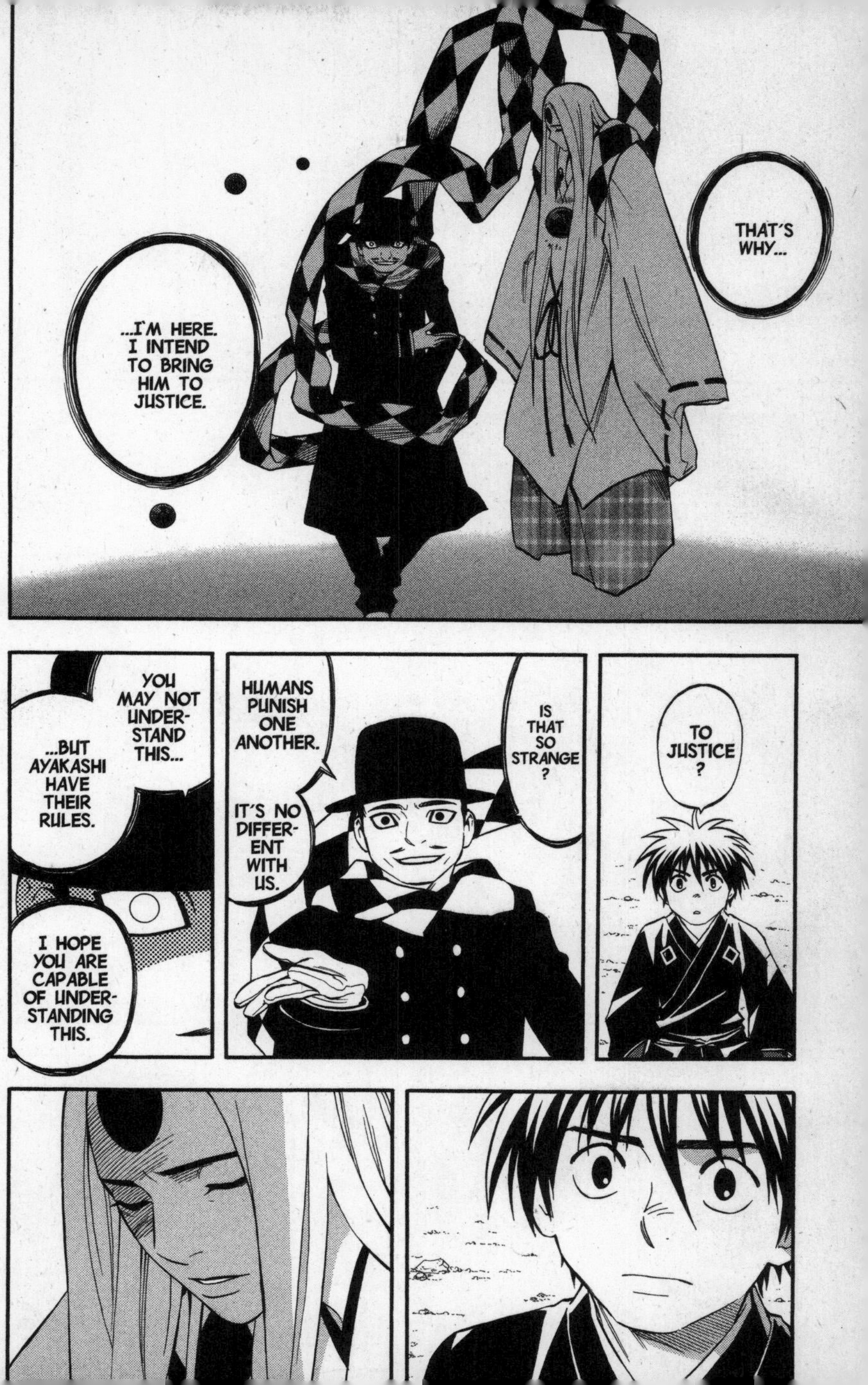
THAT'S WHY...
...I'M HERE. I INTEND TO BRING HIM TO JUSTICE.
TO JUSTICE?
IS THAT SO STRANGE?
HUMANS PUNISH ONE ANOTHER.
IT'S NO DIFFER-ENT WITH US.
YOU MAY NOT UNDER-STAND THIS...
...BUT AYAKASHI HAVE THEIR RULES.
I HOPE YOU ARE CAPABLE OF UNDER-STANDING THIS.

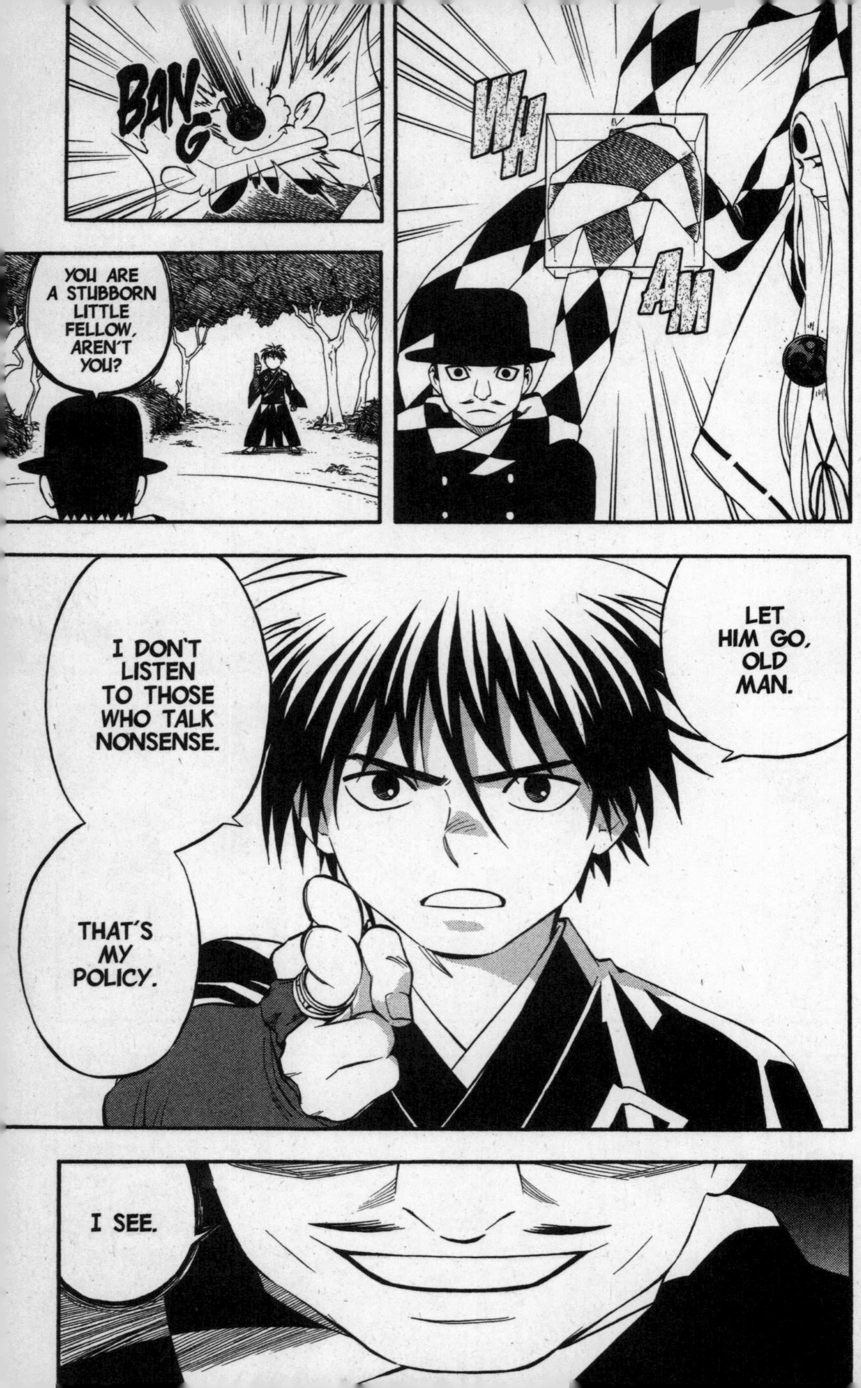
WHAM
BANG
YOU ARE A STUBBORN LITTLE FELLOW, AREN'T YOU?
LET HIM GO, OLD MAN.
I DON'T LISTEN TO THOSE WHO TALK NONSENSE.
THAT'S MY POLICY.
I SEE.

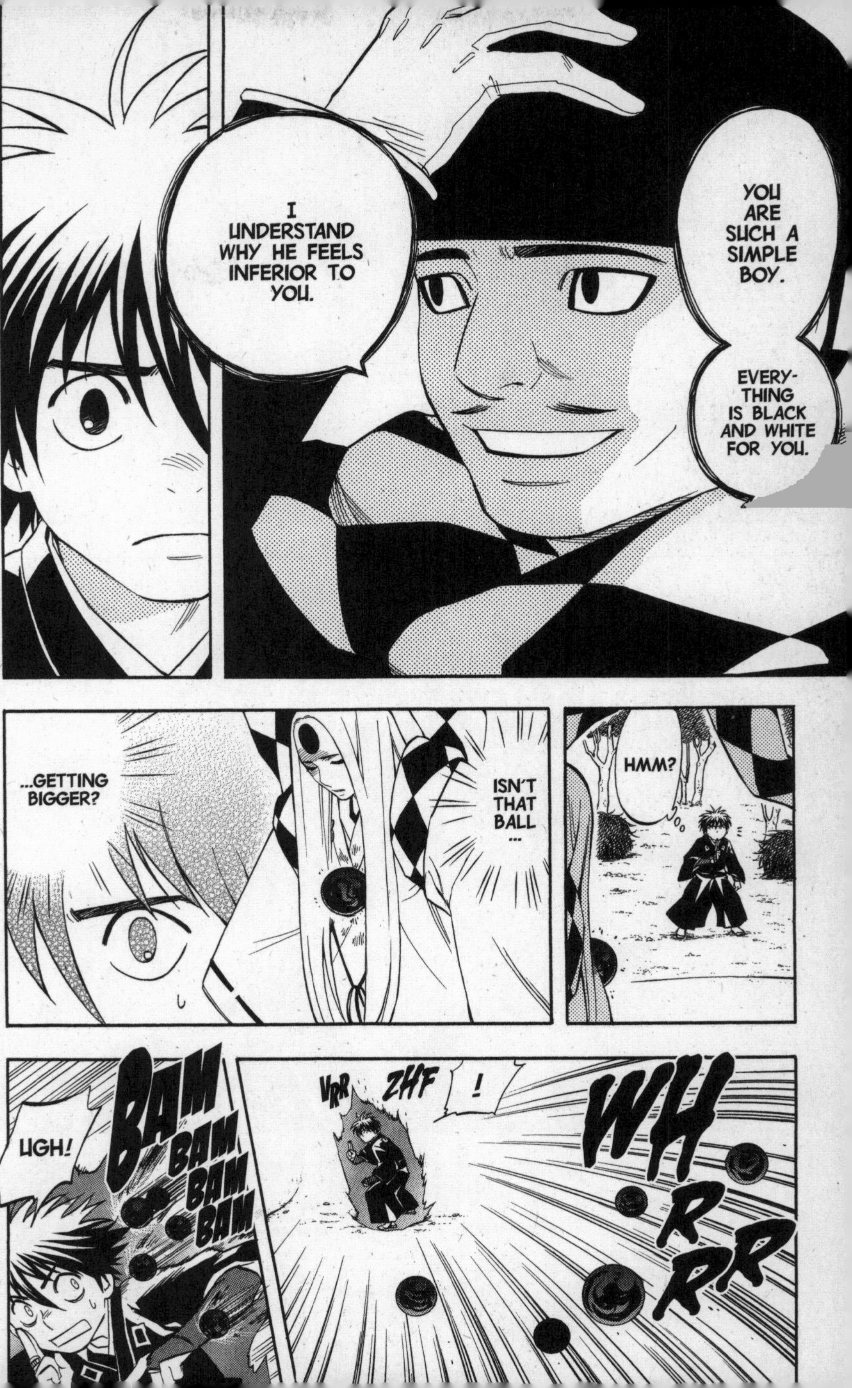
YOU ARE SUCH A SIMPLE BOY.
EVERY-THING IS BLACK AND WHITE FOR YOU.
I UNDERSTAND WHY HE FEELS INFERIOR TO YOU.
HMM?
ISN'T THAT BALL ...
...GETTING BIGGER?
WHRRR
!
ZHF
VRR
BAM BAM BAM BAM BAM
UGH!

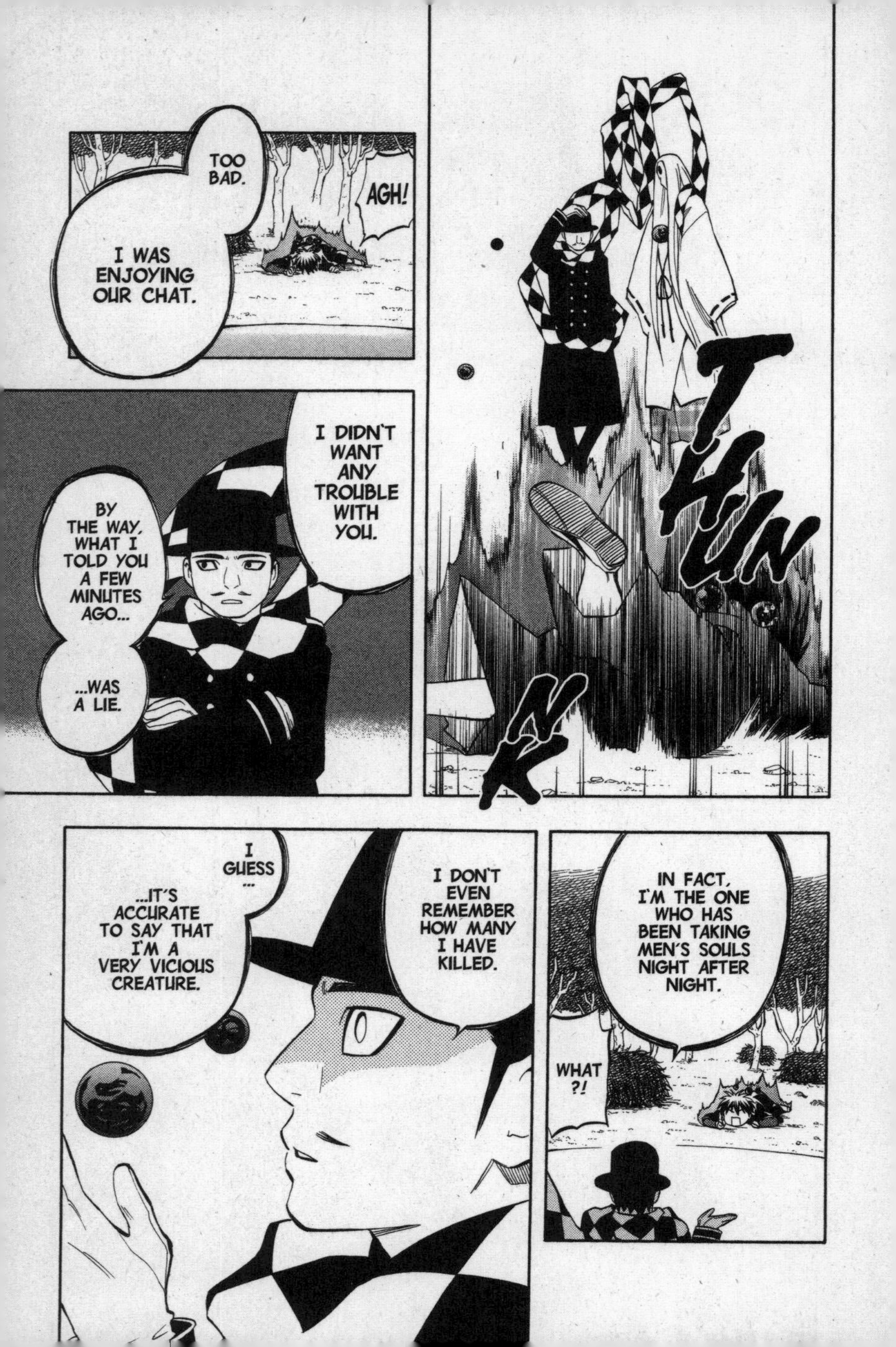
THUNK
AGH!
TOO BAD.
I WAS ENJOYING OUR CHAT.
I DIDN'T WANT ANY TROUBLE WITH YOU.
BY THE WAY, WHAT I TOLD YOU A FEW MINUTES AGO...
...WAS A LIE.
IN FACT, I'M THE ONE WHO HAS BEEN TAKING MEN'S SOULS NIGHT AFTER NIGHT.
WHAT?!
I DON'T EVEN REMEMBER HOW MANY I HAVE KILLED.
I GUESS...
...IT'S ACCURATE TO SAY THAT I'M A VERY VICIOUS CREATURE.

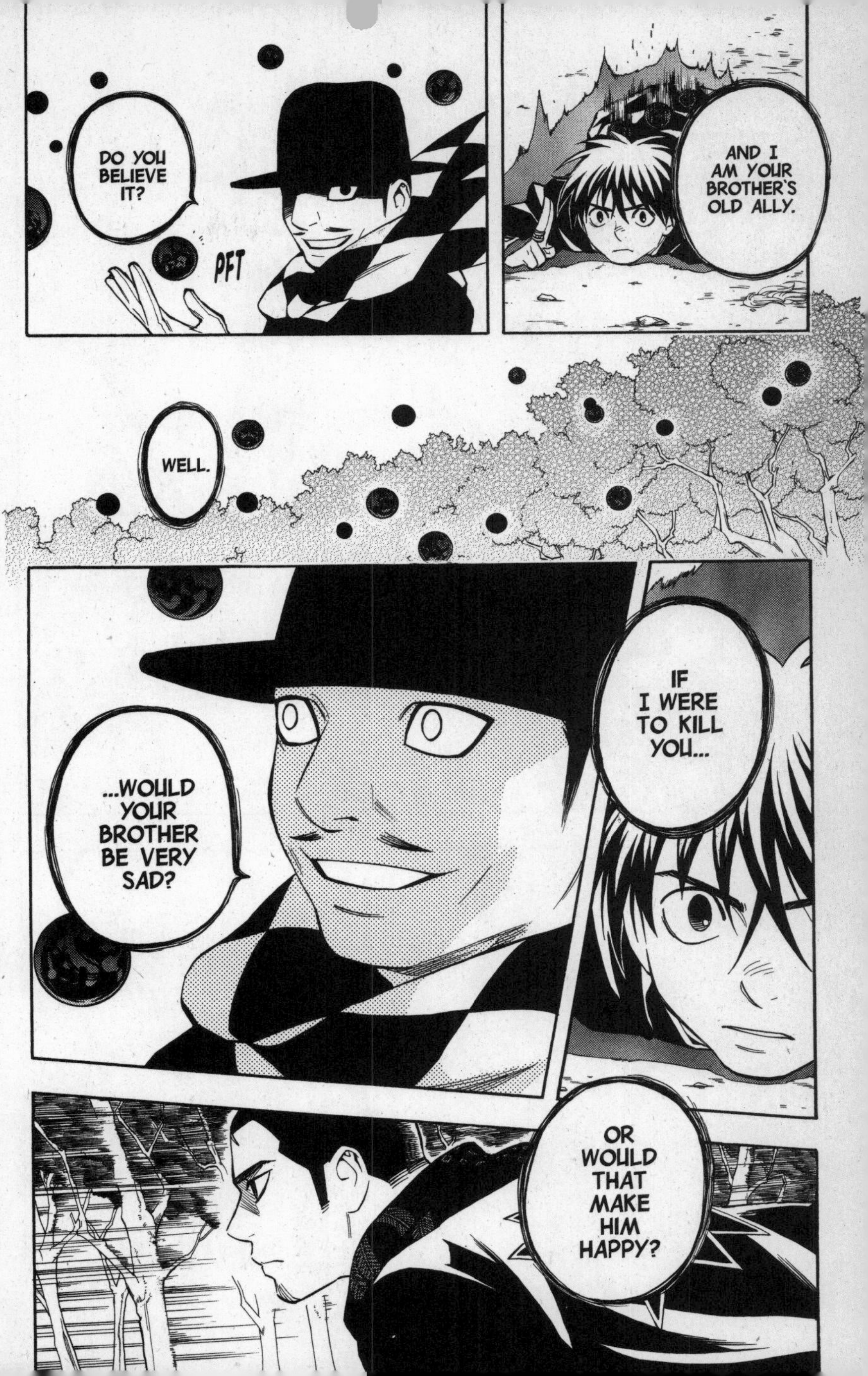
AND I AM YOUR BROTHER'S OLD ALLY.
DO YOU BELIEVE IT?
PFT
WELL.
IF I WERE TO KILL YOU...
...WOULD YOUR BROTHER BE VERY SAD?
OR WOULD THAT MAKE HIM HAPPY?

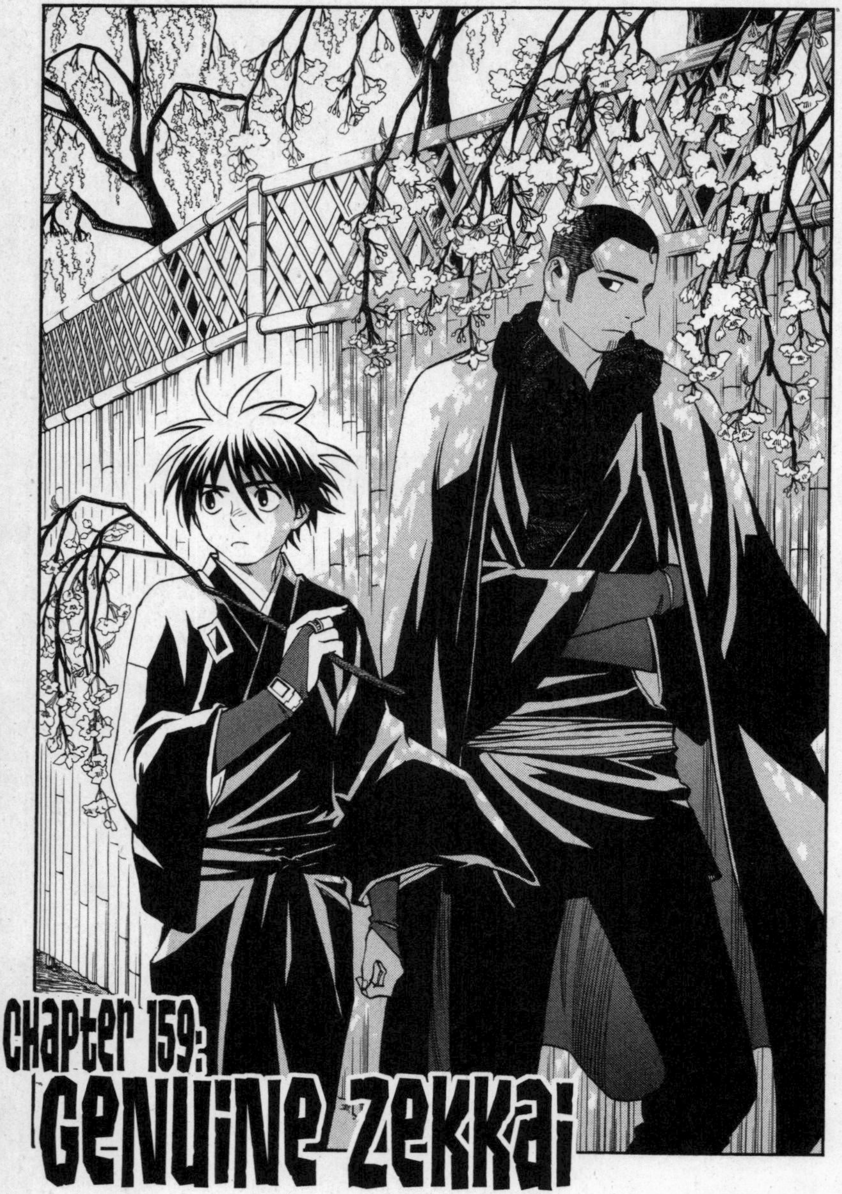
Chapter 159:
Genuine Zekkai

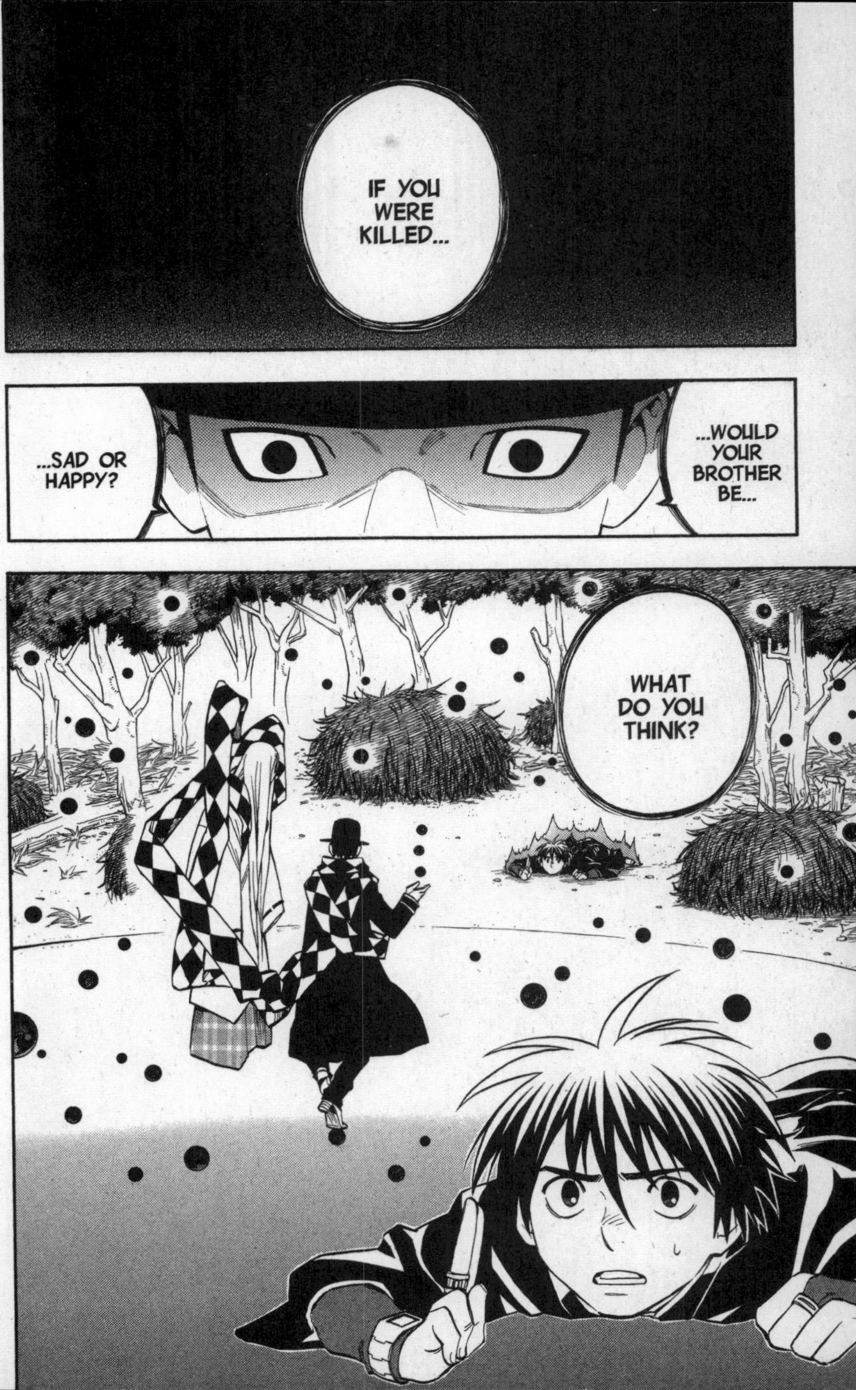
IF YOU WERE KILLED...
...WOULD YOUR BROTHER BE...
...SAD OR HAPPY?
WHAT DO YOU THINK?

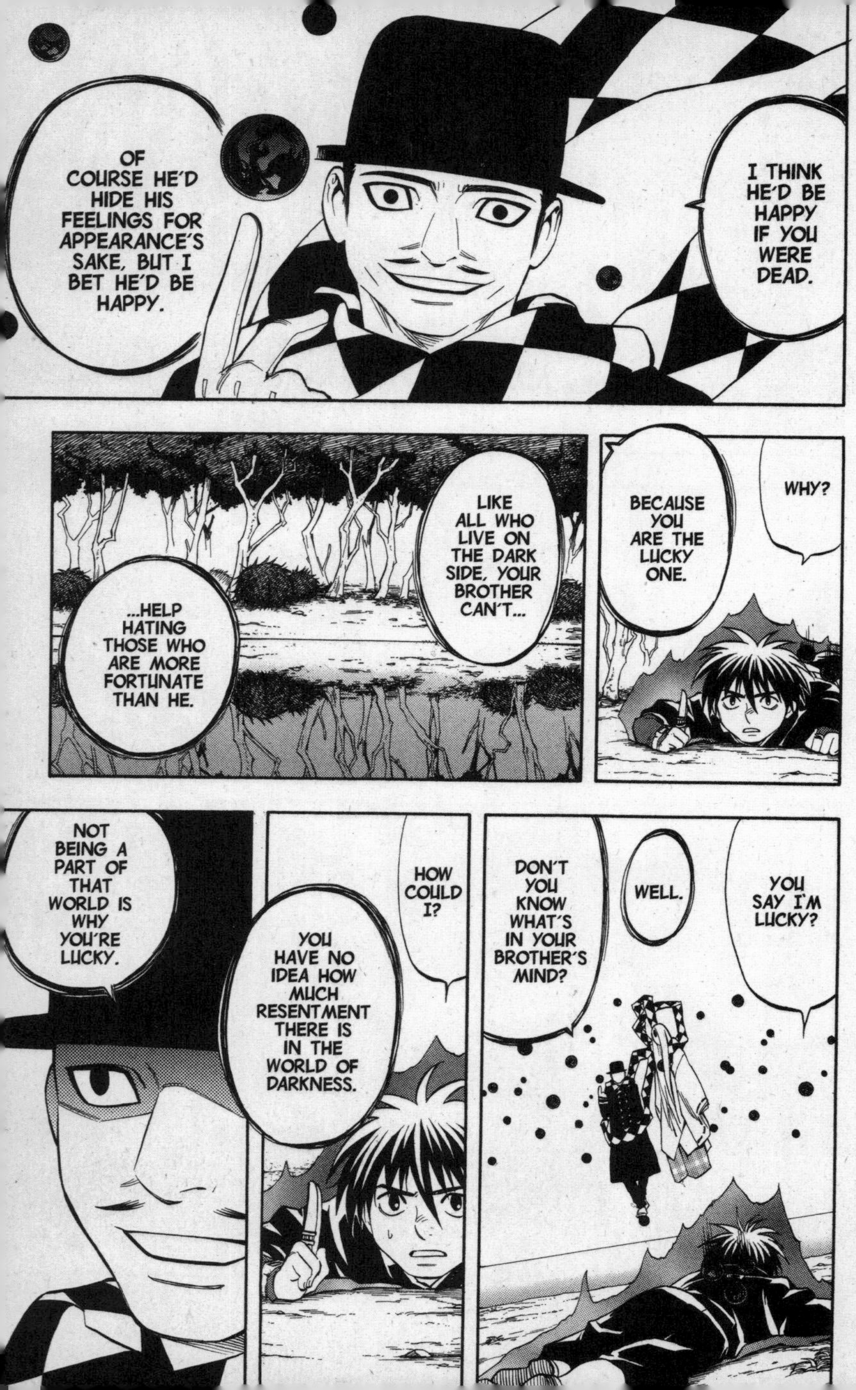
I THINK HE'D BE HAPPY IF YOU WERE DEAD.
OF COURSE HE'D HIDE HIS FEELINGS FOR APPEARANCE'S SAKE, BUT I BET HE'D BE HAPPY.
WHY?
BECAUSE YOU ARE THE LUCKY ONE.
LIKE ALL WHO LIVE ON THE DARK SIDE, YOUR BROTHER CAN'T...
...HELP HATING THOSE WHO ARE MORE FORTUNATE THAN HE.
YOU SAY I'M LUCKY?
WELL.
DON'T YOU KNOW WHAT'S IN YOUR BROTHER'S MIND?
HOW COULD I?
YOU HAVE NO IDEA HOW MUCH RESENTMENT THERE IS IN THE WORLD OF DARKNESS.
NOT BEING A PART OF THAT WORLD IS WHY YOU'RE LUCKY.

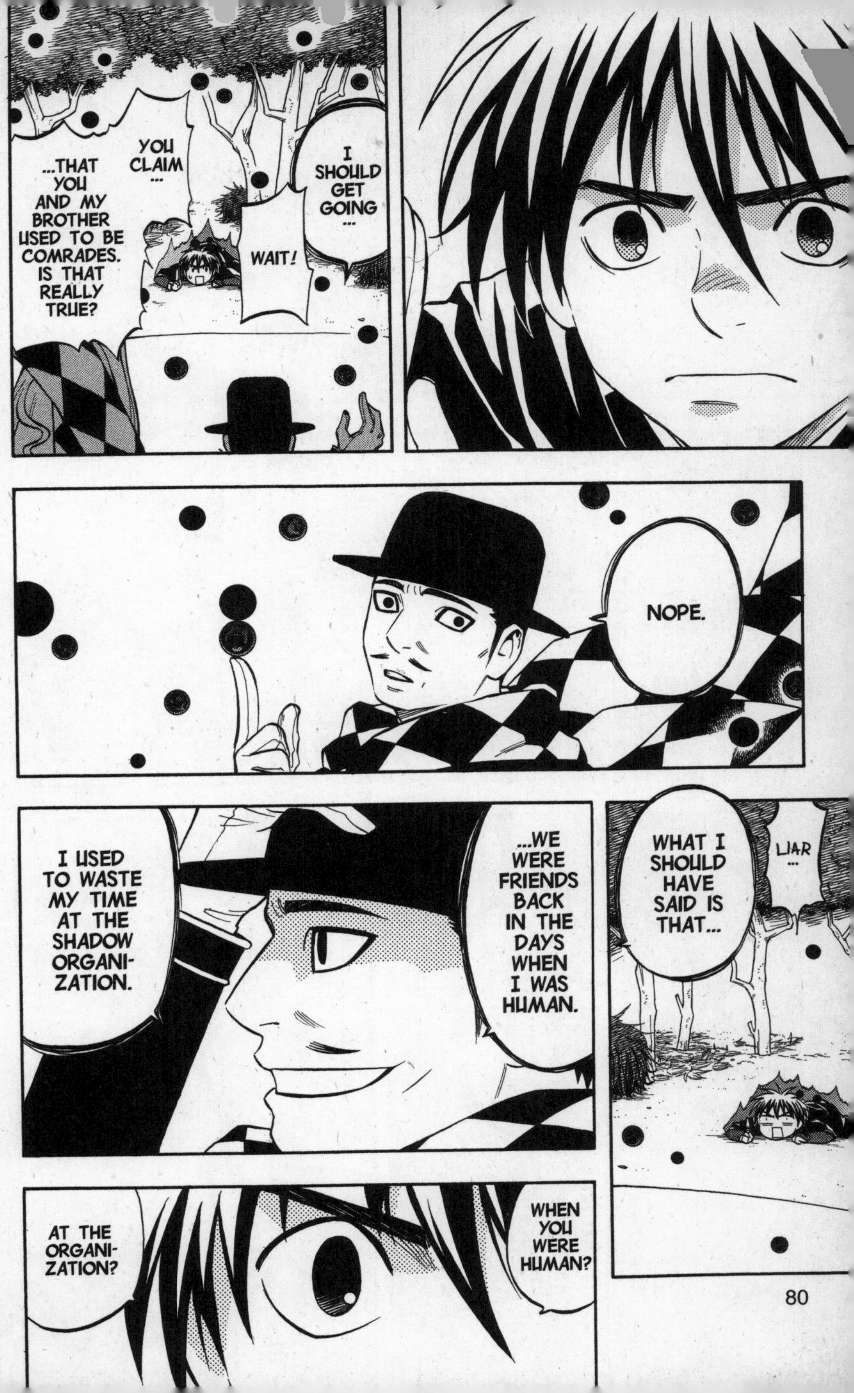
I SHOULD GET GOING ...
WAIT!
YOU CLAIM ...
...THAT YOU AND MY BROTHER USED TO BE COMRADES. IS THAT REALLY TRUE?
NOPE.
LIAR ...
WHAT I SHOULD HAVE SAID IS THAT...
...WE WERE FRIENDS BACK IN THE DAYS WHEN I WAS HUMAN.
I USED TO WASTE MY TIME AT THE SHADOW ORGANIZATION.
WHEN YOU WERE HUMAN?
AT THE ORGANIZATION?

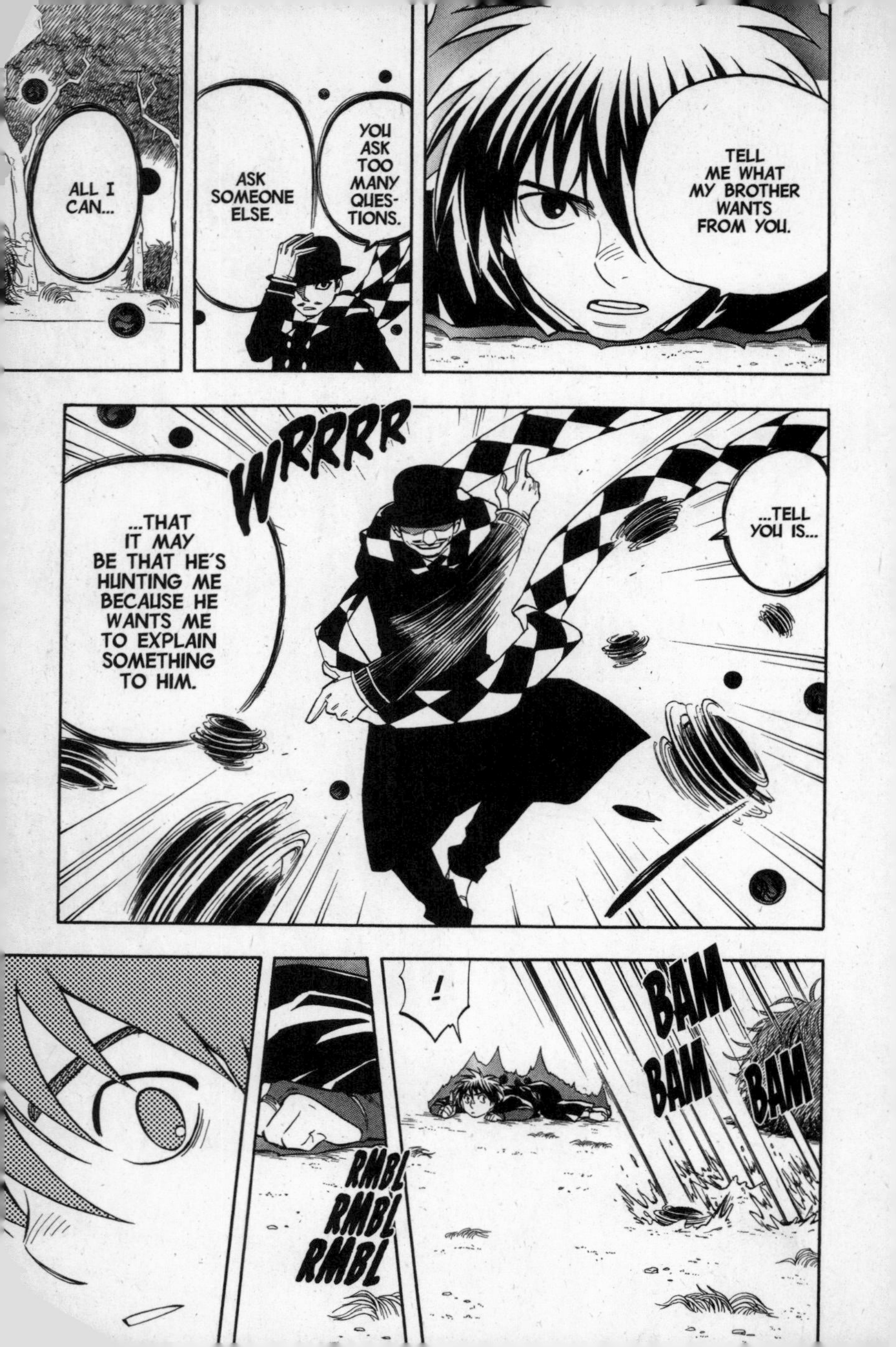
TELL ME WHAT MY BROTHER WANTS FROM YOU.
YOU ASK TOO MANY QUES-TIONS.
ASK SOMEONE ELSE.
ALL I CAN...
WRRRR
...TELL YOU IS...
...THAT IT MAY BE THAT HE'S HUNTING ME BECAUSE HE WANTS ME TO EXPLAIN SOMETHING TO HIM.
!
BAM
BAM
BAM
RMBL
RMBL
RMBL

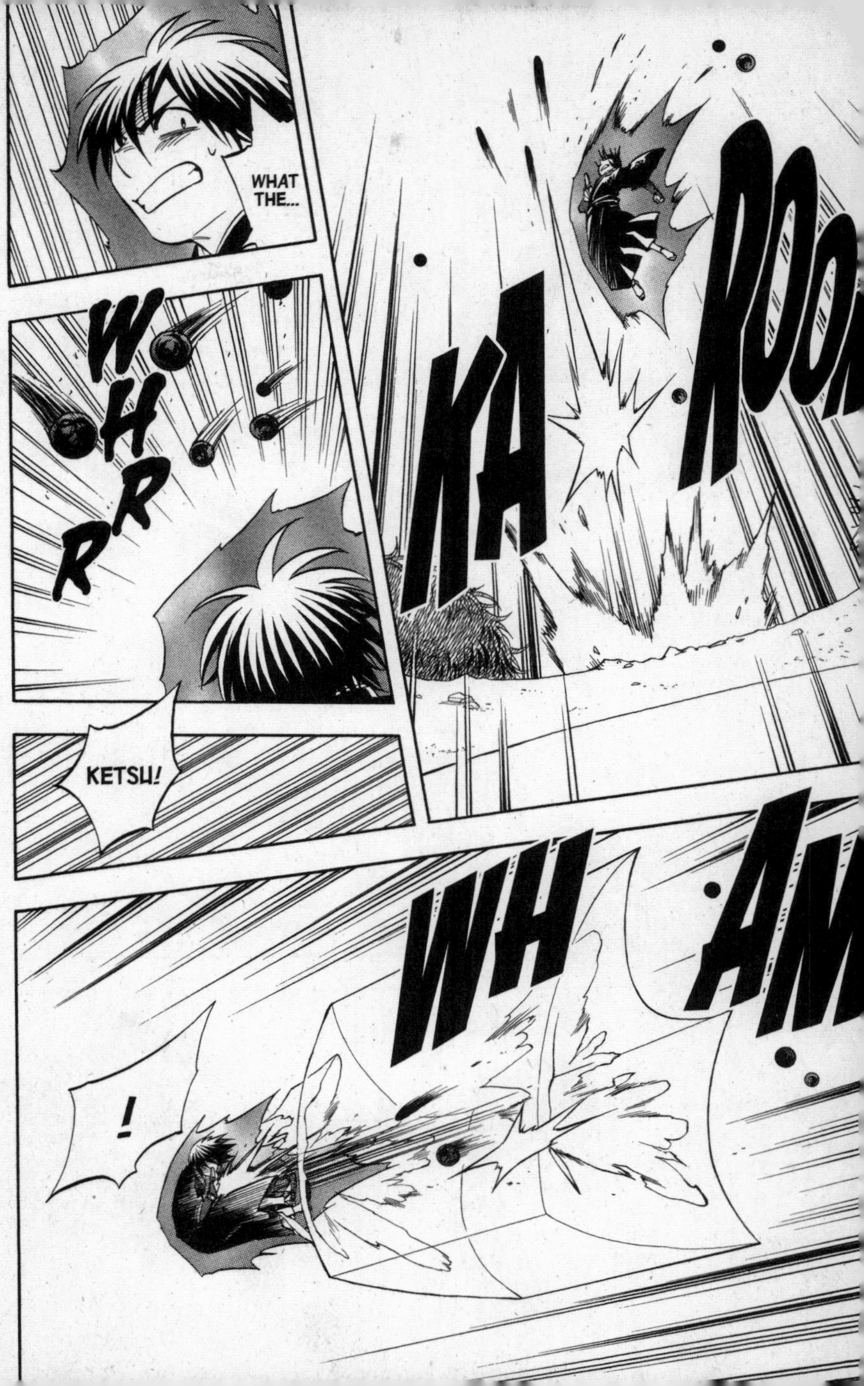
KA ROO
WHAT THE...
WHRRR
KETSU!
WH AM
!

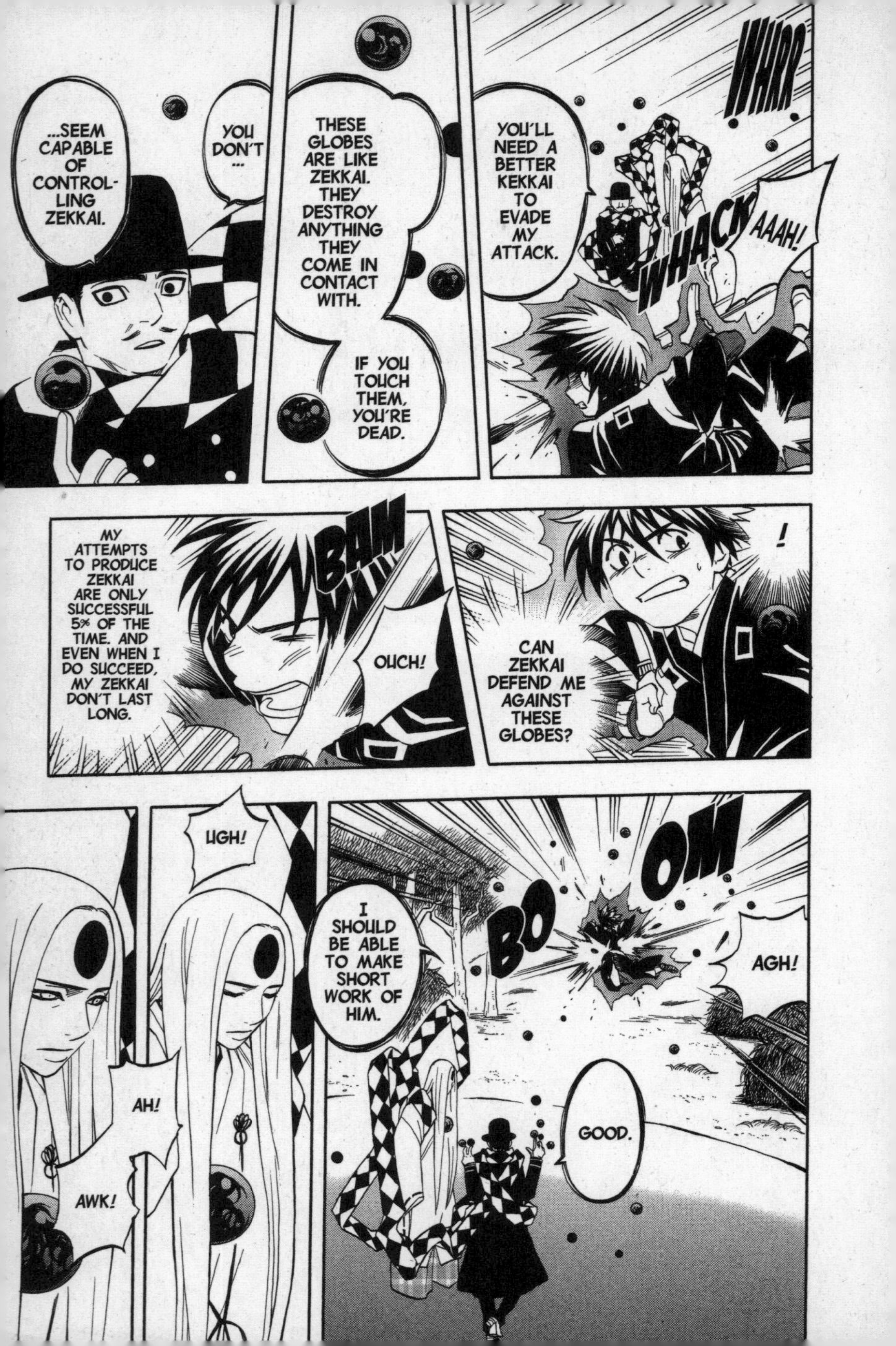
WHRR
YOU'LL NEED A BETTER KEKKAI TO EVADE MY ATTACK.
AAAH!
WHACK
THESE GLOBES ARE LIKE ZEKKAI. THEY DESTROY ANYTHING THEY COME IN CONTACT WITH.
IF YOU TOUCH THEM, YOU'RE DEAD.
YOU DON'T ...
...SEEM CAPABLE OF CONTROL-LING ZEKKAI.
!
CAN ZEKKAI DEFEND ME AGAINST THESE GLOBES?
BAM
OUCH!
MY ATTEMPTS TO PRODUCE ZEKKAI ARE ONLY SUCCESSFUL 5% OF THE TIME. AND EVEN WHEN I DO SUCCEED, MY ZEKKAI DON'T LAST LONG.
BOOM
AGH!
I SHOULD BE ABLE TO MAKE SHORT WORK OF HIM.
GOOD.
UGH!
AH!
AWK!

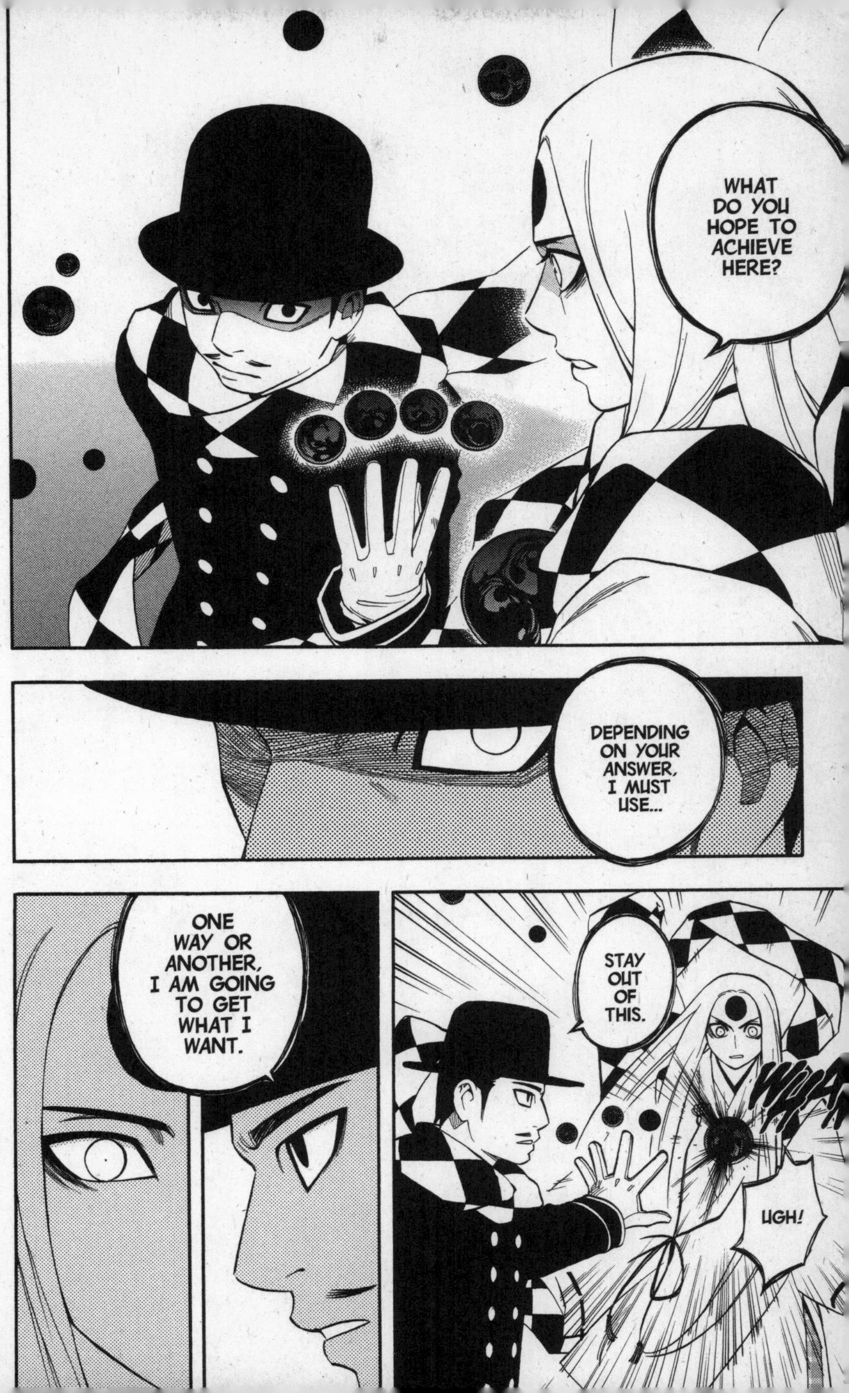
WHAT DO YOU HOPE TO ACHIEVE HERE?
DEPENDING ON YOUR ANSWER, I MUST USE...
STAY OUT OF THIS.
UGH!
ONE WAY OR ANOTHER, I AM GOING TO GET WHAT I WANT.

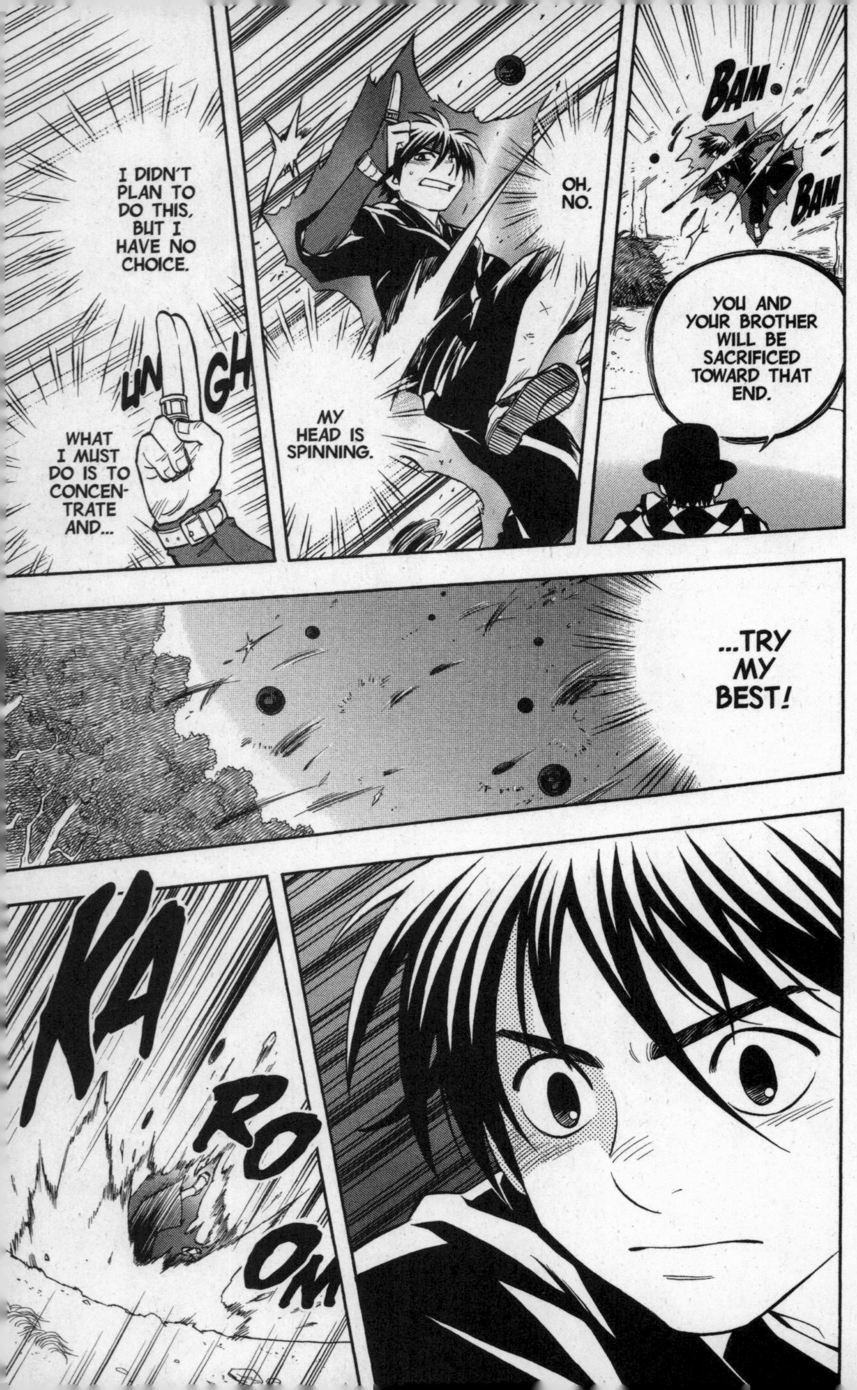
BAM
BAM
YOU AND YOUR BROTHER WILL BE SACRIFICED TOWARD THAT END.
OH, NO.
MY HEAD IS SPINNING.
I DIDN'T PLAN TO DO THIS, BUT I HAVE NO CHOICE.
UNGH
WHAT I MUST DO IS TO CONCEN-TRATE AND...
...TRY MY BEST!
KAROOM

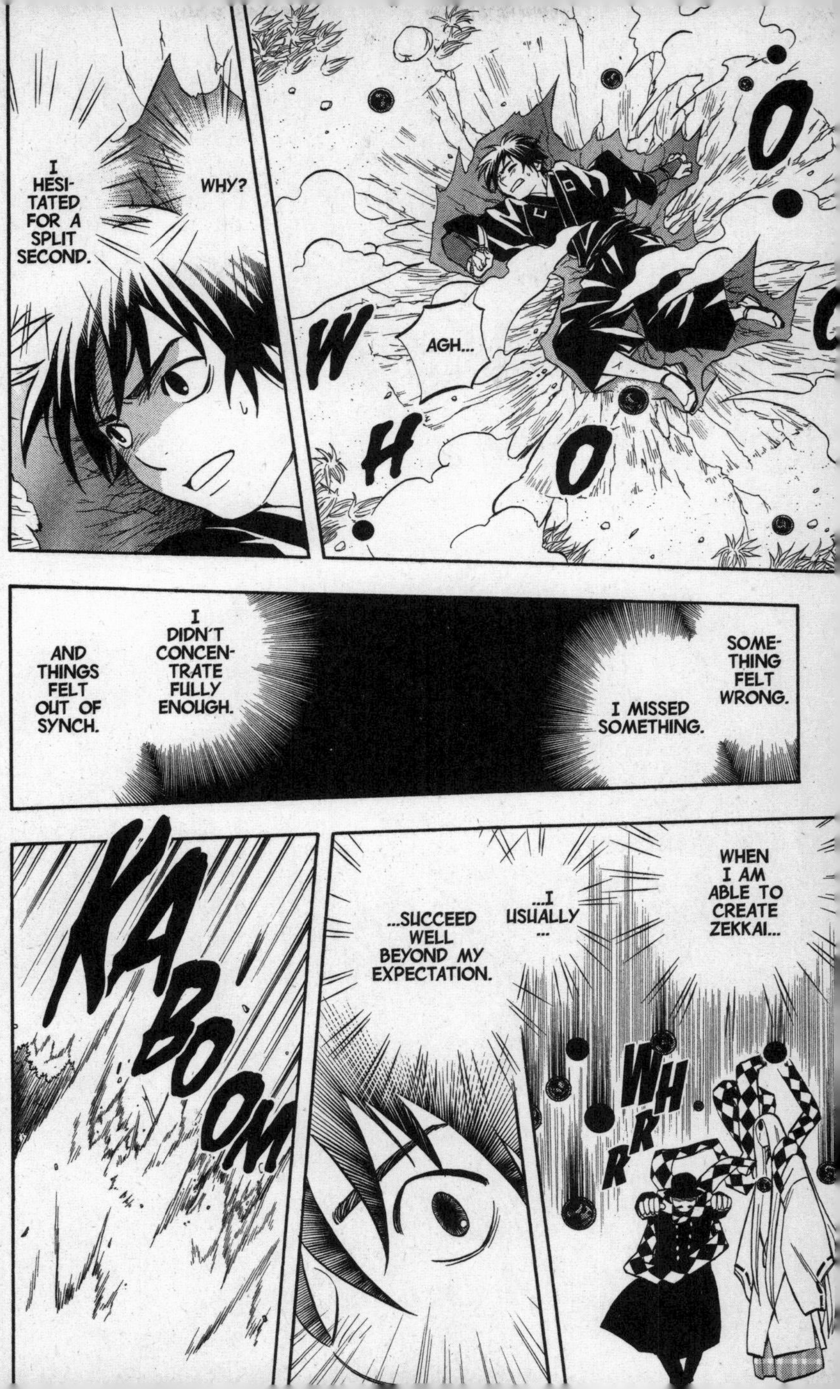
AGH...
WHOOO
WHY?
I HESITATED FOR A SPLIT SECOND.
SOMETHING FELT WRONG.
I MISSED SOMETHING.
I DIDN'T CONCENTRATE FULLY ENOUGH.
AND THINGS FELT OUT OF SYNCH.
WHEN I AM ABLE TO CREATE ZEKKAI...
...I USUALLY ...
...SUCCEED WELL BEYOND MY EXPECTATION.
WHRRR
KABOOM

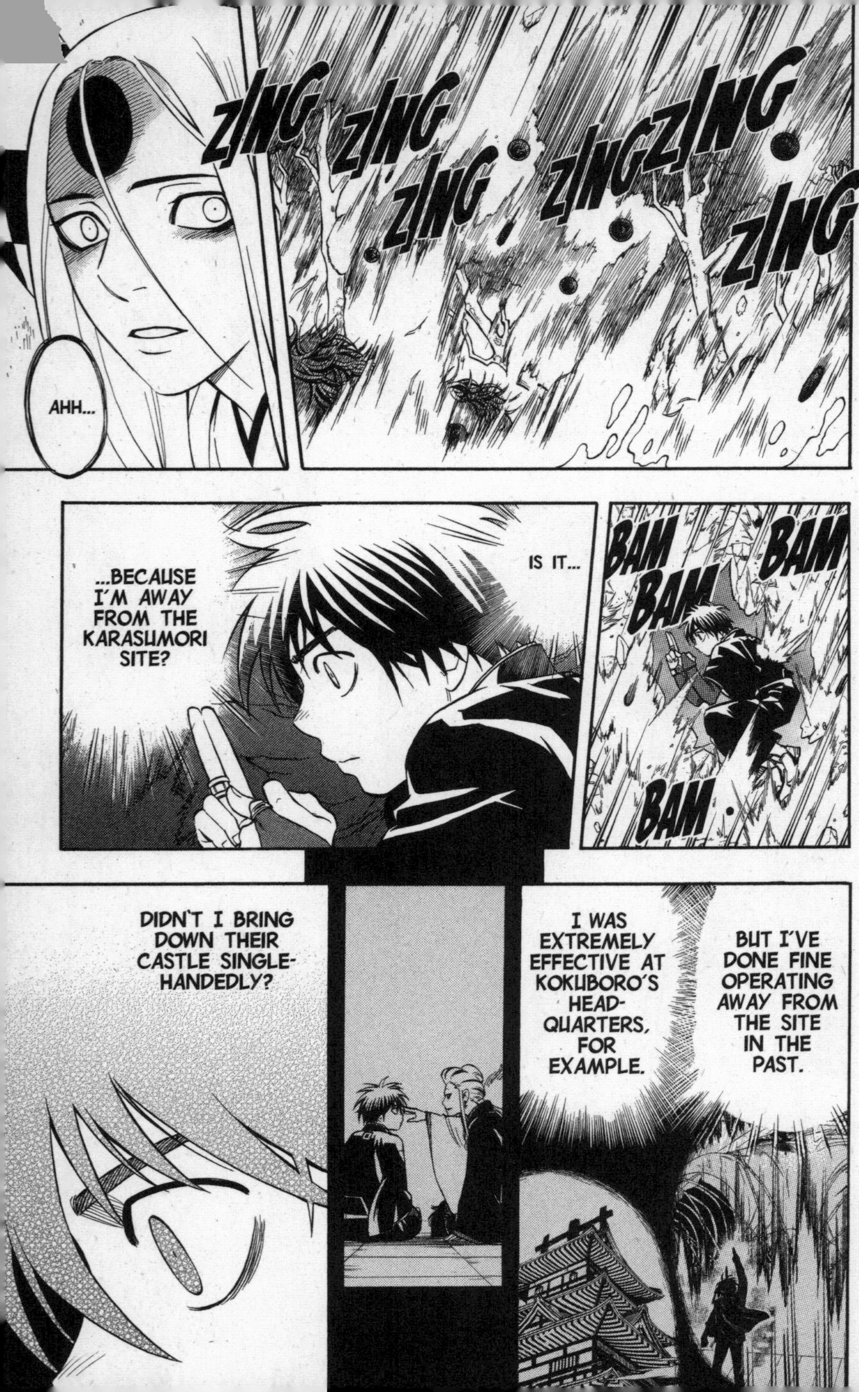
ZING
ZINGZING
ZING
ZING
ZING
AHH...
BAM
BAM
BAM
BAM
IS IT...
...BECAUSE I'M AWAY FROM THE KARASUMORI SITE?
BUT I'VE DONE FINE OPERATING AWAY FROM THE SITE IN THE PAST.
I WAS EXTREMELY EFFECTIVE AT KOKUBORO'S HEAD-QUARTERS, FOR EXAMPLE.
DIDN'T I BRING DOWN THEIR CASTLE SINGLE-HANDEDLY?

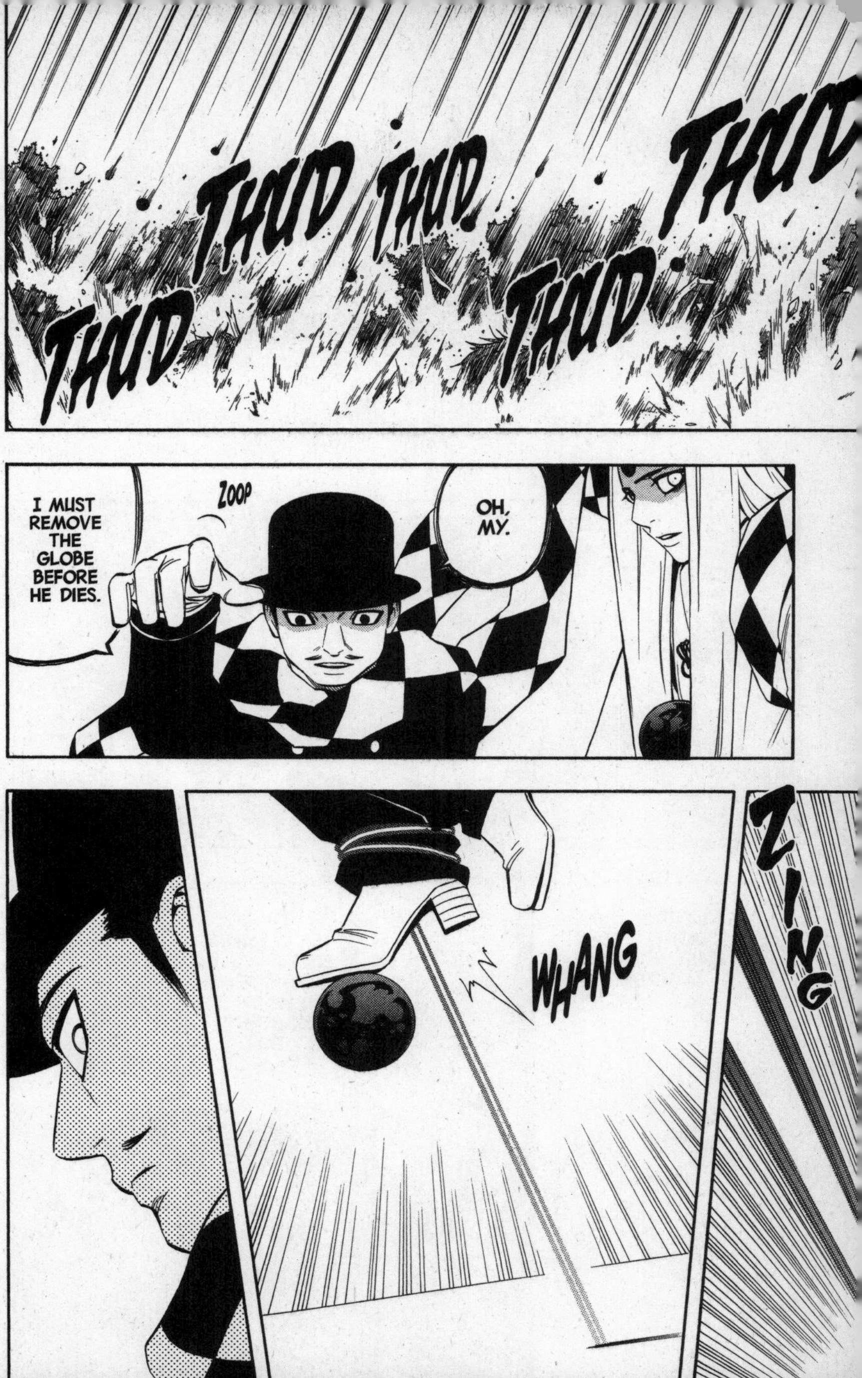
THUD
THUD
THUD
THUD
THUD
OH, MY.
ZOOP
I MUST REMOVE THE GLOBE BEFORE HE DIES.
ZING
WHANG

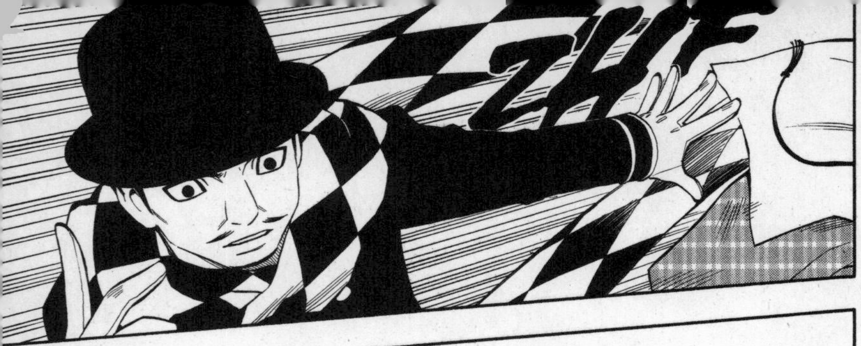
ZHF
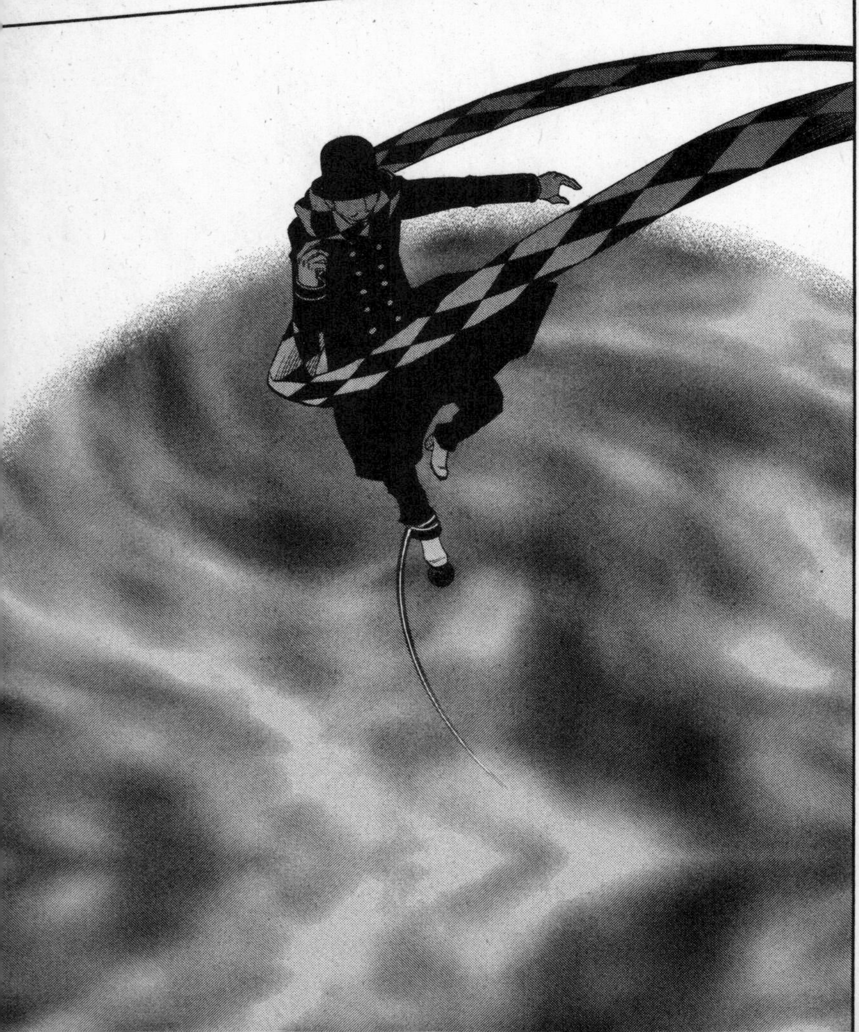

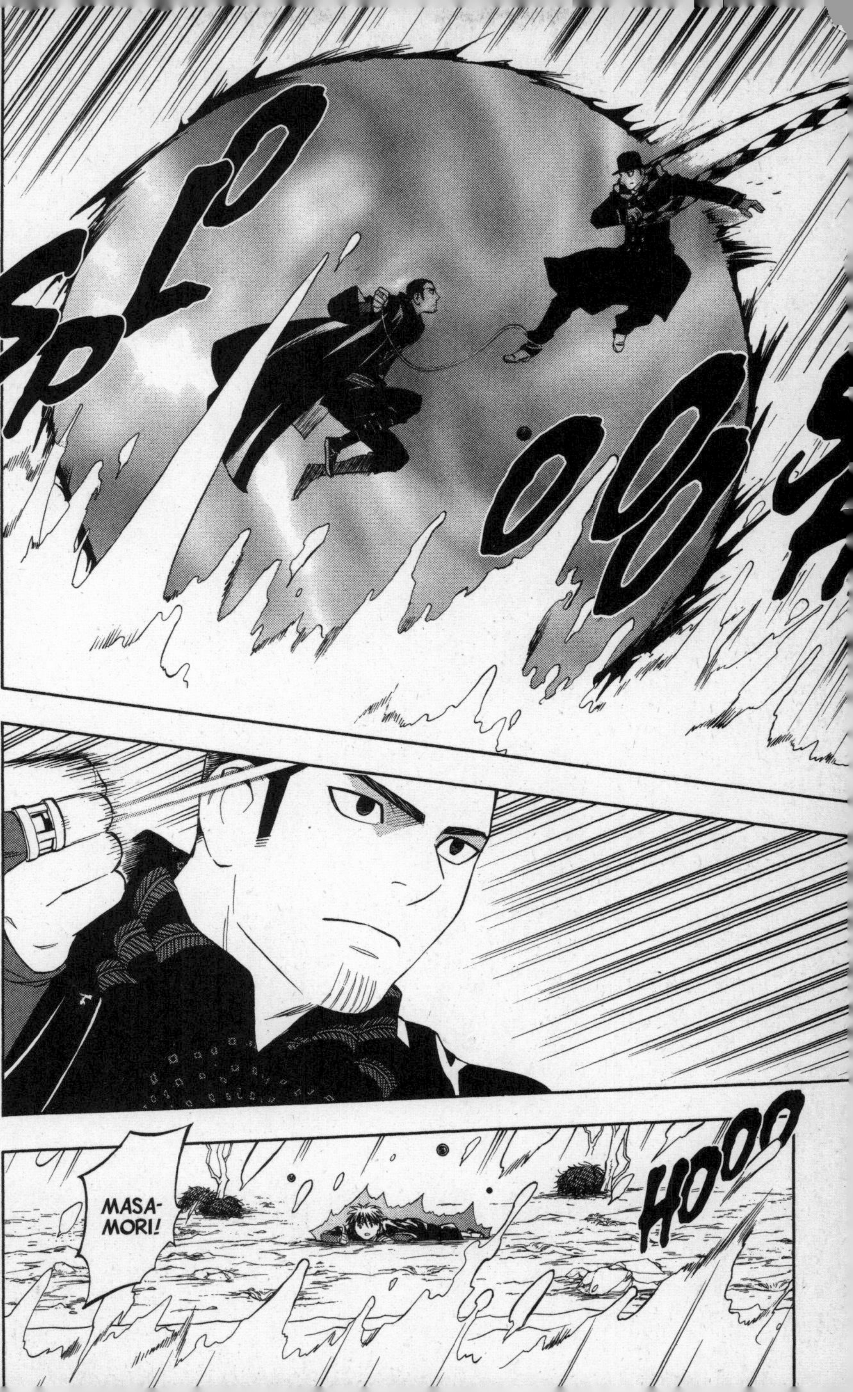
SPLOOOOSH
MASA-
MORI!
HOOOO

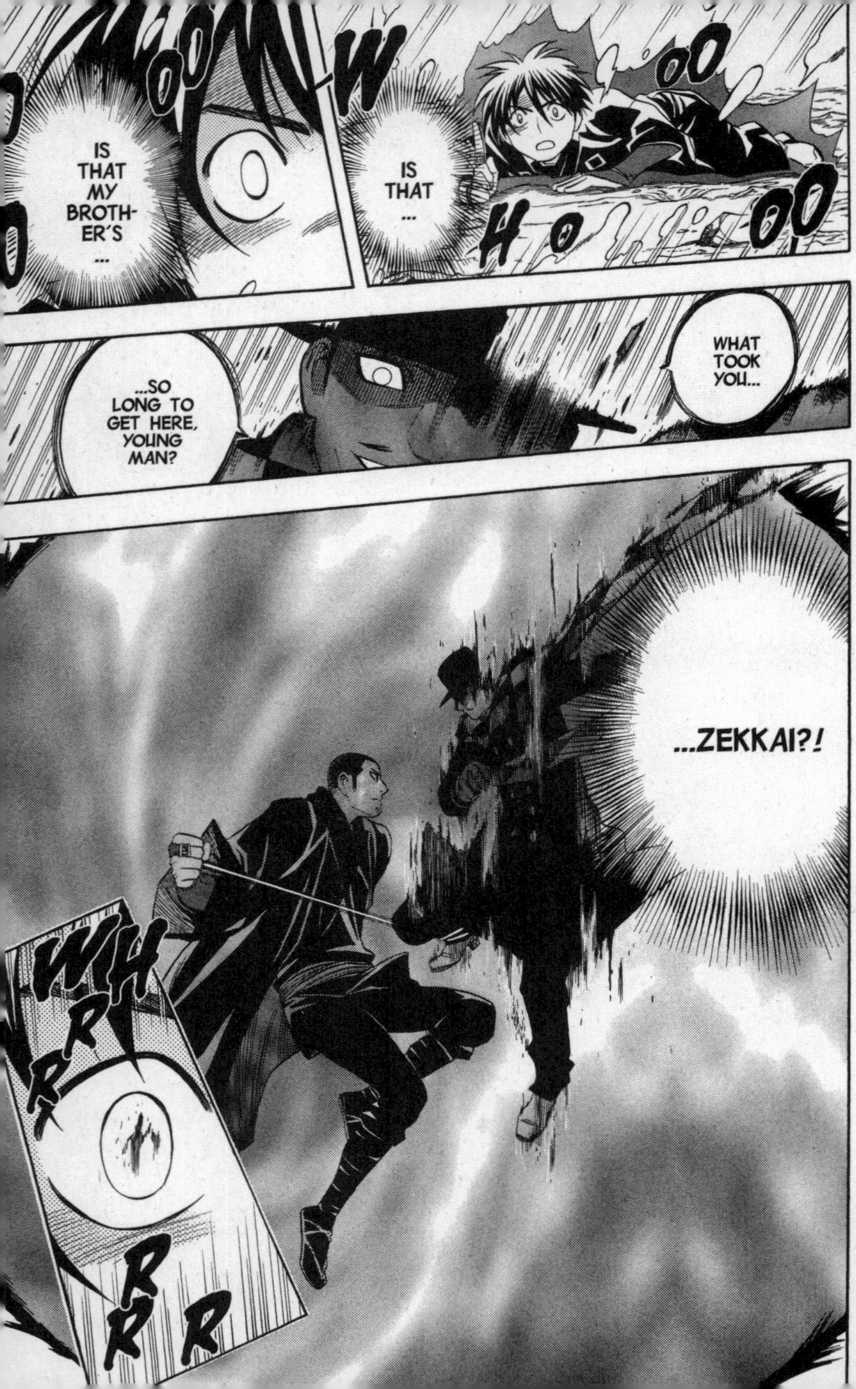
IS THAT ...
IS THAT MY BROTH-ER'S ...
WHAT TOOK YOU...
...SO LONG TO GET HERE, YOUNG MAN?
...ZEKKAI?!

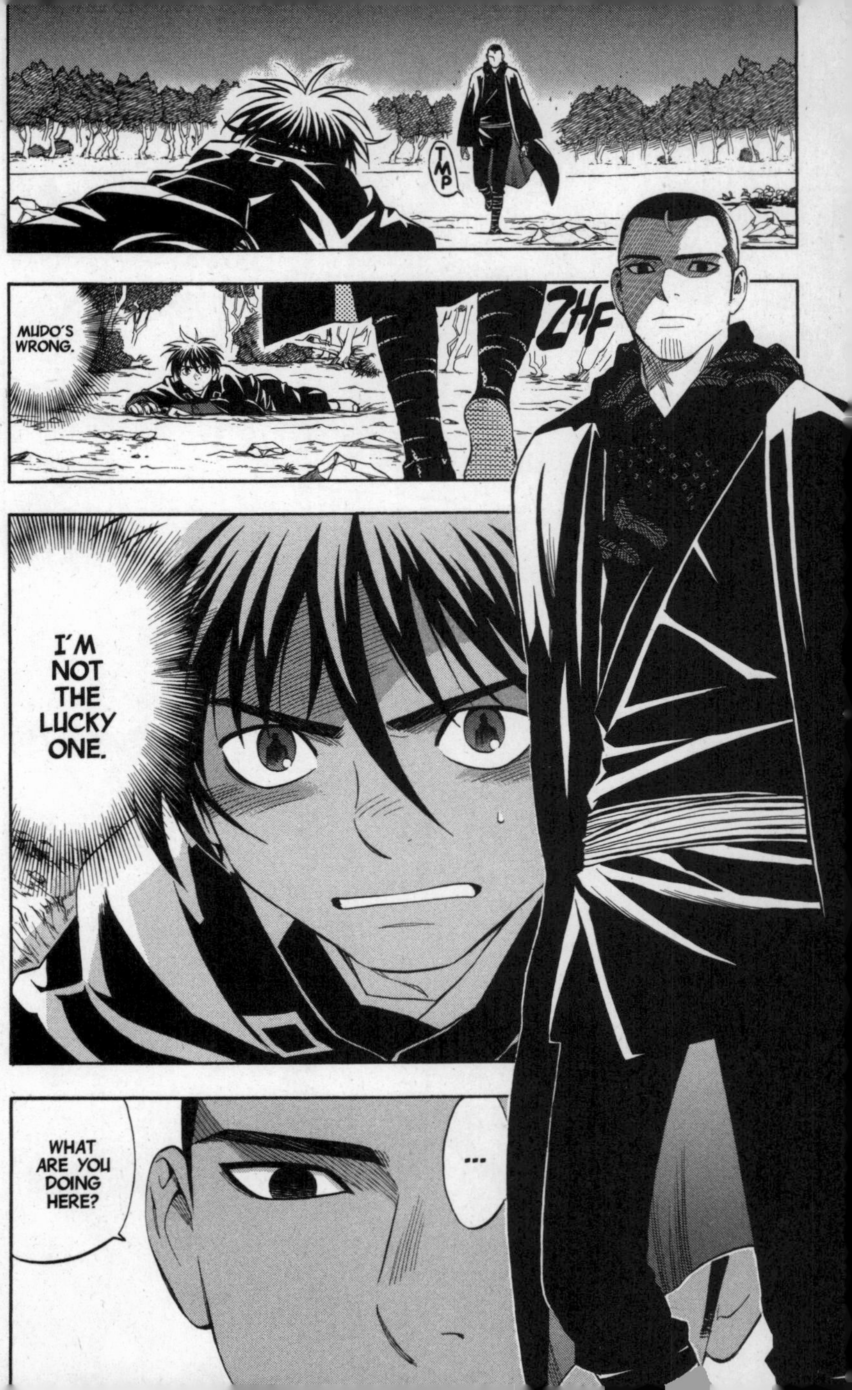
TMP
ZHF
MUDO'S WRONG.
I'M NOT THE LUCKY ONE.
...
WHAT ARE YOU DOING HERE?

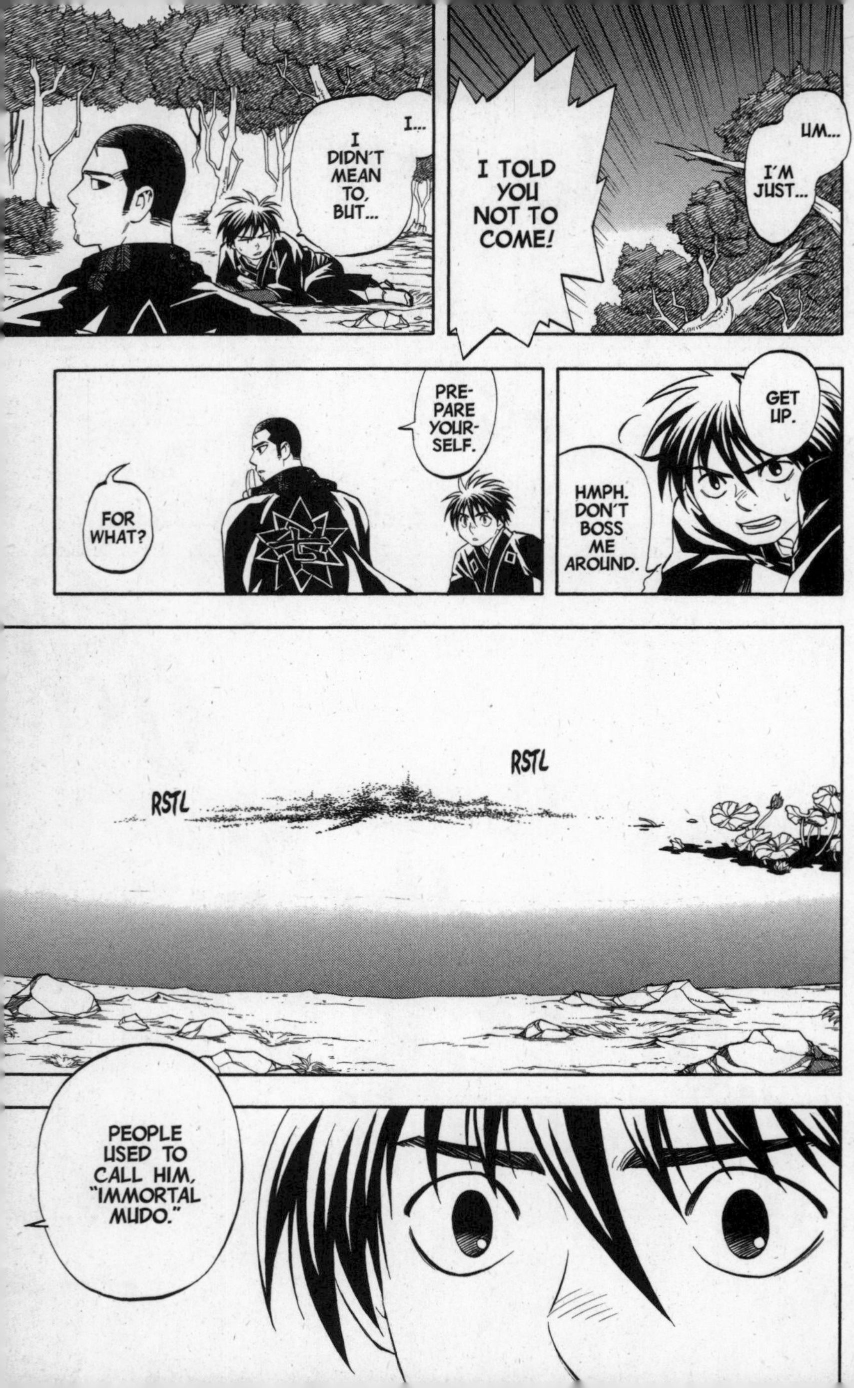
UM...
I'M JUST...
I TOLD YOU NOT TO COME!
I...
I DIDN'T MEAN TO, BUT...
GET UP.
HMPH. DON'T BOSS ME AROUND.
PRE-PARE YOUR-SELF.
FOR WHAT?
RSTL
RSTL
PEOPLE USED TO CALL HIM, "IMMORTAL MUDO."

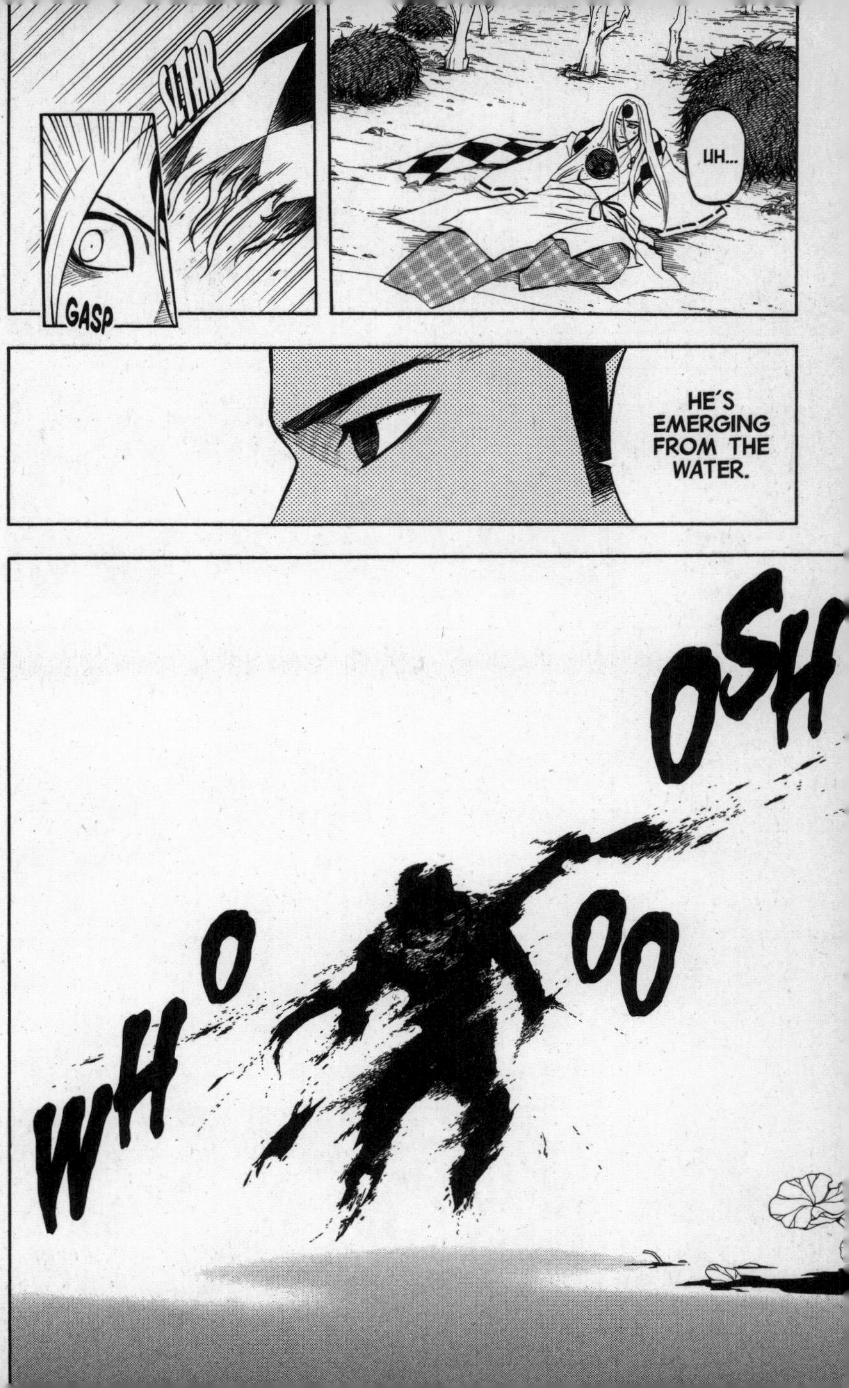
UH...
SLTHR
GASP
HE'S EMERGING FROM THE WATER.
WHOOOOSH

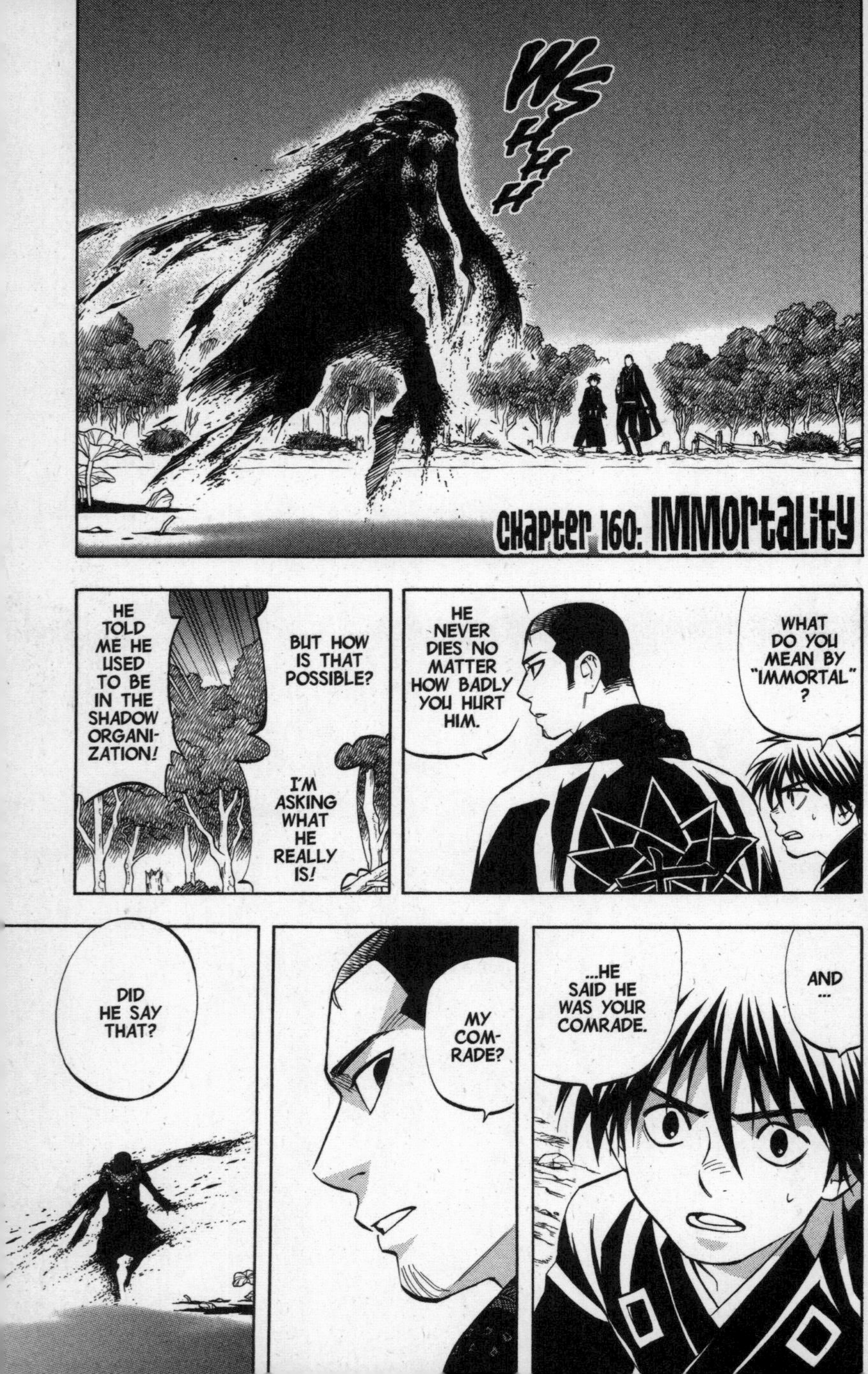
WSHHHH
Chapter 160: Immortality
WHAT DO YOU MEAN BY "IMMORTAL"?
HE NEVER DIES NO MATTER HOW BADLY YOU HURT HIM.
BUT HOW IS THAT POSSIBLE?
HE TOLD ME HE USED TO BE IN THE SHADOW ORGANIZATION!
I'M ASKING WHAT HE REALLY IS!
AND ...
...HE SAID HE WAS YOUR COMRADE.
MY COMRADE?
DID HE SAY THAT?

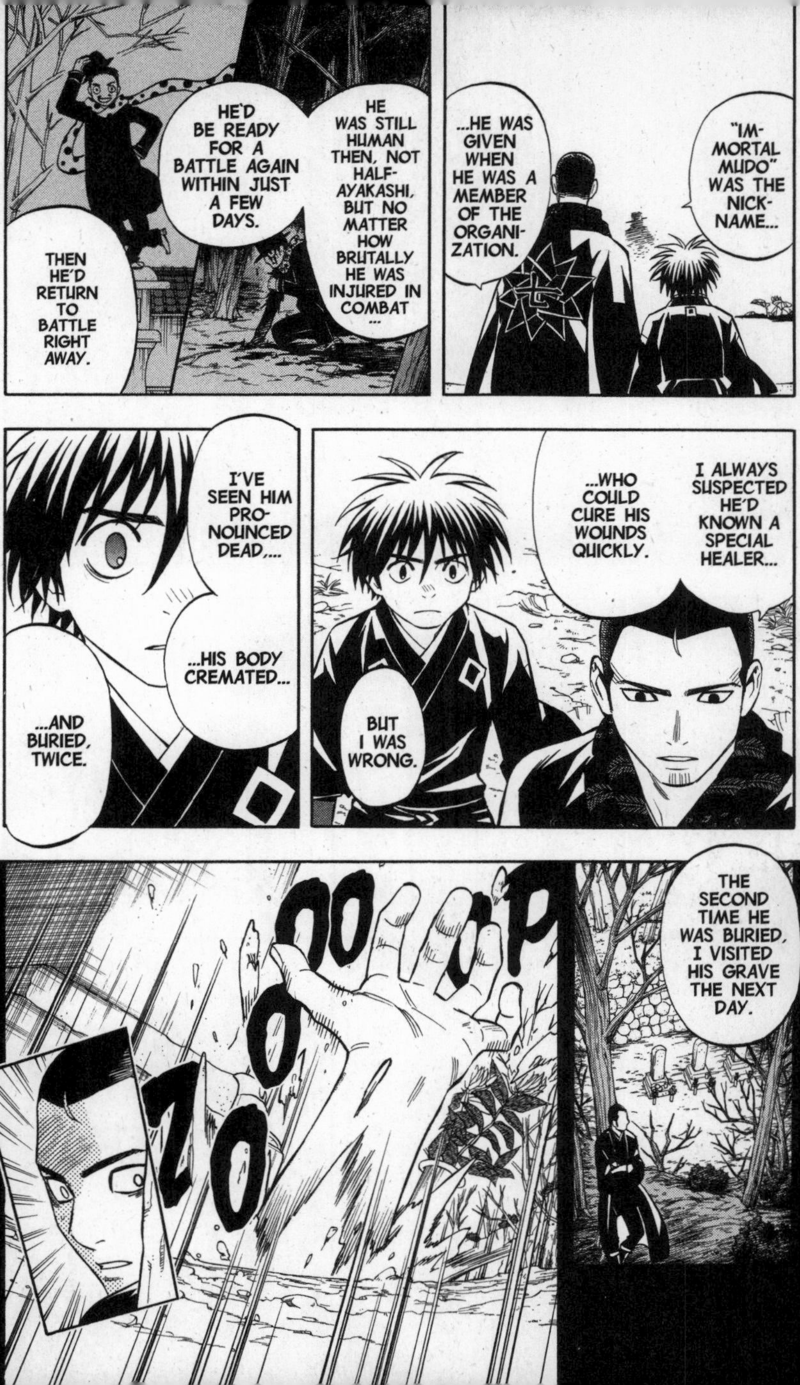
"IM-MORTAL MUDO" WAS THE NICK-NAME...
...HE WAS GIVEN WHEN HE WAS A MEMBER OF THE ORGANI-ZATION.
HE WAS STILL HUMAN THEN, NOT HALF-AYAKASHI, BUT NO MATTER HOW BRUTALLY HE WAS INJURED IN COMBAT...
HE'D BE READY FOR A BATTLE AGAIN WITHIN JUST A FEW DAYS.
THEN HE'D RETURN TO BATTLE RIGHT AWAY.
I ALWAYS SUSPECTED HE'D KNOWN A SPECIAL HEALER...
...WHO COULD CURE HIS WOUNDS QUICKLY.
BUT I WAS WRONG.
I'VE SEEN HIM PRO-NOUNCED DEAD,...
...HIS BODY CREMATED...
...AND BURIED, TWICE.
THE SECOND TIME HE WAS BURIED, I VISITED HIS GRAVE THE NEXT DAY.
ZOOOOOP

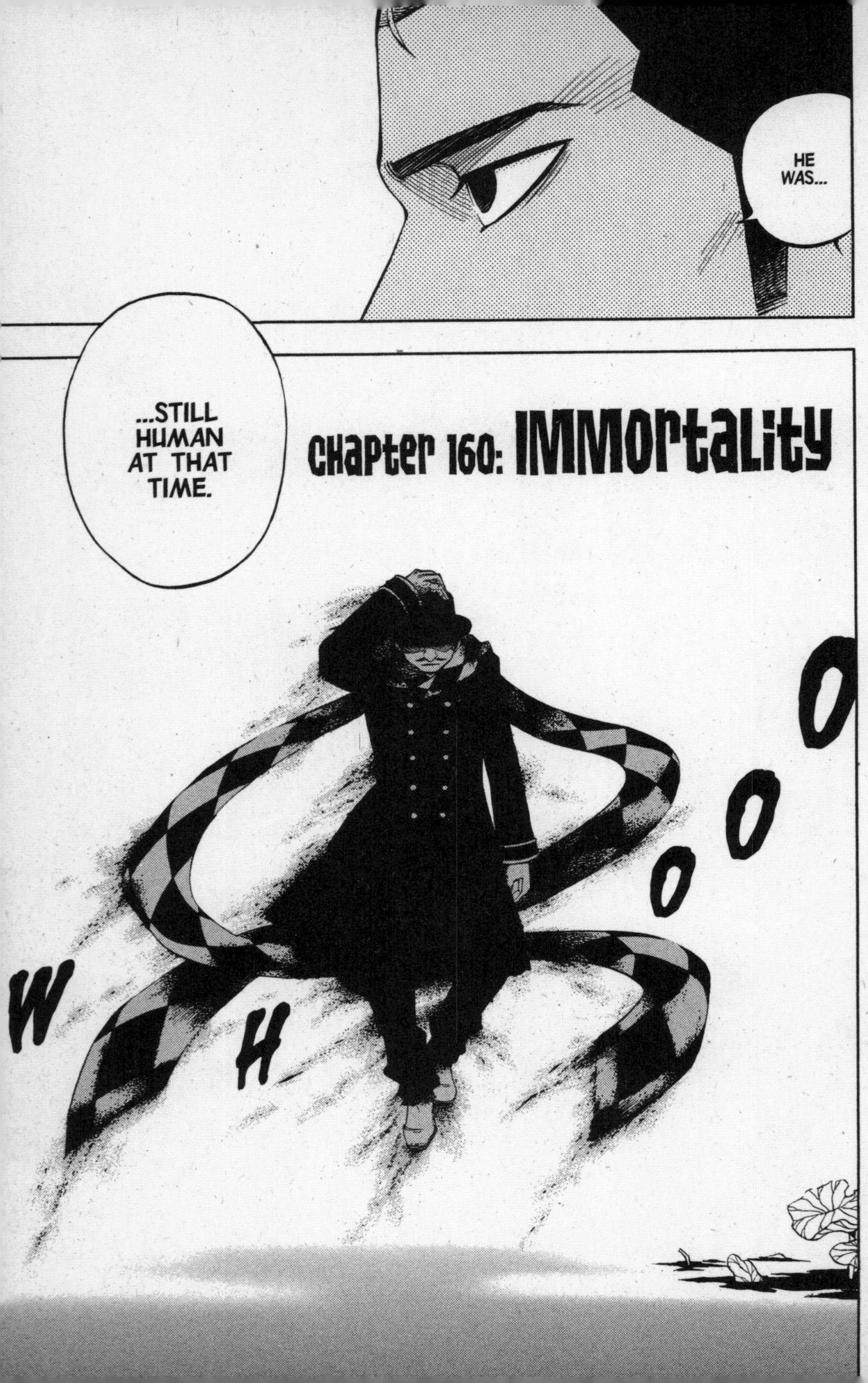
HE WAS...
...STILL HUMAN AT THAT TIME.
Chapter 160: Immortality
WHOOOOO

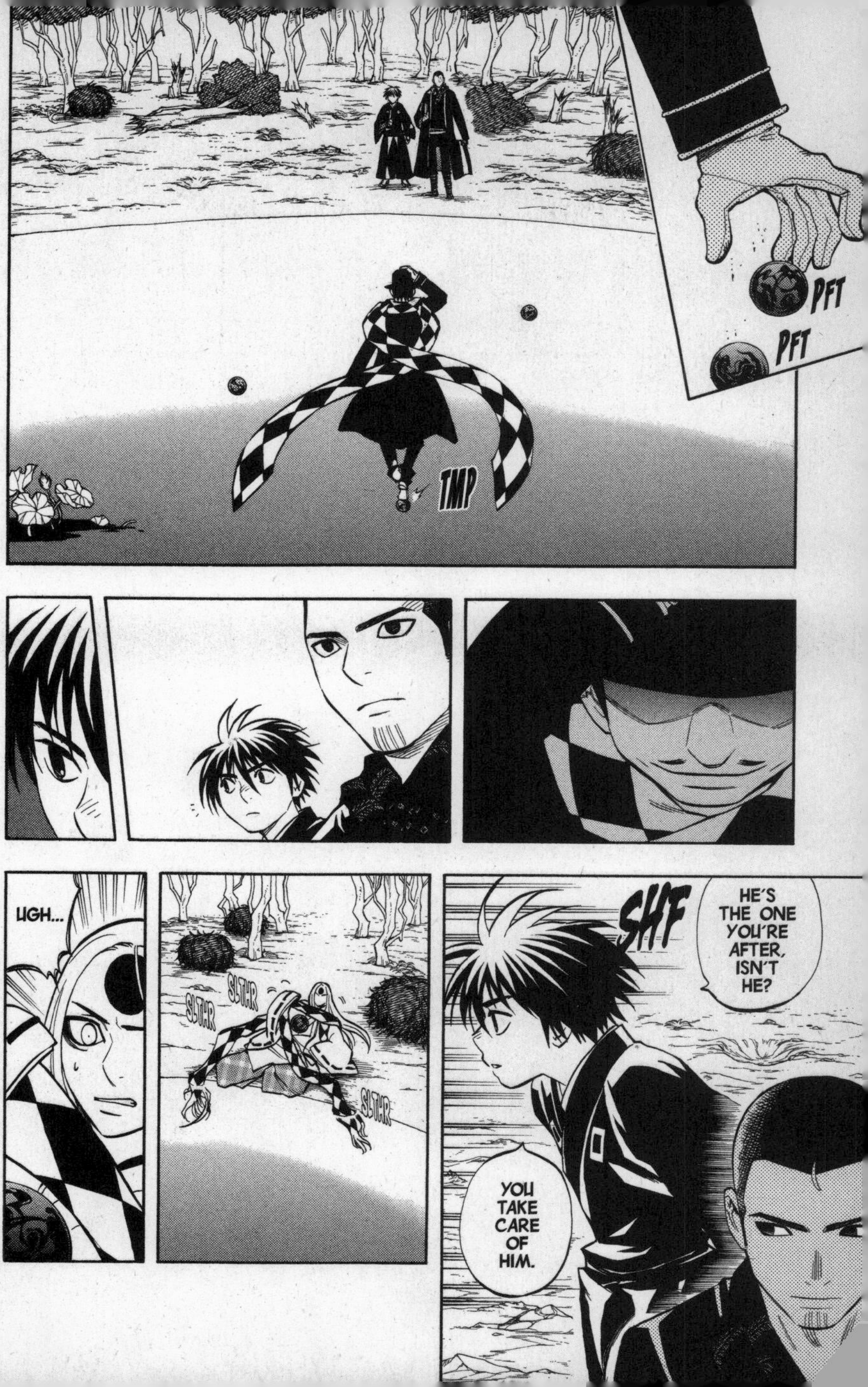
PFT
PFT
TMP
SHF
HE'S THE ONE YOU'RE AFTER, ISN'T HE?
YOU TAKE CARE OF HIM.
SLTHR
SLTHR
SLTHR
UGH...

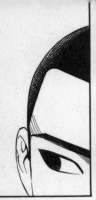

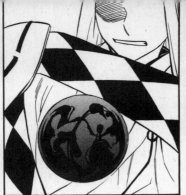

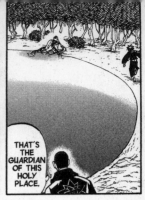

THAT'S THE GUARDIAN OF THIS HOLY PLACE.

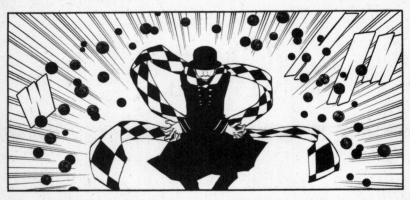

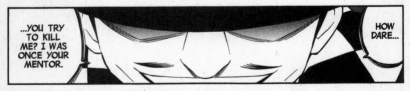

...YOU TRY TO KILL ME? I WAS ONCE YOUR MENTOR.

HOW DARE...

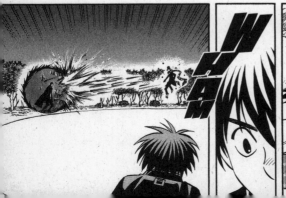

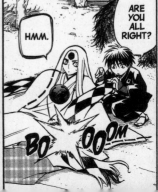

HMM.

ARE YOU ALL RIGHT?

BO OOOM

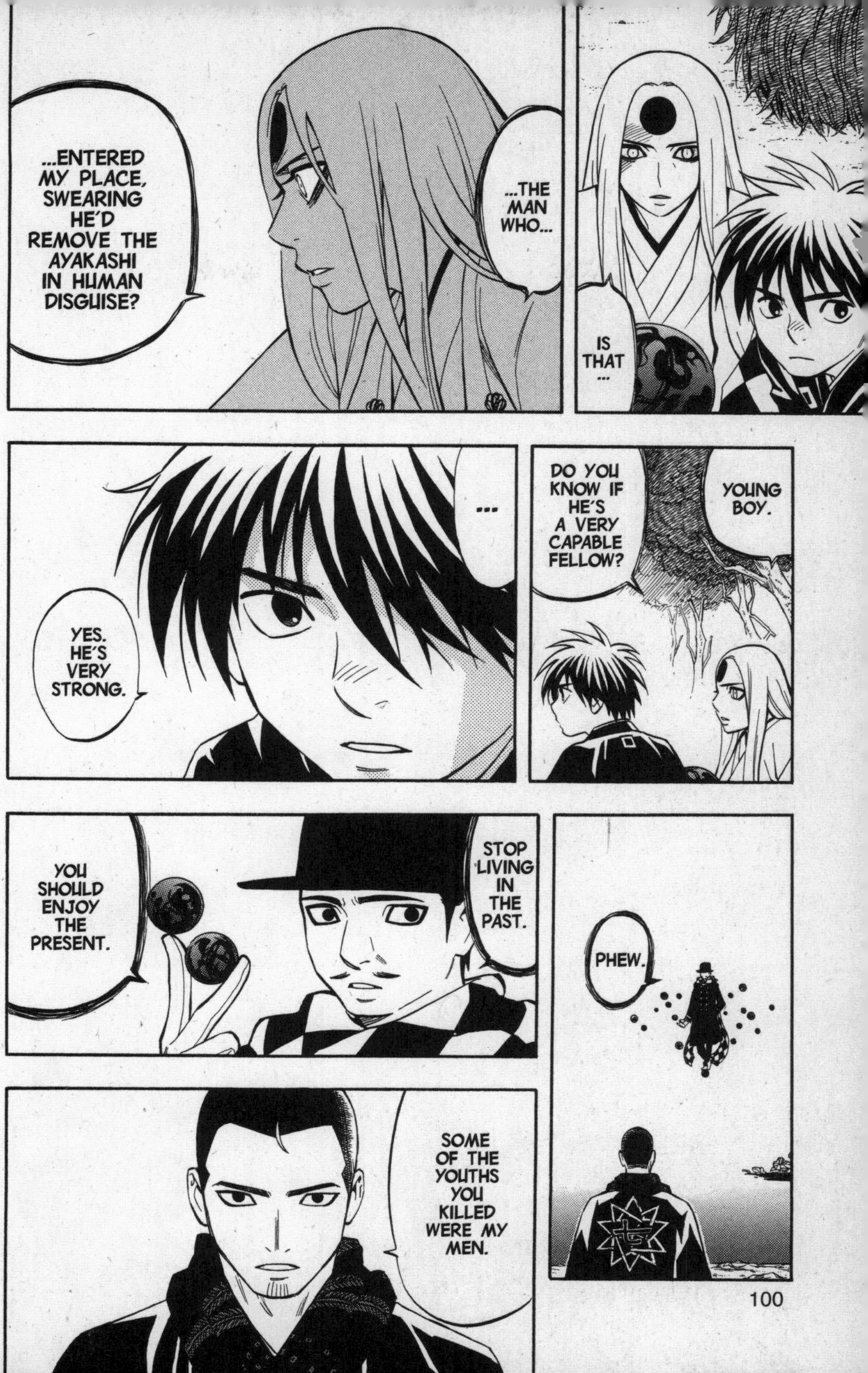
IS THAT ...
...THE MAN WHO...
...ENTERED MY PLACE, SWEARING HE'D REMOVE THE AYAKASHI IN HUMAN DISGUISE?
YOUNG BOY.
DO YOU KNOW IF HE'S A VERY CAPABLE FELLOW?
...
YES. HE'S VERY STRONG.
PHEW.
STOP LIVING IN THE PAST.
YOU SHOULD ENJOY THE PRESENT.
SOME OF THE YOUTHS YOU KILLED WERE MY MEN.

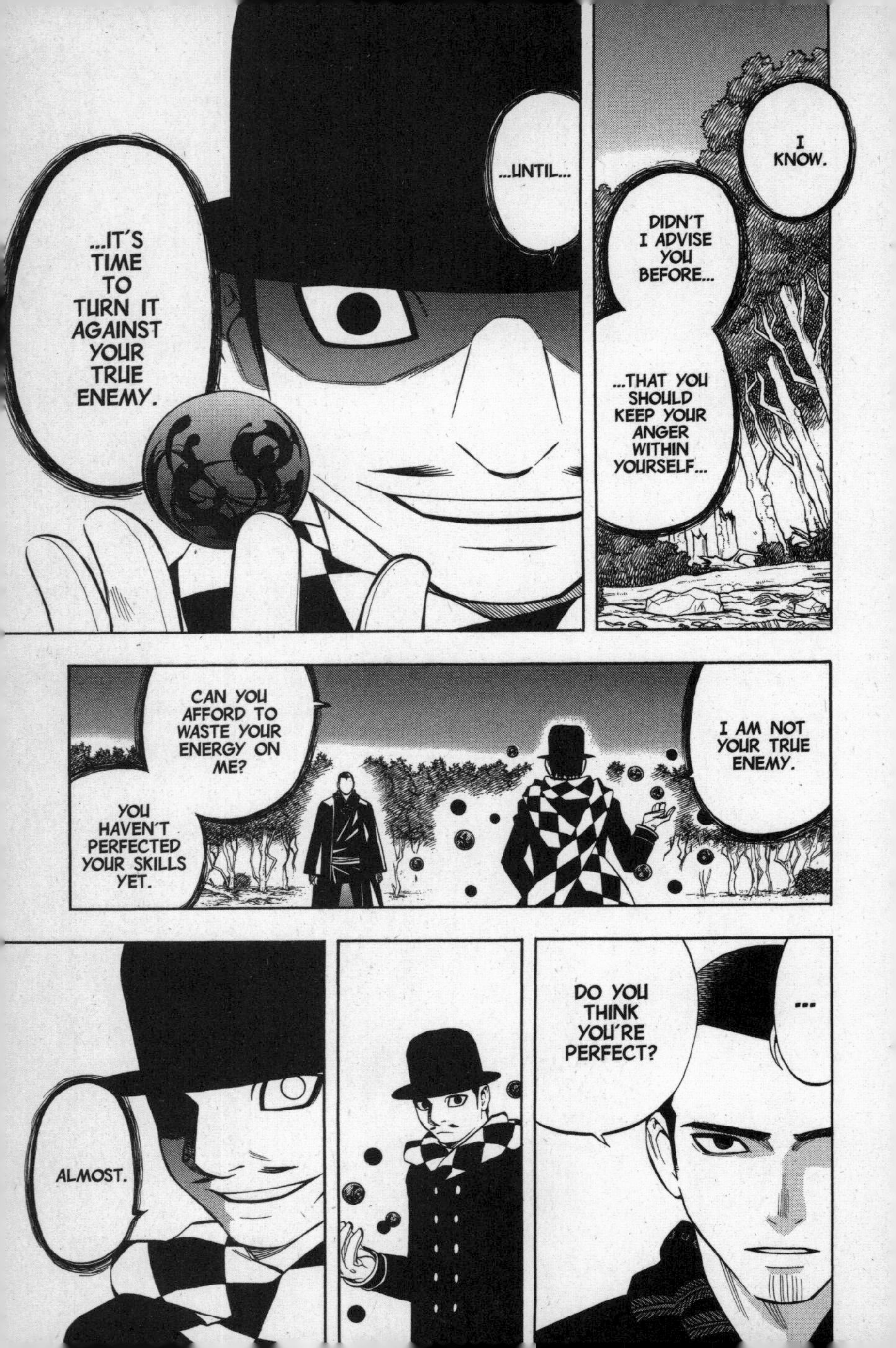
I KNOW.
DIDN'T I ADVISE YOU BEFORE...
...THAT YOU SHOULD KEEP YOUR ANGER WITHIN YOURSELF...
...UNTIL...
...IT'S TIME TO TURN IT AGAINST YOUR TRUE ENEMY.
I AM NOT YOUR TRUE ENEMY.
CAN YOU AFFORD TO WASTE YOUR ENERGY ON ME?
YOU HAVEN'T PERFECTED YOUR SKILLS YET.
...
DO YOU THINK YOU'RE PERFECT?
ALMOST.

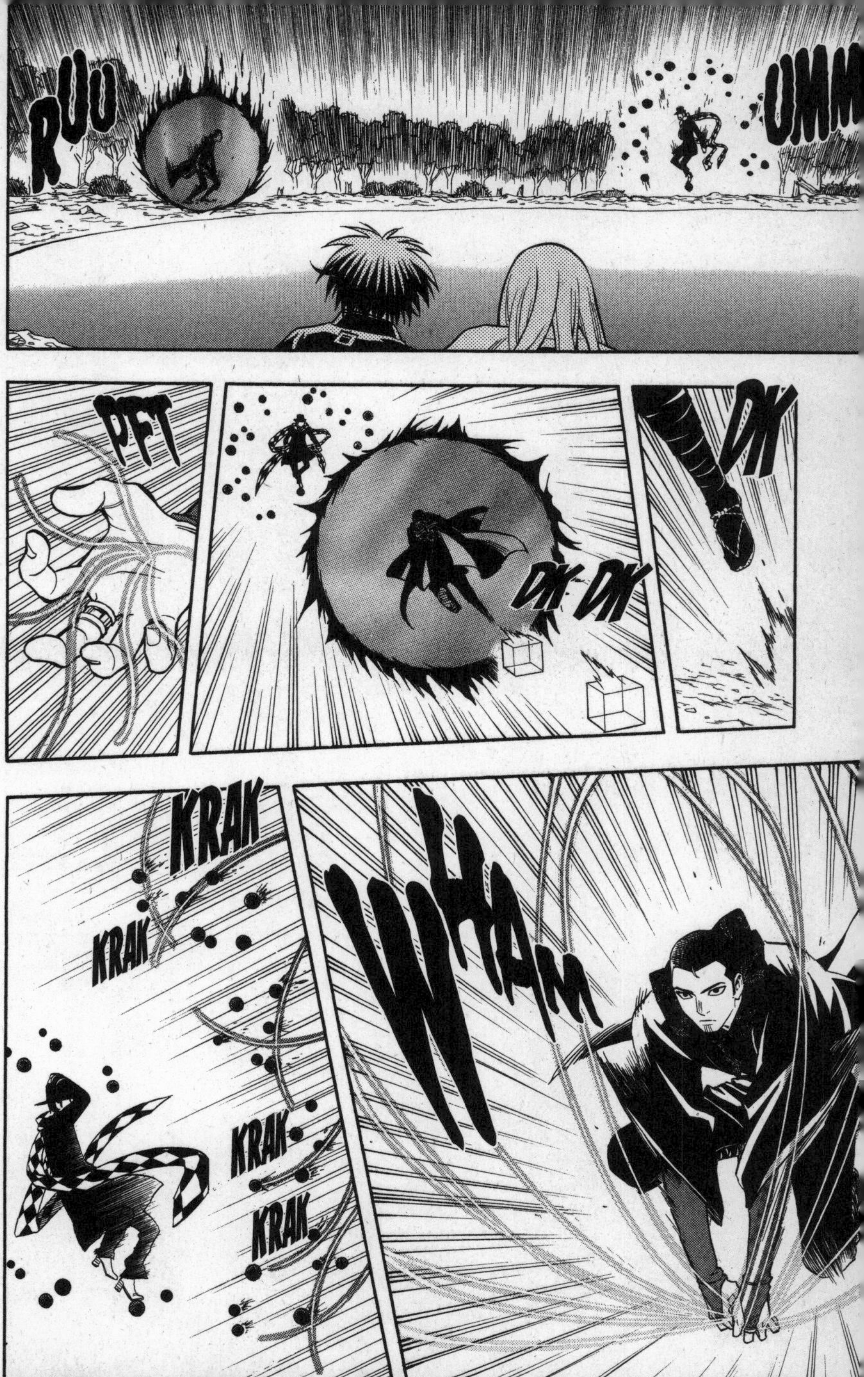
RUU
UMM
DK
DK DK
PFT
WHAM
KRAK
KRAK
KRAK
KRAK

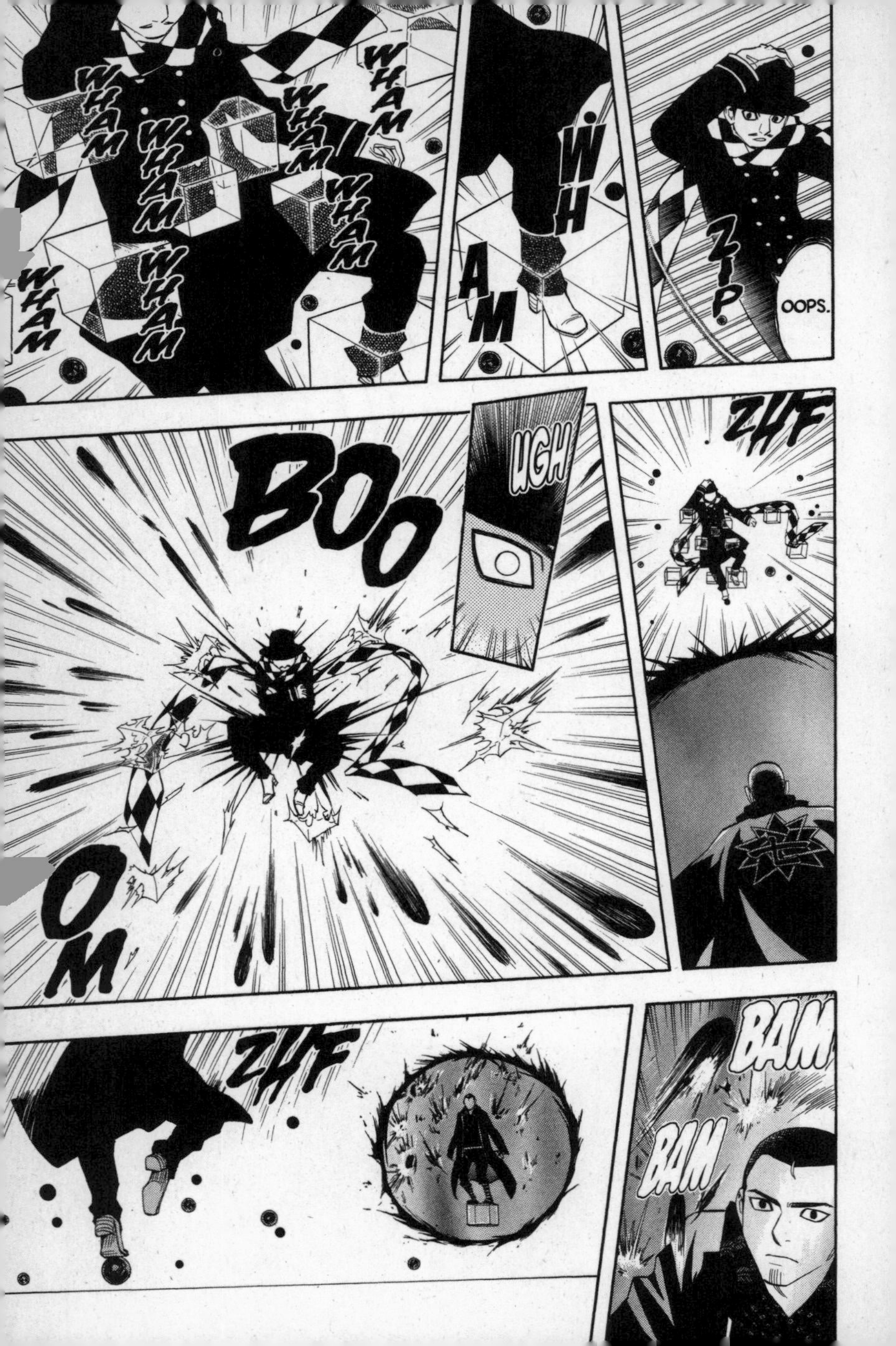

OOPS.
ZIP
WH
AM
WHAM
WHAM
WHAM
WHAM
WHAM
WHAM
WHAM
ZHF
UGH
BOO
OM
BAM
BAM
ZHF

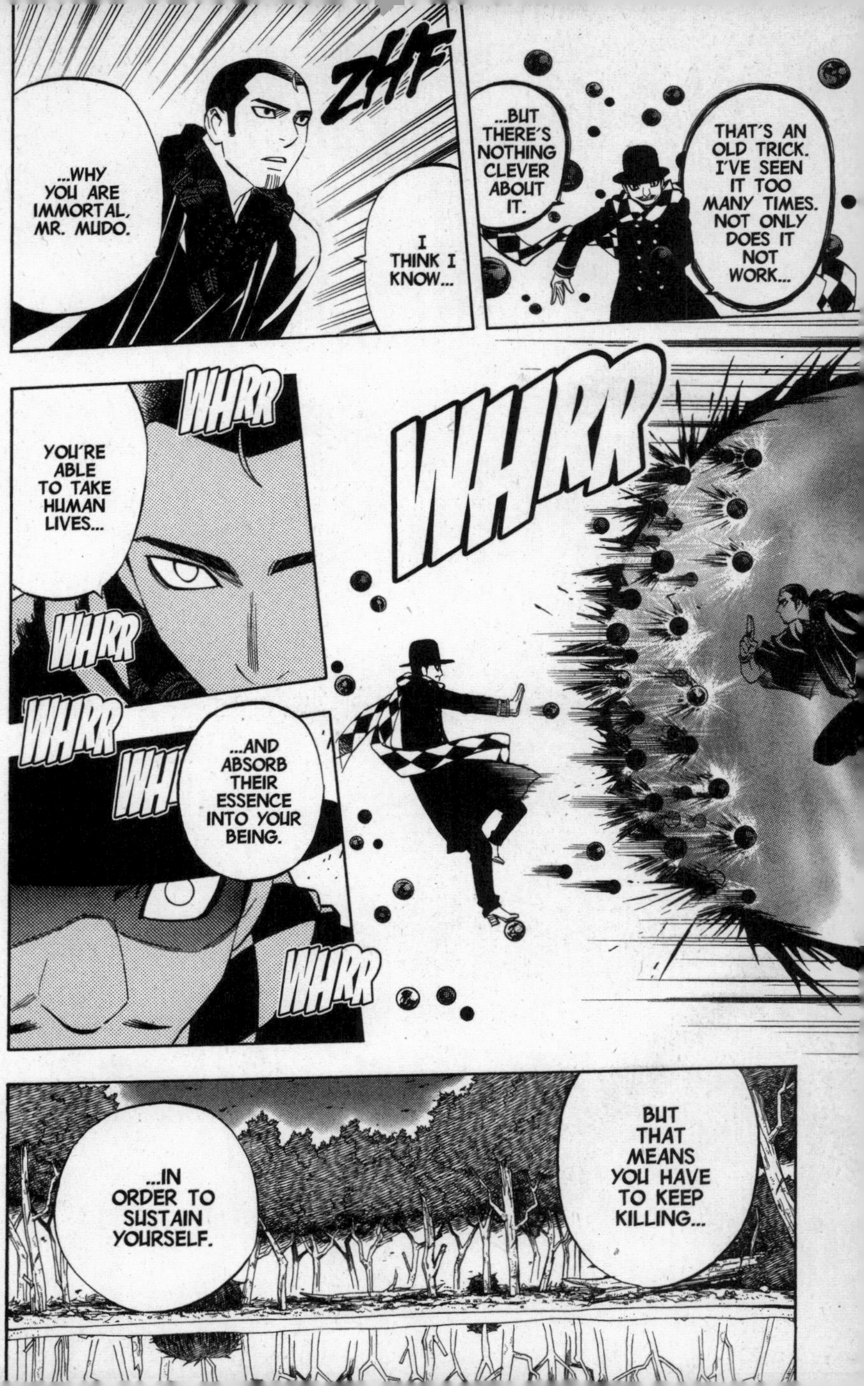
THAT'S AN OLD TRICK. I'VE SEEN IT TOO MANY TIMES. NOT ONLY DOES IT NOT WORK...
...BUT THERE'S NOTHING CLEVER ABOUT IT.
ZHF
I THINK I KNOW...
...WHY YOU ARE IMMORTAL, MR. MUDO.
WHRR
WHRR
YOU'RE ABLE TO TAKE HUMAN LIVES...
WHRR
WHRR
...AND ABSORB THEIR ESSENCE INTO YOUR BEING.
WHRR
BUT THAT MEANS YOU HAVE TO KEEP KILLING...
...IN ORDER TO SUSTAIN YOURSELF.

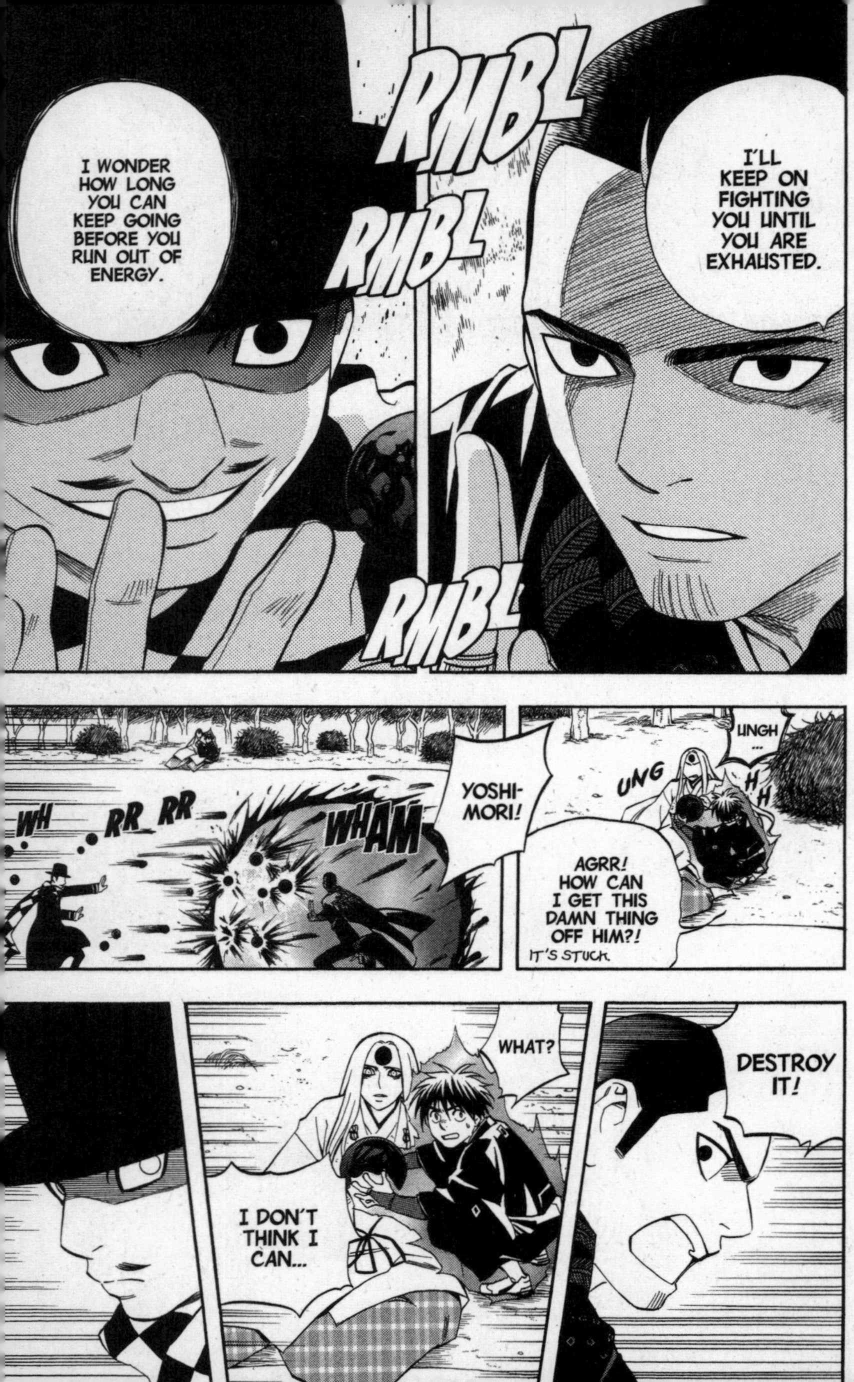
I'LL KEEP ON FIGHTING YOU UNTIL YOU ARE EXHAUSTED.
RMBL
RMBL
I WONDER HOW LONG YOU CAN KEEP GOING BEFORE YOU RUN OUT OF ENERGY.
RMBL
UNGH...
H H
YOSHI-MORI!
UNG
AGRR! HOW CAN I GET THIS DAMN THING OFF HIM?!
IT'S STUCK.
WHAM
RR RR
WH
DESTROY IT!
WHAT?
I DON'T THINK I CAN...

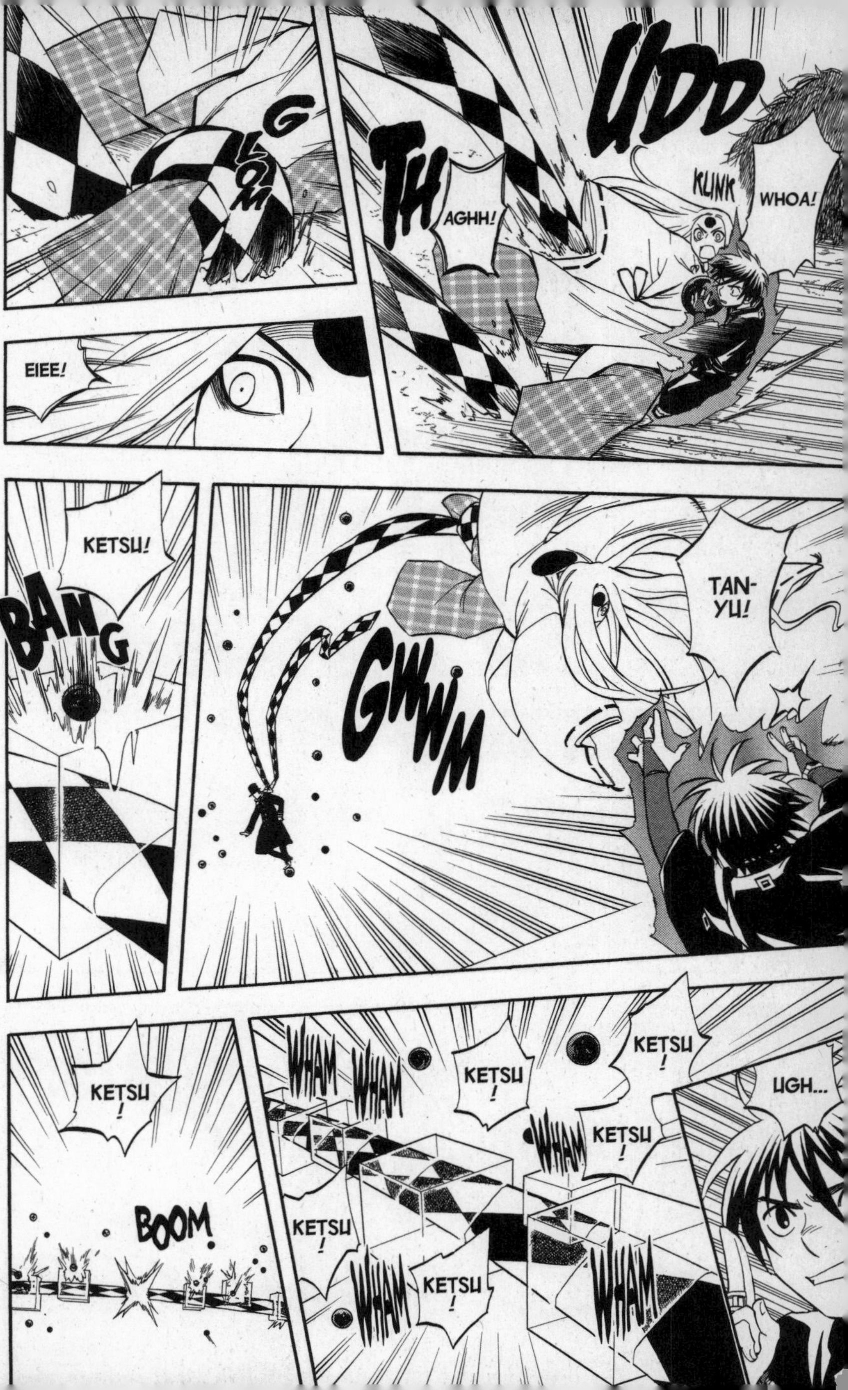
THUDD
WHOA!
KLUNK
AGHH!
GLOM
EIEE!
TAN-YU!
GWWM
KETSU!
BANG
UGH...
KETSU!
KETSU!
WHAM
KETSU!
WHAM
WHAM
WHAM
KETSU!
KETSU!
WHAM
KETSU!
BOOM

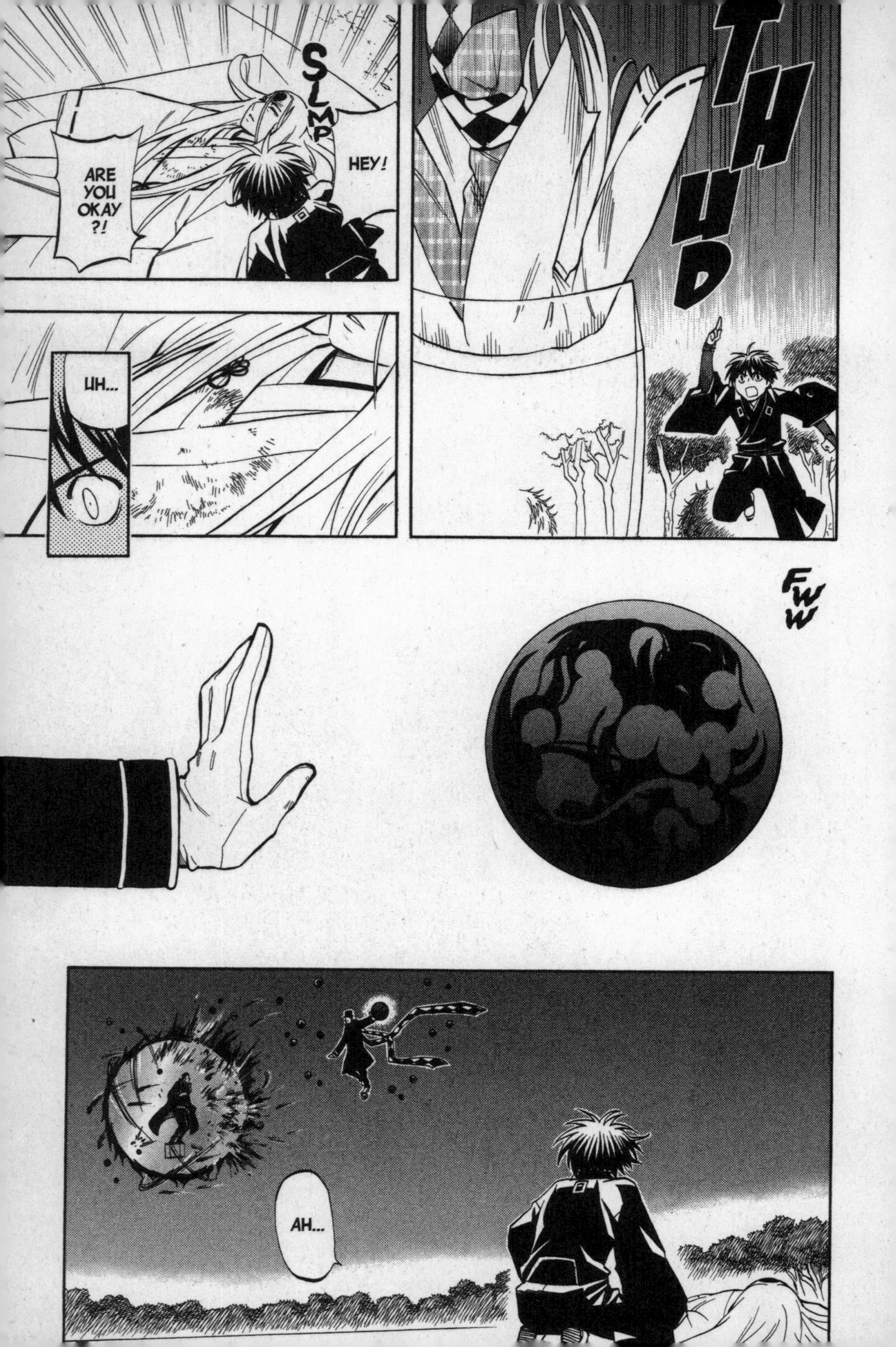
THUD
SLMP
HEY!
ARE YOU OKAY?!
UH...
FWW
AH...

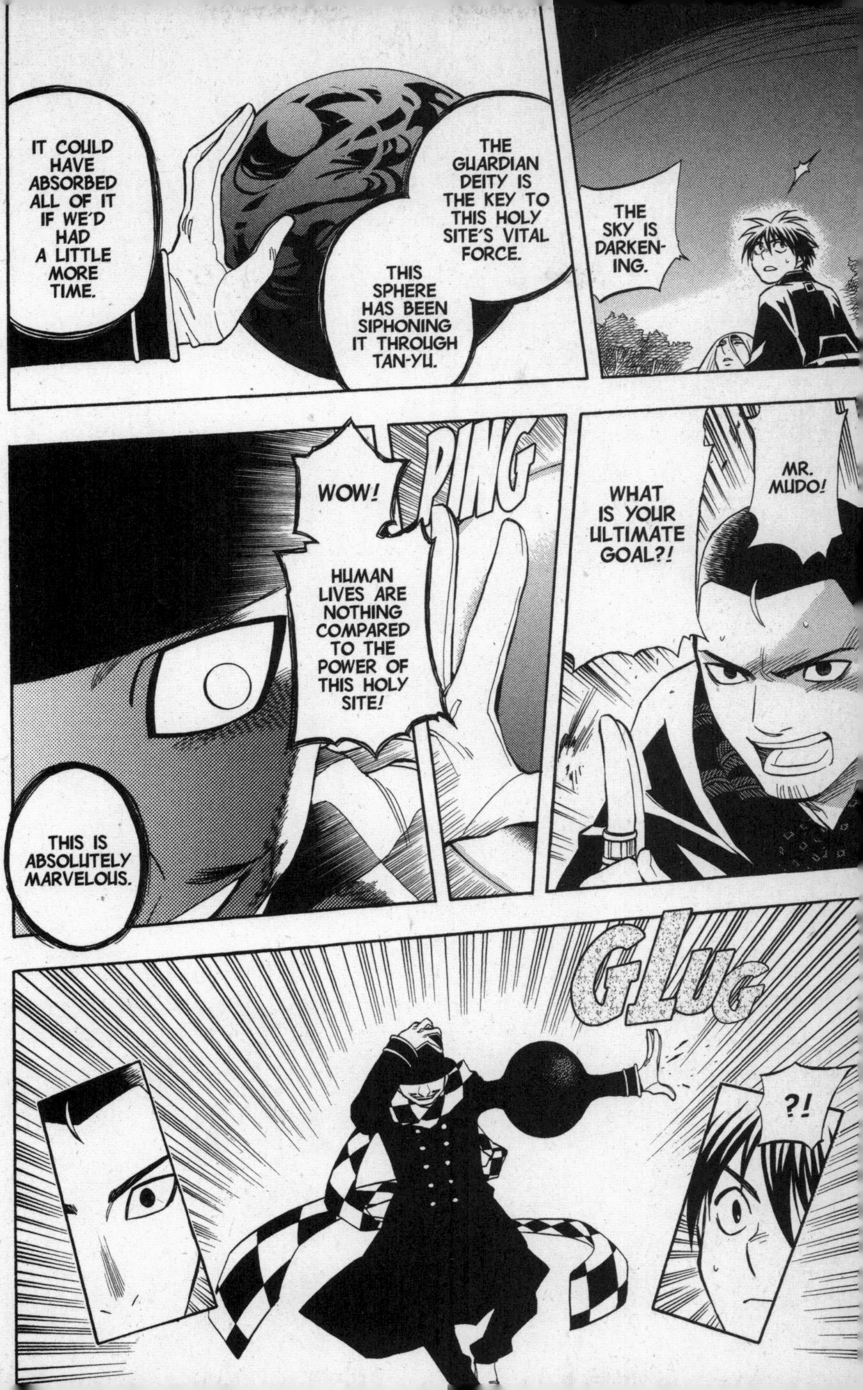
THE SKY IS DARKEN-ING.
THE GUARDIAN DEITY IS THE KEY TO THIS HOLY SITE'S VITAL FORCE.
THIS SPHERE HAS BEEN SIPHONING IT THROUGH TAN-YU.
IT COULD HAVE ABSORBED ALL OF IT IF WE'D HAD A LITTLE MORE TIME.
MR. MUDO!
WHAT IS YOUR ULTIMATE GOAL?!
PING
WOW!
HUMAN LIVES ARE NOTHING COMPARED TO THE POWER OF THIS HOLY SITE!
THIS IS ABSOLUTELY MARVELOUS.
GLUG
?!

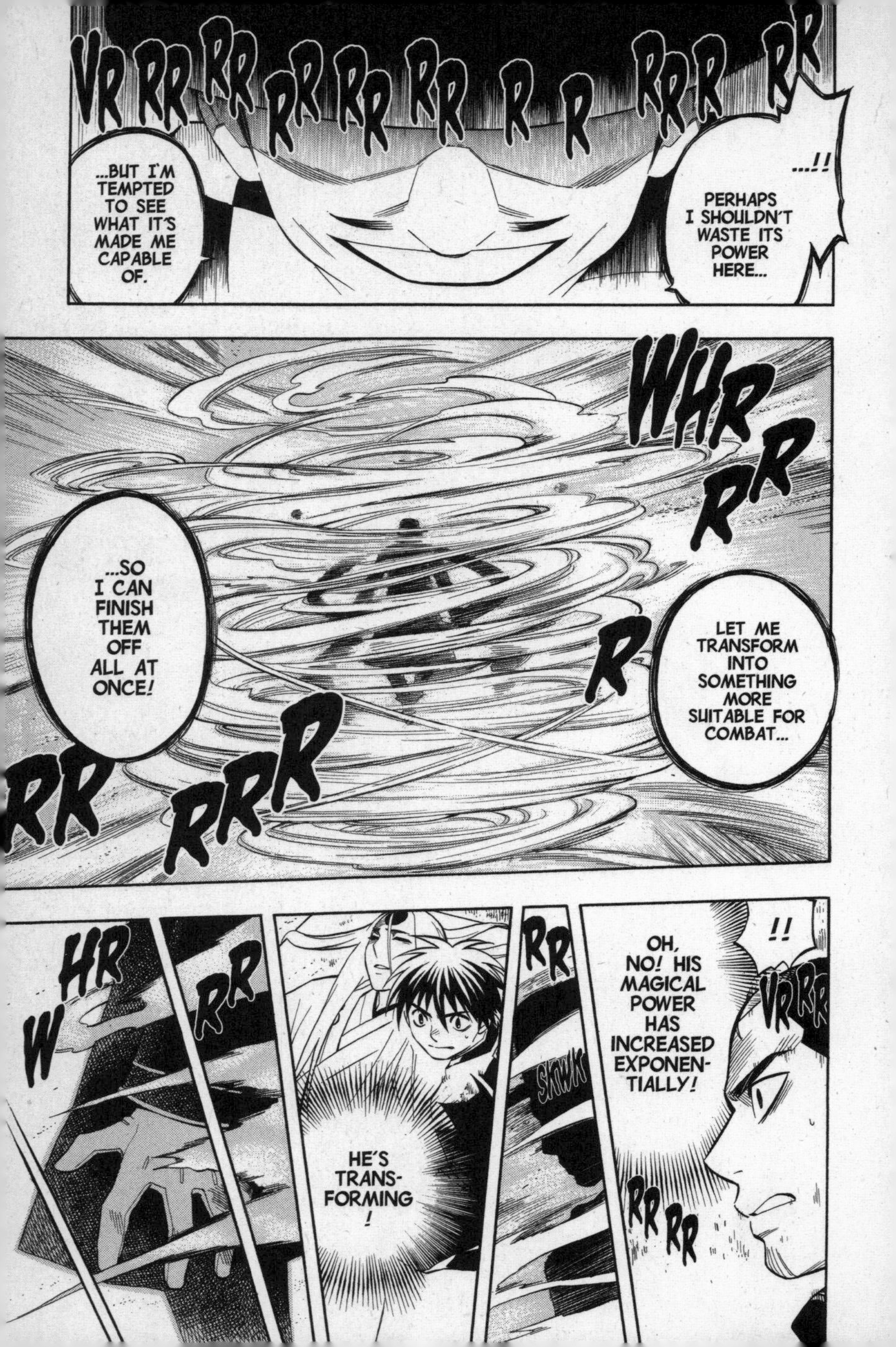
VRRRRRRRRRRRRRRRRRRR
...!!
PERHAPS I SHOULDN'T WASTE ITS POWER HERE...
...BUT I'M TEMPTED TO SEE WHAT IT'S MADE ME CAPABLE OF.
WHRRRR
LET ME TRANSFORM INTO SOMETHING MORE SUITABLE FOR COMBAT...
...SO I CAN FINISH THEM OFF ALL AT ONCE!
RRRRR
!!
VRRR
OH, NO! HIS MAGICAL POWER HAS INCREASED EXPONEN-TIALLY!
RRRR
RR
SKWK
HE'S TRANS-FORMING!
RR
WHR

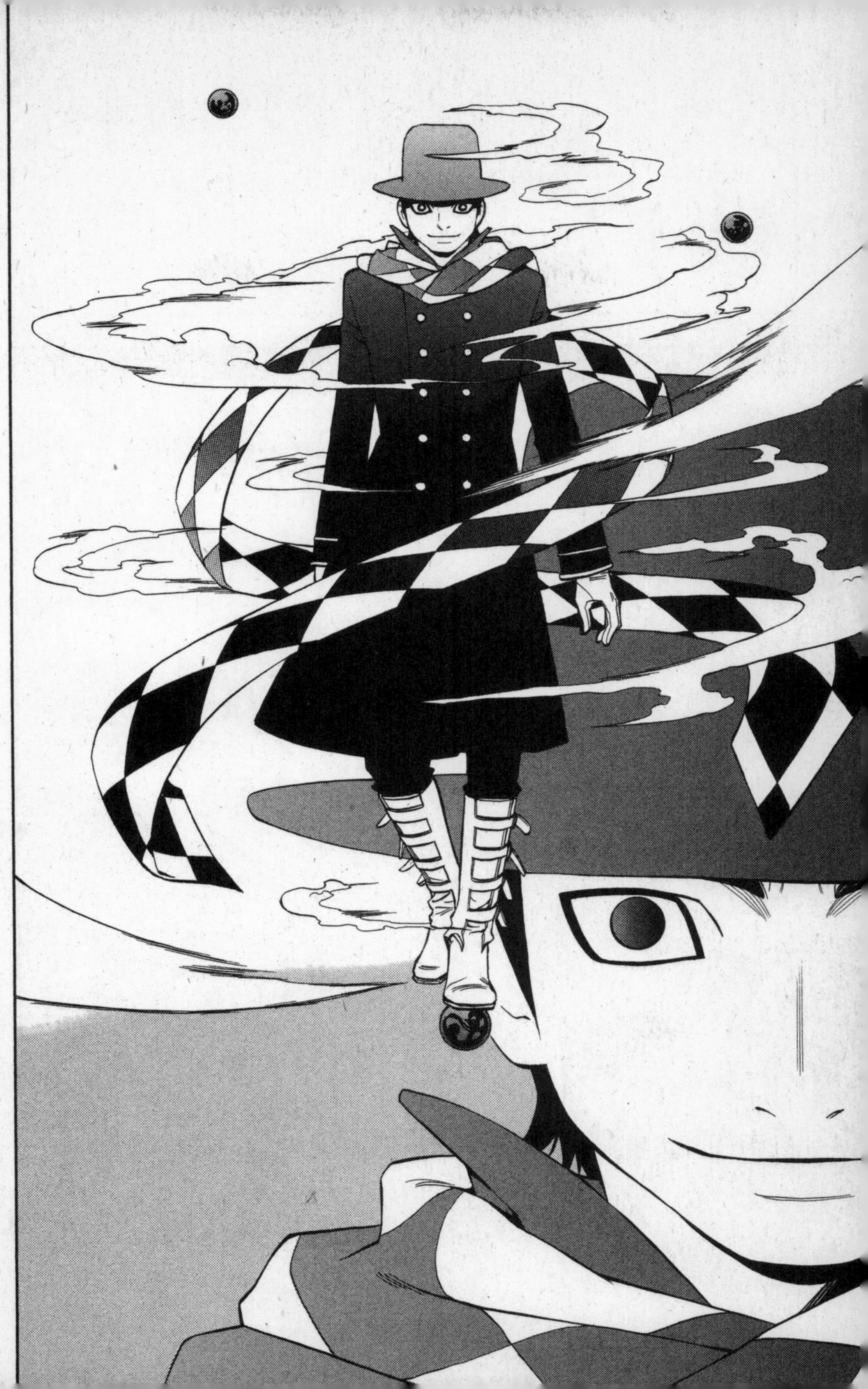

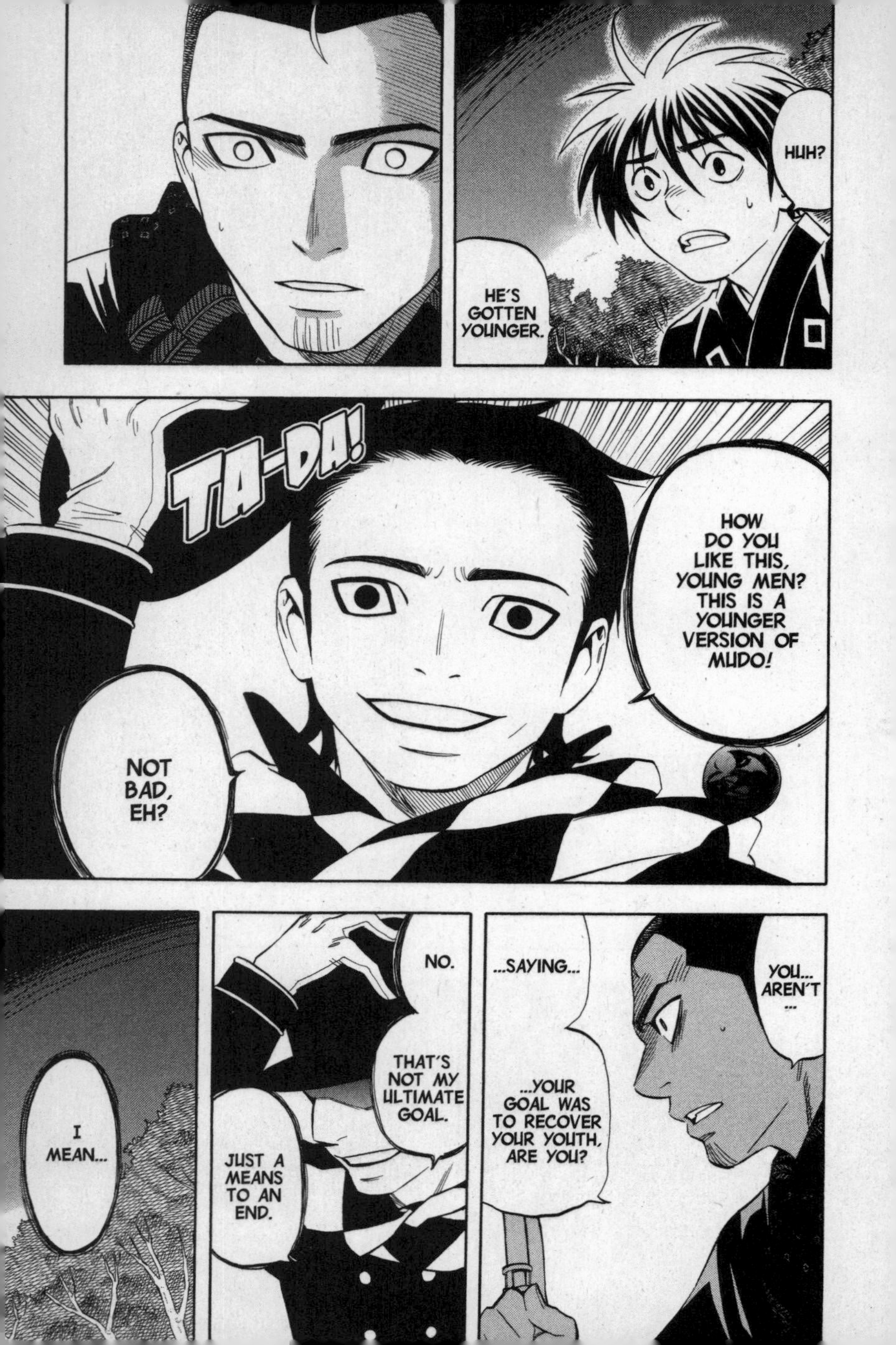
HUH?
HE'S GOTTEN YOUNGER.
TA-DA!
HOW DO YOU LIKE THIS, YOUNG MEN? THIS IS A YOUNGER VERSION OF MUDO!
NOT BAD, EH?
YOU... AREN'T ...
...SAYING...
...YOUR GOAL WAS TO RECOVER YOUR YOUTH, ARE YOU?
NO.
THAT'S NOT MY ULTIMATE GOAL.
JUST A MEANS TO AN END.
I MEAN...

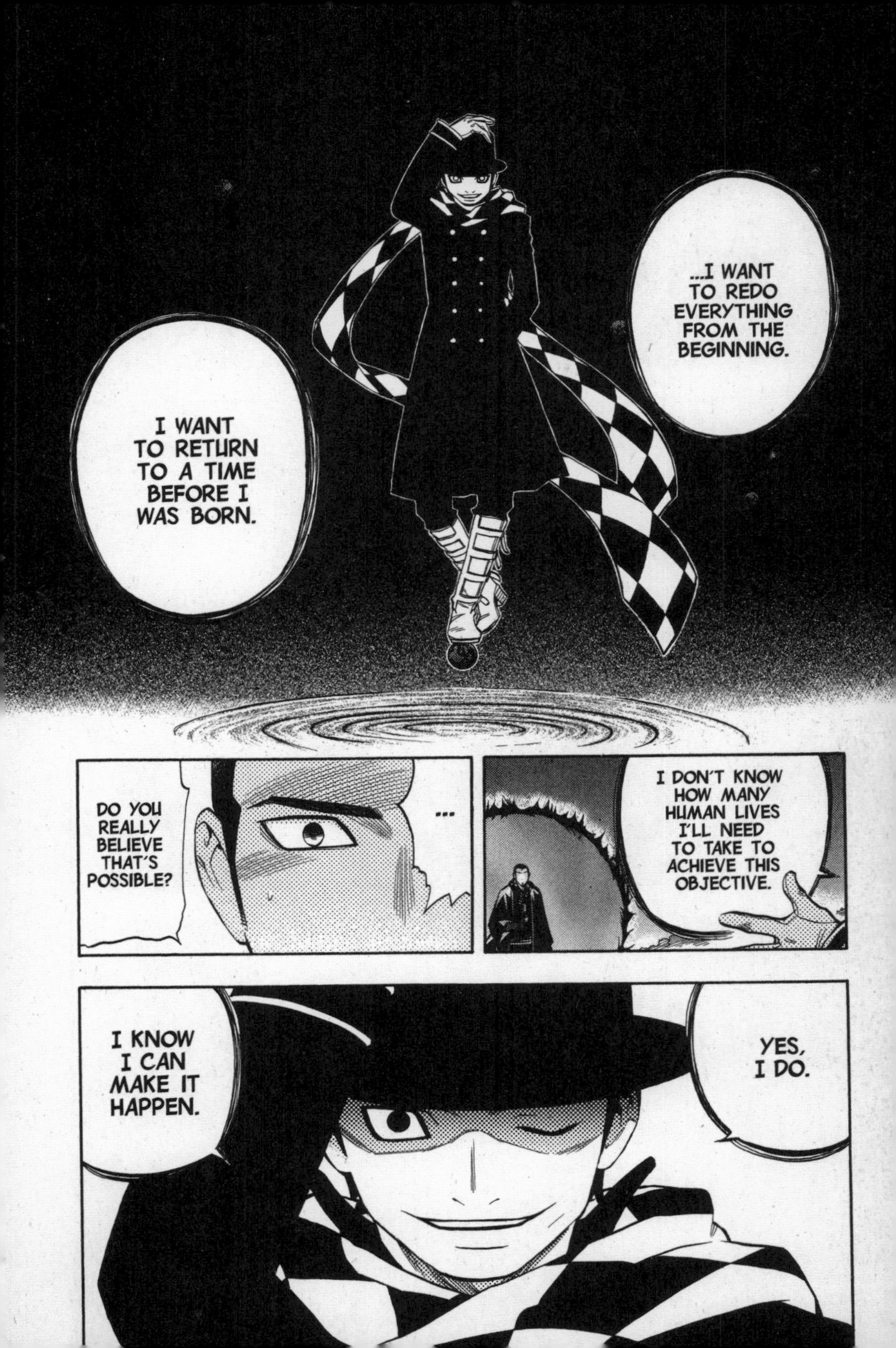
...I WANT TO REDO EVERYTHING FROM THE BEGINNING.
I WANT TO RETURN TO A TIME BEFORE I WAS BORN.
I DON'T KNOW HOW MANY HUMAN LIVES I'LL NEED TO TAKE TO ACHIEVE THIS OBJECTIVE.
...
DO YOU REALLY BELIEVE THAT'S POSSIBLE?
YES, I DO.
I KNOW I CAN MAKE IT HAPPEN.

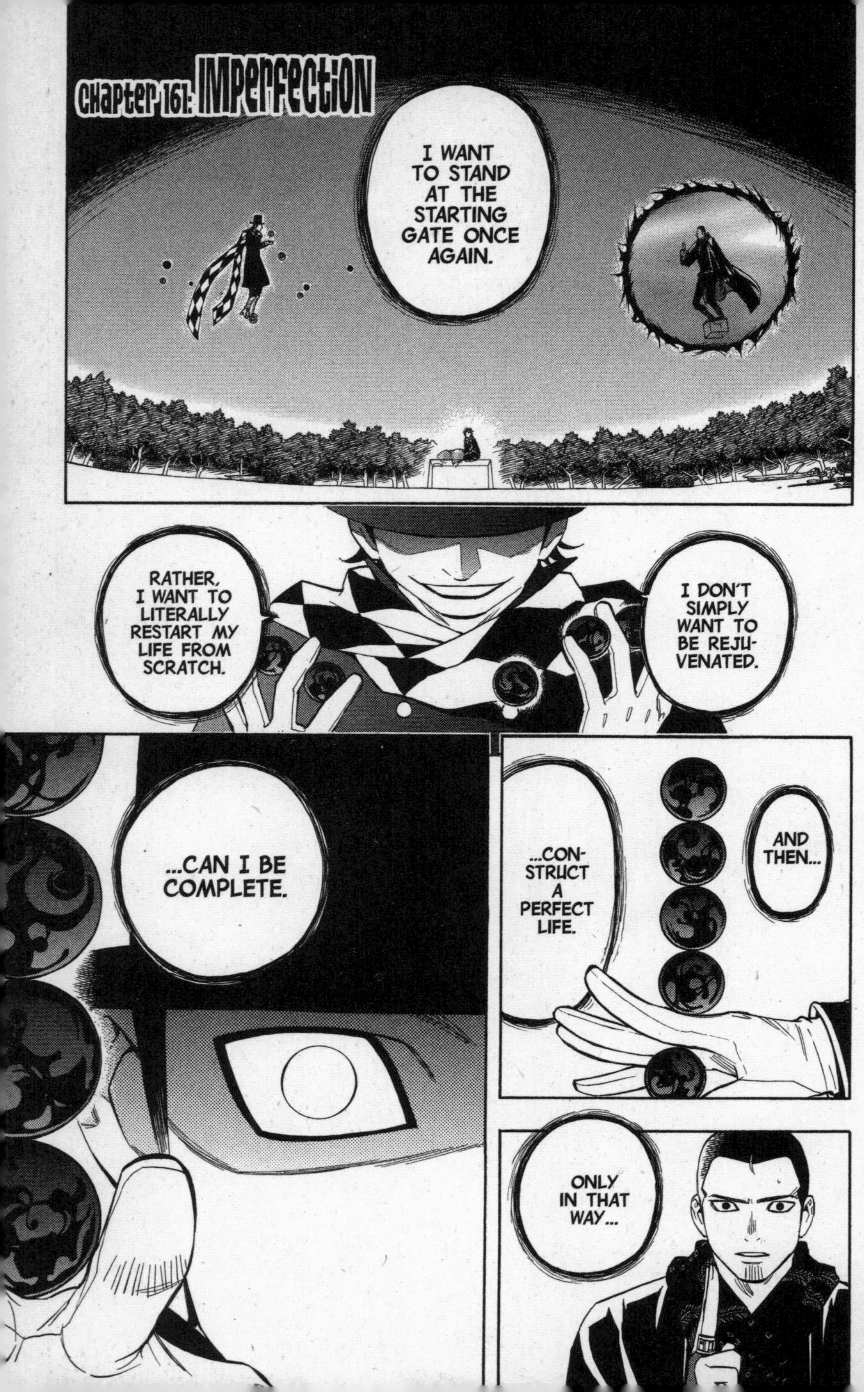
Chapter 161: Imperfection
I WANT TO STAND AT THE STARTING GATE ONCE AGAIN.
I DON'T SIMPLY WANT TO BE REJU-VENATED.
RATHER, I WANT TO LITERALLY RESTART MY LIFE FROM SCRATCH.
AND THEN...
...CON-STRUCT A PERFECT LIFE.
ONLY IN THAT WAY...
...CAN I BE COMPLETE.

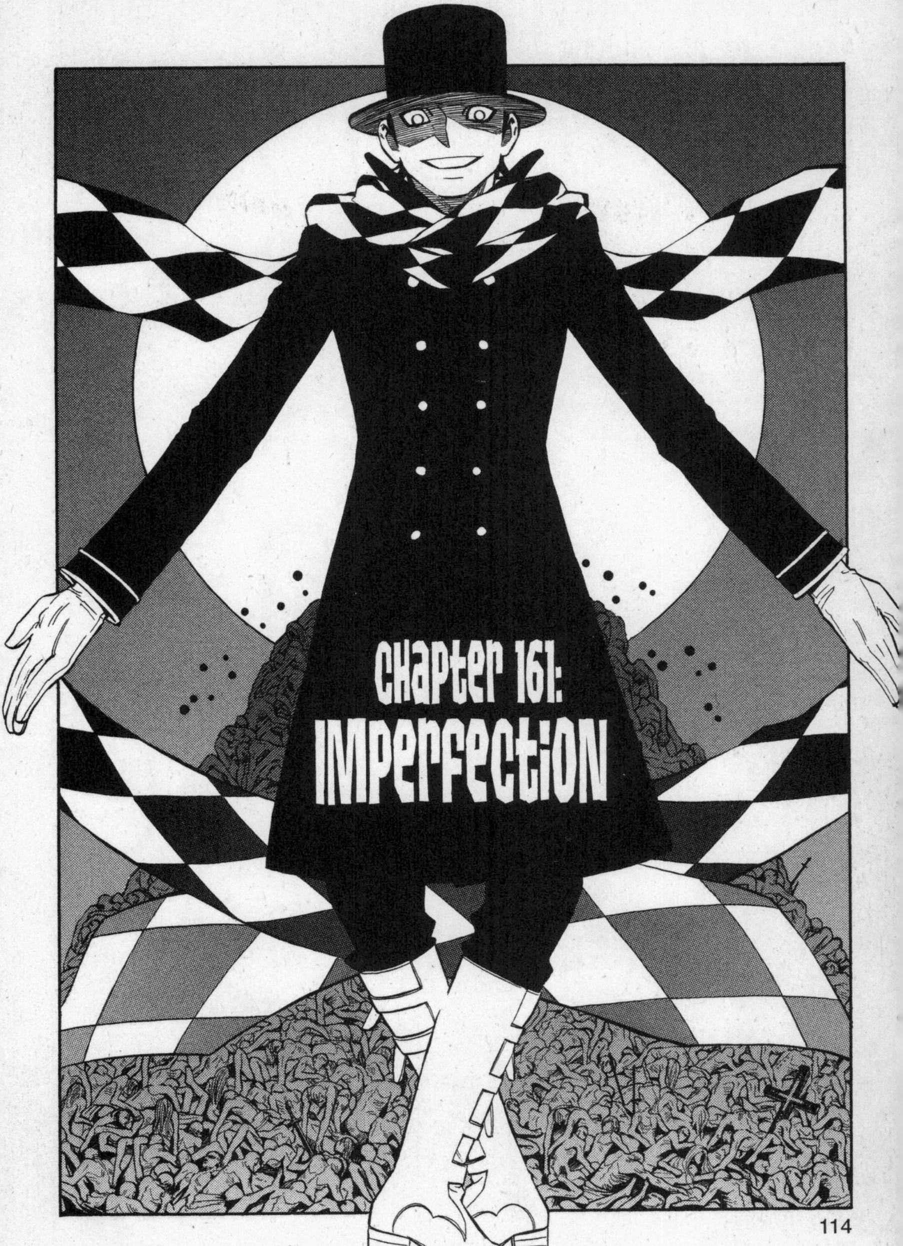
CHAPTER 161:
IMPERFECTION

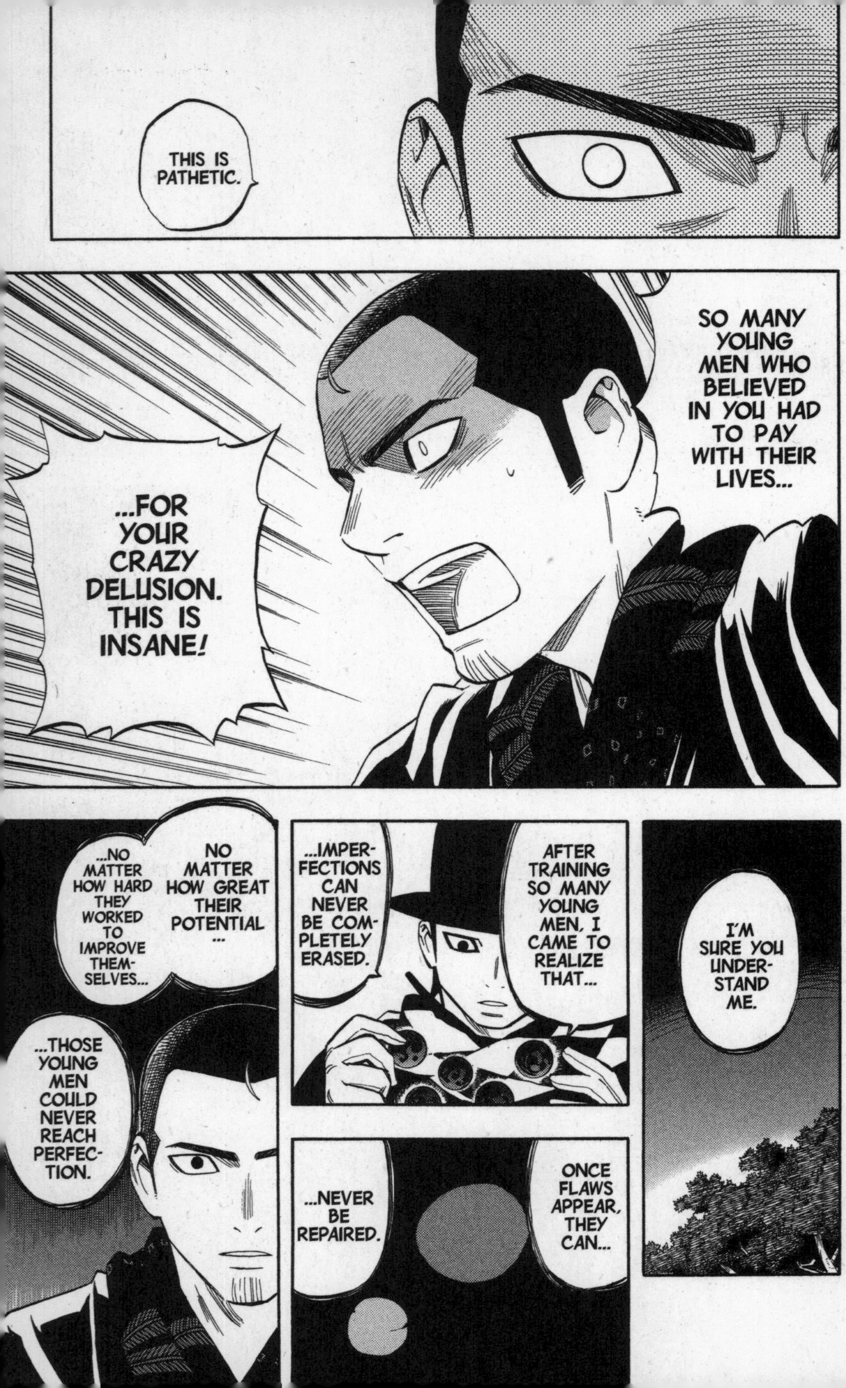
THIS IS PATHETIC.
SO MANY YOUNG MEN WHO BELIEVED IN YOU HAD TO PAY WITH THEIR LIVES...
...FOR YOUR CRAZY DELUSION. THIS IS INSANE!
I'M SURE YOU UNDERSTAND ME.
AFTER TRAINING SO MANY YOUNG MEN, I CAME TO REALIZE THAT...
...IMPERFECTIONS CAN NEVER BE COMPLETELY ERASED.
ONCE FLAWS APPEAR, THEY CAN...
...NEVER BE REPAIRED.
NO MATTER HOW GREAT THEIR POTENTIAL...
...NO MATTER HOW HARD THEY WORKED TO IMPROVE THEMSELVES...
...THOSE YOUNG MEN COULD NEVER REACH PERFECTION.

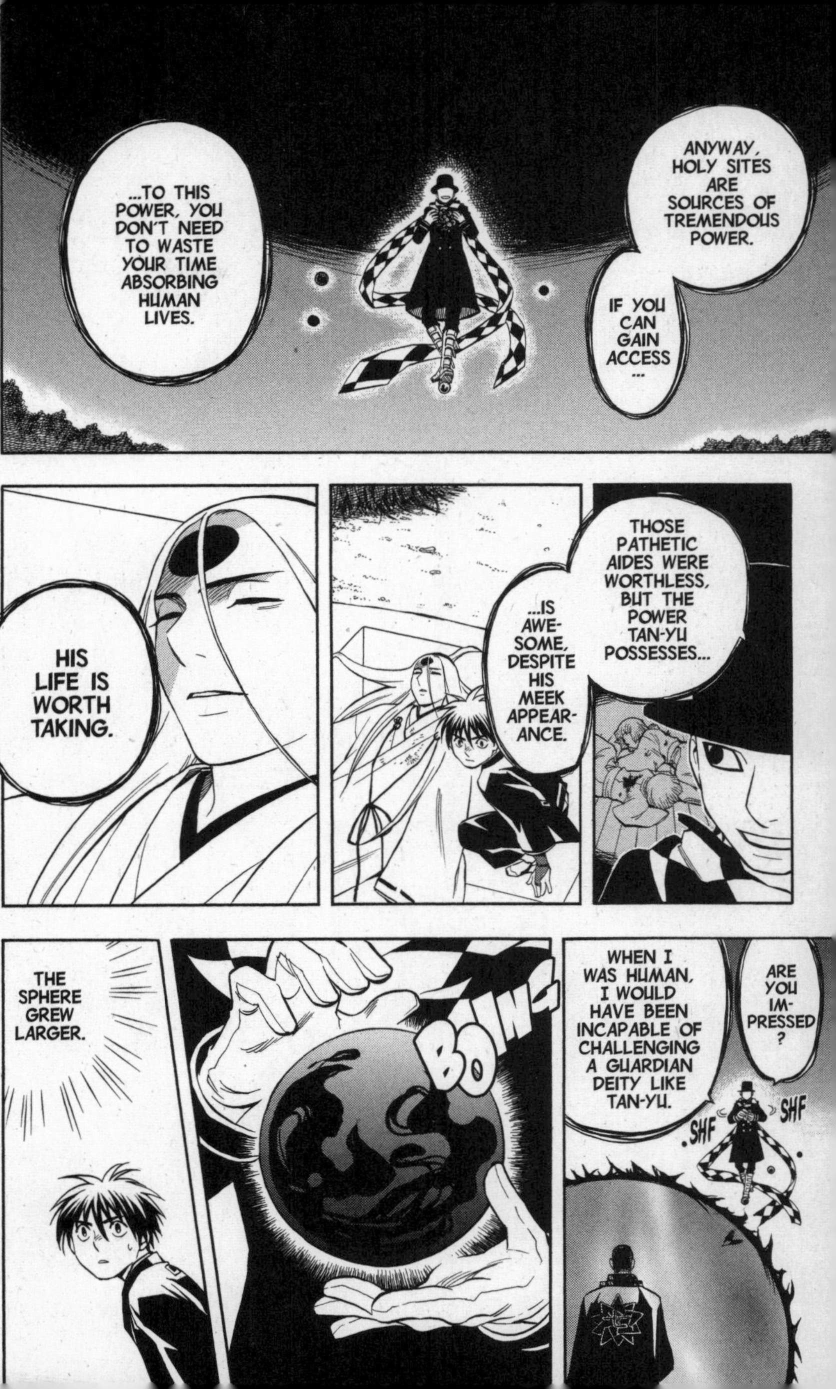
ANYWAY, HOLY SITES ARE SOURCES OF TREMENDOUS POWER.
IF YOU CAN GAIN ACCESS ...
...TO THIS POWER, YOU DON'T NEED TO WASTE YOUR TIME ABSORBING HUMAN LIVES.
THOSE PATHETIC AIDES WERE WORTHLESS, BUT THE POWER TAN-YU POSSESSES...
...IS AWESOME, DESPITE HIS MEEK APPEARANCE.
HIS LIFE IS WORTH TAKING.
ARE YOU IMPRESSED?
WHEN I WAS HUMAN, I WOULD HAVE BEEN INCAPABLE OF CHALLENGING A GUARDIAN DEITY LIKE TAN-YU.
SHF
SHF
BOING
THE SPHERE GREW LARGER.

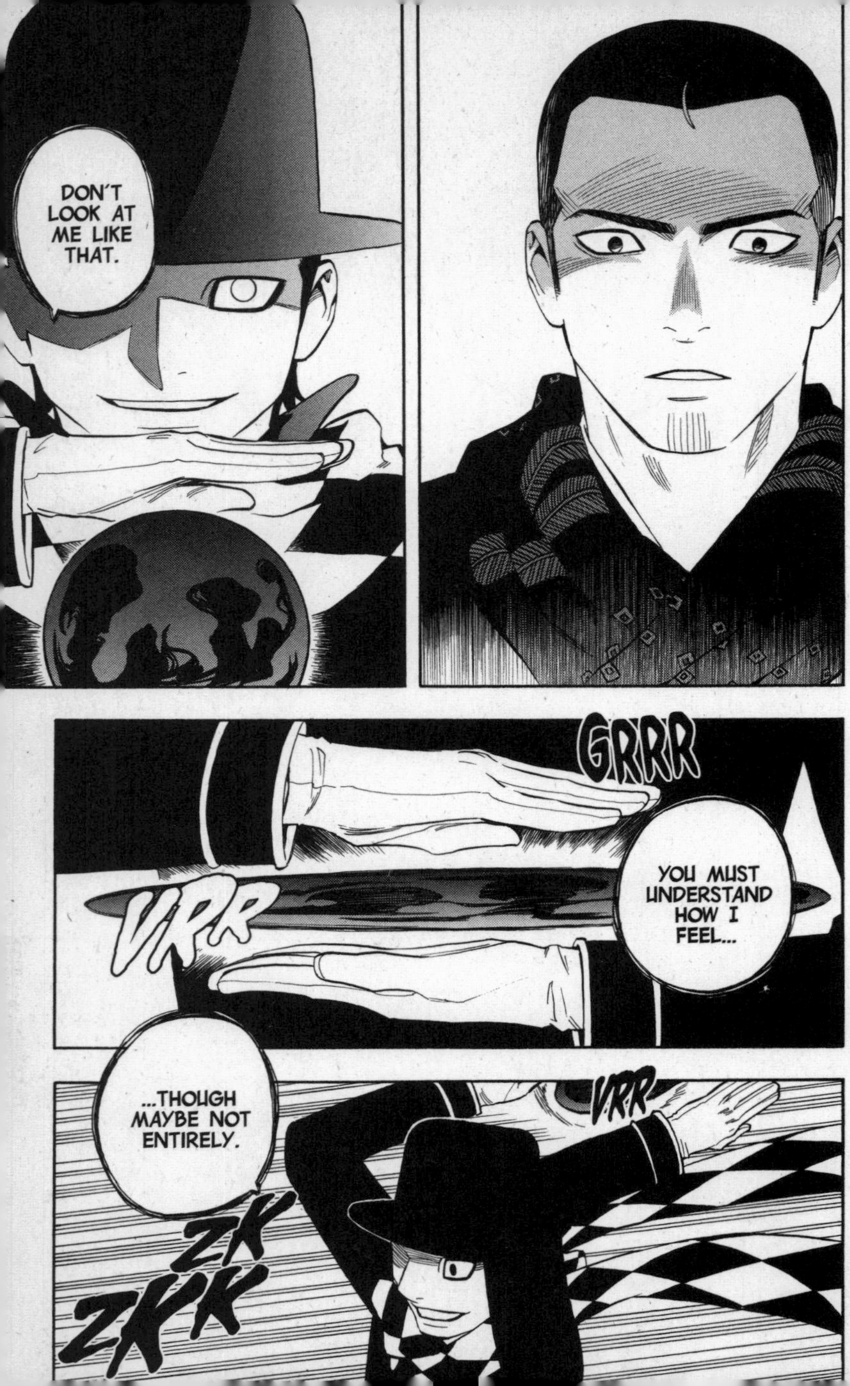
DON'T LOOK AT ME LIKE THAT.
GRRR
YOU MUST UNDERSTAND HOW I FEEL...
VRR
VRR
...THOUGH MAYBE NOT ENTIRELY.
ZK ZKK

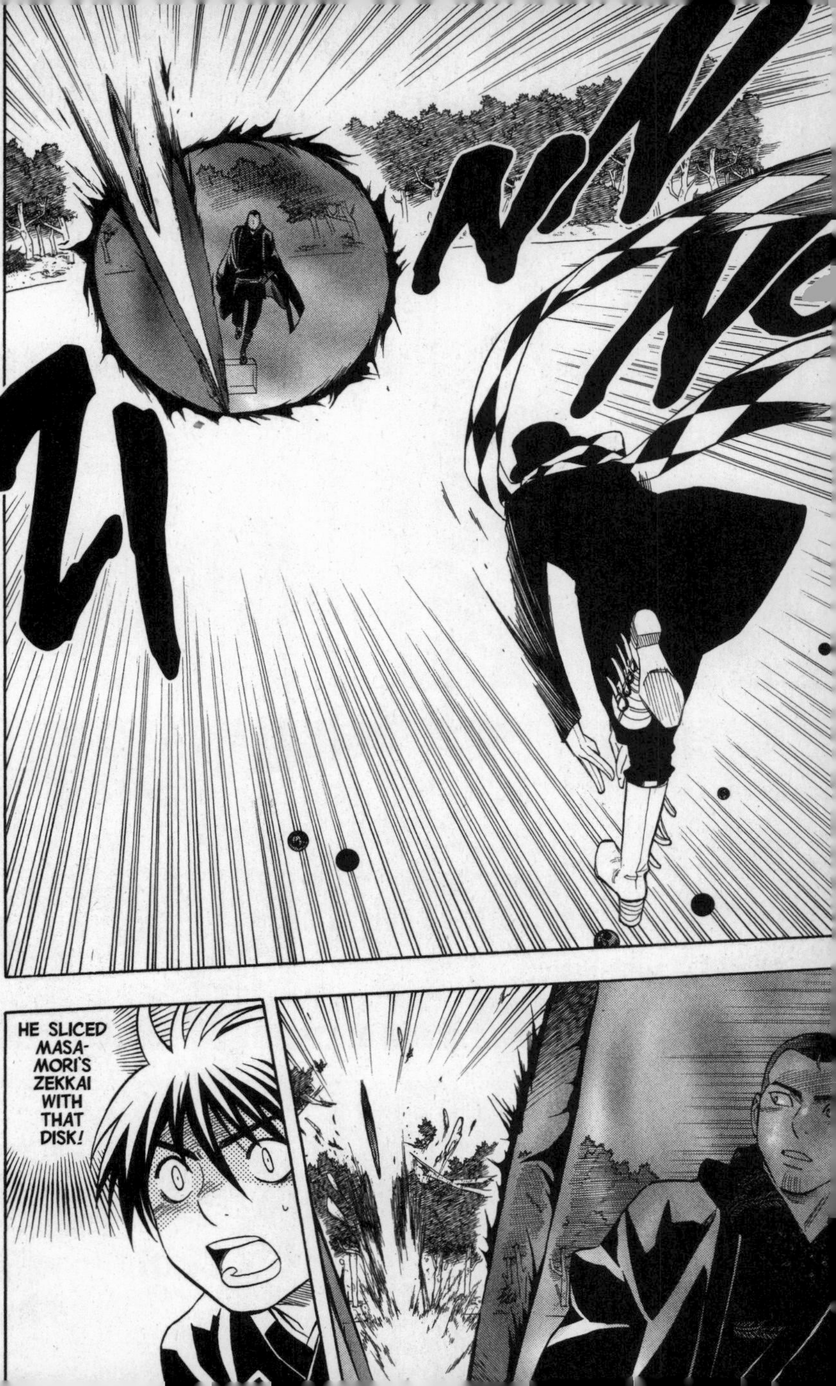
ZI
HE SLICED MASA-MORI'S ZEKKAI WITH THAT DISK!

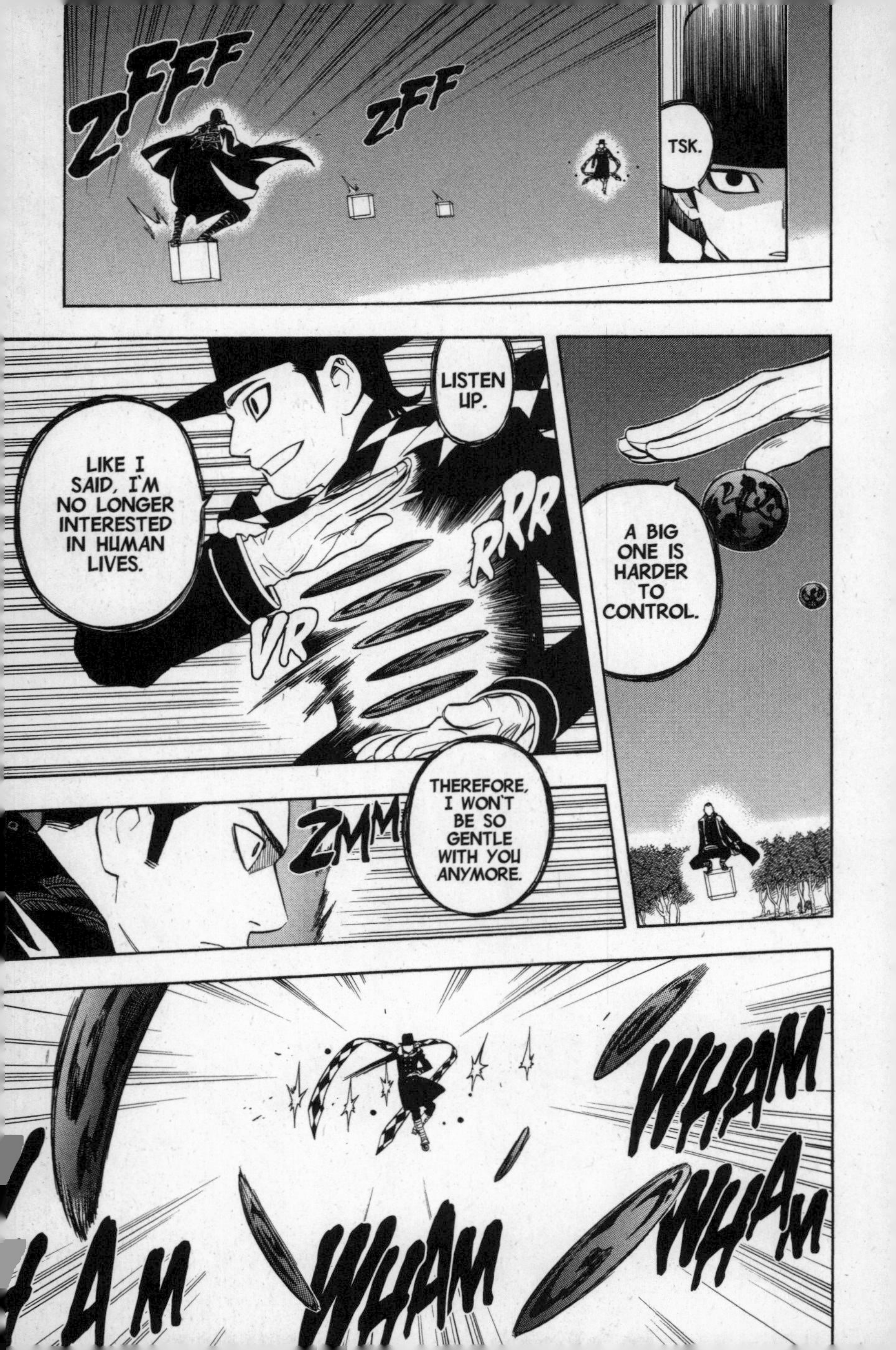
TSK.
ZFFF
ZFF
A BIG ONE IS HARDER TO CONTROL.
LISTEN UP.
LIKE I SAID, I'M NO LONGER INTERESTED IN HUMAN LIVES.
RRR
VR
THEREFORE, I WON'T BE SO GENTLE WITH YOU ANYMORE.
ZMM
WHAM
WHAM
WHAM
WHAM

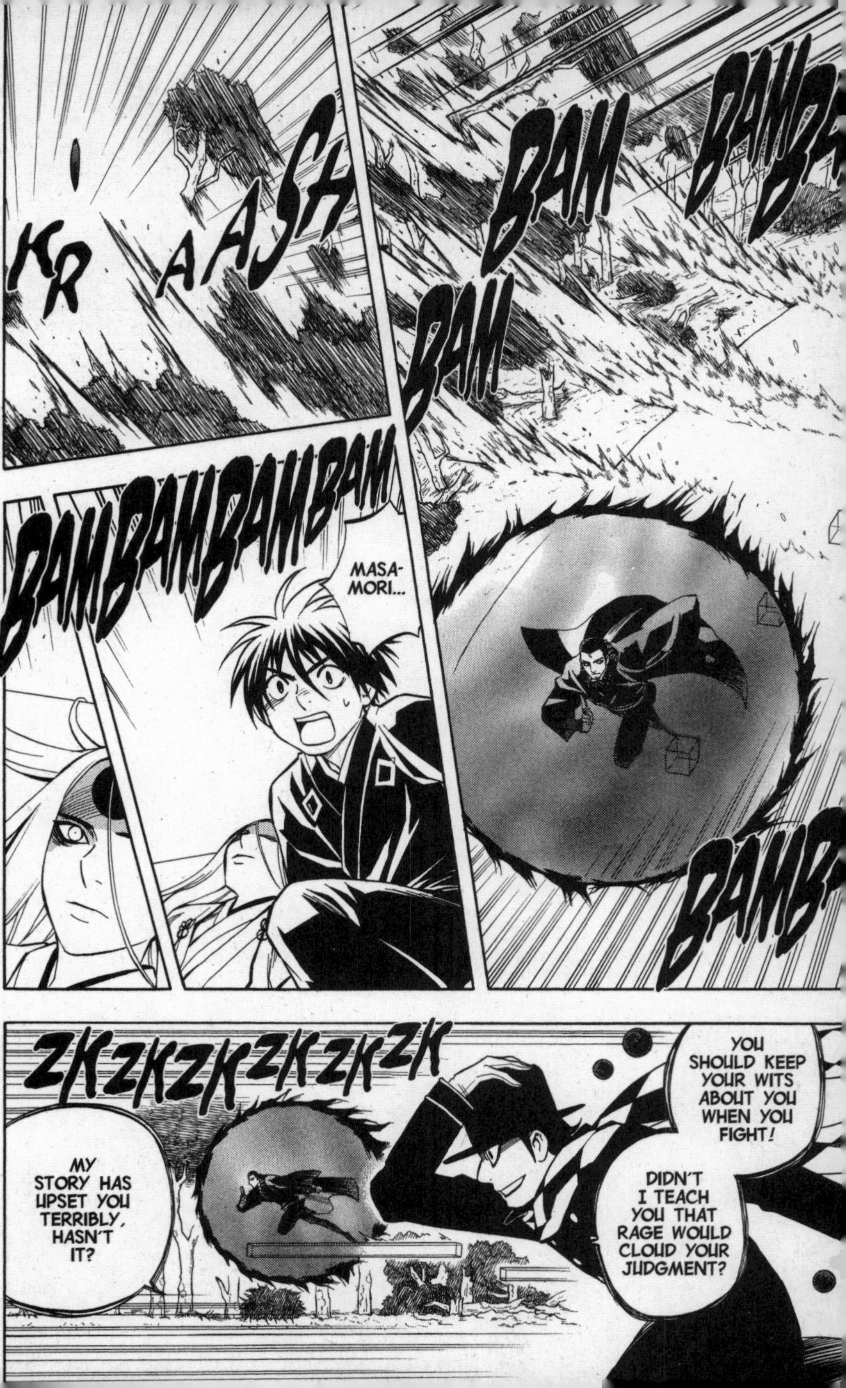

BAM BAM BAM
KRAASH
BAMBAMBAMBAM
MASA-MORI...
ZKZKZKZKZKZK
YOU SHOULD KEEP YOUR WITS ABOUT YOU WHEN YOU FIGHT!
DIDN'T I TEACH YOU THAT RAGE WOULD CLOUD YOUR JUDGMENT?
MY STORY HAS UPSET YOU TERRIBLY, HASN'T IT?

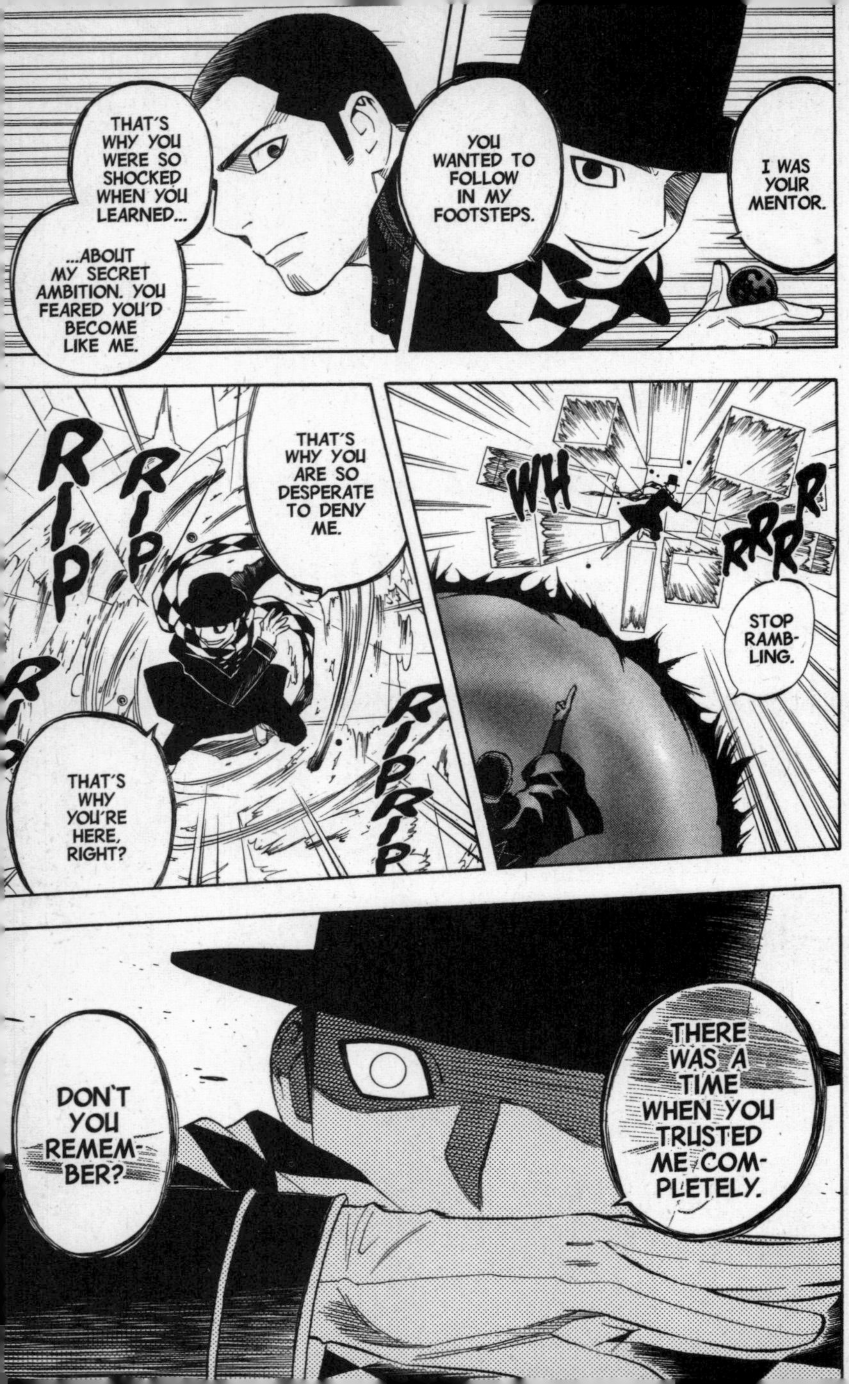
I WAS YOUR MENTOR.
YOU WANTED TO FOLLOW IN MY FOOTSTEPS.
THAT'S WHY YOU WERE SO SHOCKED WHEN YOU LEARNED...
...ABOUT MY SECRET AMBITION. YOU FEARED YOU'D BECOME LIKE ME.
WH
RRRRR
STOP RAMBLING.
THAT'S WHY YOU ARE SO DESPERATE TO DENY ME.
RIP
RIP
RIPRIP
THAT'S WHY YOU'RE HERE, RIGHT?
THERE WAS A TIME WHEN YOU TRUSTED ME COMPLETELY.
DON'T YOU REMEMBER?

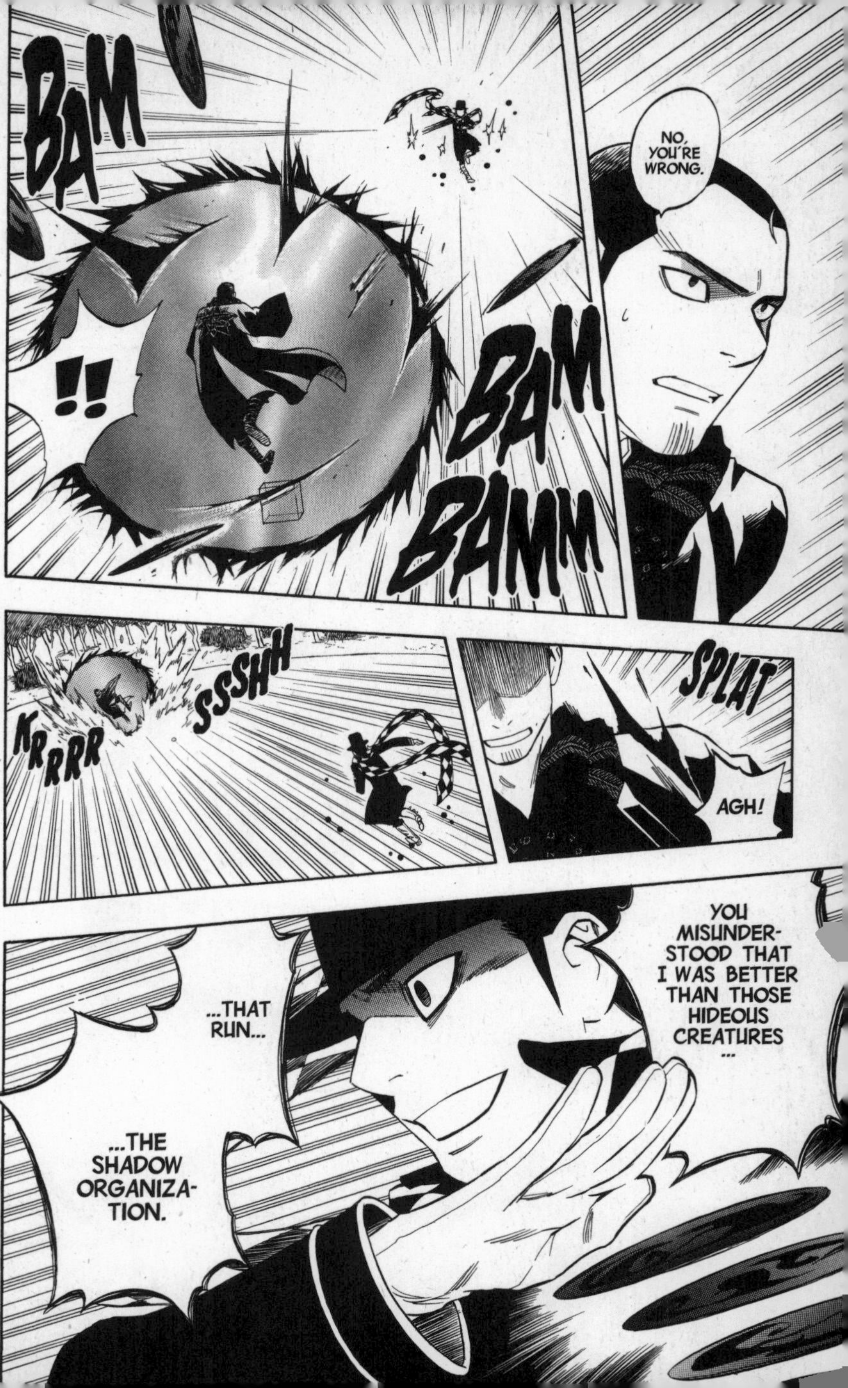
NO, YOU'RE WRONG.
BAM
BAM BAMM
!!
SPLAT
AGH!
SSSHH
KRRRR
YOU MISUNDER-STOOD THAT I WAS BETTER THAN THOSE HIDEOUS CREATURES ...
...THAT RUN...
...THE SHADOW ORGANIZA-TION.

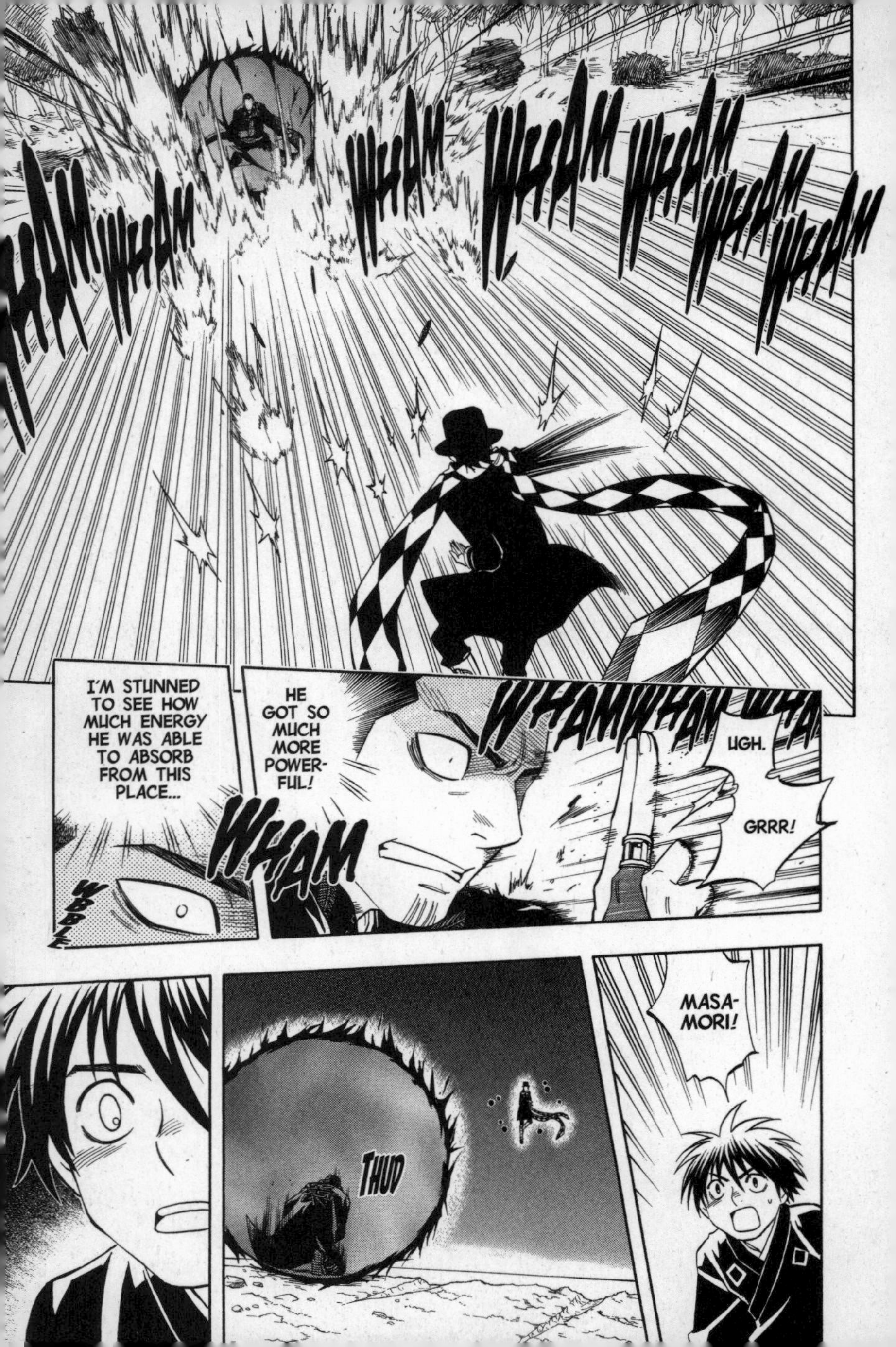

WHAM WHAM WHAM WHAM
WHAM WHAM WHAM
UGH.
GRRR!
WHAMWHAM WHAM
HE GOT SO MUCH MORE POWERFUL!
WHAM
I'M STUNNED TO SEE HOW MUCH ENERGY HE WAS ABLE TO ABSORB FROM THIS PLACE...
WOBBLE
MASA-MORI!
THUD

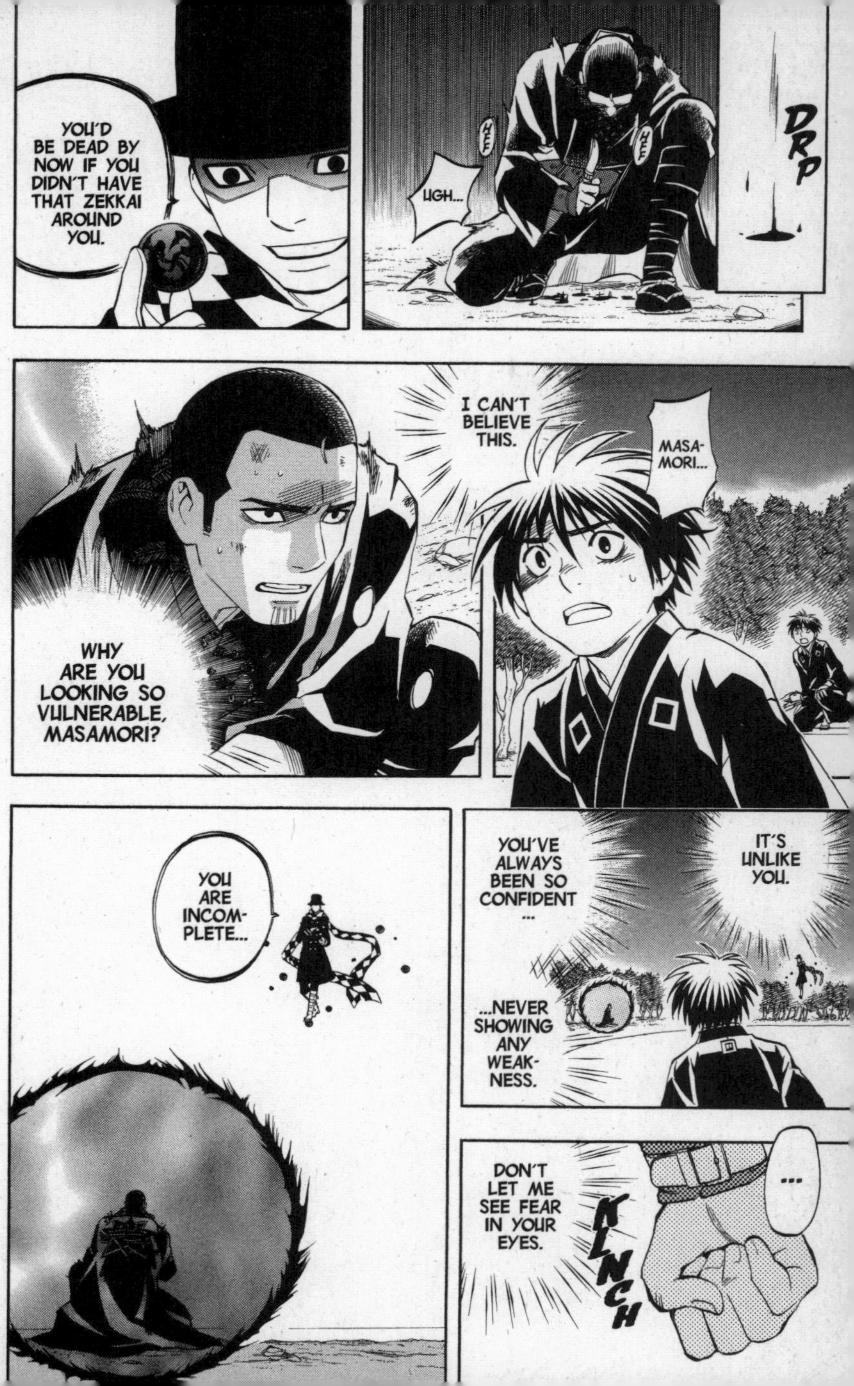
DRP
HFF
HFF
UGH...
YOU'D BE DEAD BY NOW IF YOU DIDN'T HAVE THAT ZEKKAI AROUND YOU.
MASA-MORI...
I CAN'T BELIEVE THIS.
WHY ARE YOU LOOKING SO VULNERABLE, MASAMORI?
IT'S UNLIKE YOU.
YOU'VE ALWAYS BEEN SO CONFIDENT ...
...NEVER SHOWING ANY WEAK-NESS.
...
KLNCH
DON'T LET ME SEE FEAR IN YOUR EYES.
YOU ARE INCOMP-PLETE...

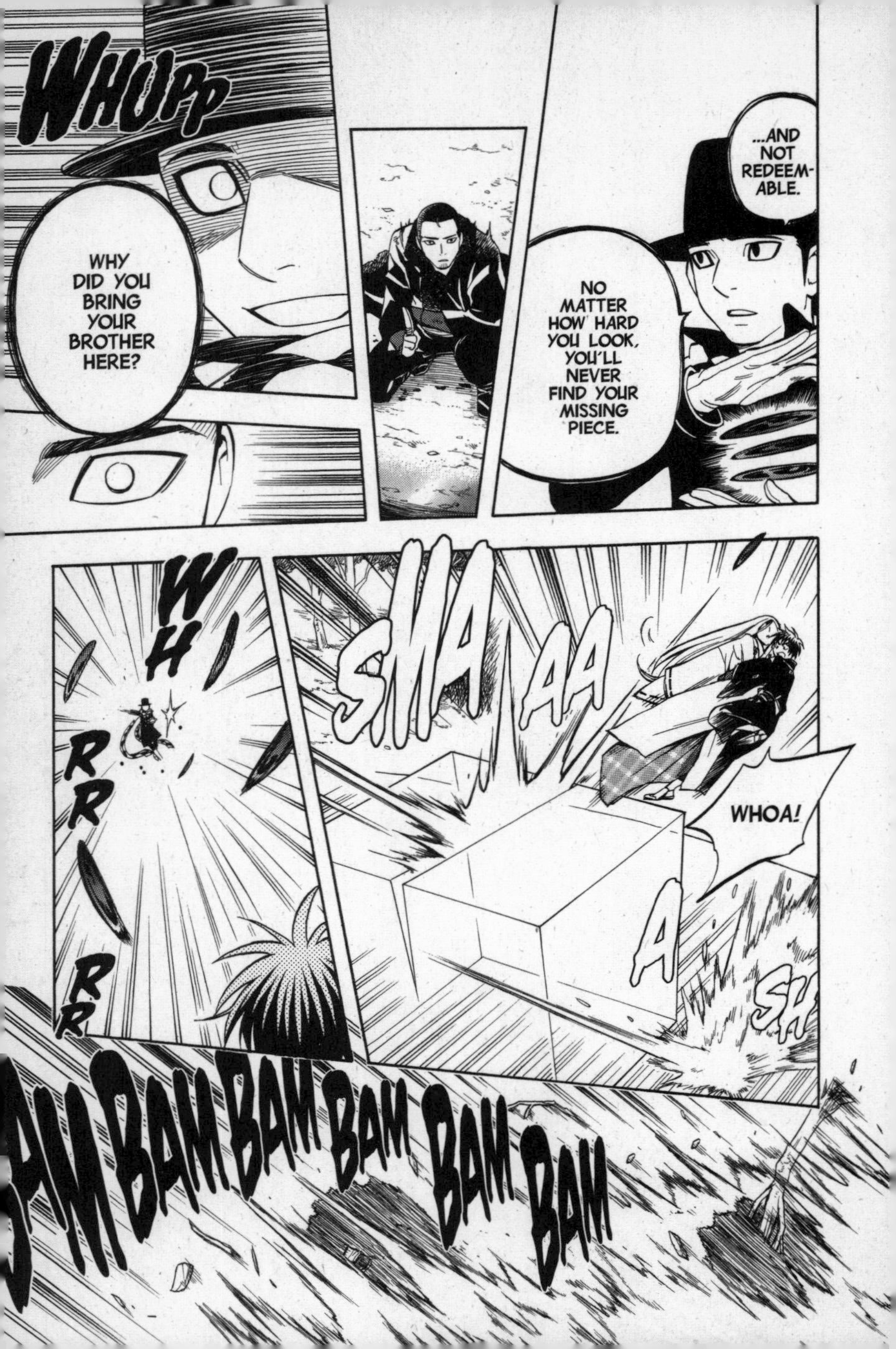
...AND NOT REDEEMABLE.
NO MATTER HOW HARD YOU LOOK, YOU'LL NEVER FIND YOUR MISSING PIECE.
WHUPP
WHY DID YOU BRING YOUR BROTHER HERE?
SHAAAA
WHOA!
SH
WHIRRRR
BAM BAM BAM BAM BAM BAM BAM

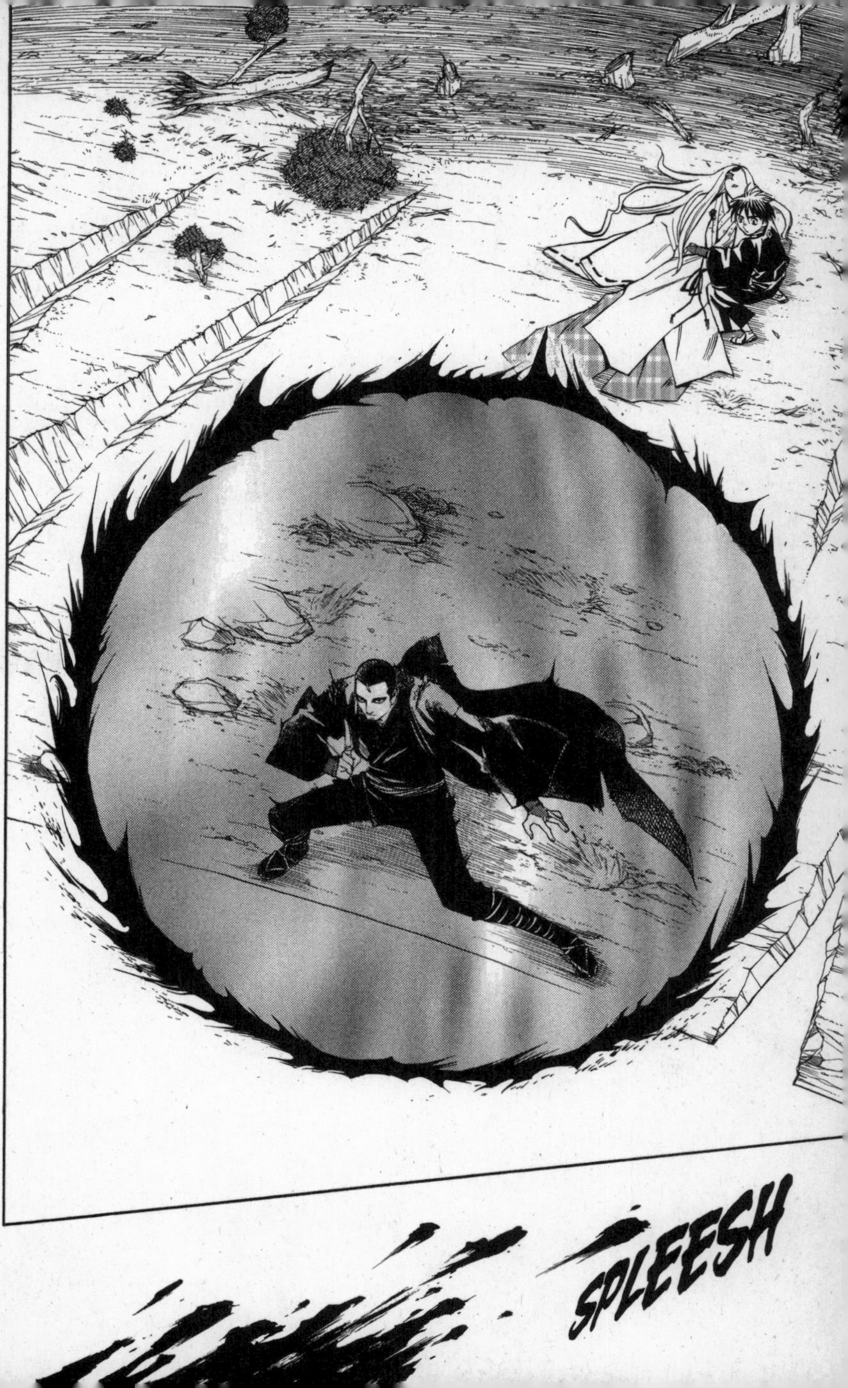
SPLEESH

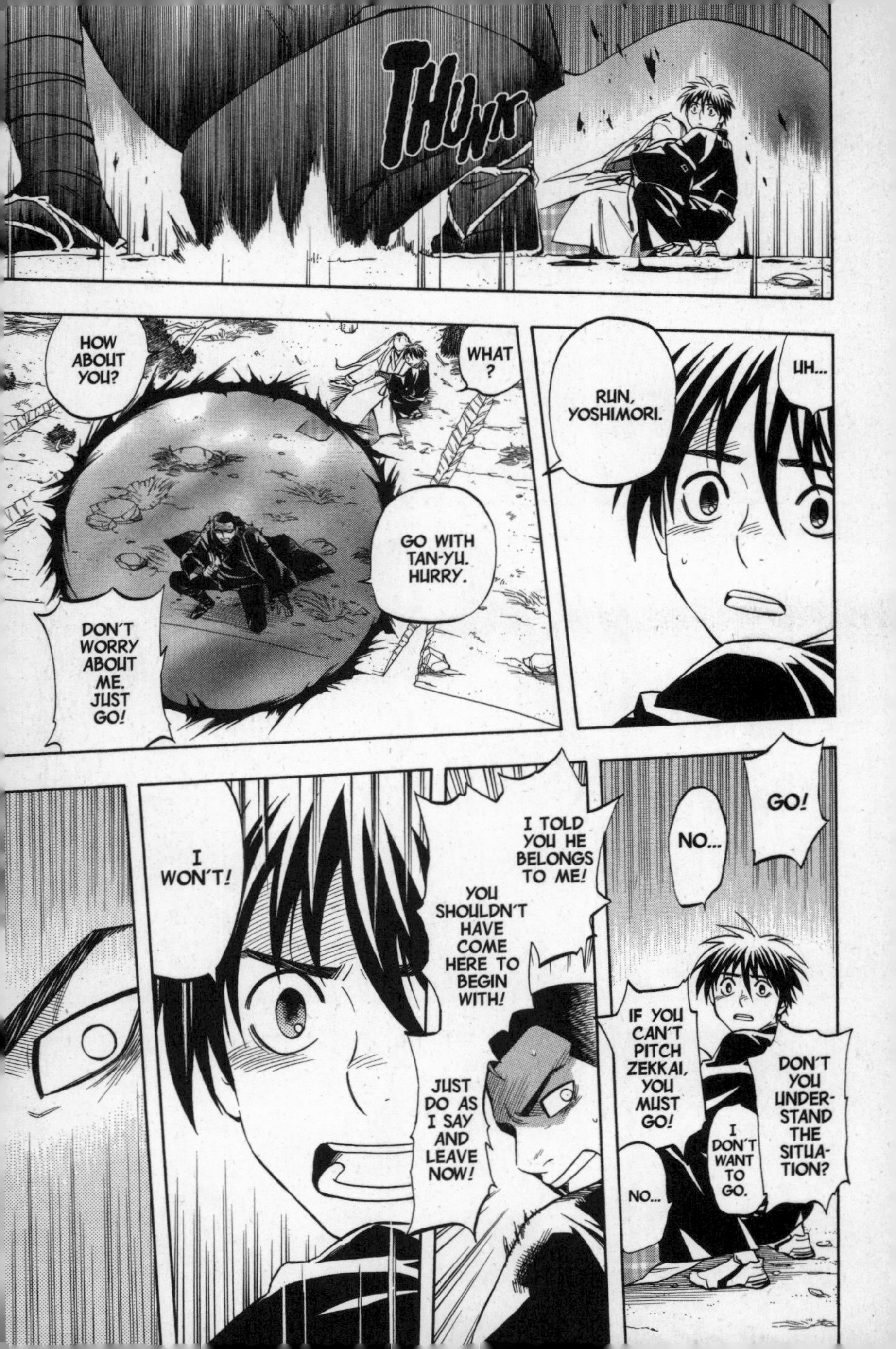
THUNK
RUN, YOSHIMORI.
UH...
WHAT?
GO WITH TAN-YU. HURRY.
HOW ABOUT YOU?
DON'T WORRY ABOUT ME. JUST GO!
GO!
NO...
DON'T YOU UNDERSTAND THE SITUATION?
IF YOU CAN'T PITCH ZEKKAI, YOU MUST GO!
I DON'T WANT TO GO.
NO...
I TOLD YOU HE BELONGS TO ME!
YOU SHOULDN'T HAVE COME HERE TO BEGIN WITH!
I WON'T!
JUST DO AS I SAY AND LEAVE NOW!

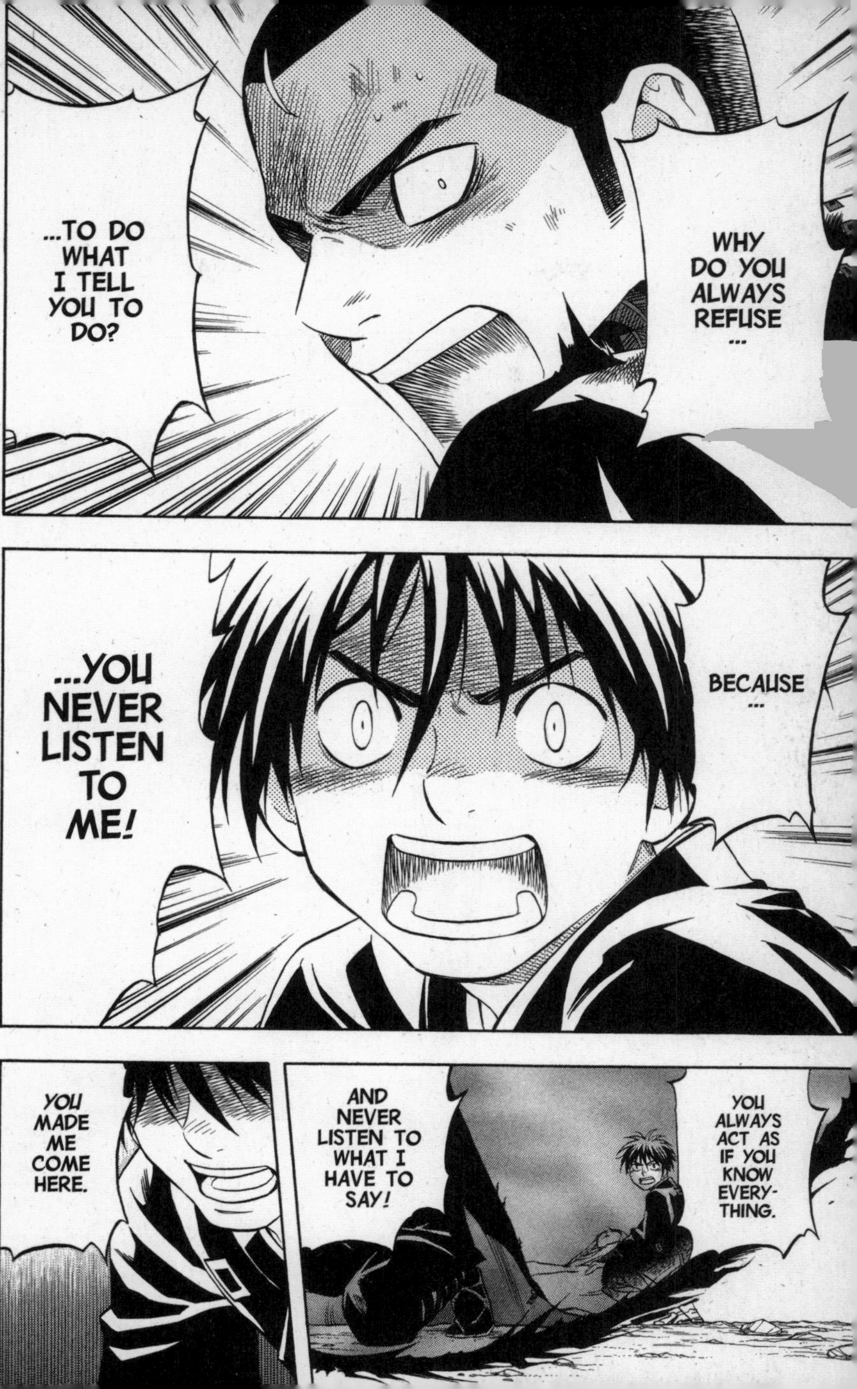
WHY DO YOU ALWAYS REFUSE ...
...TO DO WHAT I TELL YOU TO DO?
BECAUSE ...
...YOU NEVER LISTEN TO ME!
YOU ALWAYS ACT AS IF YOU KNOW EVERY-THING.
AND NEVER LISTEN TO WHAT I HAVE TO SAY!
YOU MADE ME COME HERE.

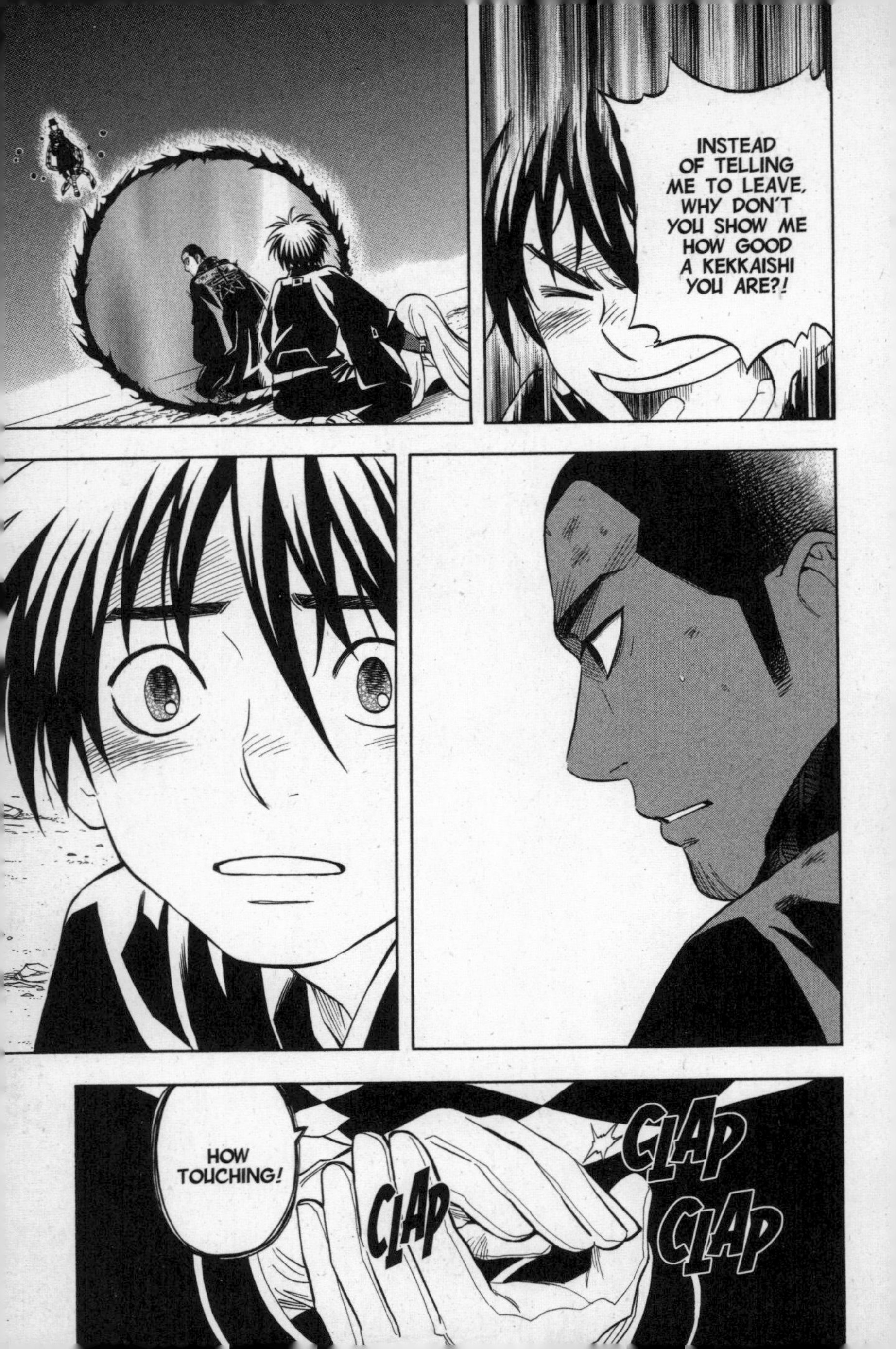
INSTEAD OF TELLING ME TO LEAVE, WHY DON'T YOU SHOW ME HOW GOOD A KEKKAISHI YOU ARE?!
CLAP
CLAP
HOW TOUCHING!
CLAP

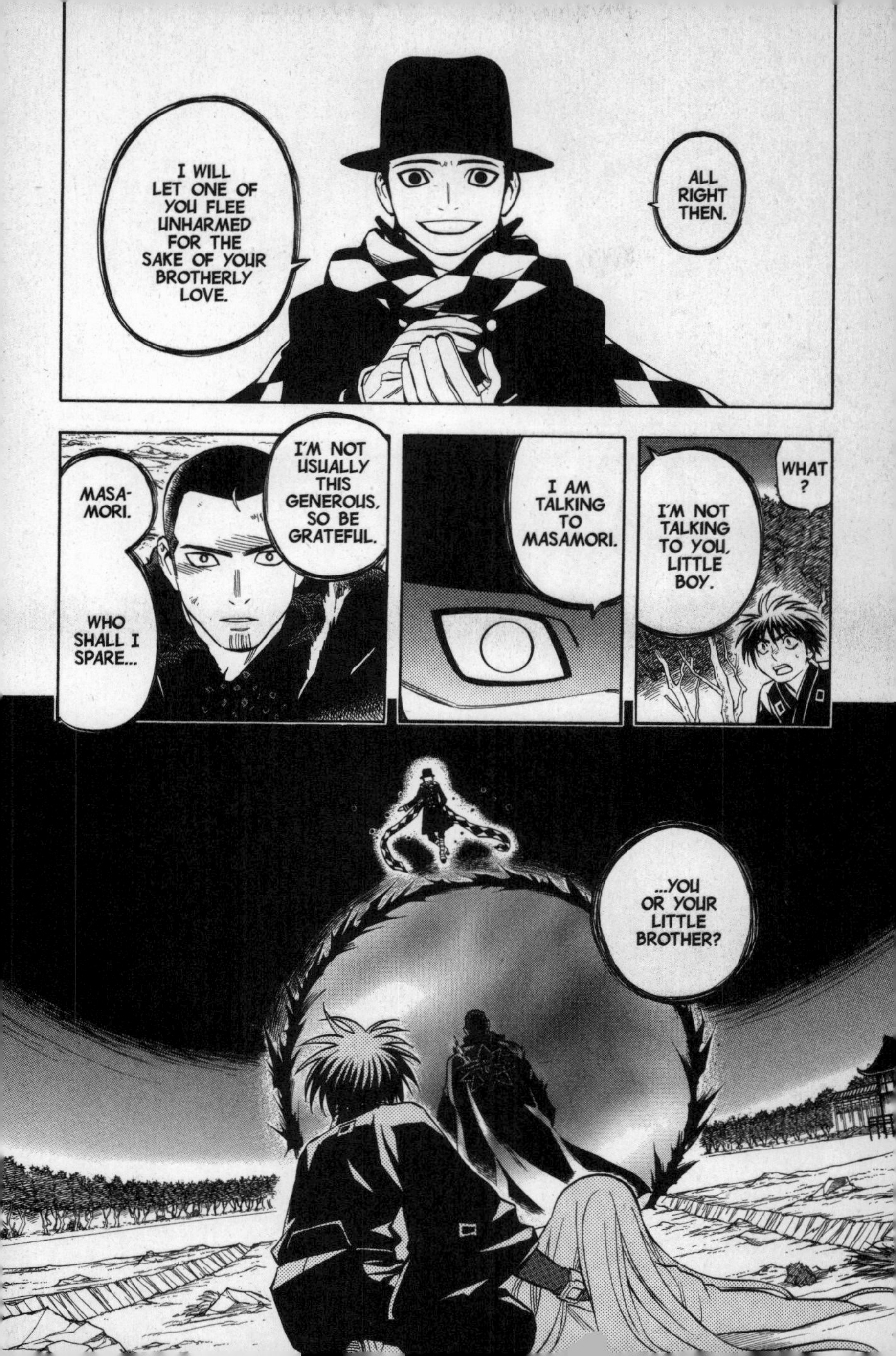
ALL RIGHT THEN.
I WILL LET ONE OF YOU FLEE UNHARMED FOR THE SAKE OF YOUR BROTHERLY LOVE.
WHAT?
I'M NOT TALKING TO YOU, LITTLE BOY.
I AM TALKING TO MASAMORI.
I'M NOT USUALLY THIS GENEROUS, SO BE GRATEFUL.
MASAMORI.
WHO SHALL I SPARE...
...YOU OR YOUR LITTLE BROTHER?

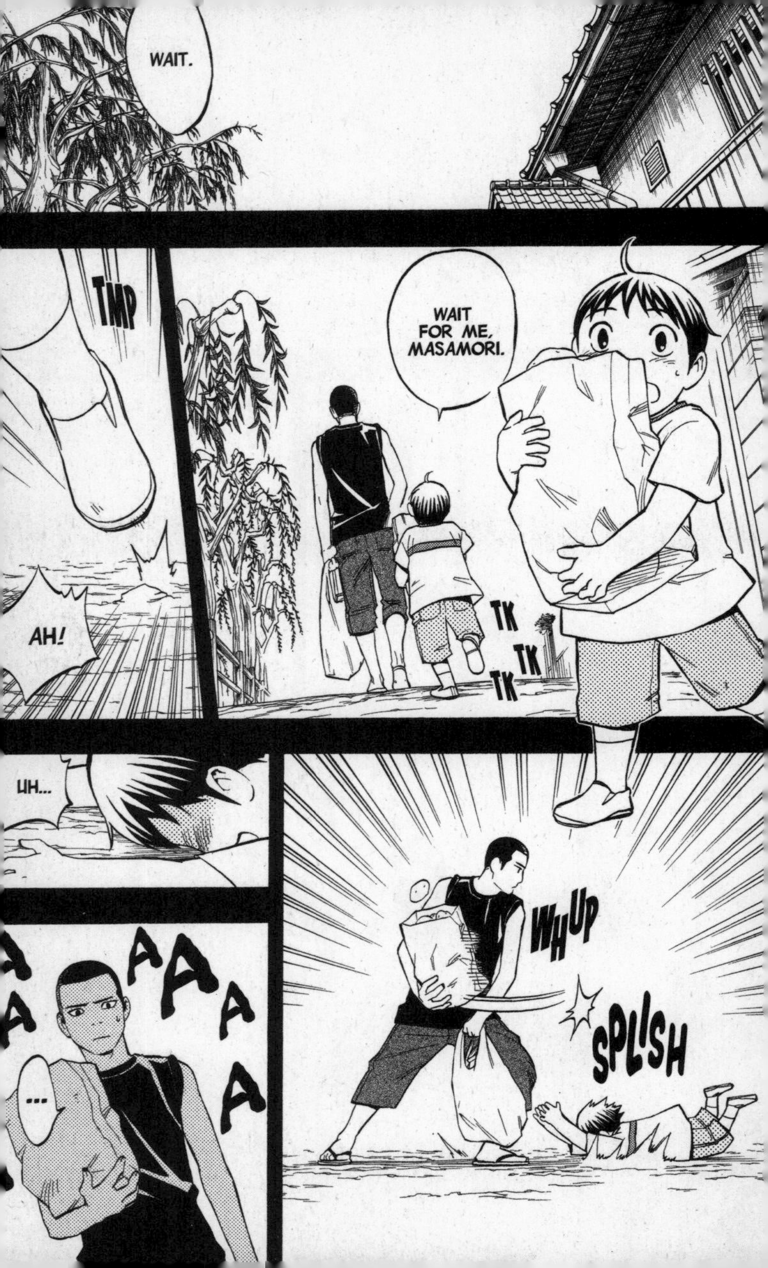
WAIT.
WAIT FOR ME, MASAMORI.
TK TK TK
TMP
AH!
WHUP
SPLISH
UH...
AAAAAAA
...

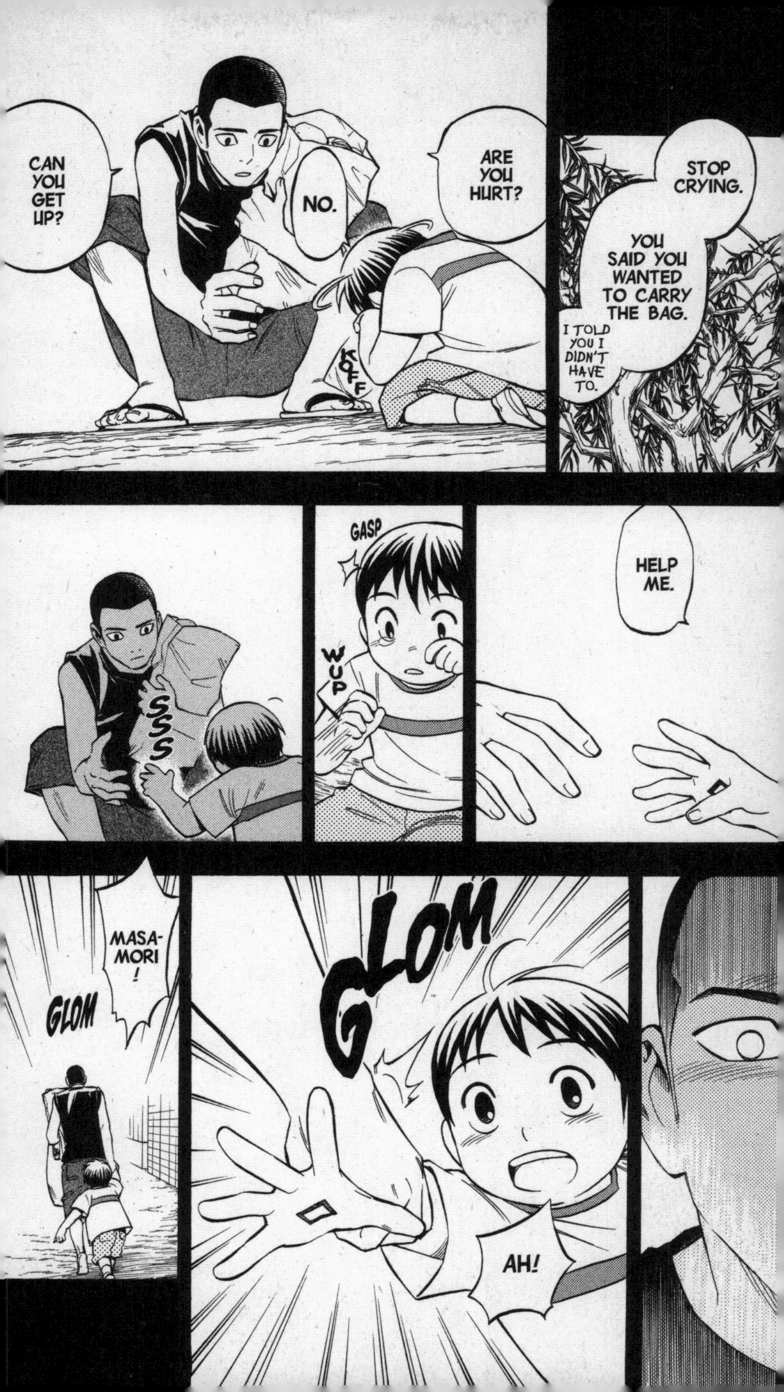
STOP CRYING.
YOU SAID YOU WANTED TO CARRY THE BAG.
I TOLD YOU I DIDN'T HAVE TO.
ARE YOU HURT?
NO.
KOFF
CAN YOU GET UP?
HELP ME.
GASP
WUP
SSS
GLOM
AH!
MASA-MORI!
GLOM

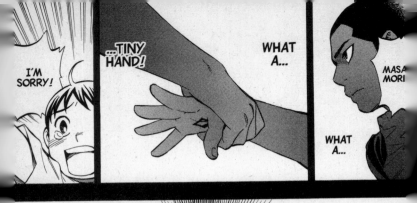

I'M SORRY!

...TINY HAND!

WHAT A...

WHAT A...

MASA-MORI

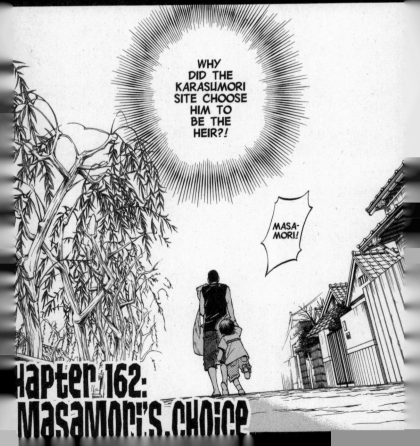

WHY DID THE KARASUMORI SITE CHOOSE HIM TO BE THE HEIR?!

MASA-MORI!

Chapter 162: Masamori's Choice

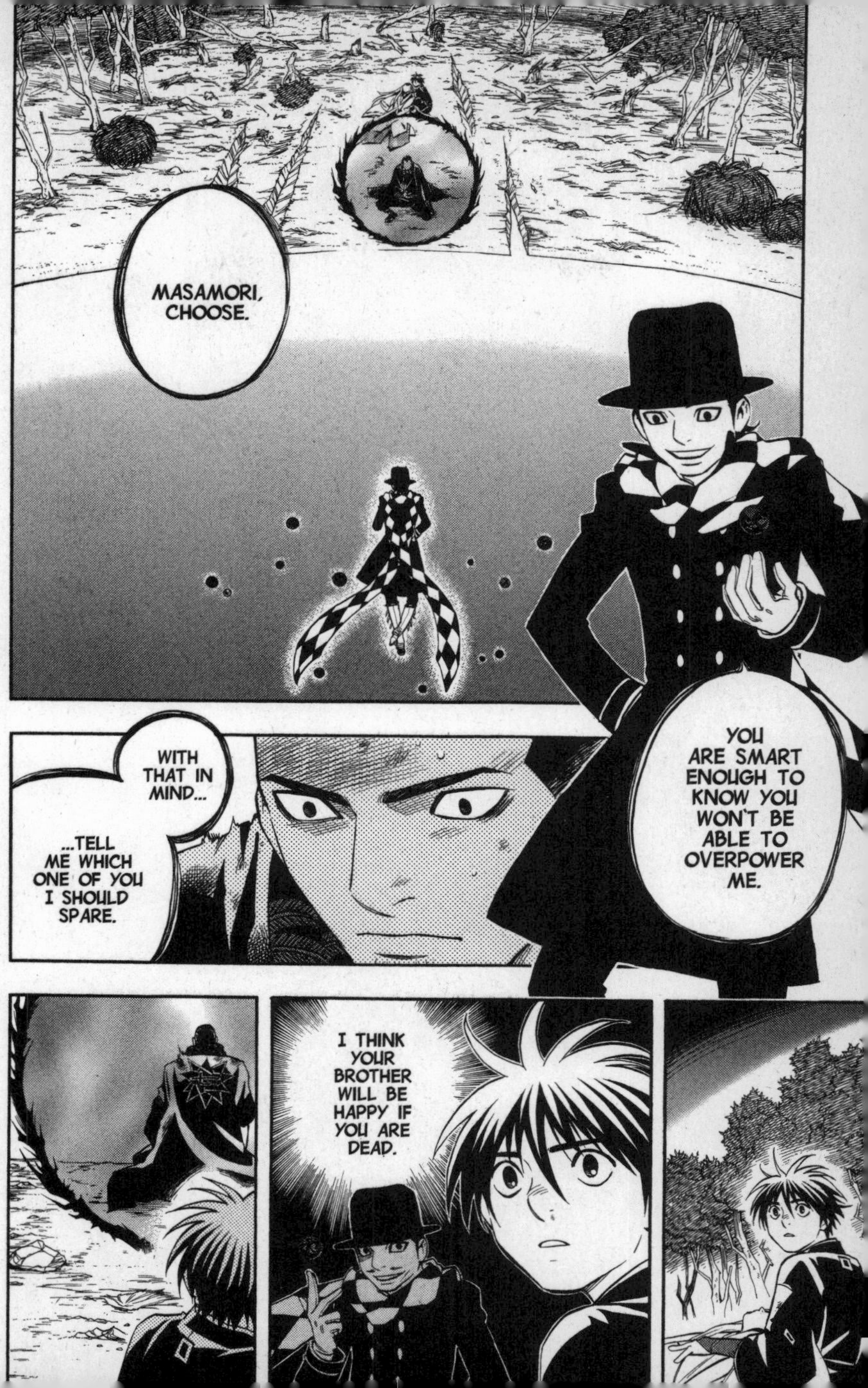
MASAMORI, CHOOSE.
YOU ARE SMART ENOUGH TO KNOW YOU WON'T BE ABLE TO OVERPOWER ME.
WITH THAT IN MIND...
...TELL ME WHICH ONE OF YOU I SHOULD SPARE.
I THINK YOUR BROTHER WILL BE HAPPY IF YOU ARE DEAD.

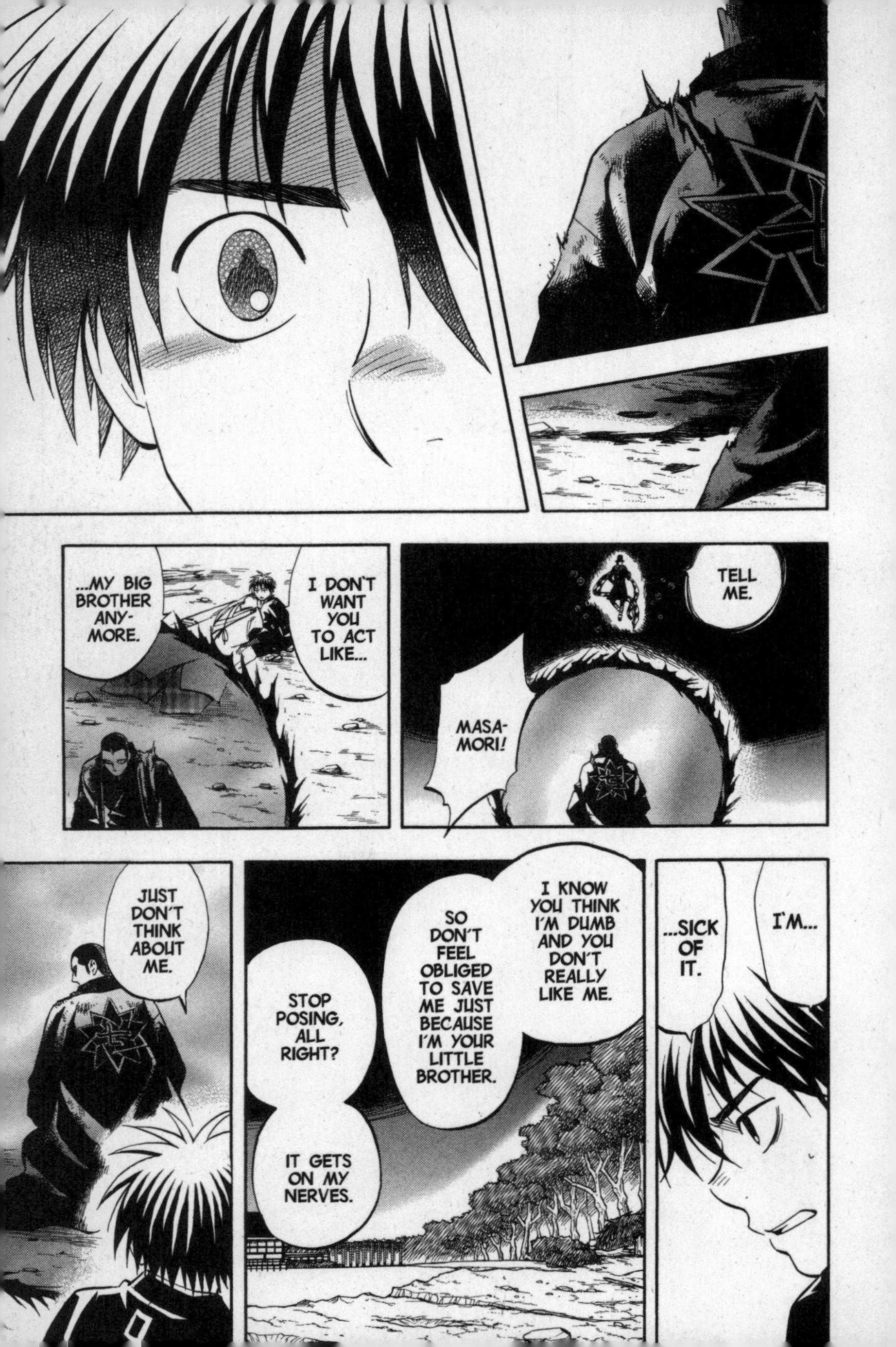
TELL ME.
MASA-MORI!
I DON'T WANT YOU TO ACT LIKE...
...MY BIG BROTHER ANYMORE.
I'M...
...SICK OF IT.
I KNOW YOU THINK I'M DUMB AND YOU DON'T REALLY LIKE ME.
SO DON'T FEEL OBLIGED TO SAVE ME JUST BECAUSE I'M YOUR LITTLE BROTHER.
STOP POSING, ALL RIGHT?
IT GETS ON MY NERVES.
JUST DON'T THINK ABOUT ME.

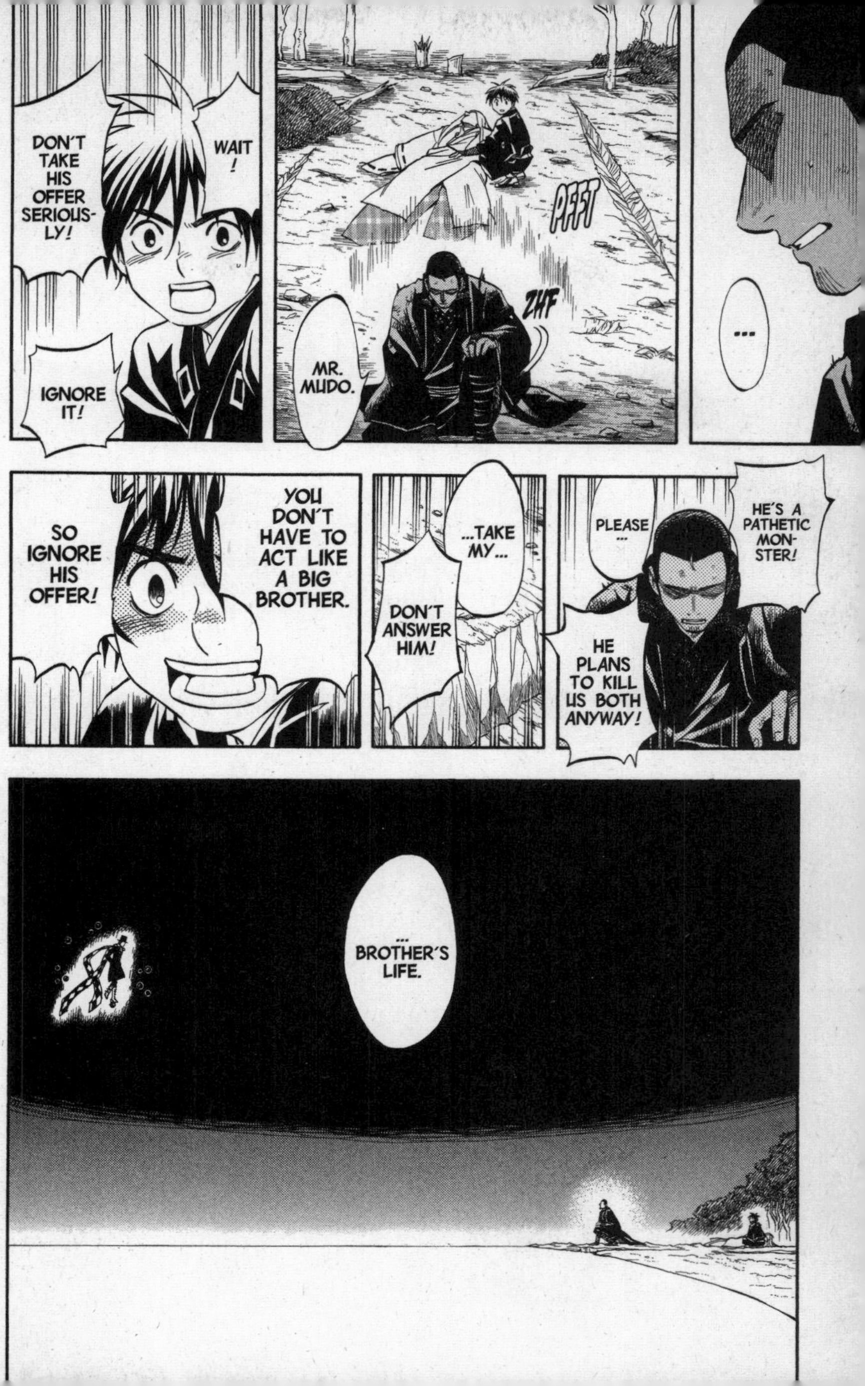
...
PFFT
ZHF
MR. MUDO.
WAIT!
DON'T TAKE HIS OFFER SERIOUSLY!
IGNORE IT!
HE'S A PATHETIC MONSTER!
PLEASE...
HE PLANS TO KILL US BOTH ANYWAY!
...TAKE MY...
DON'T ANSWER HIM!
YOU DON'T HAVE TO ACT LIKE A BIG BROTHER.
SO IGNORE HIS OFFER!
...BROTHER'S LIFE.

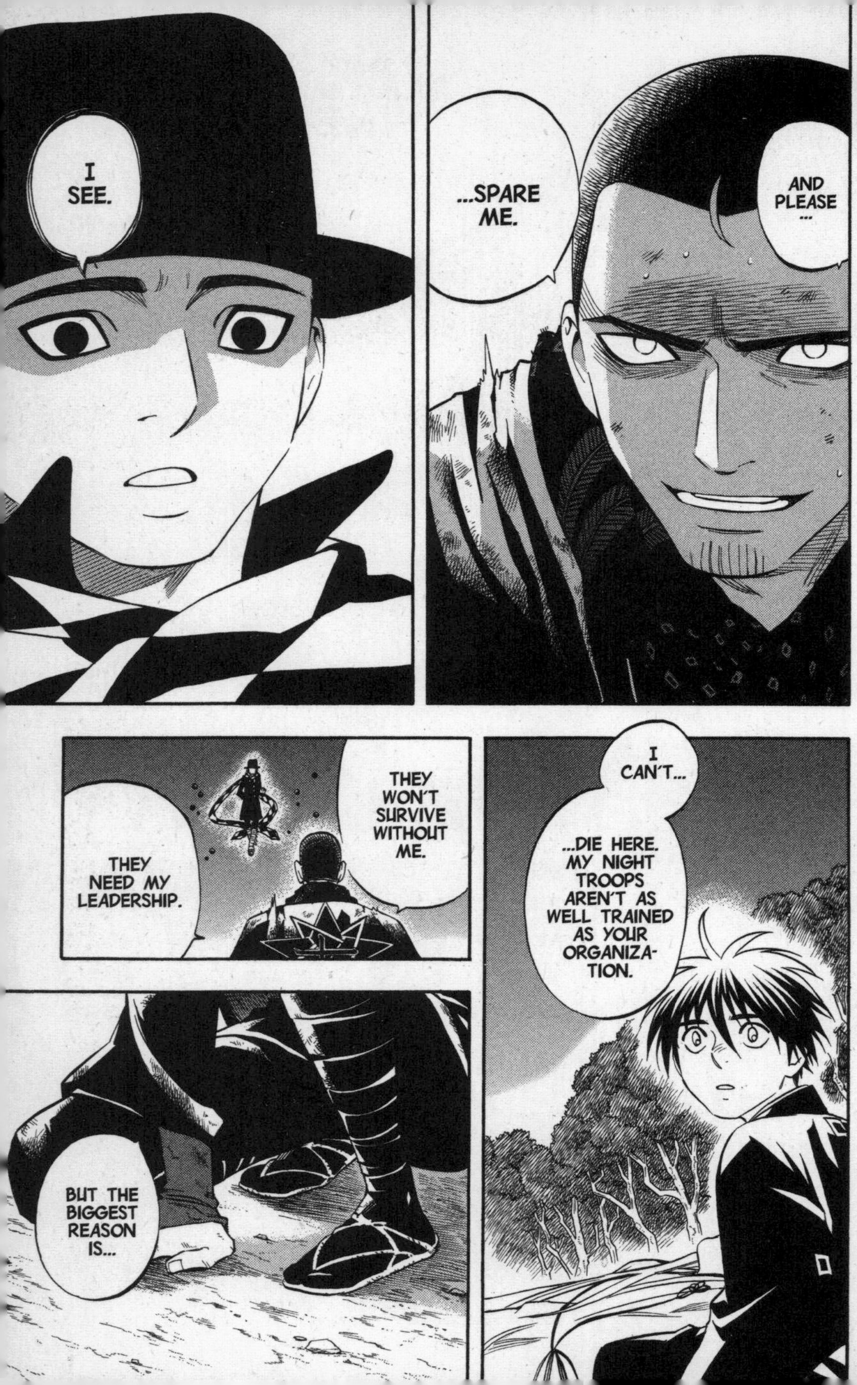
AND PLEASE ...
...SPARE ME.
I SEE.
I CAN'T...
...DIE HERE. MY NIGHT TROOPS AREN'T AS WELL TRAINED AS YOUR ORGANIZA-TION.
THEY WON'T SURVIVE WITHOUT ME.
THEY NEED MY LEADERSHIP.
BUT THE BIGGEST REASON IS...

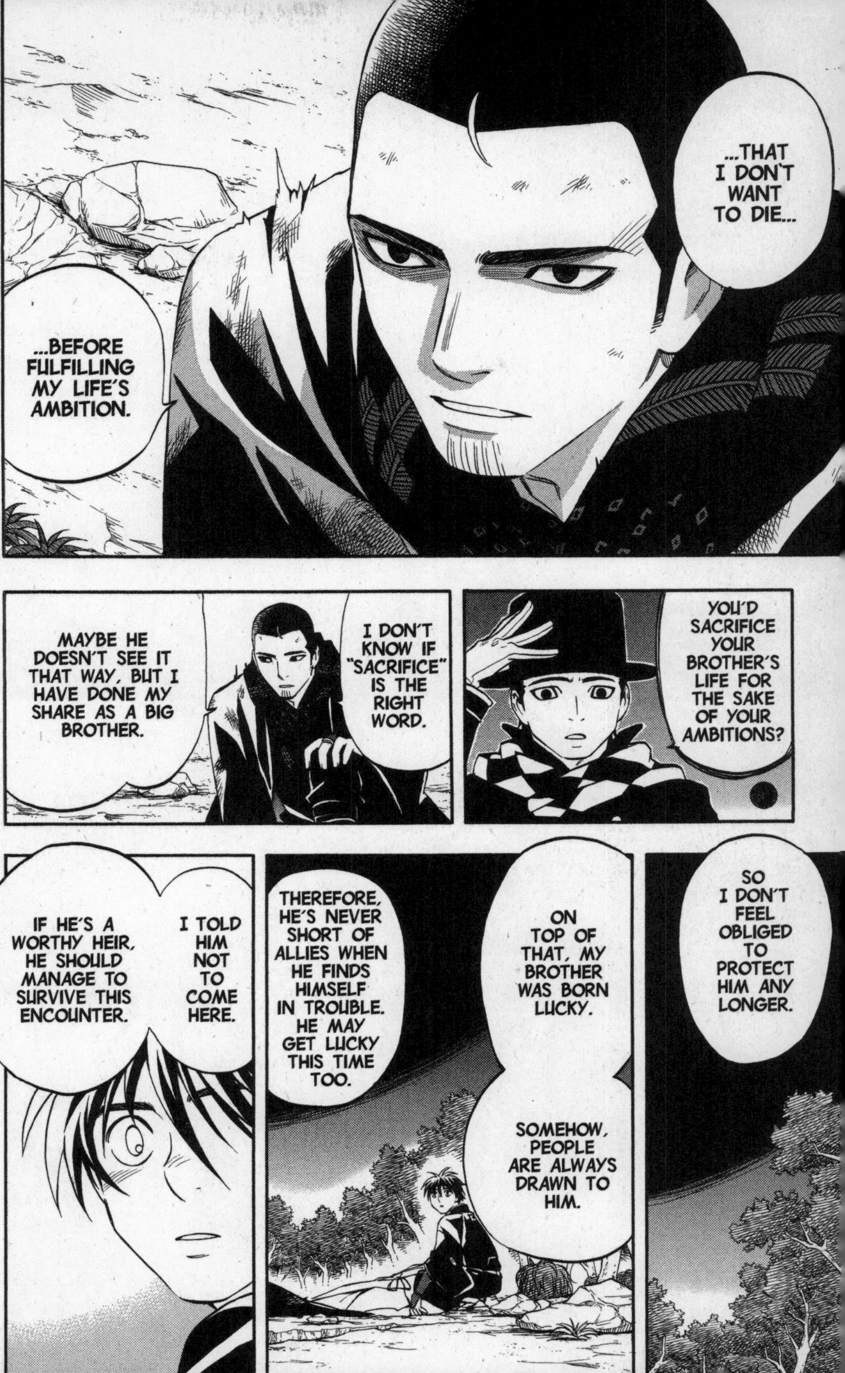
...THAT I DON'T WANT TO DIE...
...BEFORE FULFILLING MY LIFE'S AMBITION.
YOU'D SACRIFICE YOUR BROTHER'S LIFE FOR THE SAKE OF YOUR AMBITIONS?
I DON'T KNOW IF "SACRIFICE" IS THE RIGHT WORD.
MAYBE HE DOESN'T SEE IT THAT WAY, BUT I HAVE DONE MY SHARE AS A BIG BROTHER.
SO I DON'T FEEL OBLIGED TO PROTECT HIM ANY LONGER.
ON TOP OF THAT, MY BROTHER WAS BORN LUCKY.
SOMEHOW, PEOPLE ARE ALWAYS DRAWN TO HIM.
THEREFORE, HE'S NEVER SHORT OF ALLIES WHEN HE FINDS HIMSELF IN TROUBLE. HE MAY GET LUCKY THIS TIME TOO.
I TOLD HIM NOT TO COME HERE.
IF HE'S A WORTHY HEIR, HE SHOULD MANAGE TO SURVIVE THIS ENCOUNTER.

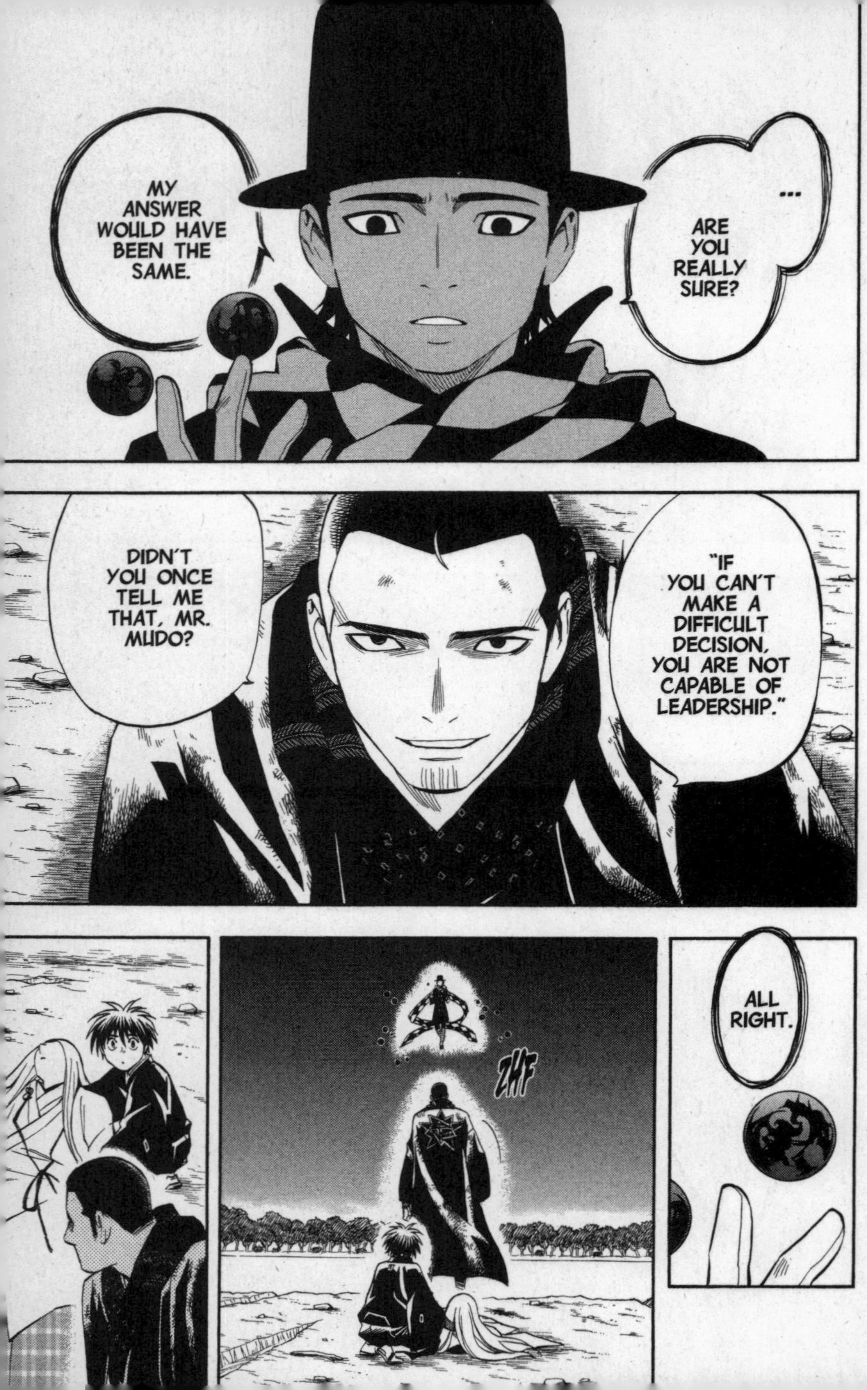
...
ARE YOU REALLY SURE?
MY ANSWER WOULD HAVE BEEN THE SAME.
"IF YOU CAN'T MAKE A DIFFICULT DECISION, YOU ARE NOT CAPABLE OF LEADERSHIP."
DIDN'T YOU ONCE TELL ME THAT, MR. MUDO?
ALL RIGHT.
ZHF

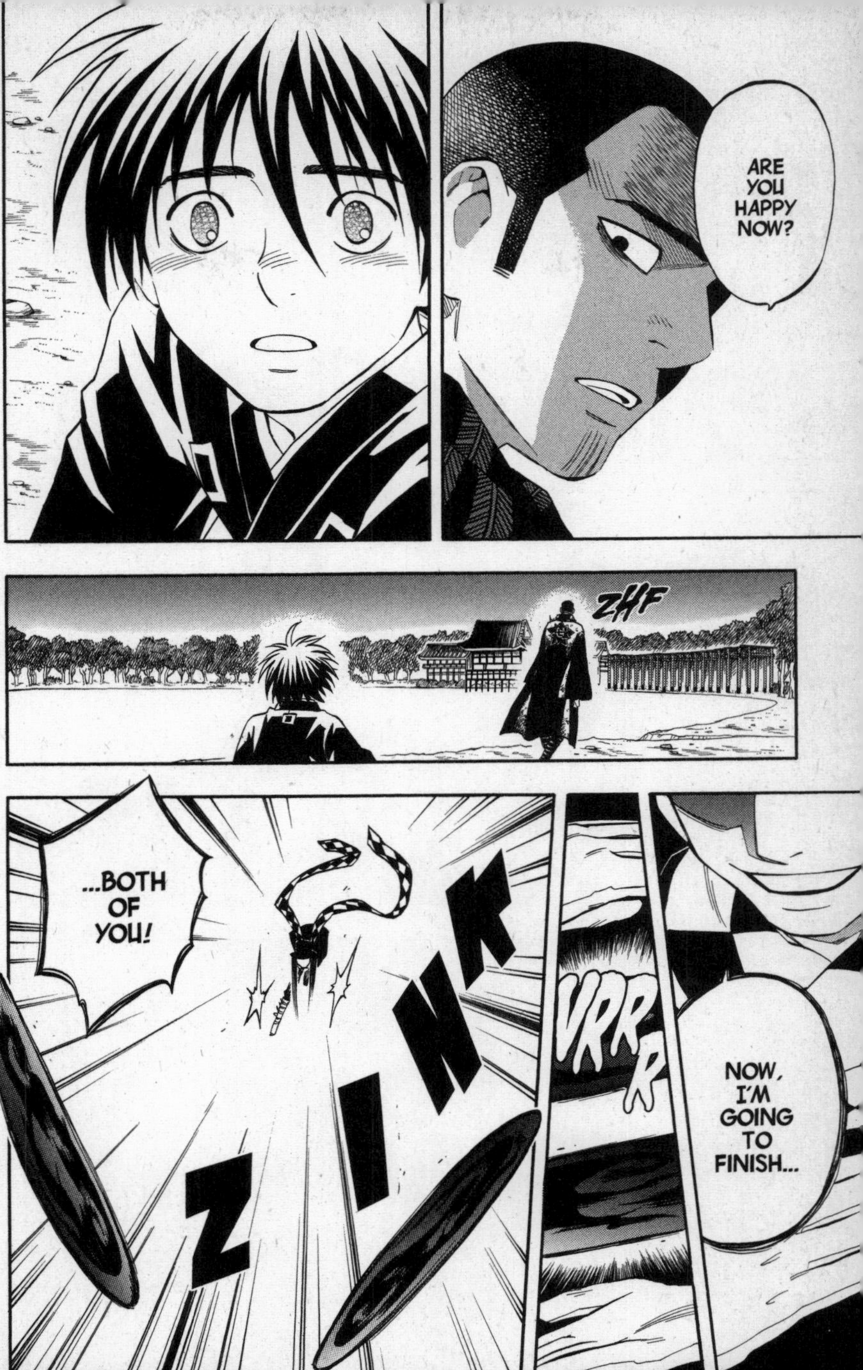
ARE YOU HAPPY NOW?
ZHF
VRRR
NOW, I'M GOING TO FINISH...
...BOTH OF YOU!
ZINK

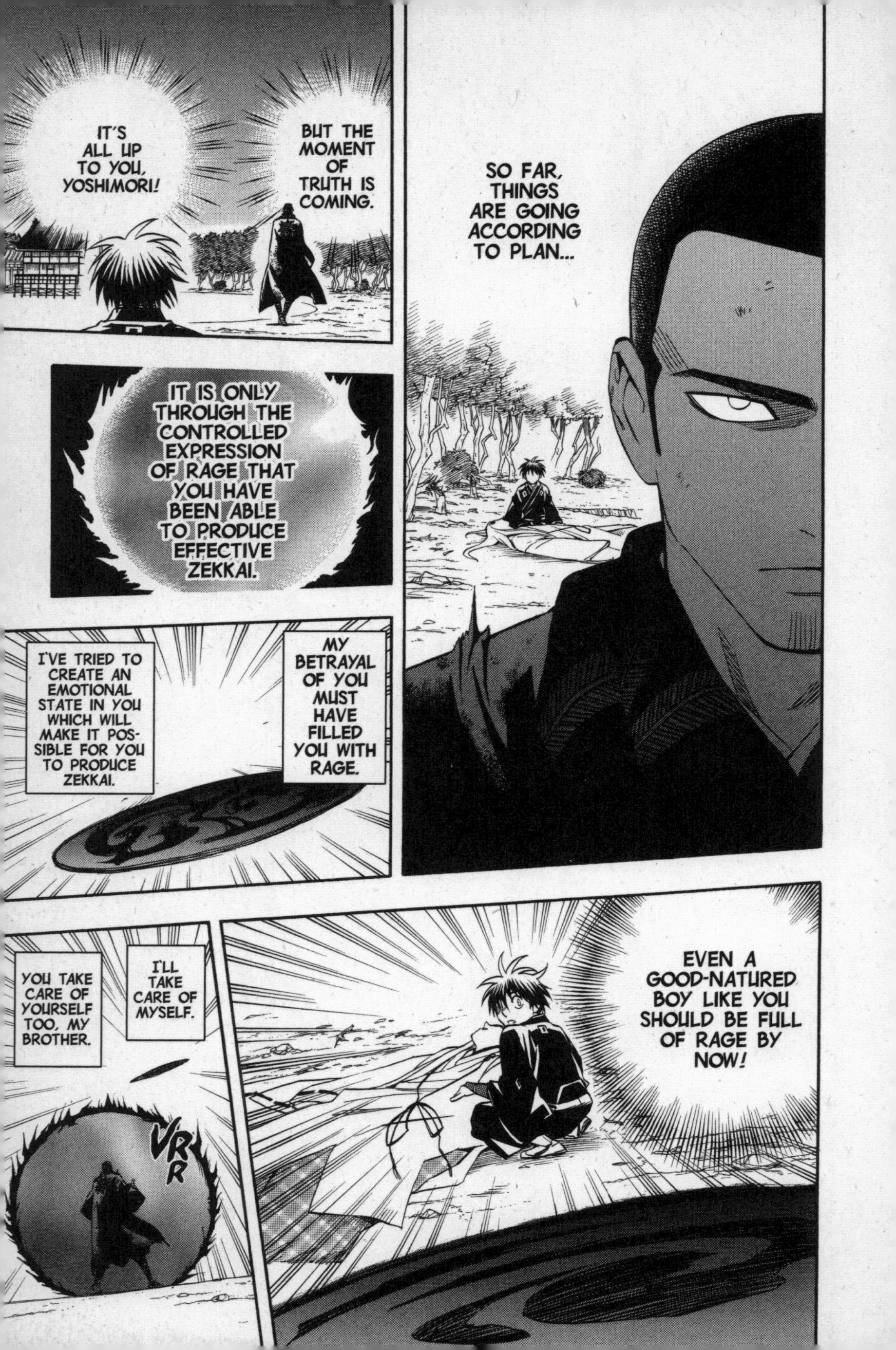
SO FAR, THINGS ARE GOING ACCORDING TO PLAN...
BUT THE MOMENT OF TRUTH IS COMING.
IT'S ALL UP TO YOU, YOSHIMORI!
IT IS ONLY THROUGH THE CONTROLLED EXPRESSION OF RAGE THAT YOU HAVE BEEN ABLE TO PRODUCE EFFECTIVE ZEKKAI.
MY BETRAYAL OF YOU MUST HAVE FILLED YOU WITH RAGE.
I'VE TRIED TO CREATE AN EMOTIONAL STATE IN YOU WHICH WILL MAKE IT POSSIBLE FOR YOU TO PRODUCE ZEKKAI.
EVEN A GOOD-NATURED BOY LIKE YOU SHOULD BE FULL OF RAGE BY NOW!
I'LL TAKE CARE OF MYSELF.
YOU TAKE CARE OF YOURSELF TOO, MY BROTHER.
VRR

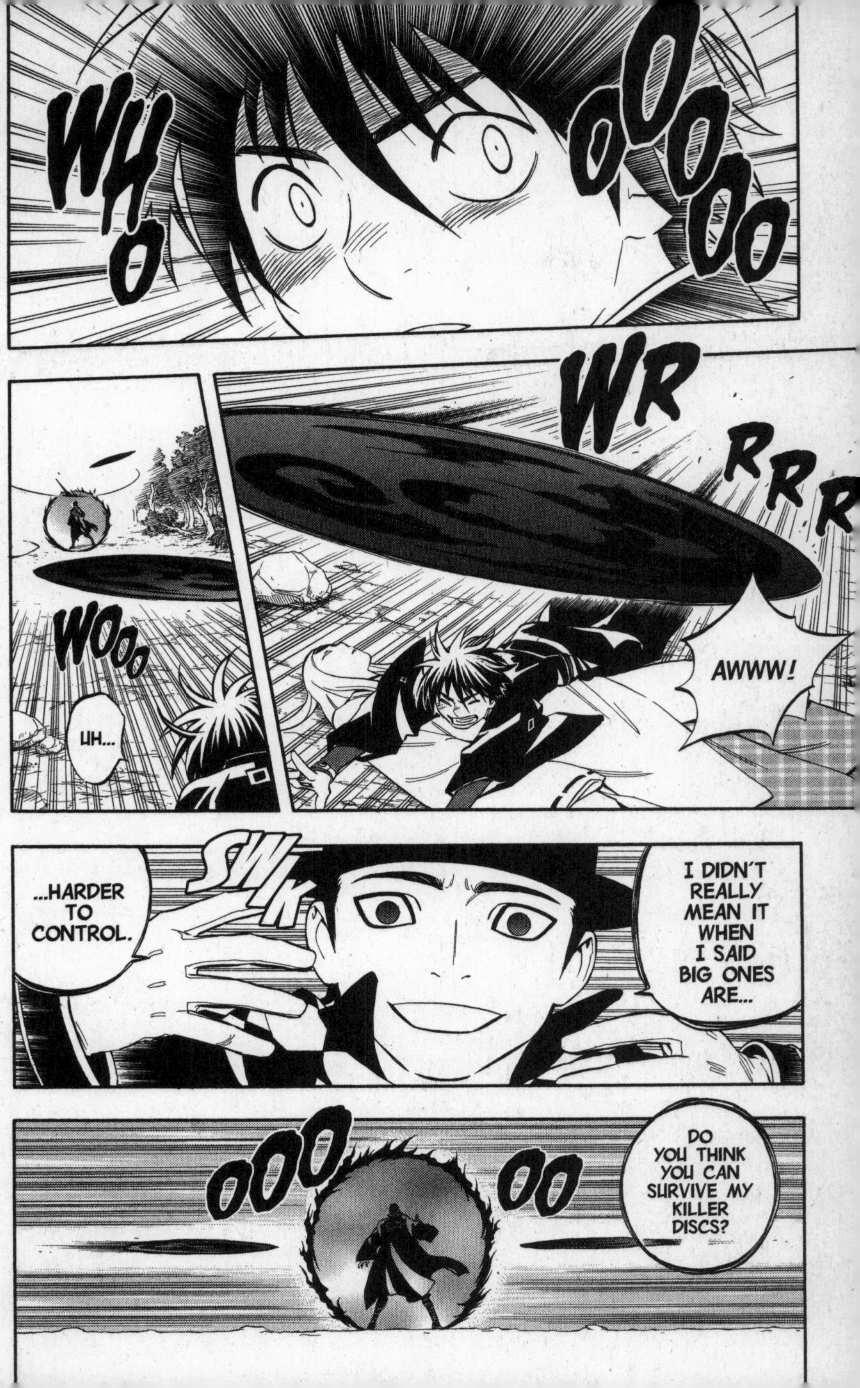
WHOO
OOOOOO
WR
RRRR
AWWW!
WOOO
UH...
SWK
I DIDN'T REALLY MEAN IT WHEN I SAID BIG ONES ARE...
...HARDER TO CONTROL.
OOO
OO
DO YOU THINK YOU CAN SURVIVE MY KILLER DISCS?

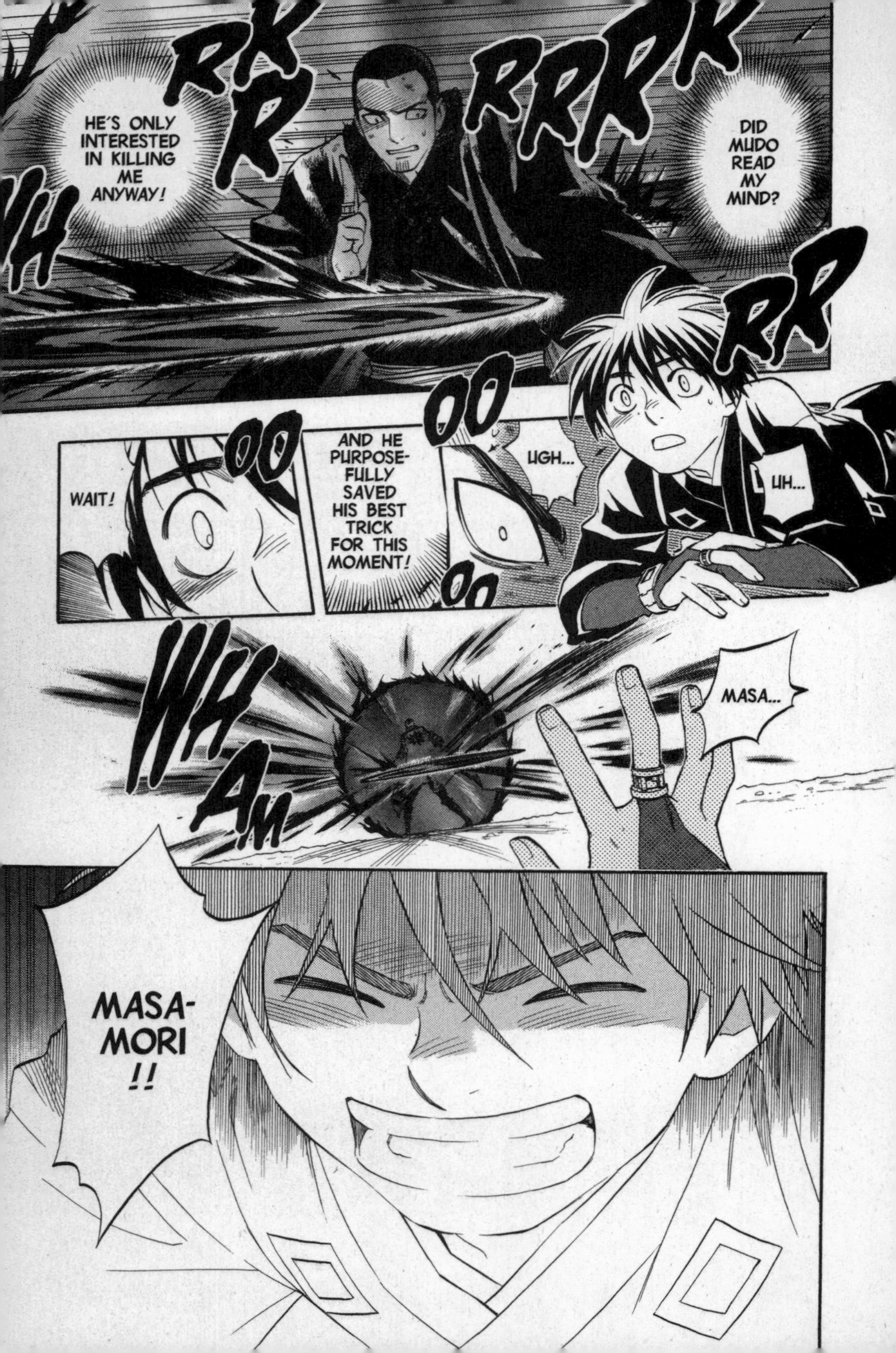

RRRRK
DID MUDO READ MY MIND?
RKR
HE'S ONLY INTERESTED IN KILLING ME ANYWAY!
WH
RR
UH...
UGH...
OO
AND HE PURPOSE-FULLY SAVED HIS BEST TRICK FOR THIS MOMENT!
OO
WAIT!
OO
MASA...
WHAM
MASA-MORI!!

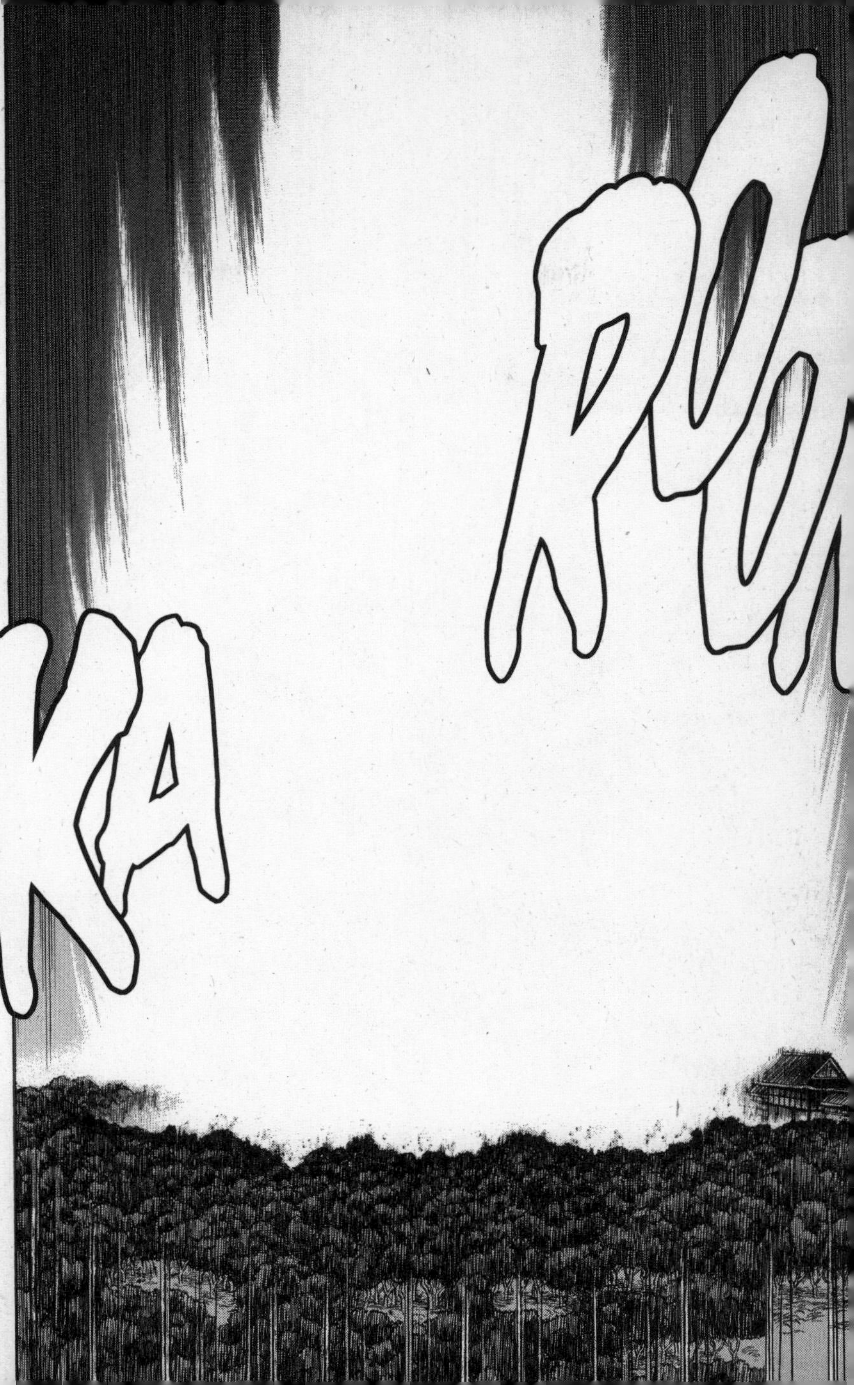
KA
PO

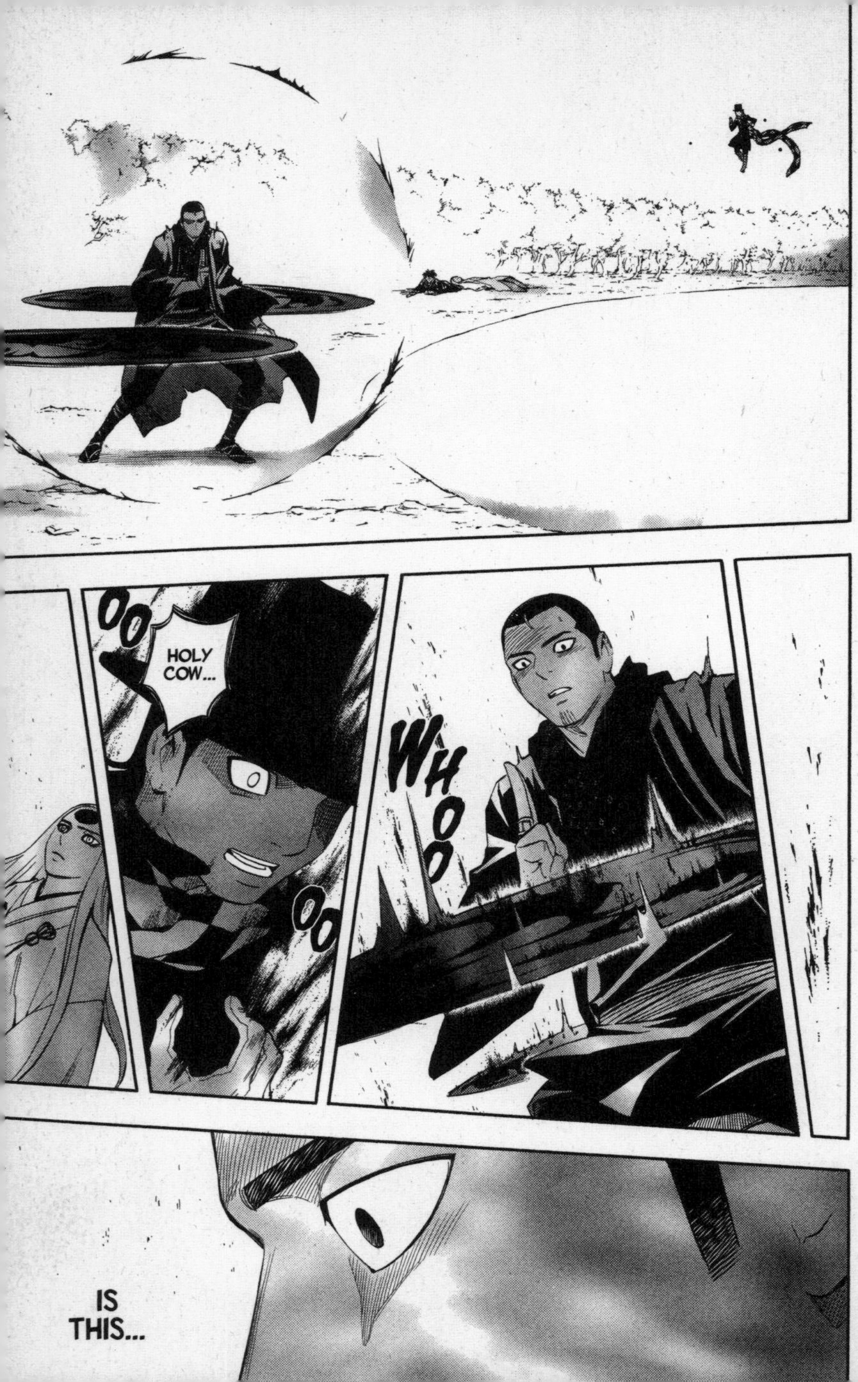
WHOOO
OO
HOLY COW...
OO
IS THIS...

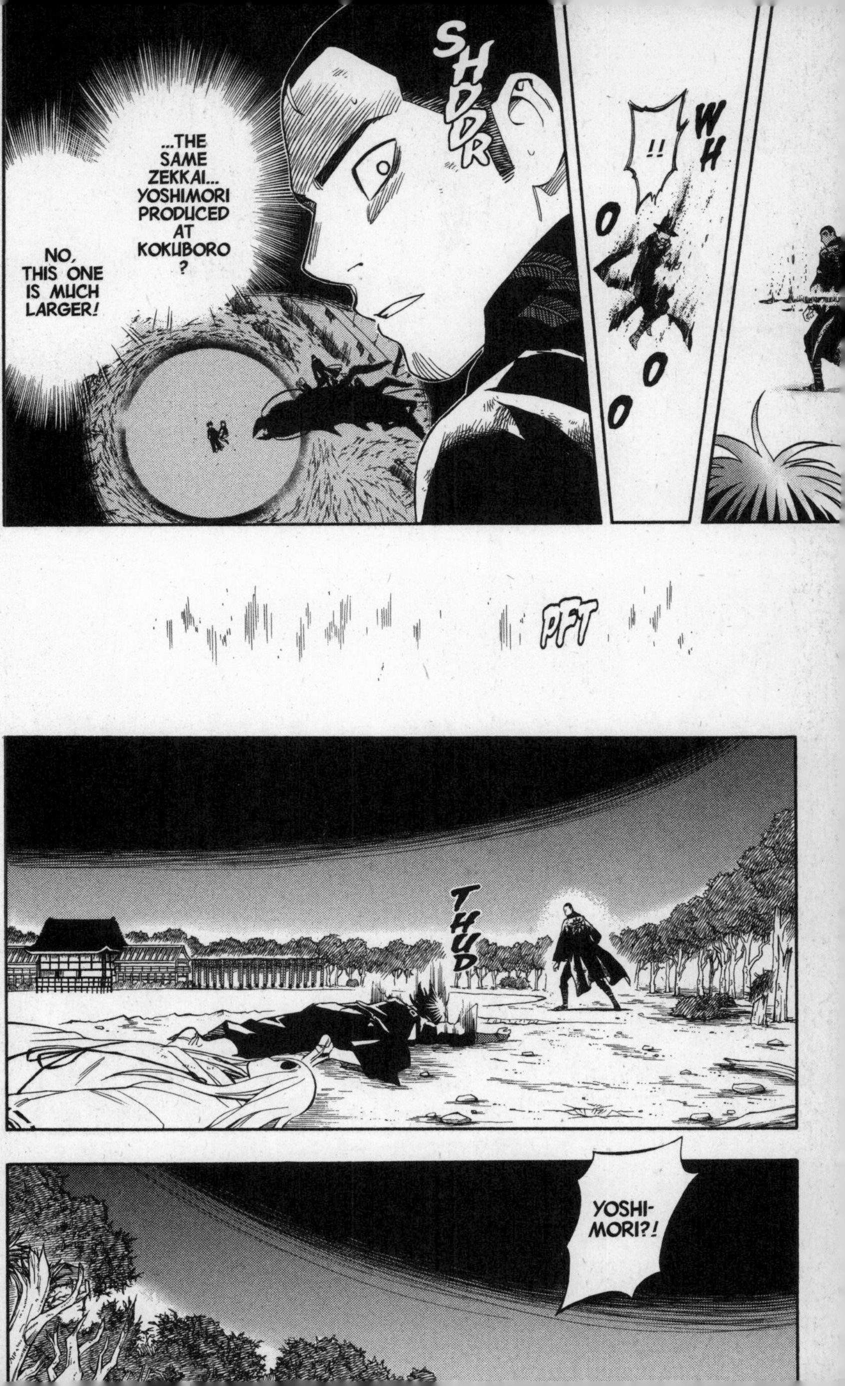
!!
WHOOOO
SHDDR
...THE SAME ZEKKAI... YOSHIMORI PRODUCED AT KOKUBORO?
NO, THIS ONE IS MUCH LARGER!
PFT
THUD
YOSHI-MORI?!

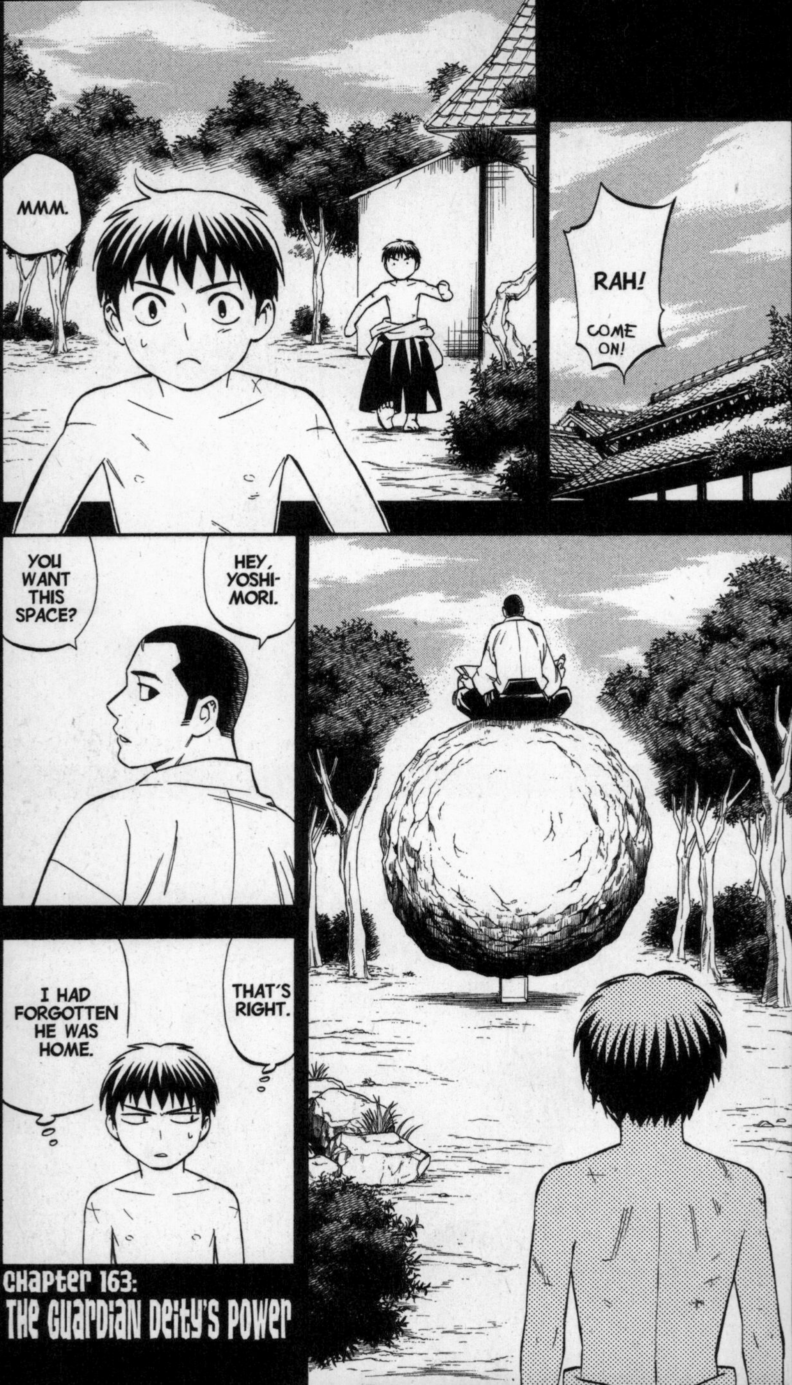
RAH!
COME ON!
MMM.
HEY, YOSHIMORI.
YOU WANT THIS SPACE?
THAT'S RIGHT.
I HAD FORGOTTEN HE WAS HOME.
Chapter 163:
The Guardian Deity's Power

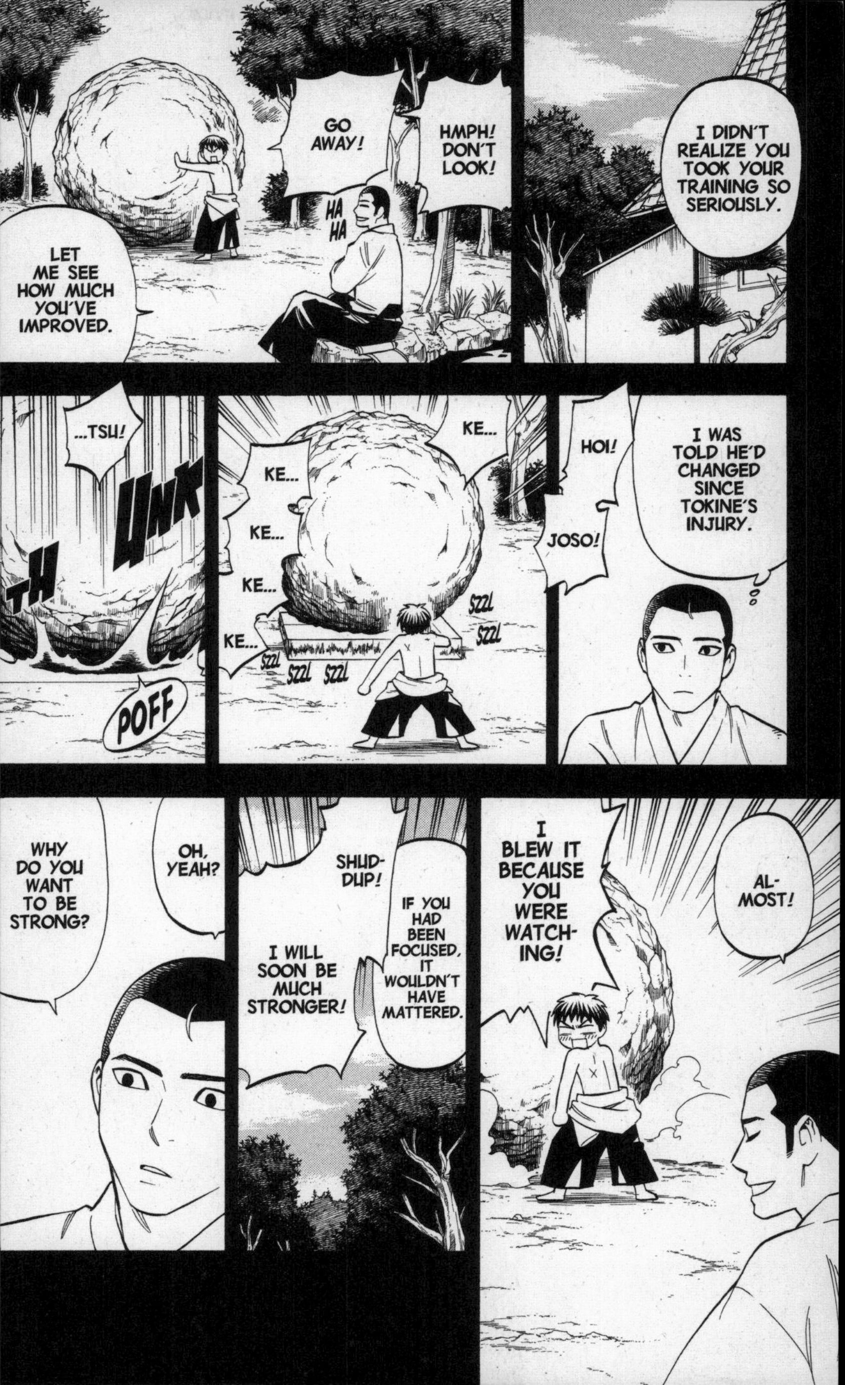
I DIDN'T REALIZE YOU TOOK YOUR TRAINING SO SERIOUSLY.
HMPH! DON'T LOOK!
GO AWAY!
HA HA
LET ME SEE HOW MUCH YOU'VE IMPROVED.
I WAS TOLD HE'D CHANGED SINCE TOKINE'S INJURY.
HOI!
JOSO!
KE...
KE...
KE...
KE...
KE...
SZZL SZZL SZZL SZZL SZZL
...TSU!
THUNK
POFF
AL-MOST!
I BLEW IT BECAUSE YOU WERE WATCHING!
IF YOU HAD BEEN FOCUSED, IT WOULDN'T HAVE MATTERED.
SHUD-DUP!
I WILL SOON BE MUCH STRONGER!
OH, YEAH?
WHY DO YOU WANT TO BE STRONG?

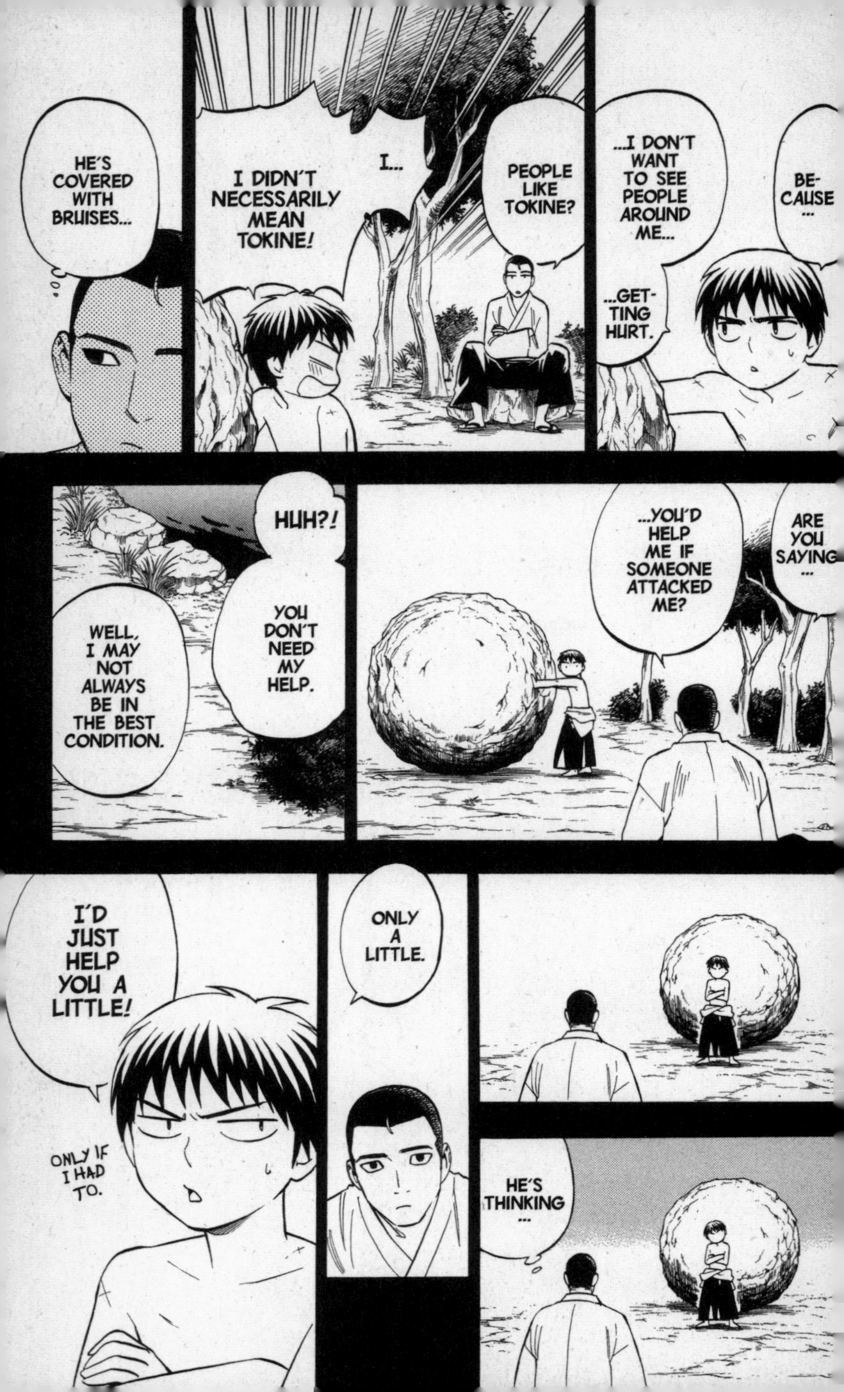
BE-CAUSE ...
...I DON'T WANT TO SEE PEOPLE AROUND ME...
...GET-TING HURT.
PEOPLE LIKE TOKINE?
I...
I DIDN'T NECESSARILY MEAN TOKINE!
HE'S COVERED WITH BRUISES...
ARE YOU SAYING ...
...YOU'D HELP ME IF SOMEONE ATTACKED ME?
HUH?!
YOU DON'T NEED MY HELP.
WELL, I MAY NOT ALWAYS BE IN THE BEST CONDITION.
HE'S THINKING ...
ONLY A LITTLE.
I'D JUST HELP YOU A LITTLE!
ONLY IF I HAD TO.

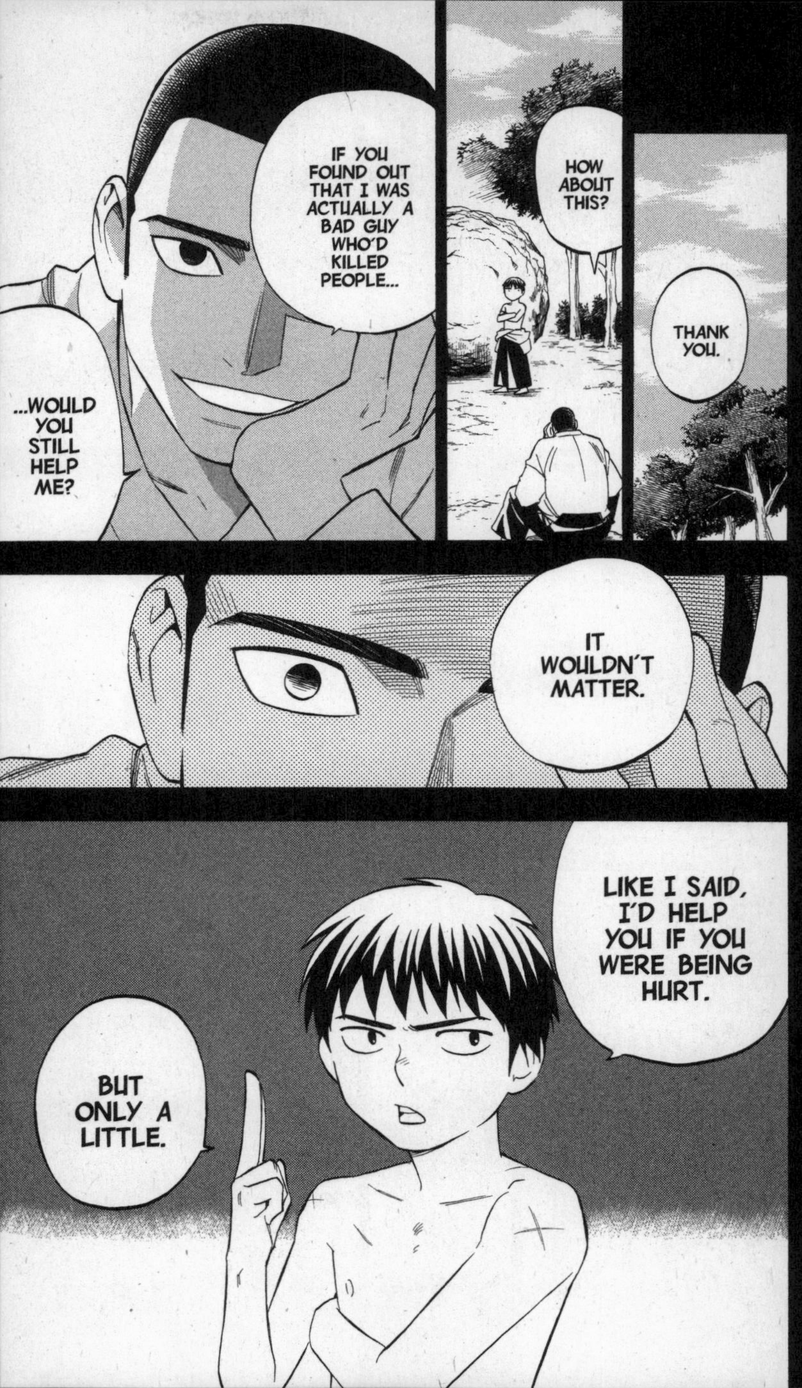
THANK YOU.
HOW ABOUT THIS?
IF YOU FOUND OUT THAT I WAS ACTUALLY A BAD GUY WHO'D KILLED PEOPLE...
...WOULD YOU STILL HELP ME?
IT WOULDN'T MATTER.
LIKE I SAID, I'D HELP YOU IF YOU WERE BEING HURT.
BUT ONLY A LITTLE.

Chapter 163: The Guardian Deity's Power

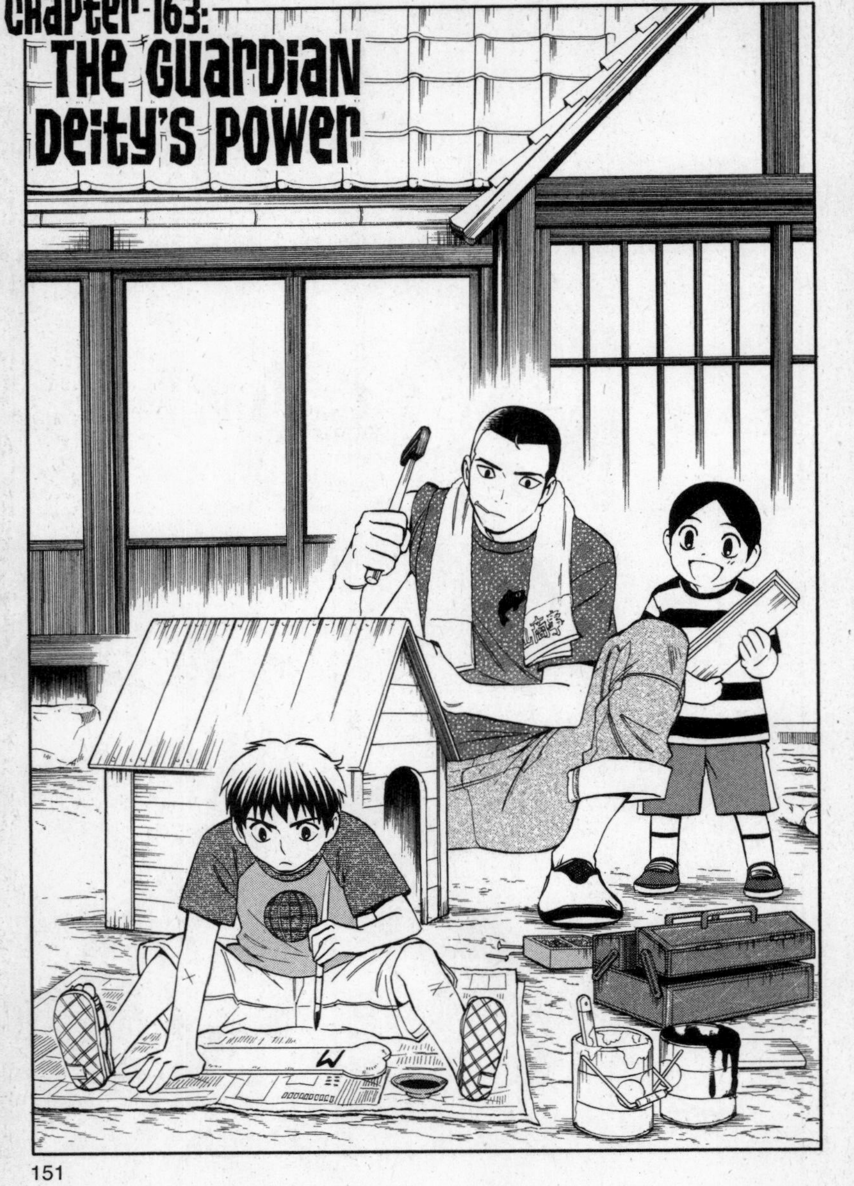

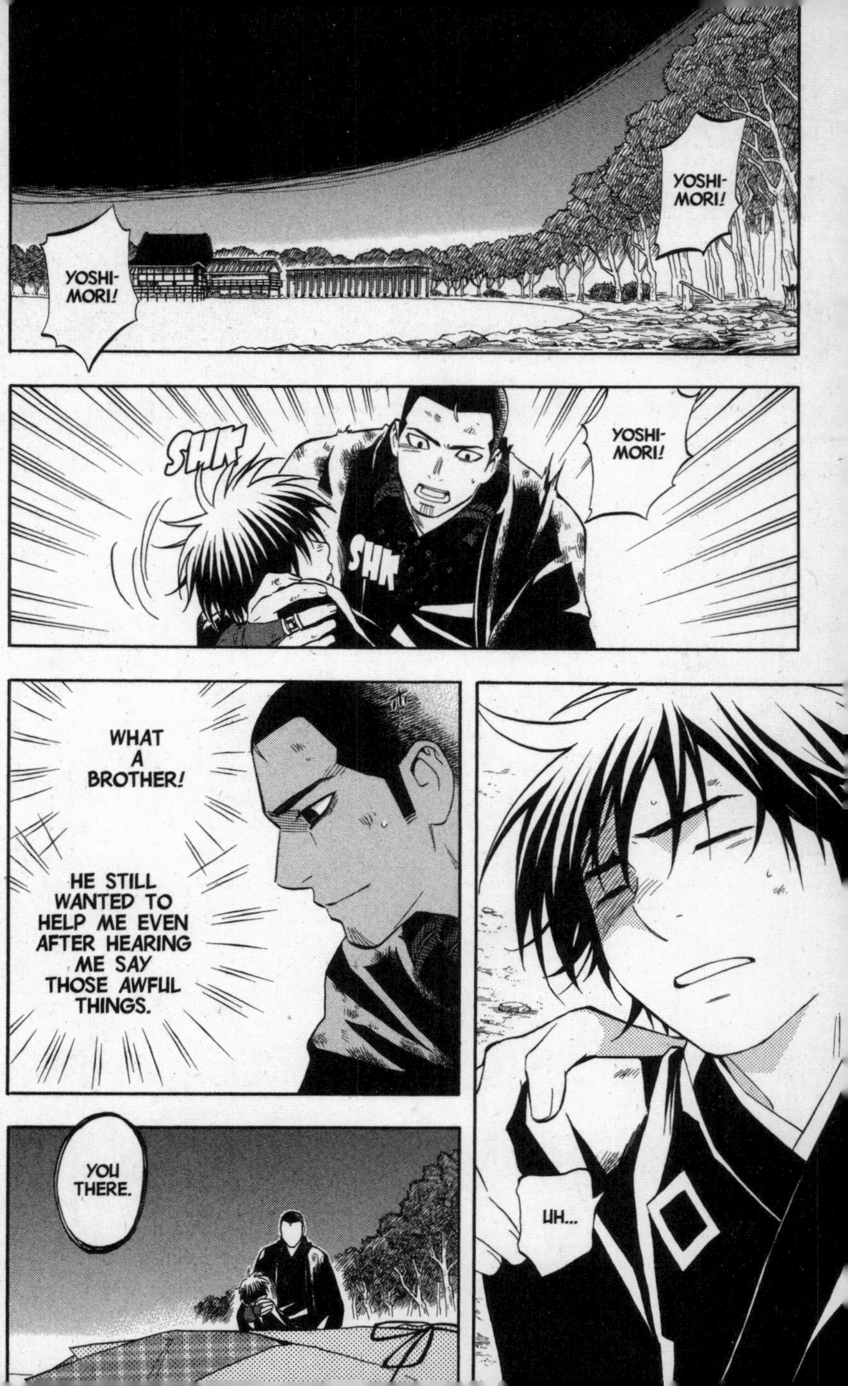
YOSHI-MORI!
YOSHI-MORI!
SHK
SHK
YOSHI-MORI!
WHAT A BROTHER!
HE STILL WANTED TO HELP ME EVEN AFTER HEARING ME SAY THOSE AWFUL THINGS.
YOU THERE.
UH...

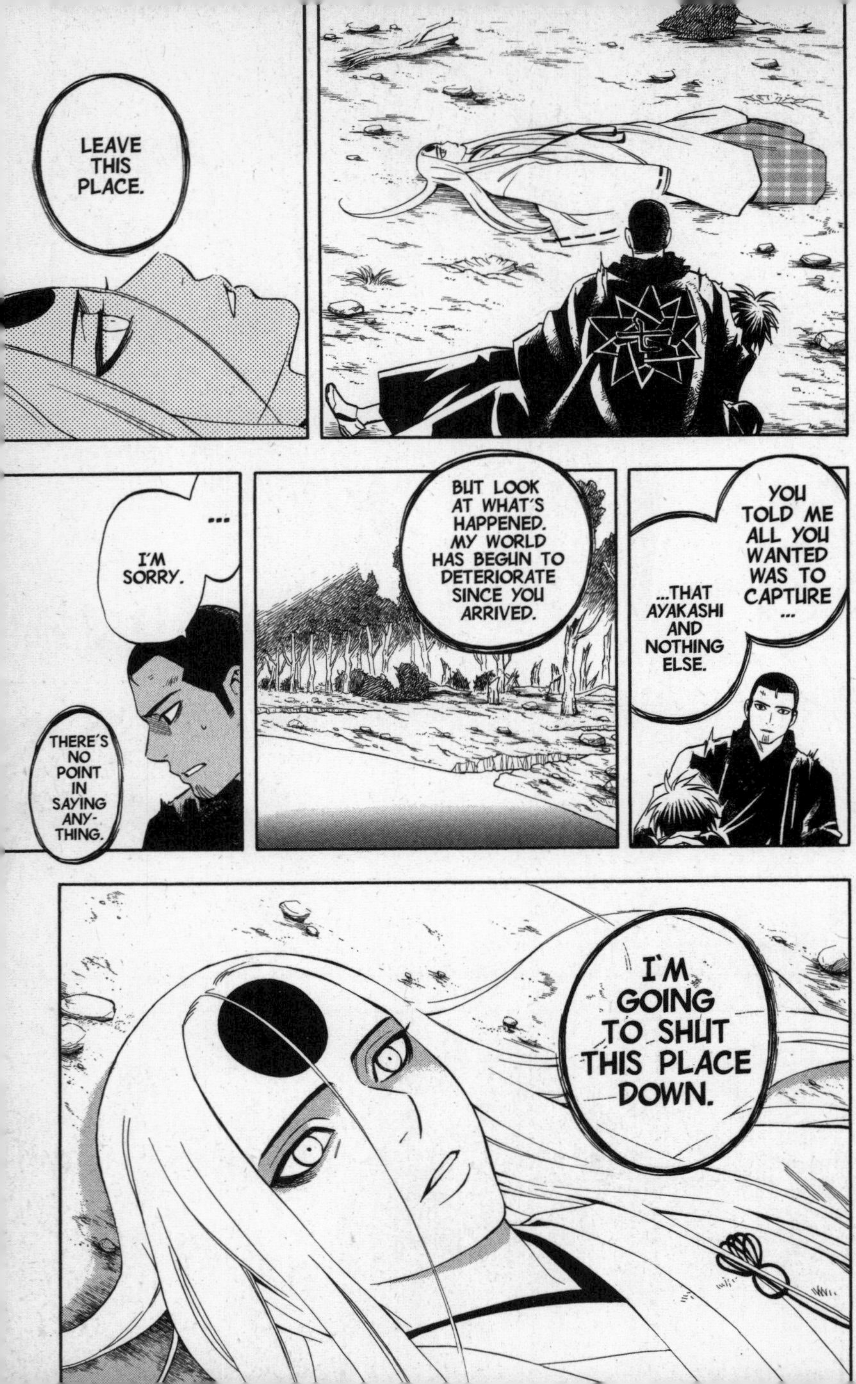
LEAVE THIS PLACE.
YOU TOLD ME ALL YOU WANTED WAS TO CAPTURE ...
...THAT AYAKASHI AND NOTHING ELSE.
BUT LOOK AT WHAT'S HAPPENED. MY WORLD HAS BEGUN TO DETERIORATE SINCE YOU ARRIVED.
...
I'M SORRY.
THERE'S NO POINT IN SAYING ANY-THING.
I'M GOING TO SHUT THIS PLACE DOWN.

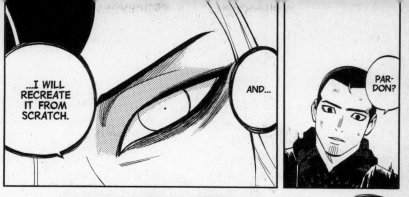

...I WILL RECREATE IT FROM SCRATCH.

AND...

PAR-DON?

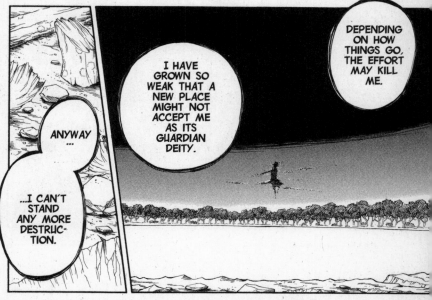

DEPENDING ON HOW THINGS GO, THE EFFORT MAY KILL ME.

I HAVE GROWN SO WEAK THAT A NEW PLACE MIGHT NOT ACCEPT ME AS ITS GUARDIAN DEITY.

ANYWAY...

...I CAN'T STAND ANY MORE DESTRUC-TION.

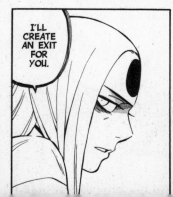

I'LL CREATE AN EXIT FOR YOU.

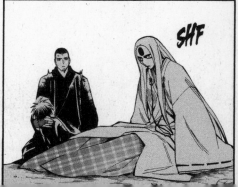

SHF

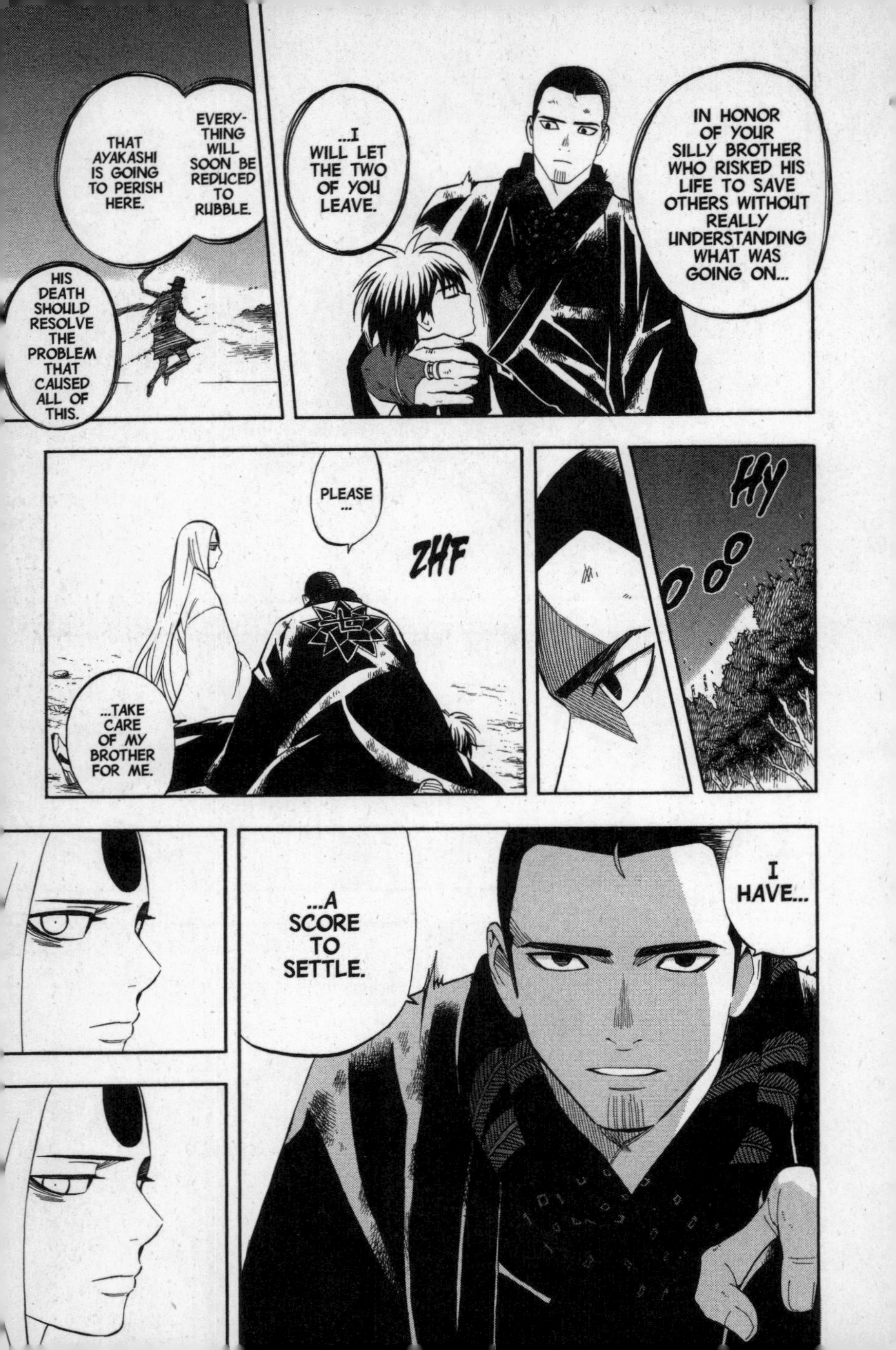
IN HONOR OF YOUR SILLY BROTHER WHO RISKED HIS LIFE TO SAVE OTHERS WITHOUT REALLY UNDERSTANDING WHAT WAS GOING ON...
...I WILL LET THE TWO OF YOU LEAVE.
EVERY-THING WILL SOON BE REDUCED TO RUBBLE.
THAT AYAKASHI IS GOING TO PERISH HERE.
HIS DEATH SHOULD RESOLVE THE PROBLEM THAT CAUSED ALL OF THIS.
HYOOO
PLEASE...
ZHF
...TAKE CARE OF MY BROTHER FOR ME.
I HAVE...
...A SCORE TO SETTLE.

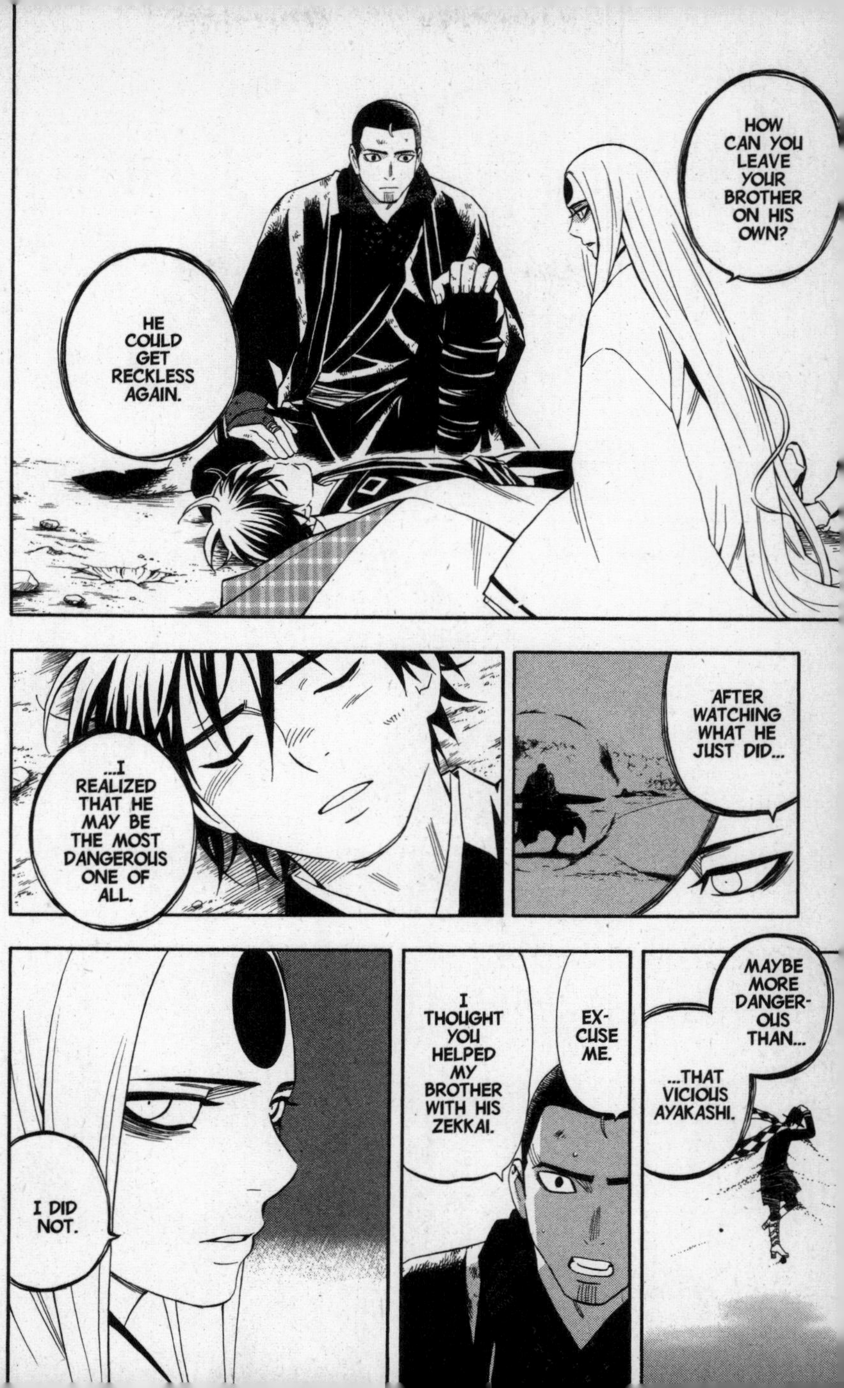
HOW CAN YOU LEAVE YOUR BROTHER ON HIS OWN?
HE COULD GET RECKLESS AGAIN.
AFTER WATCHING WHAT HE JUST DID...
...I REALIZED THAT HE MAY BE THE MOST DANGEROUS ONE OF ALL.
MAYBE MORE DANGER-OUS THAN...
...THAT VICIOUS AYAKASHI.
EX-CUSE ME.
I THOUGHT YOU HELPED MY BROTHER WITH HIS ZEKKAI.
I DID NOT.

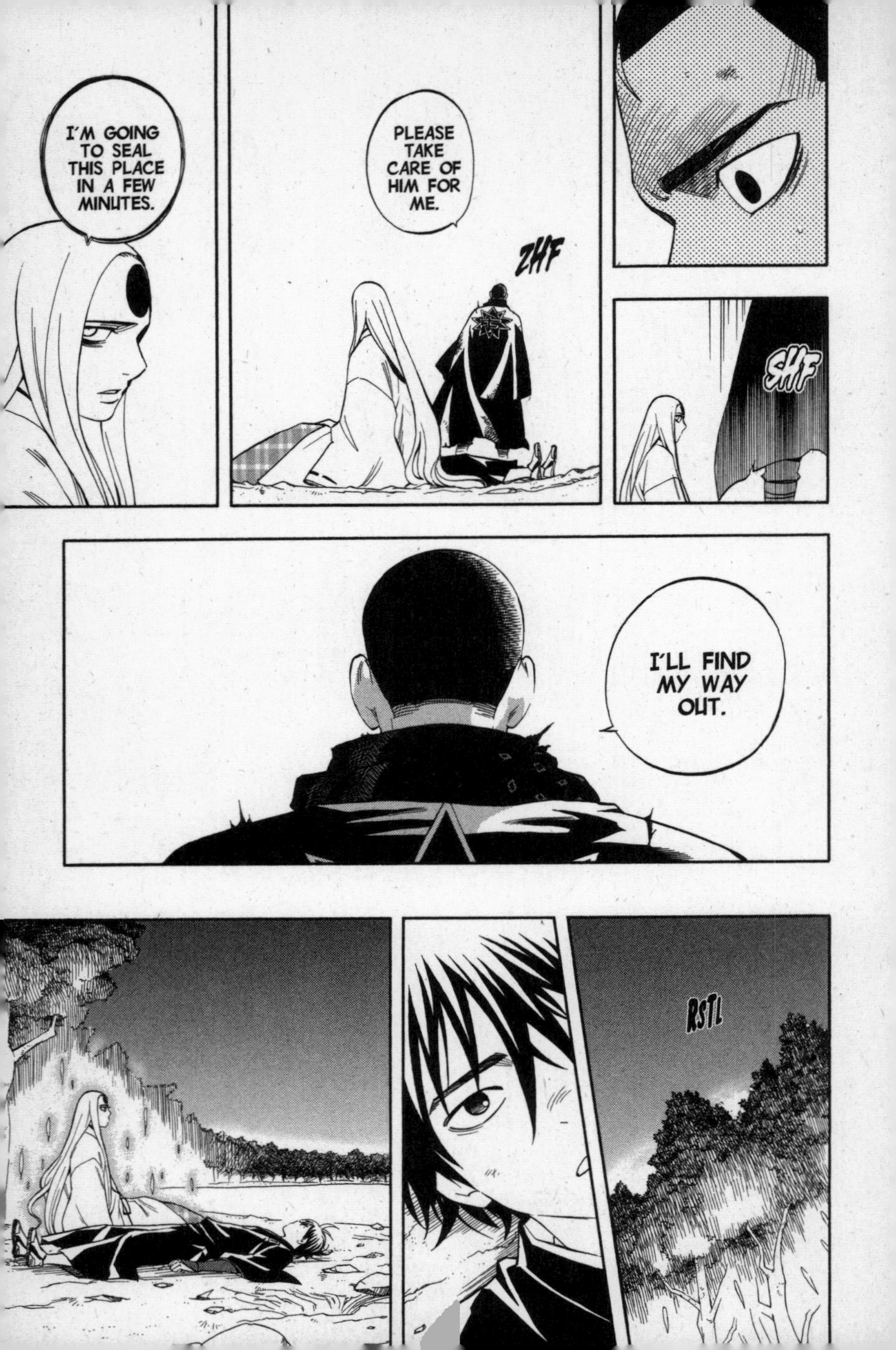
SHF
PLEASE TAKE CARE OF HIM FOR ME.
ZHF
I'M GOING TO SEAL THIS PLACE IN A FEW MINUTES.
I'LL FIND MY WAY OUT.
RSTL

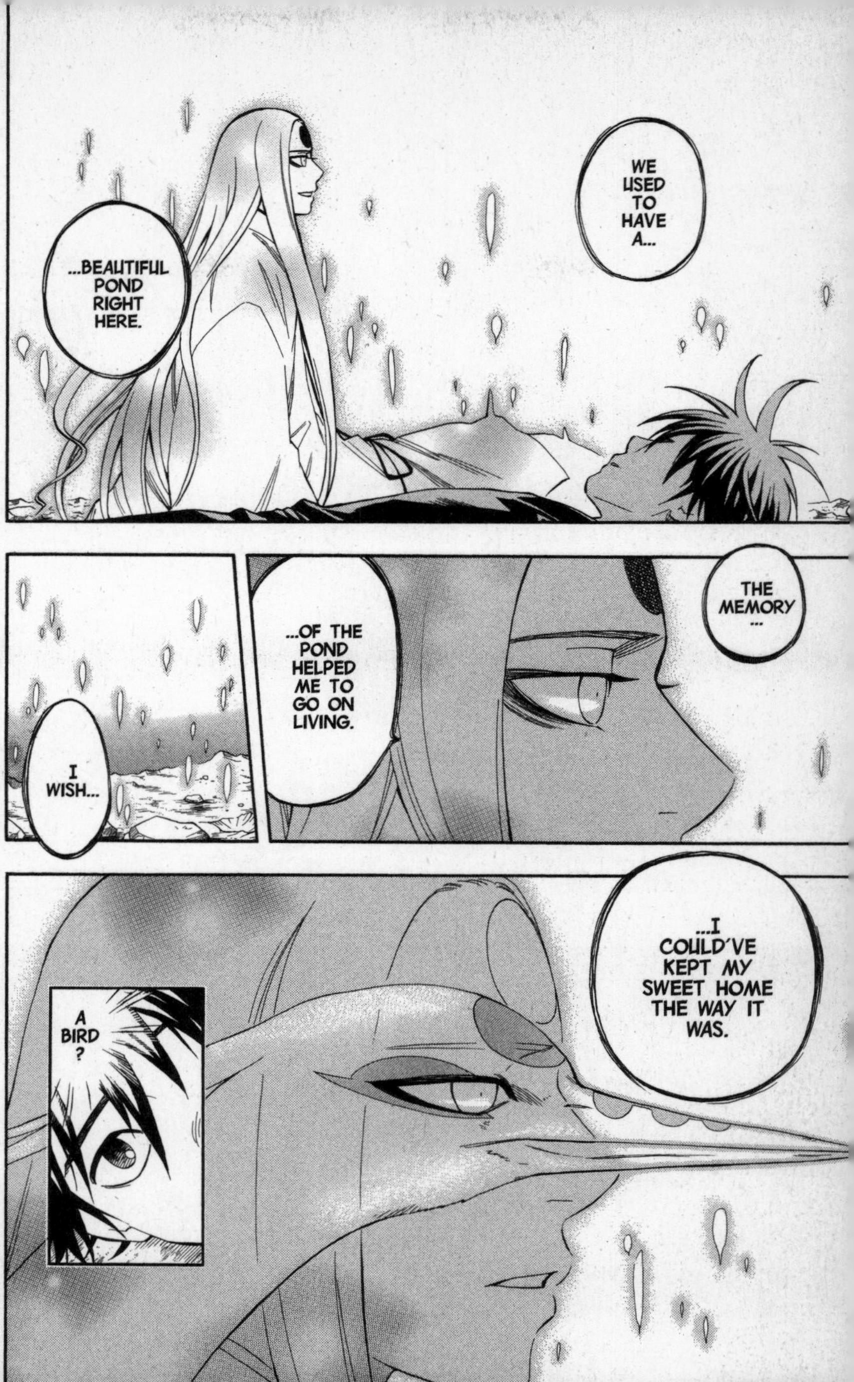
WE USED TO HAVE A...
...BEAUTIFUL POND RIGHT HERE.
THE MEMORY ...
...OF THE POND HELPED ME TO GO ON LIVING.
I WISH...
...I COULD'VE KEPT MY SWEET HOME THE WAY IT WAS.
A BIRD ?

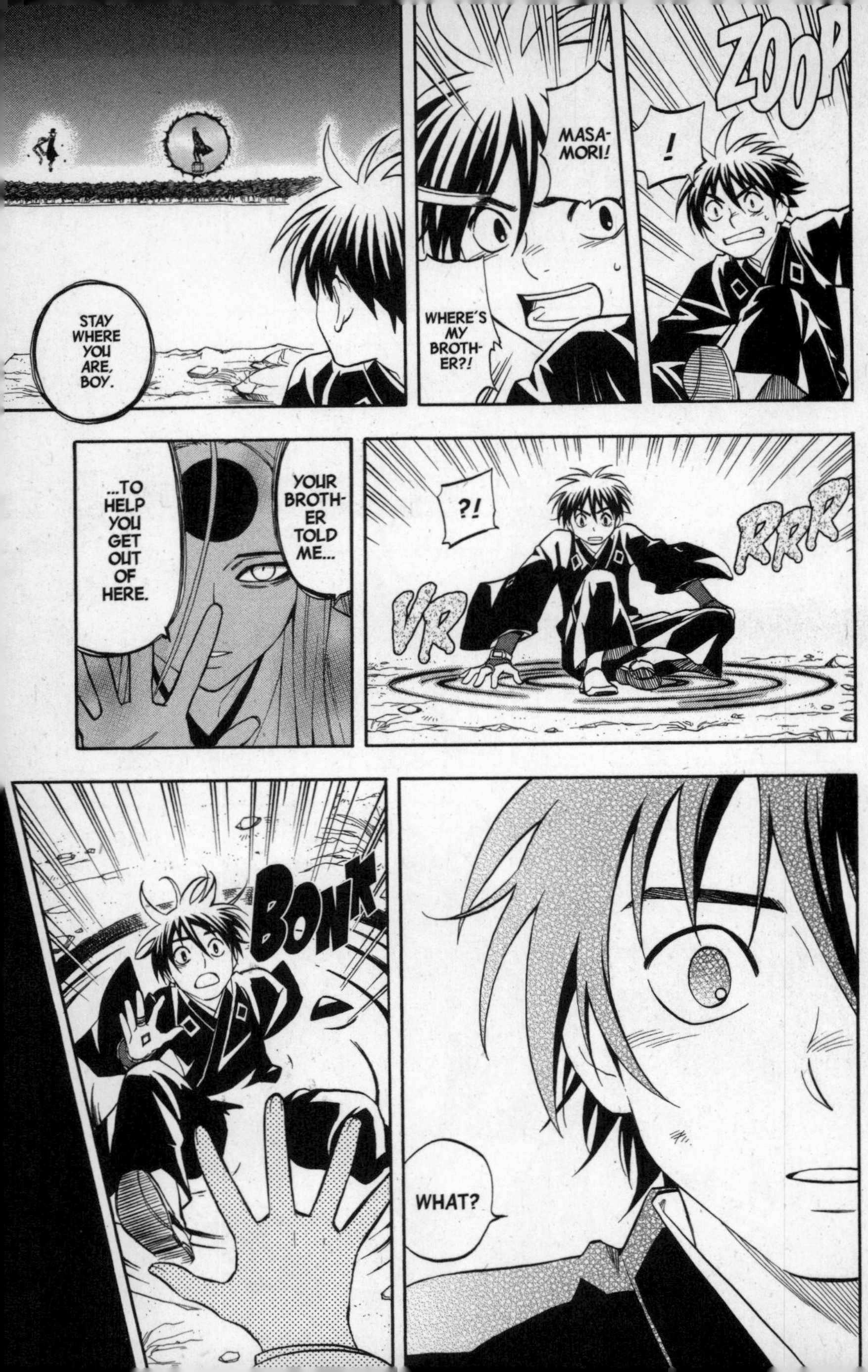
ZOOP
!
MASA-MORI!
WHERE'S MY BROTH-ER?!
STAY WHERE YOU ARE, BOY.
?!
RRR
VR
YOUR BROTH-ER TOLD ME...
...TO HELP YOU GET OUT OF HERE.
WHAT?
BONK

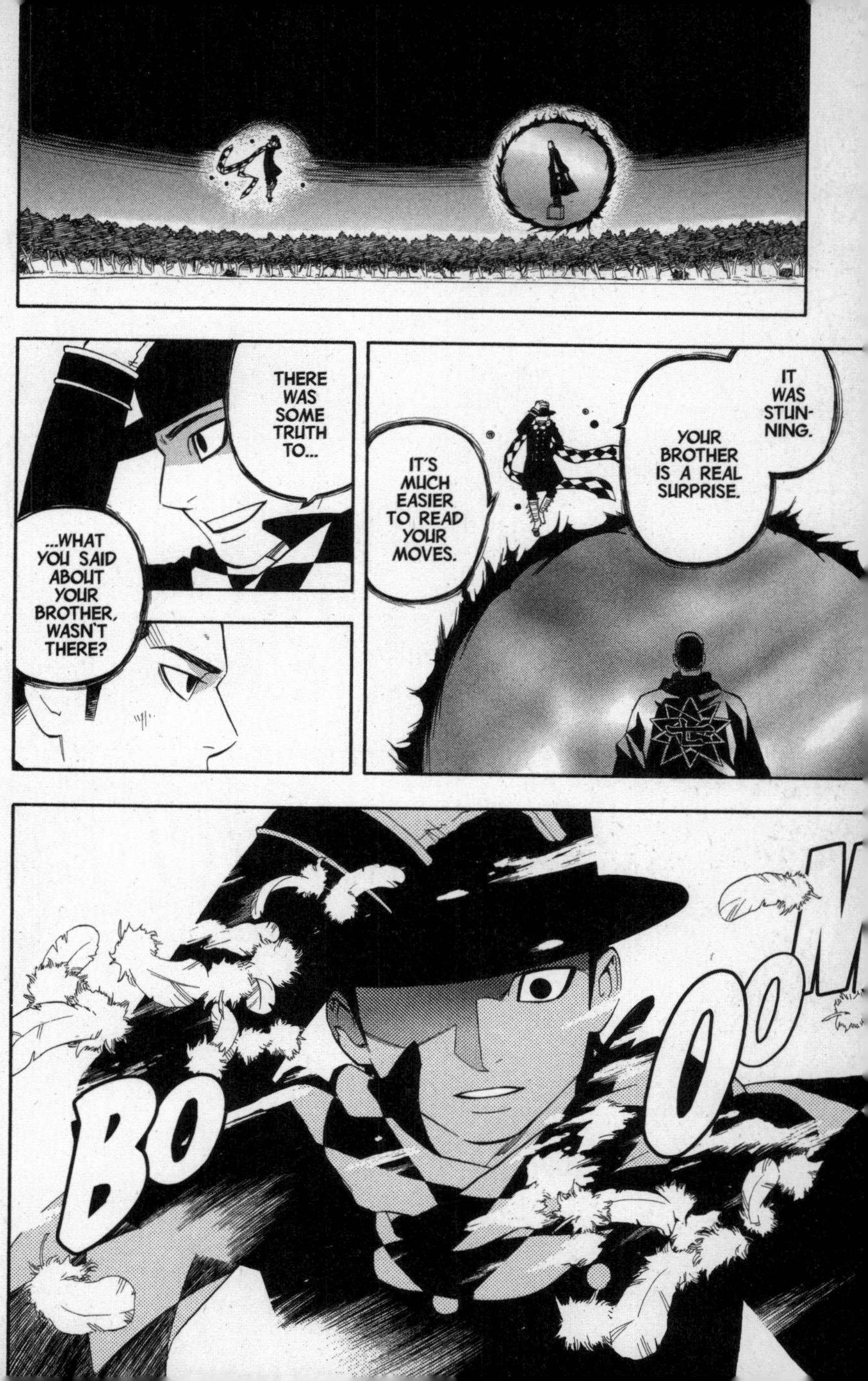
IT WAS STUN-NING.
YOUR BROTHER IS A REAL SURPRISE.
IT'S MUCH EASIER TO READ YOUR MOVES.
THERE WAS SOME TRUTH TO...
...WHAT YOU SAID ABOUT YOUR BROTHER, WASN'T THERE?
BOOOOM

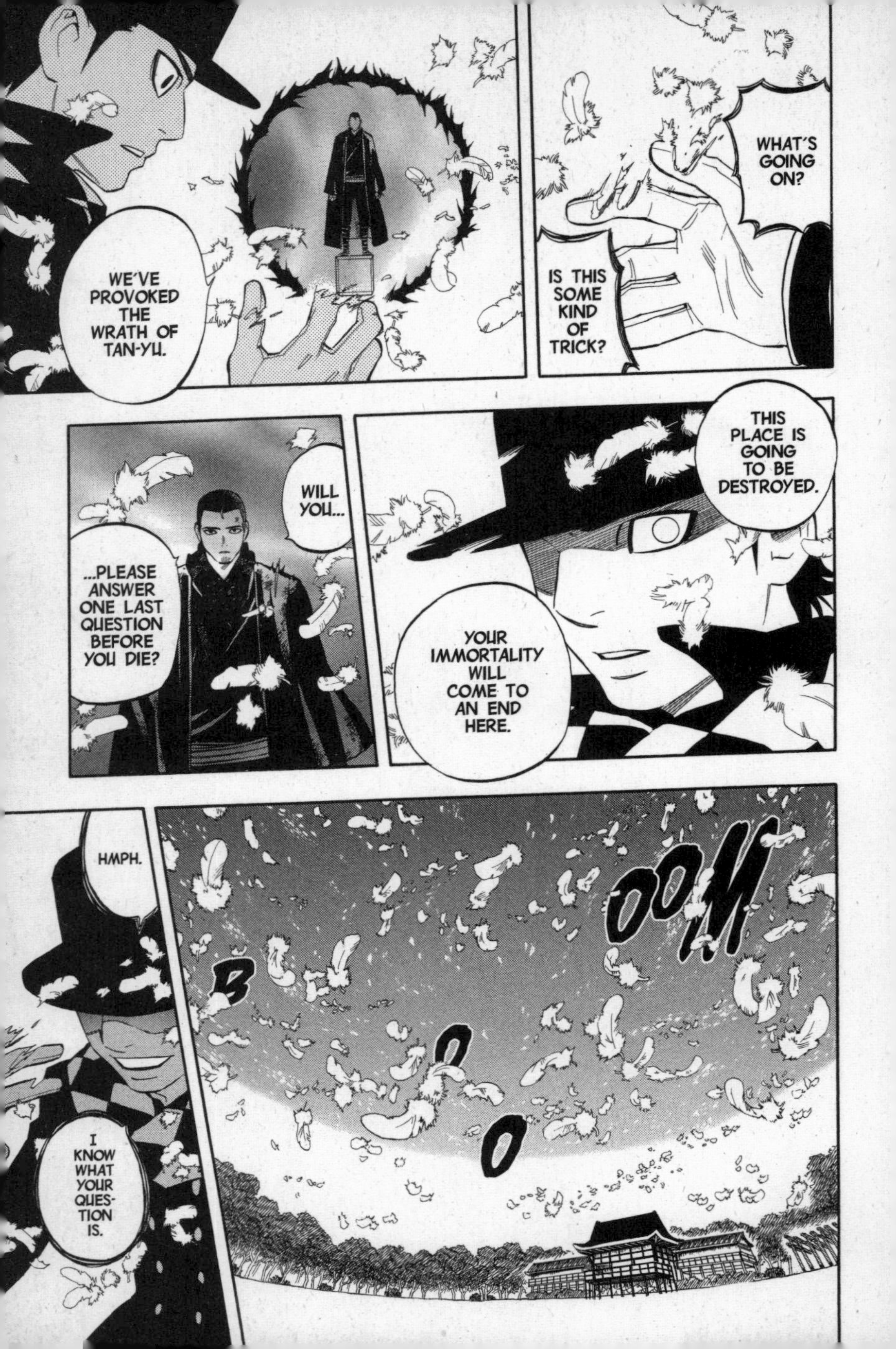
WHAT'S GOING ON?
IS THIS SOME KIND OF TRICK?
WE'VE PROVOKED THE WRATH OF TAN-YU.
THIS PLACE IS GOING TO BE DESTROYED.
YOUR IMMORTALITY WILL COME TO AN END HERE.
WILL YOU...
...PLEASE ANSWER ONE LAST QUESTION BEFORE YOU DIE?
BOOOOM
HMPH.
I KNOW WHAT YOUR QUESTION IS.

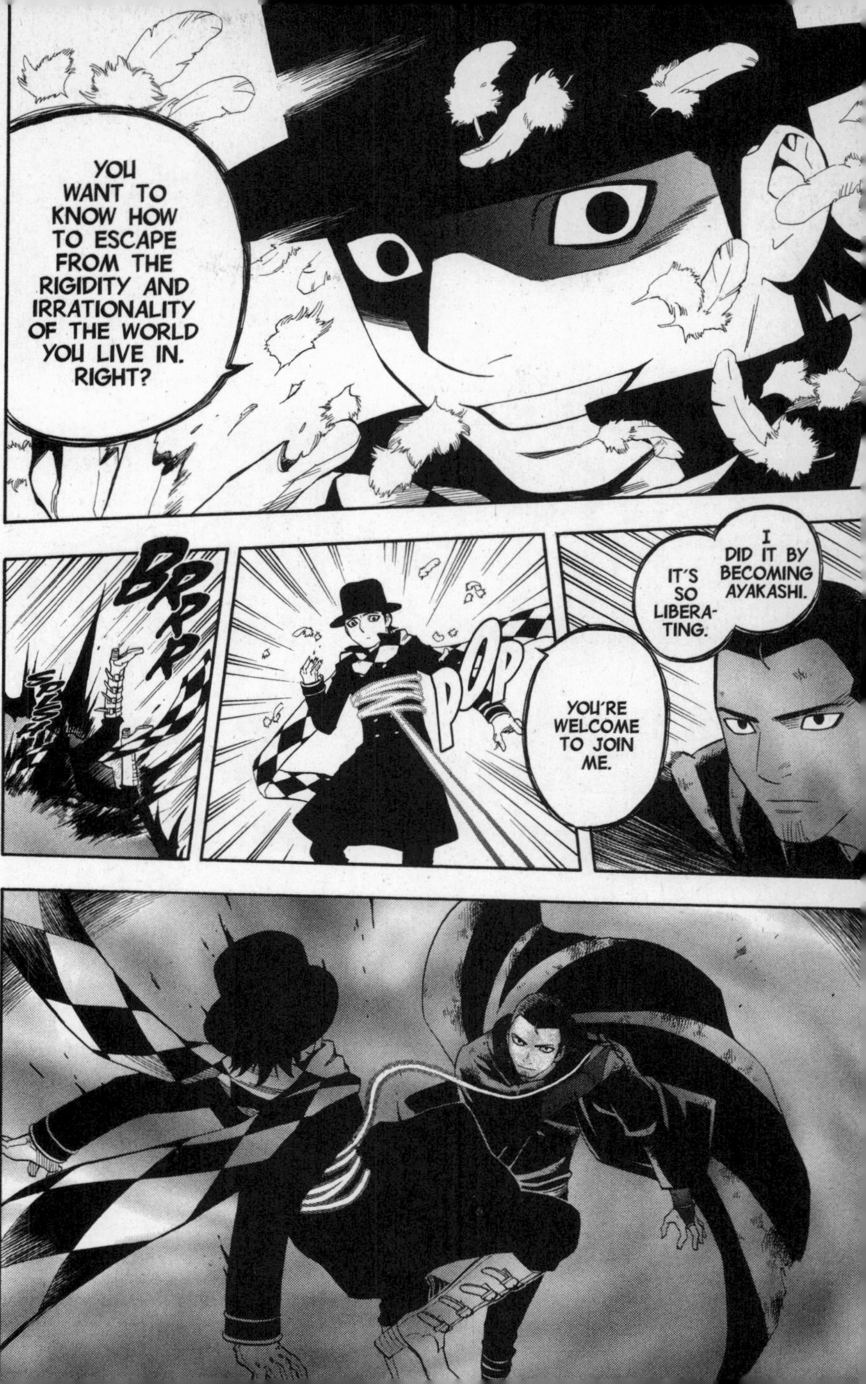
YOU WANT TO KNOW HOW TO ESCAPE FROM THE RIGIDITY AND IRRATIONALITY OF THE WORLD YOU LIVE IN. RIGHT?
I DID IT BY BECOMING AYAKASHI.
IT'S SO LIBERA-TING.
YOU'RE WELCOME TO JOIN ME.
POP
BRRR

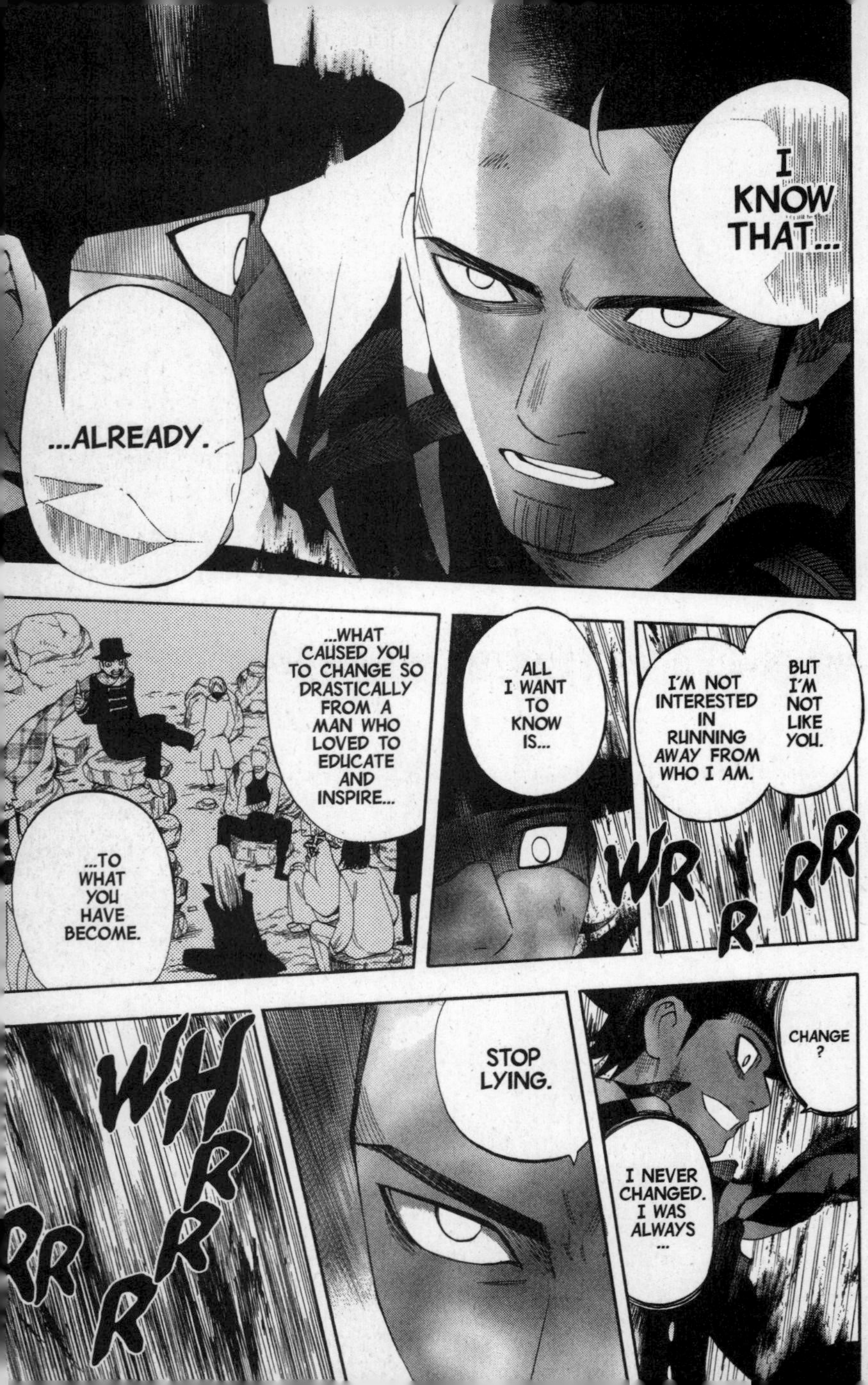
I KNOW THAT...
...ALREADY.
BUT I'M NOT LIKE YOU.
I'M NOT INTERESTED IN RUNNING AWAY FROM WHO I AM.
WRRRR
ALL I WANT TO KNOW IS...
...WHAT CAUSED YOU TO CHANGE SO DRASTICALLY FROM A MAN WHO LOVED TO EDUCATE AND INSPIRE...
...TO WHAT YOU HAVE BECOME.
CHANGE?
I NEVER CHANGED. I WAS ALWAYS ...
STOP LYING.
WHRRRRRR

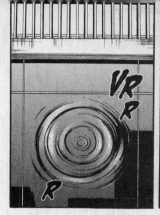
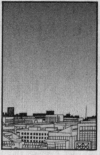

VRR R

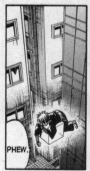

PHEW.

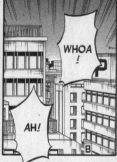

WHOA!

AH!

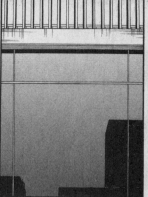

AW!

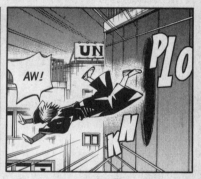

UN

PLO

KN

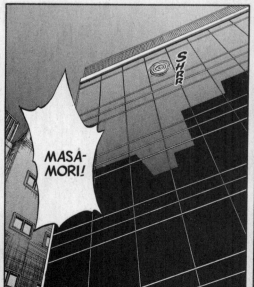

SHRR

MASA-MORI!

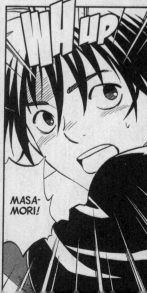

WH UP

MASA-MORI!

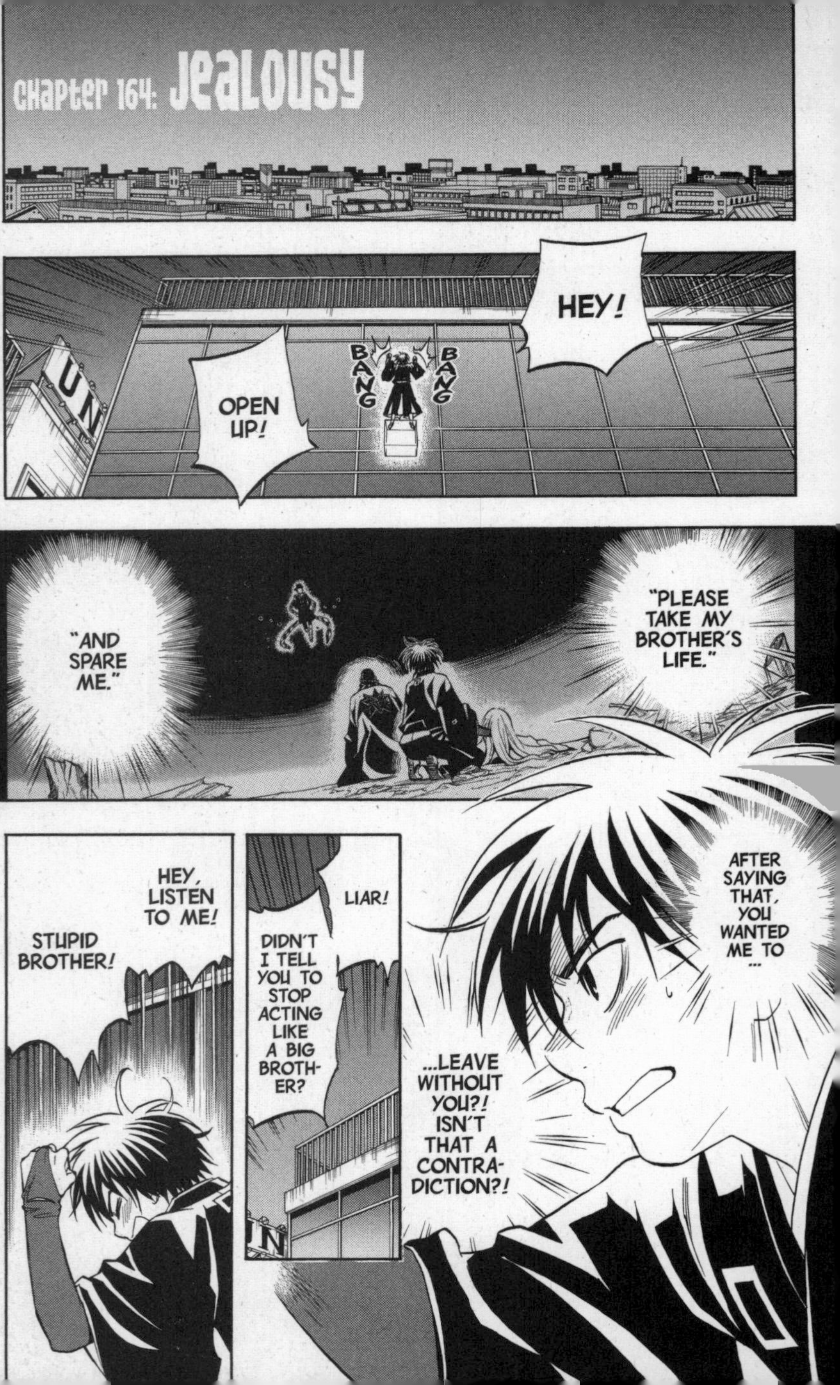
Chapter 164: Jealousy
HEY!
BANG BANG
OPEN UP!
"PLEASE TAKE MY BROTHER'S LIFE."
"AND SPARE ME."
AFTER SAYING THAT, YOU WANTED ME TO ...
...LEAVE WITHOUT YOU?! ISN'T THAT A CONTRADICTION?!
LIAR!
DIDN'T I TELL YOU TO STOP ACTING LIKE A BIG BROTHER?
HEY, LISTEN TO ME!
STUPID BROTHER!

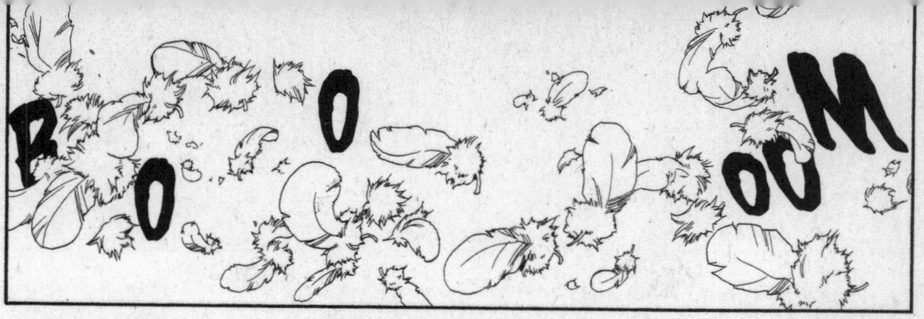
BOOOOOM

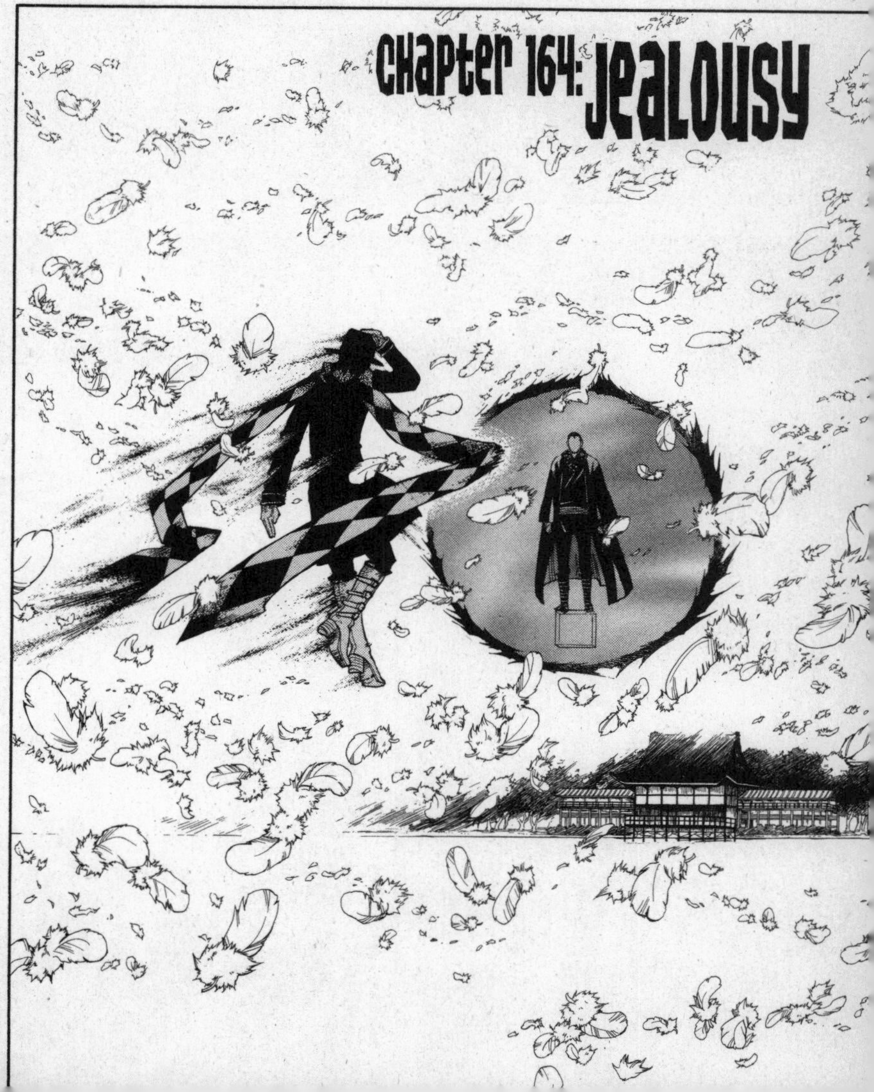
Chapter 164: Jealousy

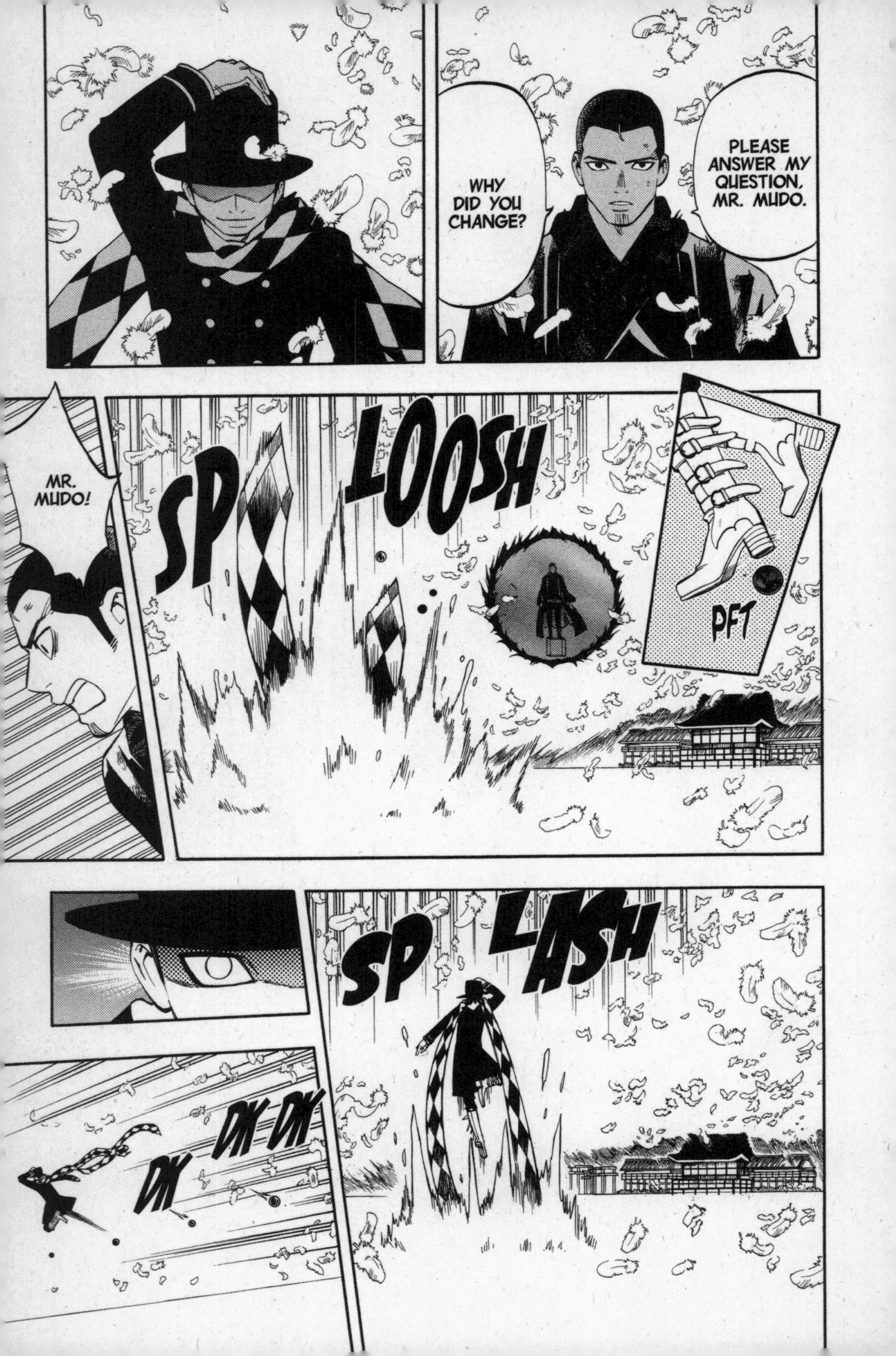
PLEASE ANSWER MY QUESTION, MR. MUDO.
WHY DID YOU CHANGE?
PFT
SPLOOSH
MR. MUDO!
SPLASH
DK DK DK

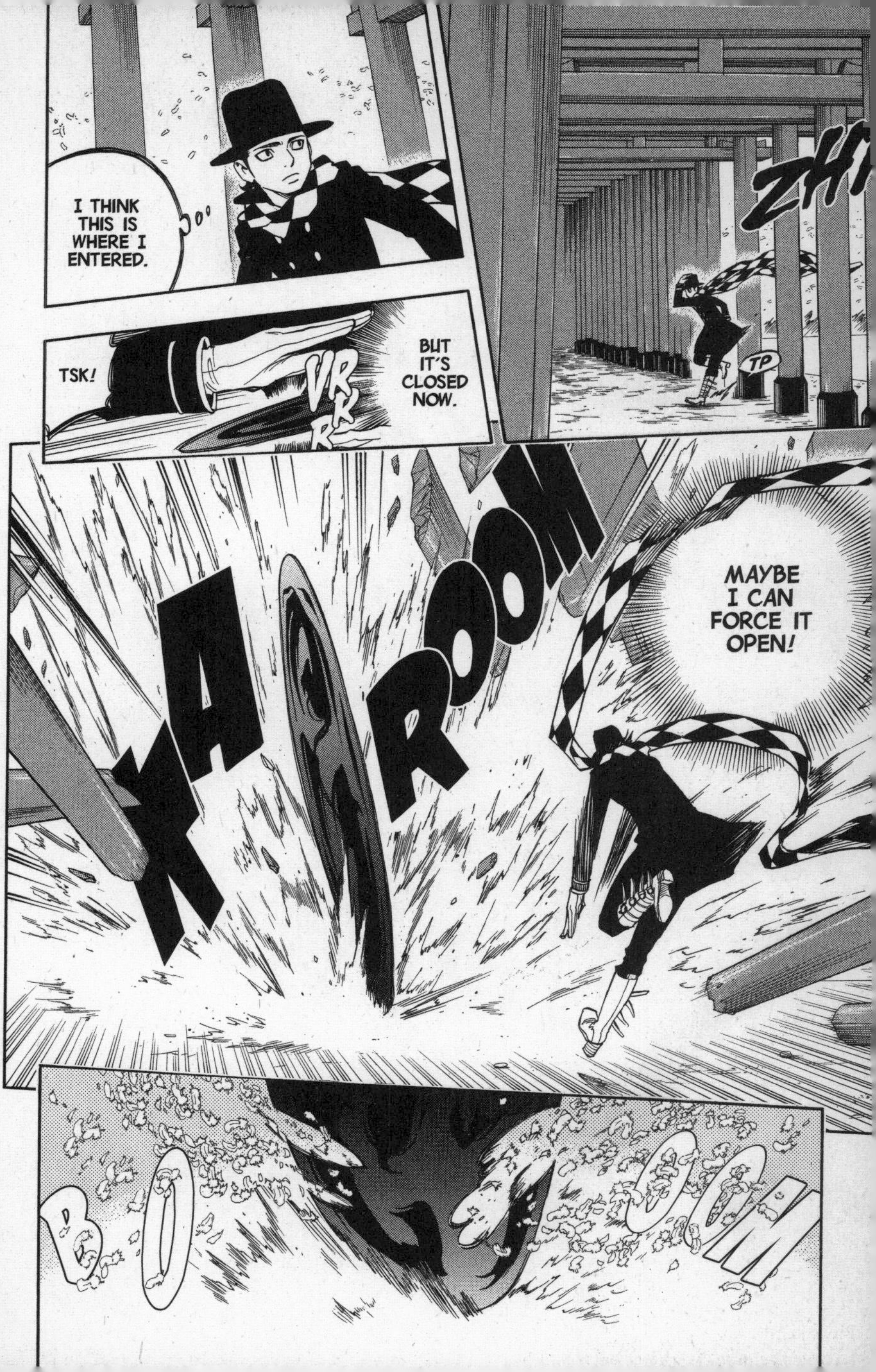
ZH
TP
I THINK THIS IS WHERE I ENTERED.
BUT IT'S CLOSED NOW.
TSK!
VRRR
MAYBE I CAN FORCE IT OPEN!
KAROOOM

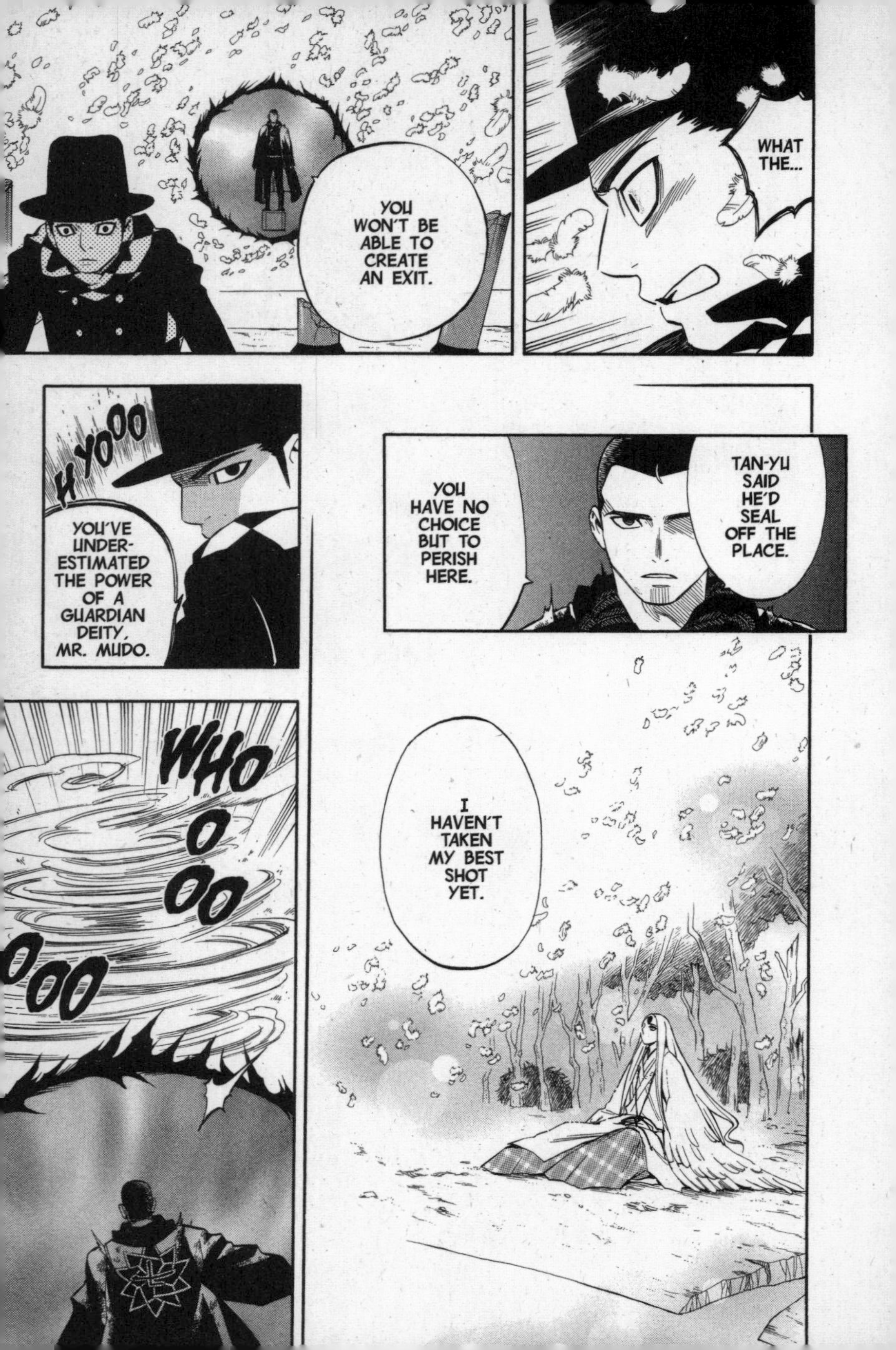
WHAT THE...
YOU WON'T BE ABLE TO CREATE AN EXIT.
TAN-YU SAID HE'D SEAL OFF THE PLACE.
YOU HAVE NO CHOICE BUT TO PERISH HERE.
I HAVEN'T TAKEN MY BEST SHOT YET.
HYOOO
YOU'VE UNDER-ESTIMATED THE POWER OF A GUARDIAN DEITY, MR. MUDO.
WHOOOOOOOO

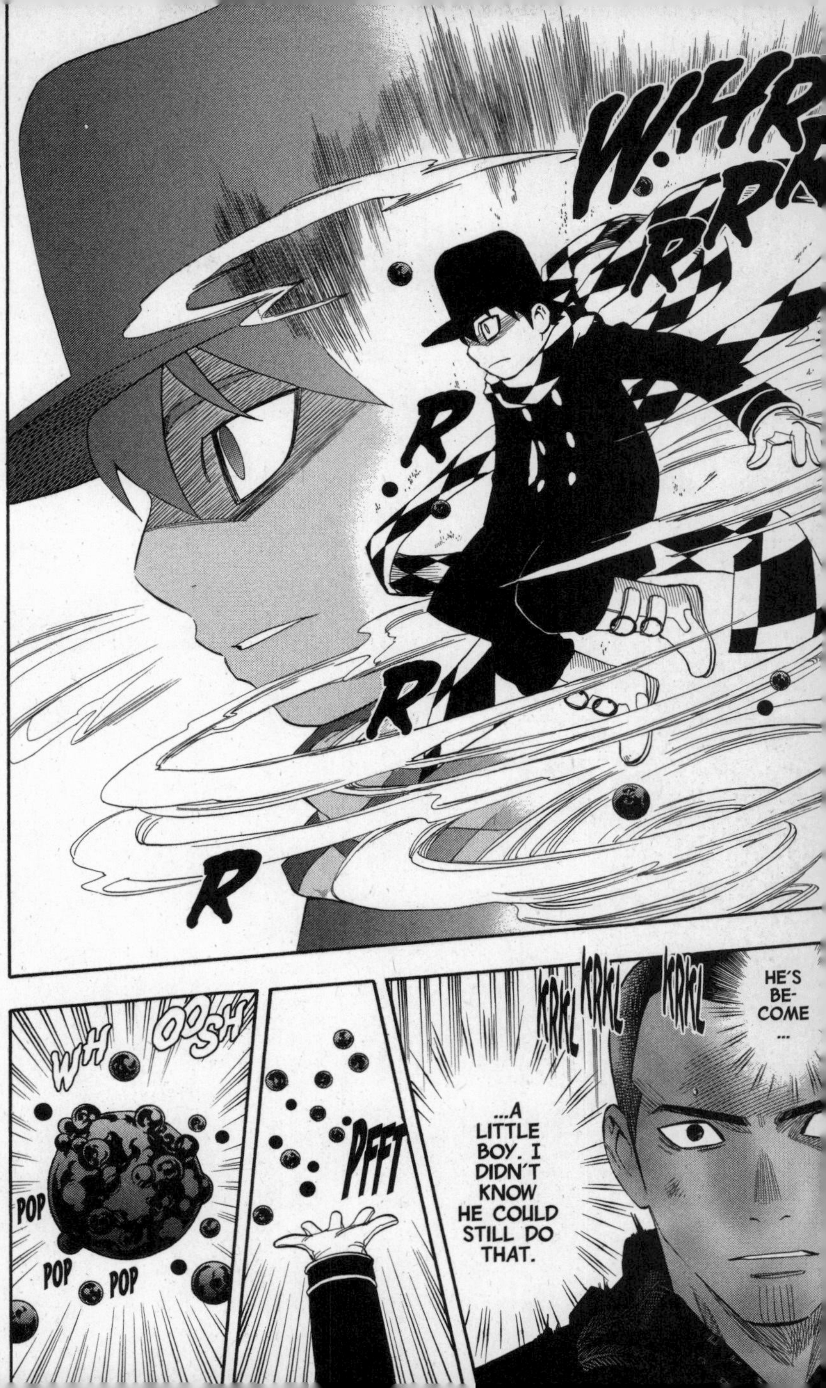
WHR
RRR
R
R
R
KRKL
KRKL
KRKL
HE'S BE-COME ...
...A LITTLE BOY. I DIDN'T KNOW HE COULD STILL DO THAT.
PFFT
WHOOSH
POP
POP
POP

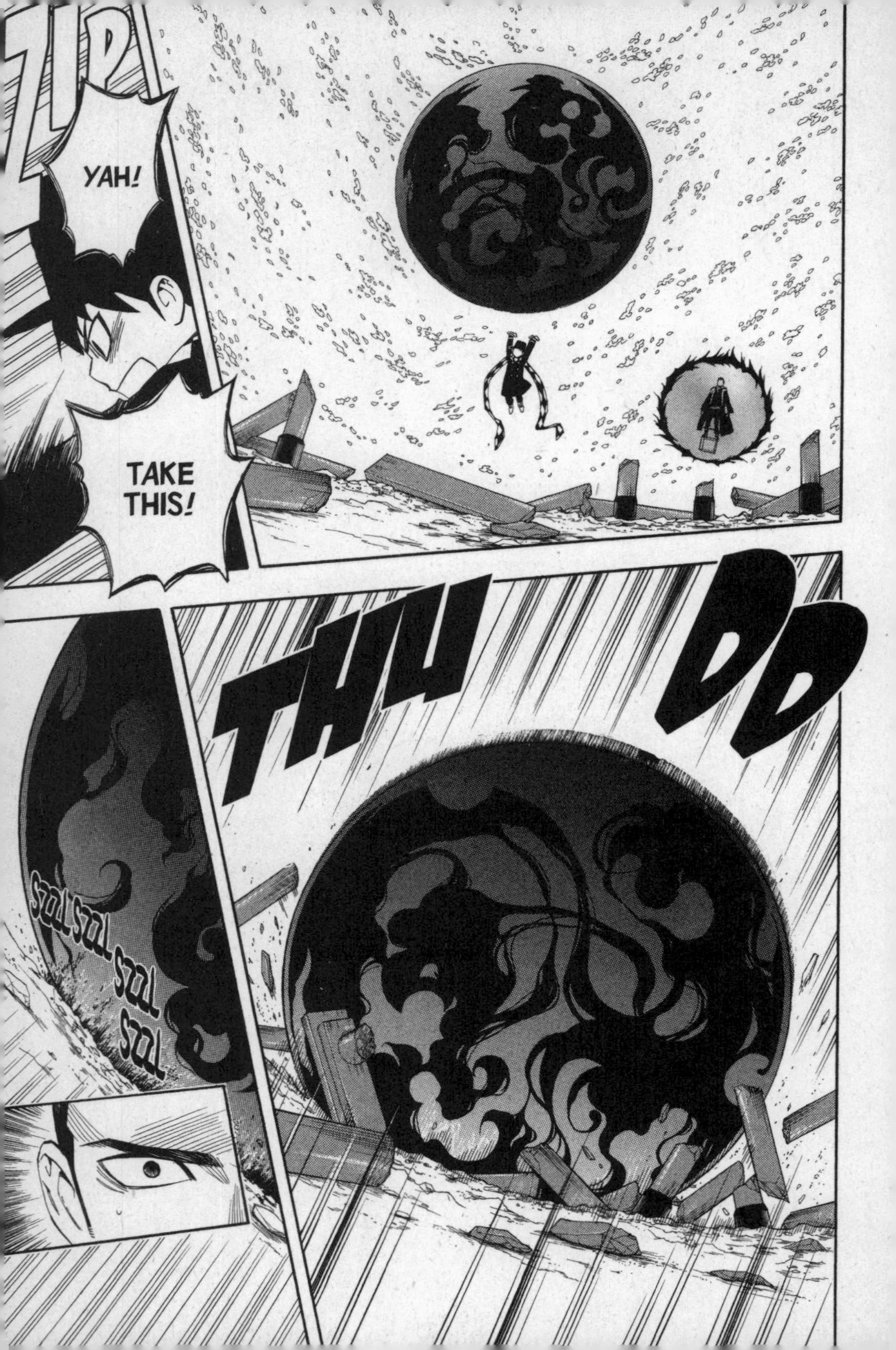
ZIP
YAH!
TAKE THIS!
THUDD
SZZL SZZL
SZZL SZZL

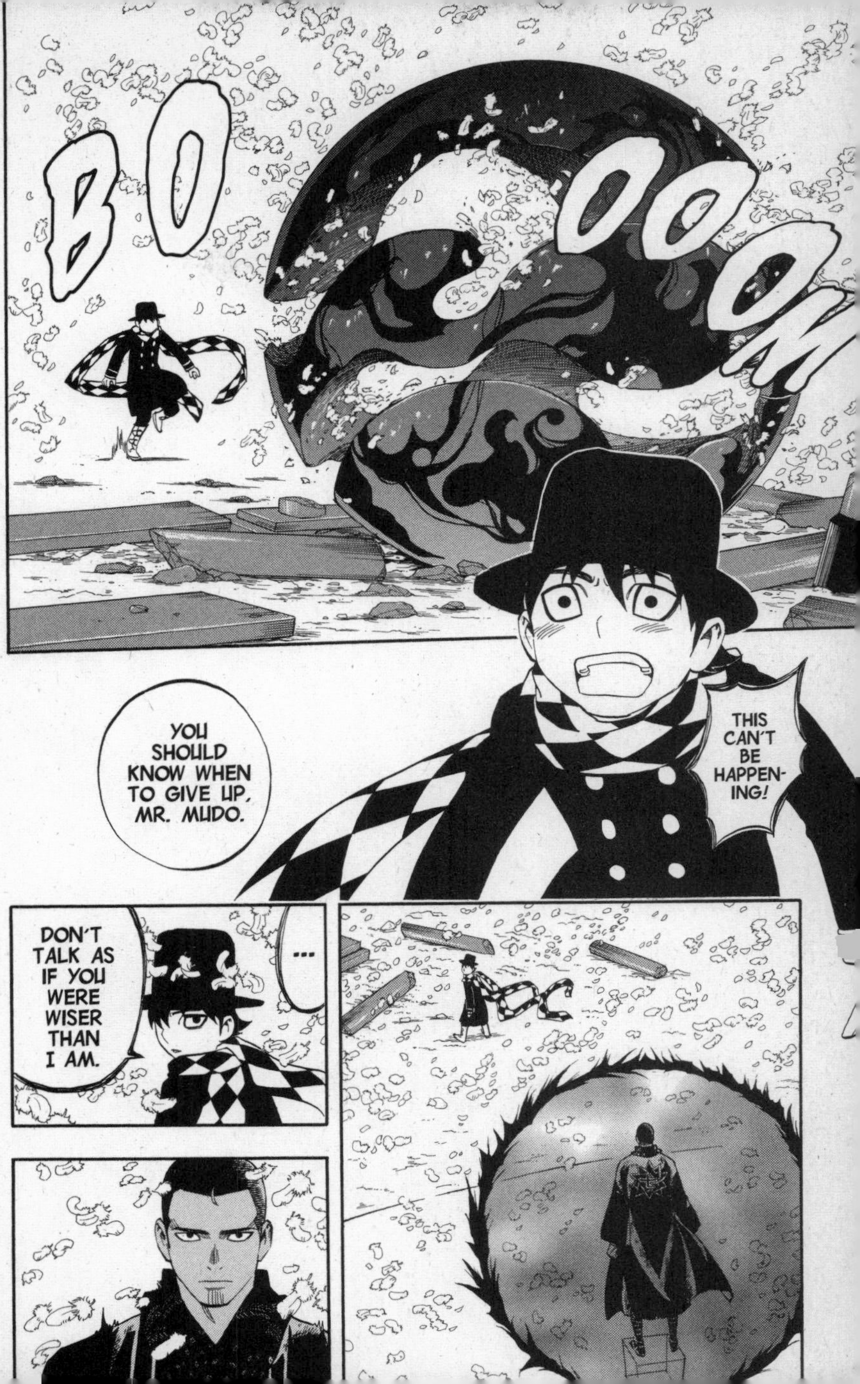
BOOOOM
THIS CAN'T BE HAPPENING!
YOU SHOULD KNOW WHEN TO GIVE UP, MR. MUDO.
...
DON'T TALK AS IF YOU WERE WISER THAN I AM.

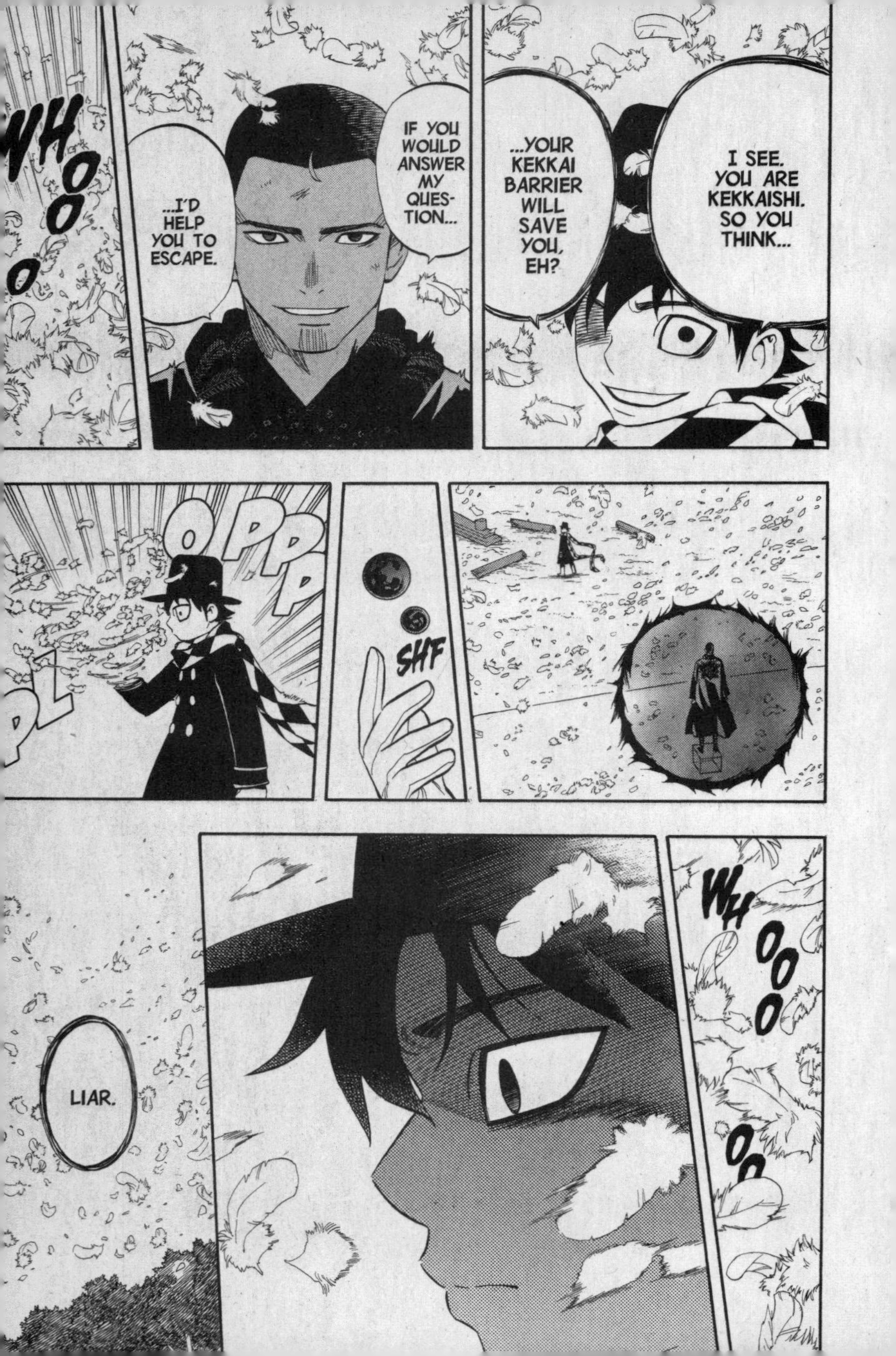
I SEE. YOU ARE KEKKAISHI. SO YOU THINK...
...YOUR KEKKAI BARRIER WILL SAVE YOU, EH?
IF YOU WOULD ANSWER MY QUES-TION...
...I'D HELP YOU TO ESCAPE.
WHOOOO
SHF
OPPP
PL
WHOOOOO
LIAR.

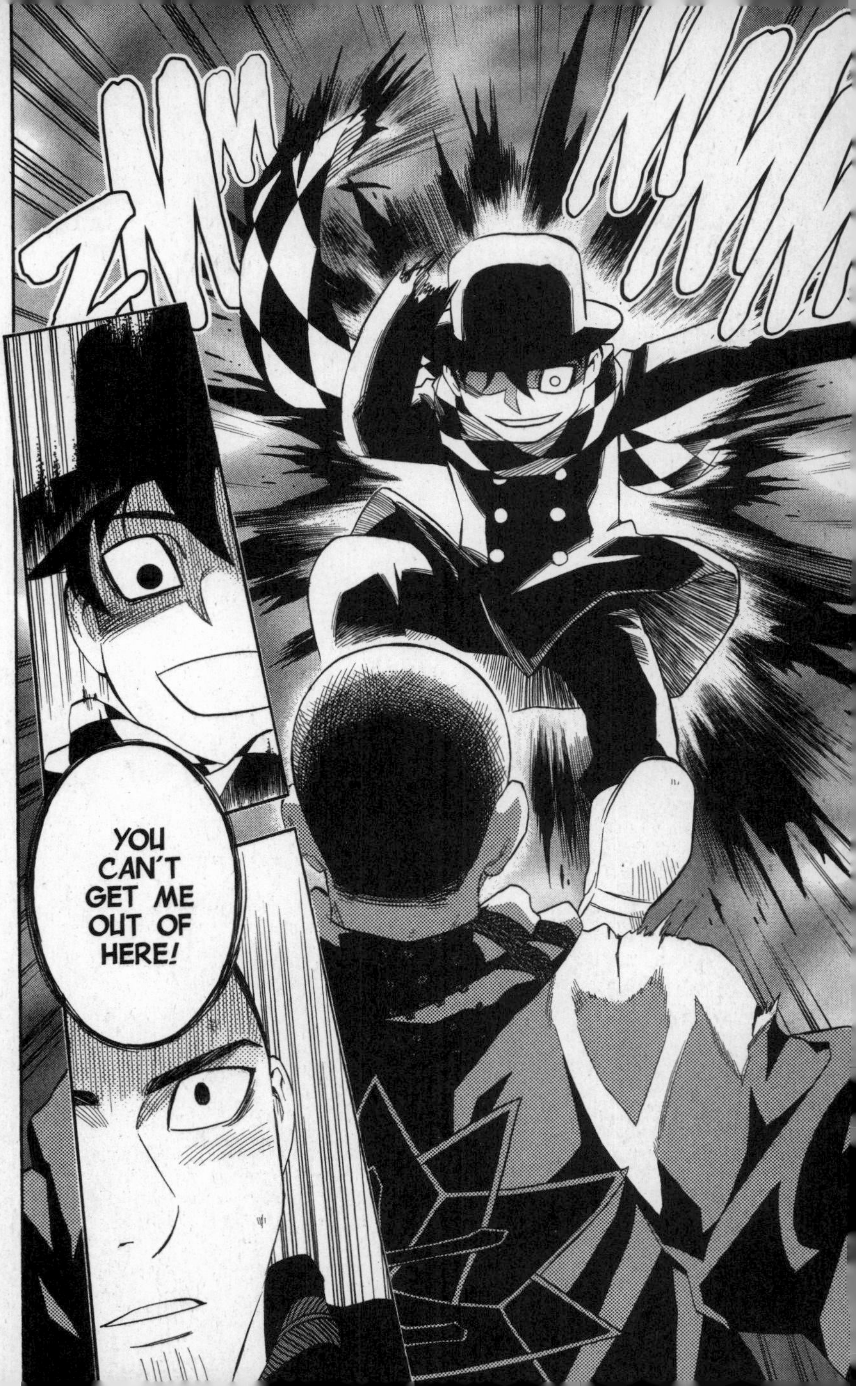
YOU CAN'T GET ME OUT OF HERE!

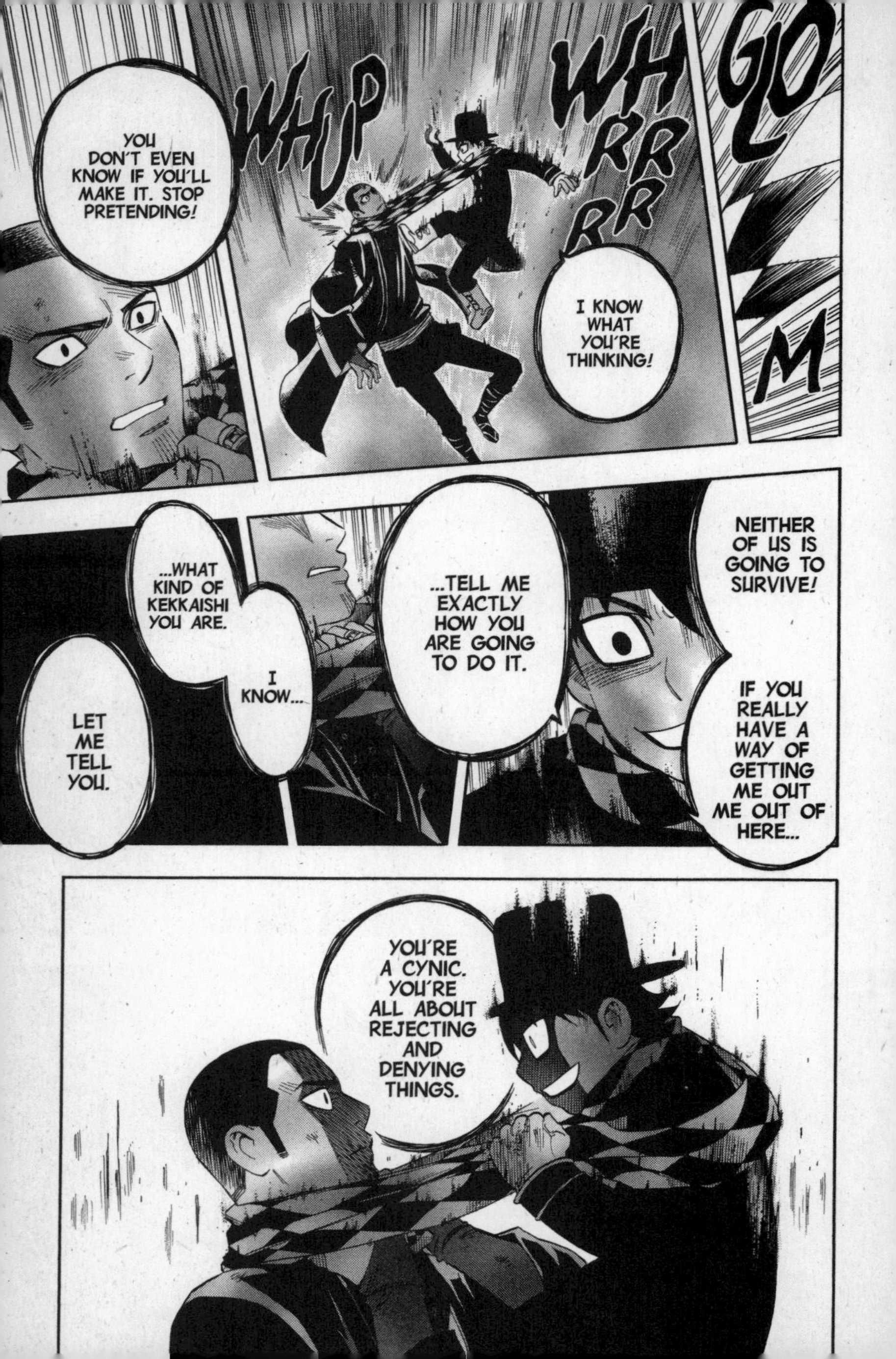
WHUP
WHRRRRR
I KNOW WHAT YOU'RE THINKING!
YOU DON'T EVEN KNOW IF YOU'LL MAKE IT. STOP PRETENDING!
NEITHER OF US IS GOING TO SURVIVE!
IF YOU REALLY HAVE A WAY OF GETTING ME OUT ME OUT OF HERE...
...TELL ME EXACTLY HOW YOU ARE GOING TO DO IT.
I KNOW...
...WHAT KIND OF KEKKAISHI YOU ARE.
LET ME TELL YOU.
YOU'RE A CYNIC. YOU'RE ALL ABOUT REJECTING AND DENYING THINGS.

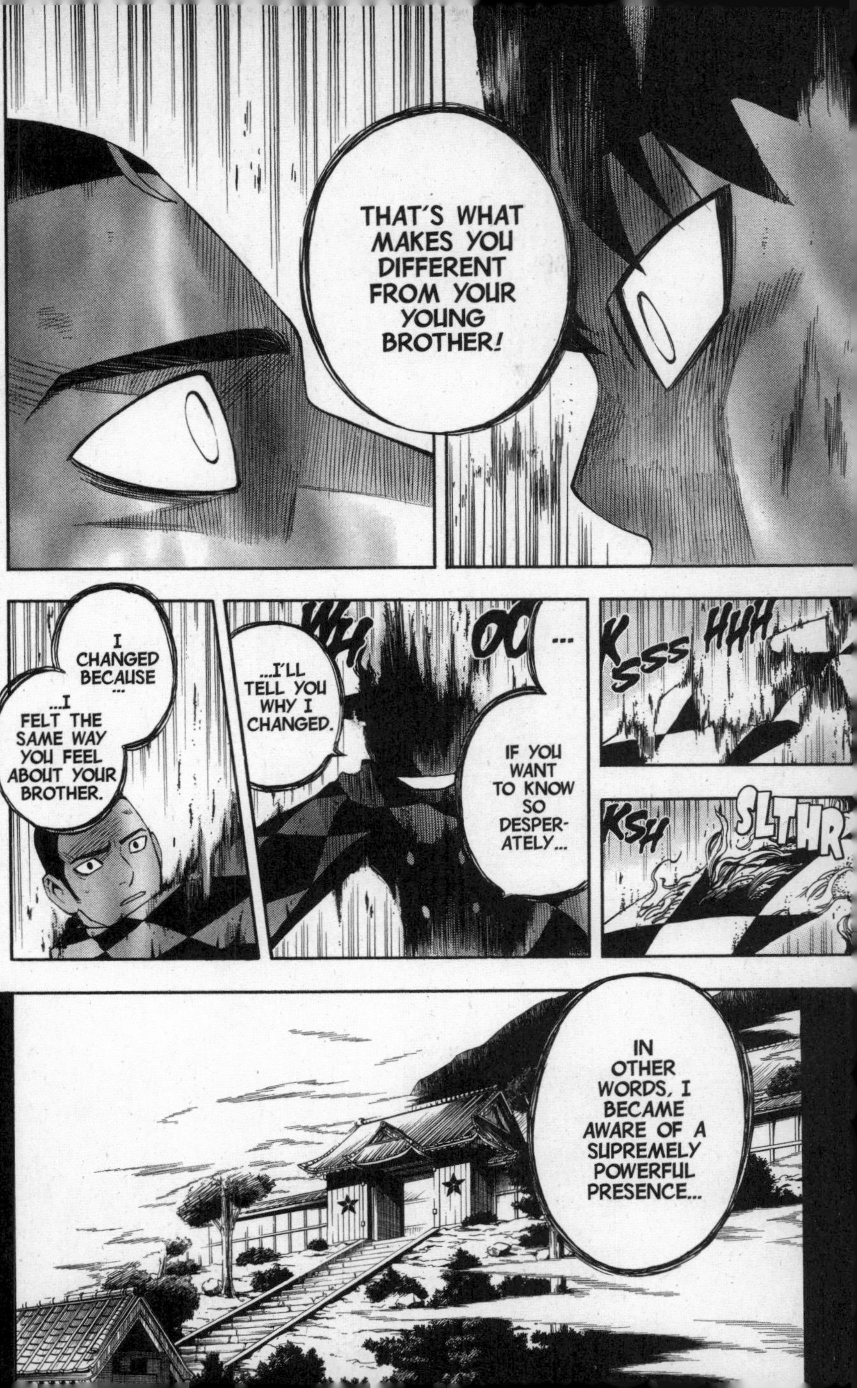
THAT'S WHAT MAKES YOU DIFFERENT FROM YOUR YOUNG BROTHER!
KSSS
HHH
KSH
SLTHR
WHOO...
IF YOU WANT TO KNOW SO DESPER-ATELY...
...I'LL TELL YOU WHY I CHANGED.
I CHANGED BECAUSE...
...I FELT THE SAME WAY YOU FEEL ABOUT YOUR BROTHER.
IN OTHER WORDS, I BECAME AWARE OF A SUPREMELY POWERFUL PRESENCE...

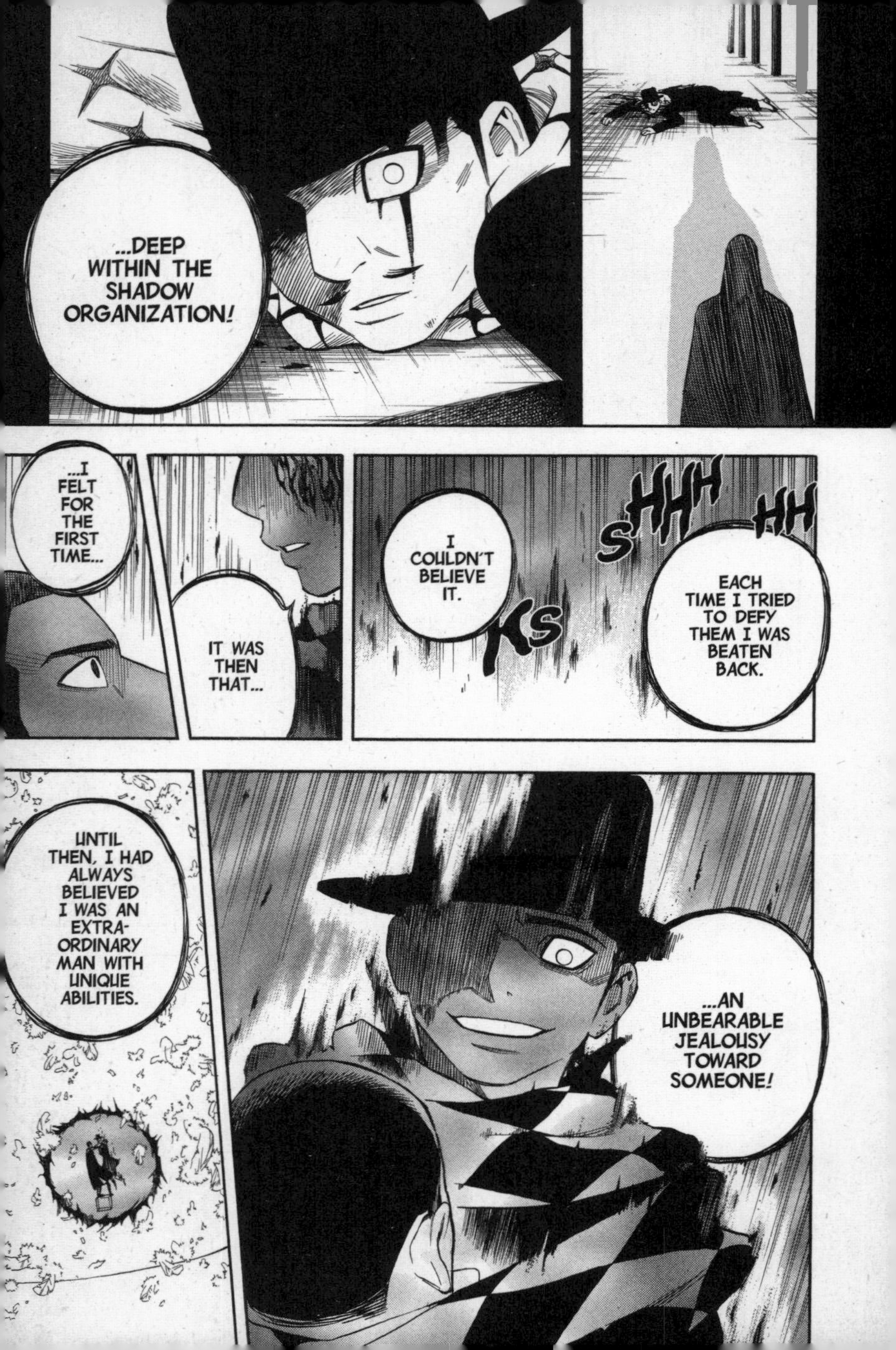
...DEEP WITHIN THE SHADOW ORGANIZATION!
SHHHHH
EACH TIME I TRIED TO DEFY THEM I WAS BEATEN BACK.
I COULDN'T BELIEVE IT.
KS
IT WAS THEN THAT...
...I FELT FOR THE FIRST TIME...
...AN UNBEARABLE JEALOUSY TOWARD SOMEONE!
UNTIL THEN, I HAD ALWAYS BELIEVED I WAS AN EXTRA-ORDINARY MAN WITH UNIQUE ABILITIES.

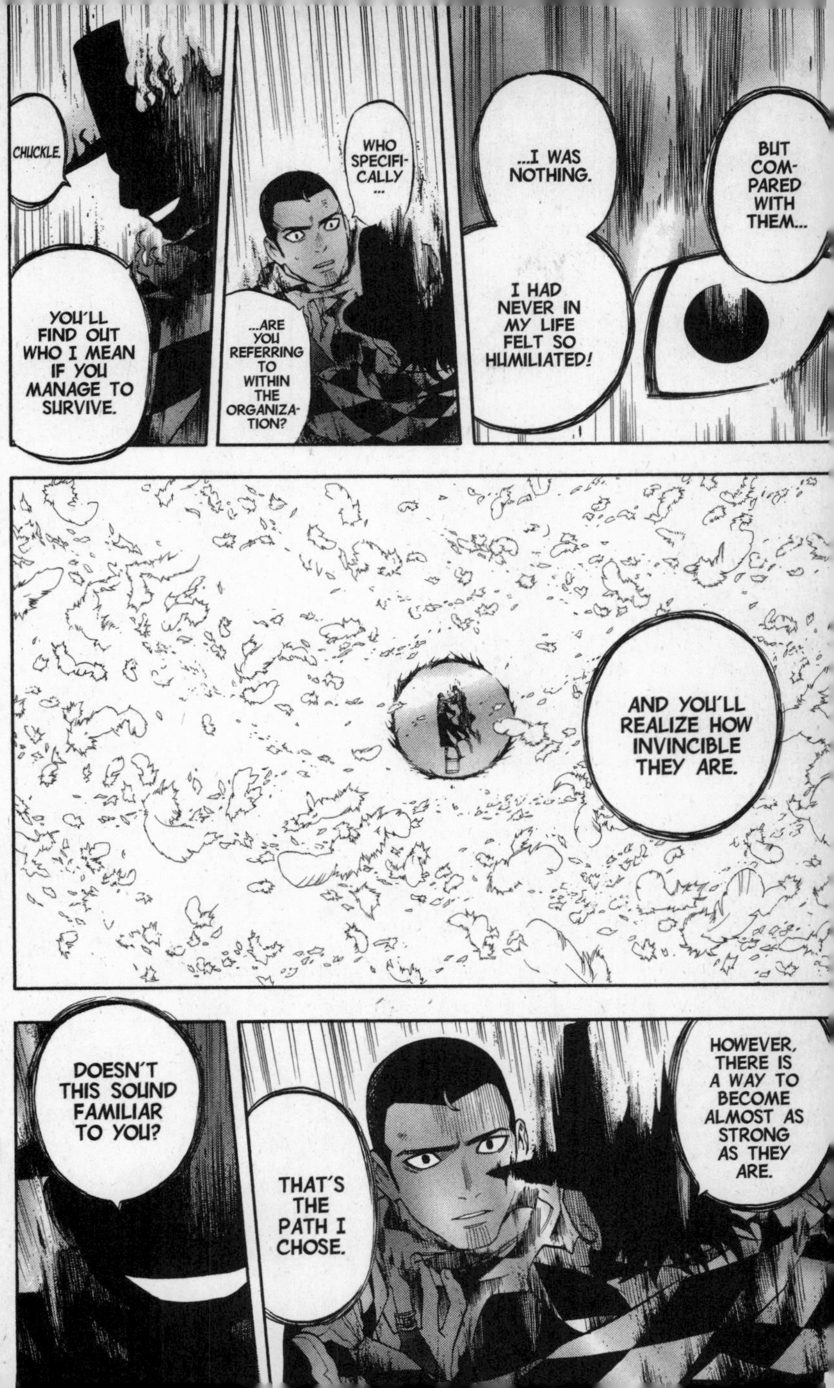
BUT COM-PARED WITH THEM...
...I WAS NOTHING.
I HAD NEVER IN MY LIFE FELT SO HUMILIATED!
WHO SPECIFI-CALLY ...
...ARE YOU REFERRING TO WITHIN THE ORGANIZA-TION?
CHUCKLE.
YOU'LL FIND OUT WHO I MEAN IF YOU MANAGE TO SURVIVE.
AND YOU'LL REALIZE HOW INVINCIBLE THEY ARE.
HOWEVER, THERE IS A WAY TO BECOME ALMOST AS STRONG AS THEY ARE.
THAT'S THE PATH I CHOSE.
DOESN'T THIS SOUND FAMILIAR TO YOU?

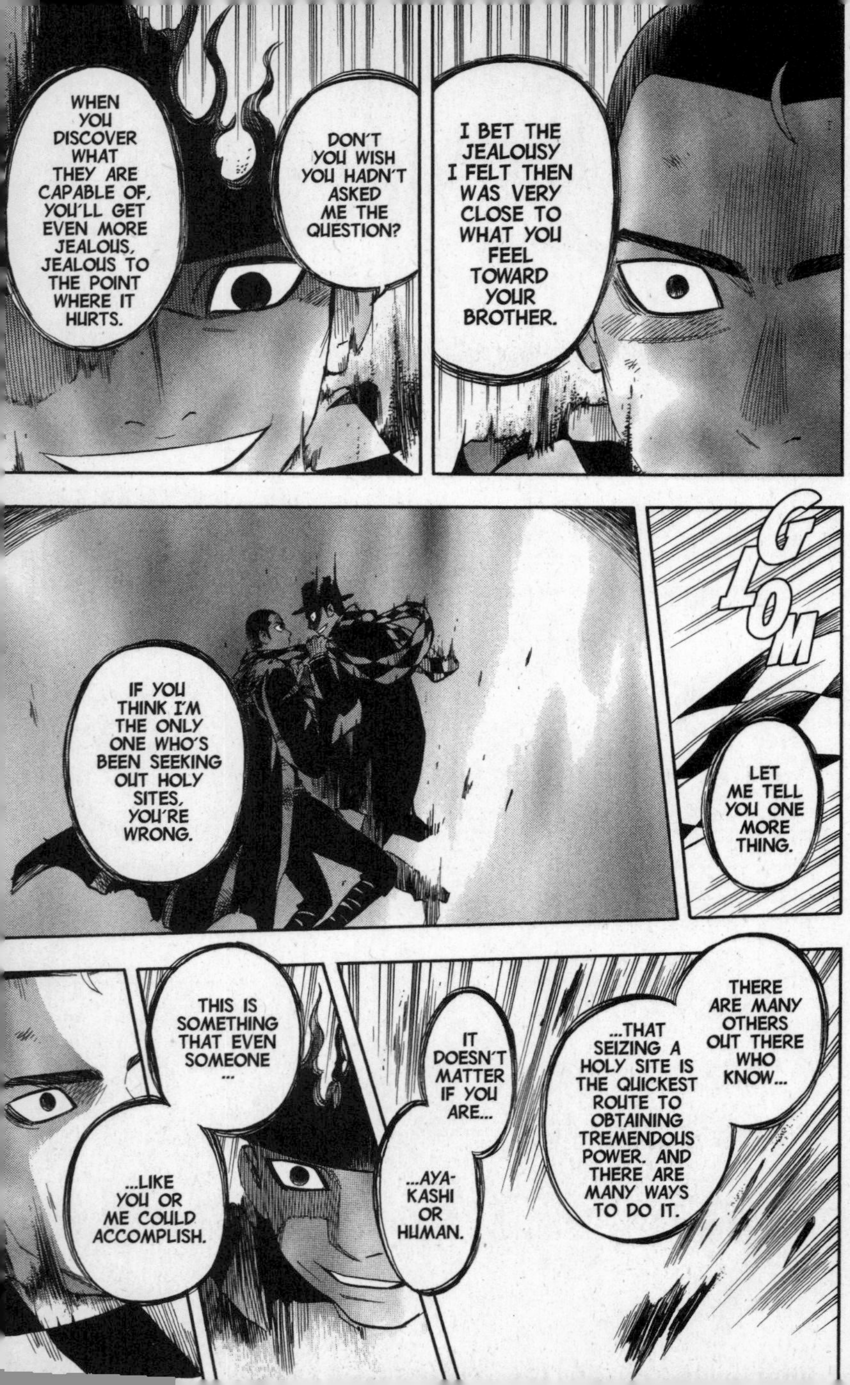
I BET THE JEALOUSY I FELT THEN WAS VERY CLOSE TO WHAT YOU FEEL TOWARD YOUR BROTHER.
DON'T YOU WISH YOU HADN'T ASKED ME THE QUESTION?
WHEN YOU DISCOVER WHAT THEY ARE CAPABLE OF, YOU'LL GET EVEN MORE JEALOUS, JEALOUS TO THE POINT WHERE IT HURTS.
GLOM
LET ME TELL YOU ONE MORE THING.
IF YOU THINK I'M THE ONLY ONE WHO'S BEEN SEEKING OUT HOLY SITES, YOU'RE WRONG.
THERE ARE MANY OTHERS OUT THERE WHO KNOW...
...THAT SEIZING A HOLY SITE IS THE QUICKEST ROUTE TO OBTAINING TREMENDOUS POWER. AND THERE ARE MANY WAYS TO DO IT.
IT DOESN'T MATTER IF YOU ARE...
...AYAKASHI OR HUMAN.
THIS IS SOMETHING THAT EVEN SOMEONE ...
...LIKE YOU OR ME COULD ACCOMPLISH.

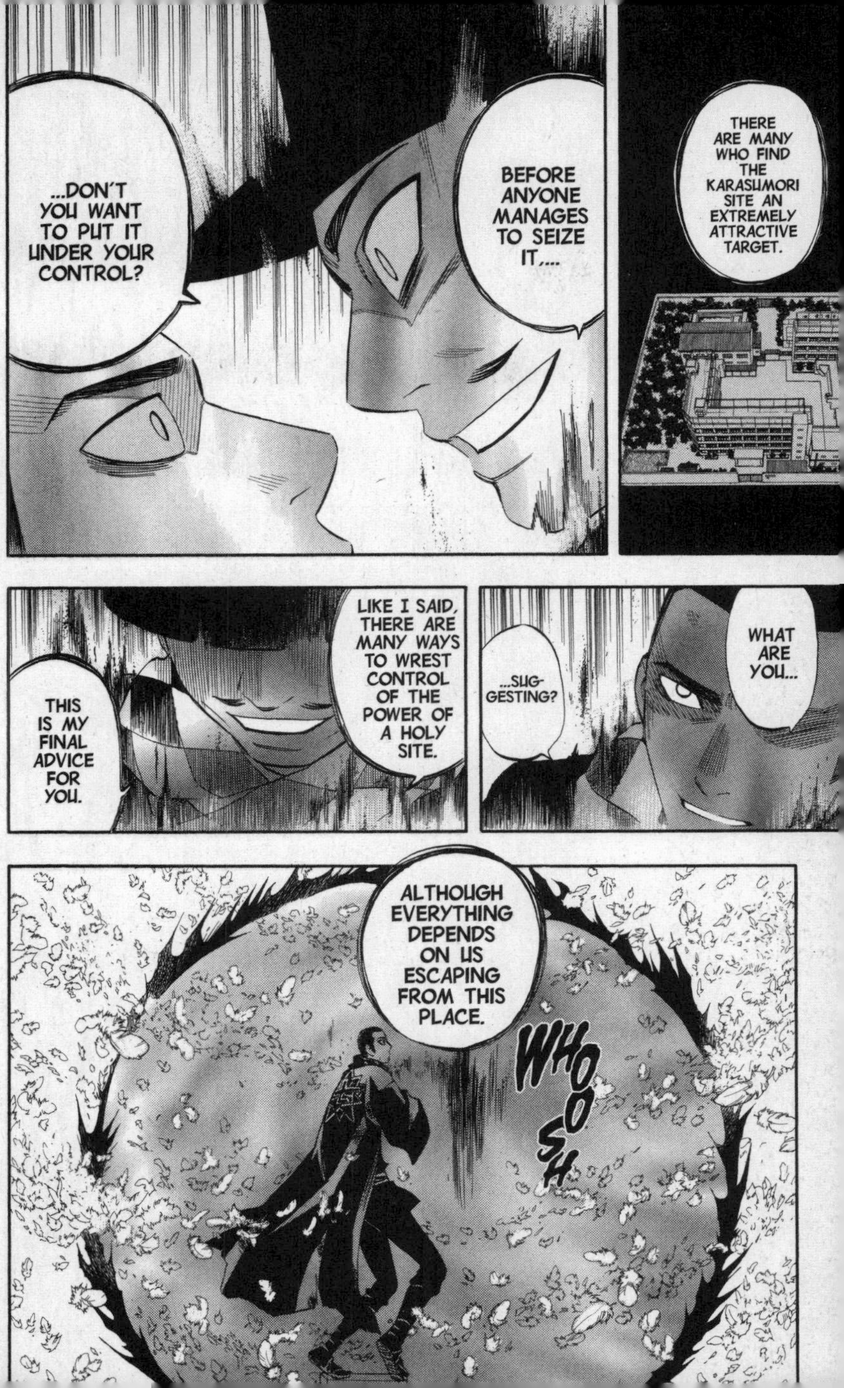
THERE ARE MANY WHO FIND THE KARASUMORI SITE AN EXTREMELY ATTRACTIVE TARGET.
BEFORE ANYONE MANAGES TO SEIZE IT,...
...DON'T YOU WANT TO PUT IT UNDER YOUR CONTROL?
WHAT ARE YOU...
...SUG-GESTING?
LIKE I SAID, THERE ARE MANY WAYS TO WREST CONTROL OF THE POWER OF A HOLY SITE.
THIS IS MY FINAL ADVICE FOR YOU.
ALTHOUGH EVERYTHING DEPENDS ON US ESCAPING FROM THIS PLACE.
WHOOSH

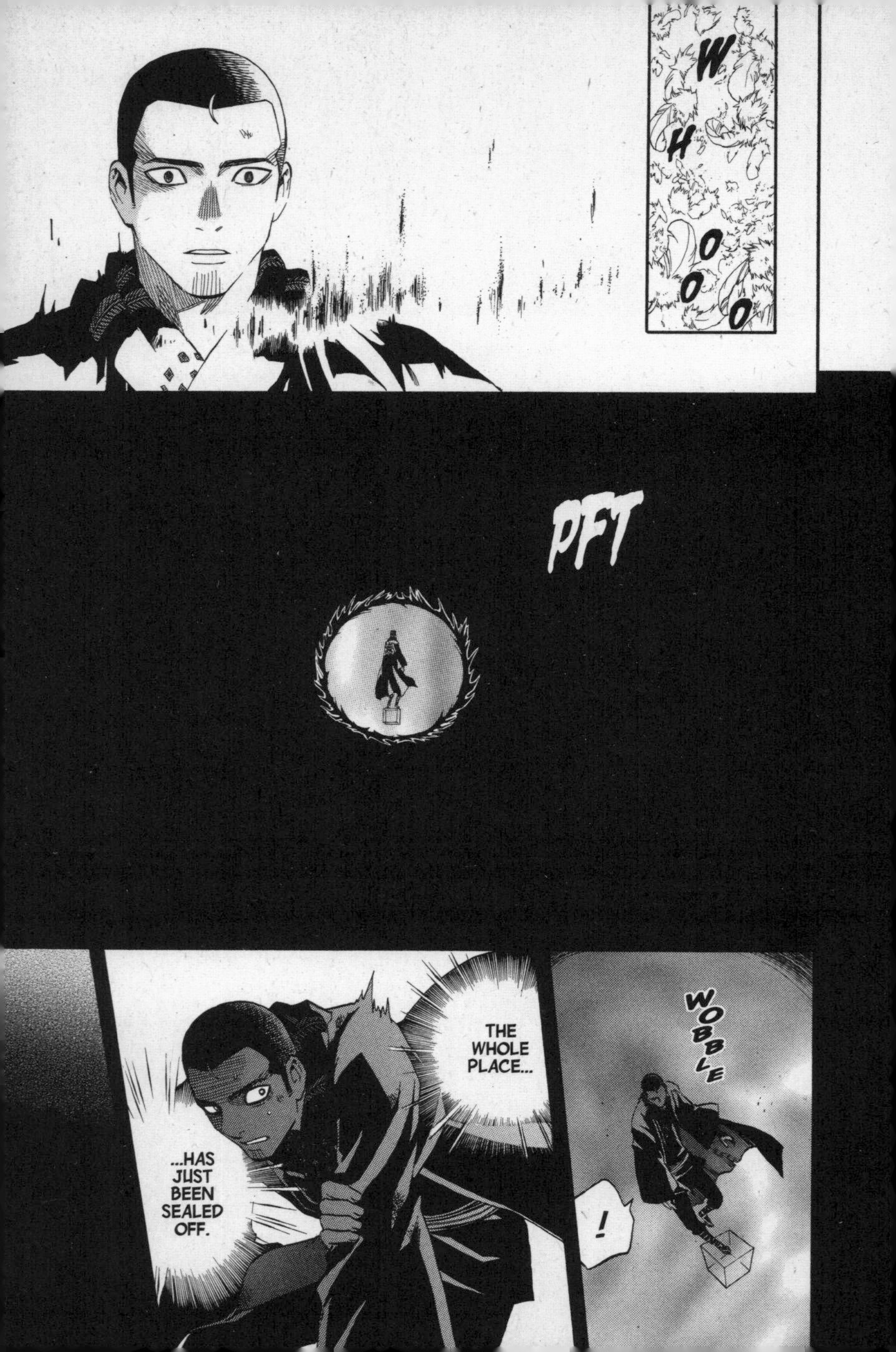
WHOOOO
PFT
WOBBLE
!
THE WHOLE PLACE...
...HAS JUST BEEN SEALED OFF.

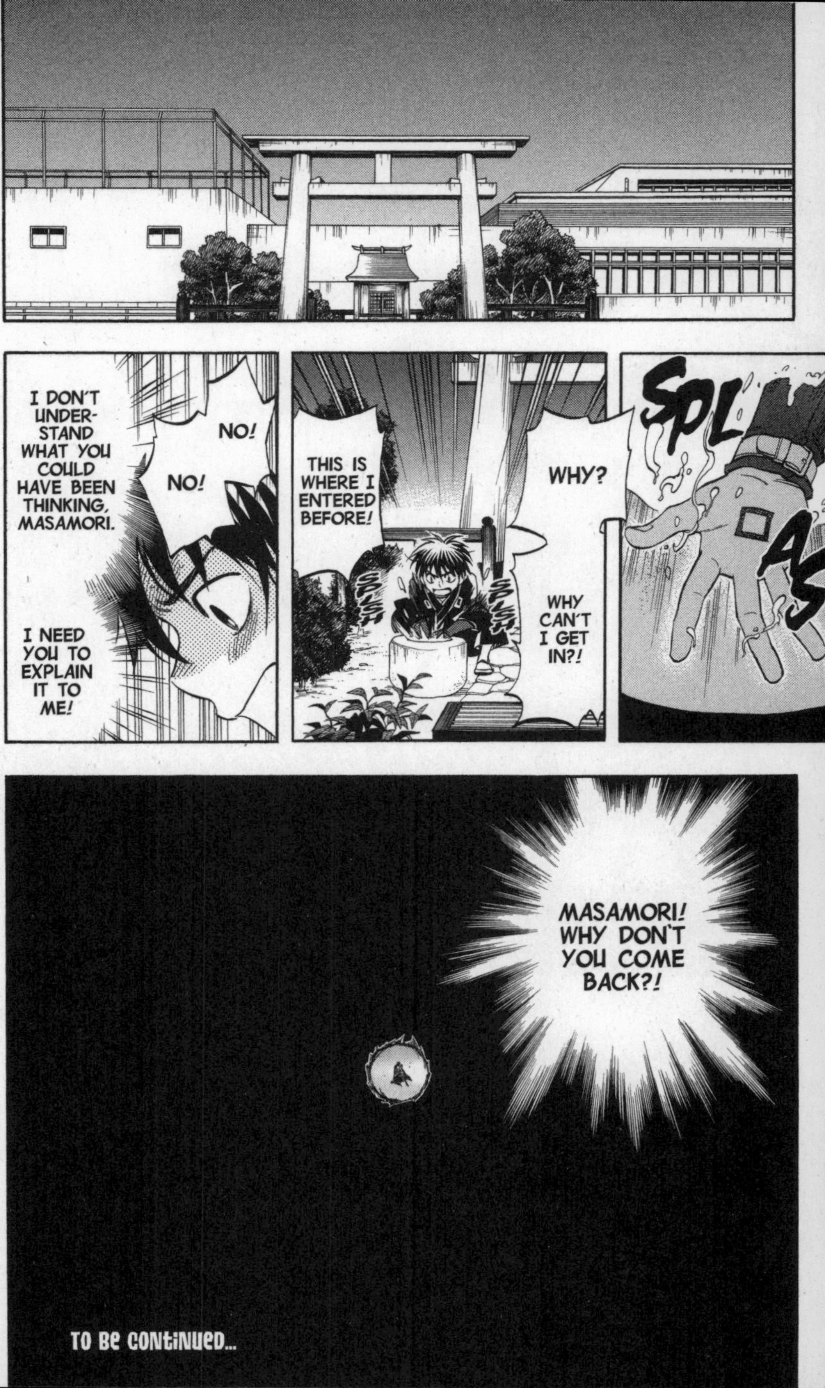
SPLASH
WHY?
WHY CAN'T I GET IN?!
THIS IS WHERE I ENTERED BEFORE!
SPLISH
SPLISH
NO!
NO!
I DON'T UNDERSTAND WHAT YOU COULD HAVE BEEN THINKING, MASAMORI.
I NEED YOU TO EXPLAIN IT TO ME!
MASAMORI! WHY DON'T YOU COME BACK?!
TO BE CONTINUED...

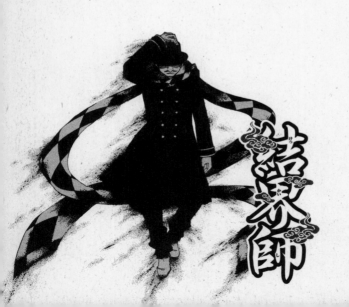

結界師

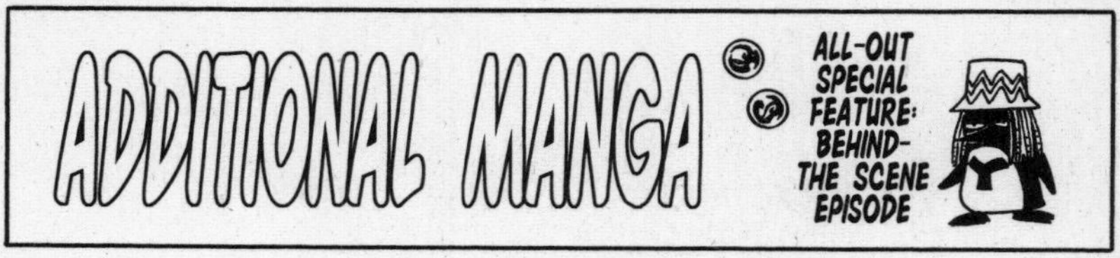
ADDITIONAL MANGA ③ ⑤
ALL-OUT SPECIAL FEATURE: BEHIND-THE SCENE EPISODE

UNTOLD STORY OF A NEW CHARACTER !!

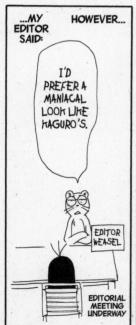

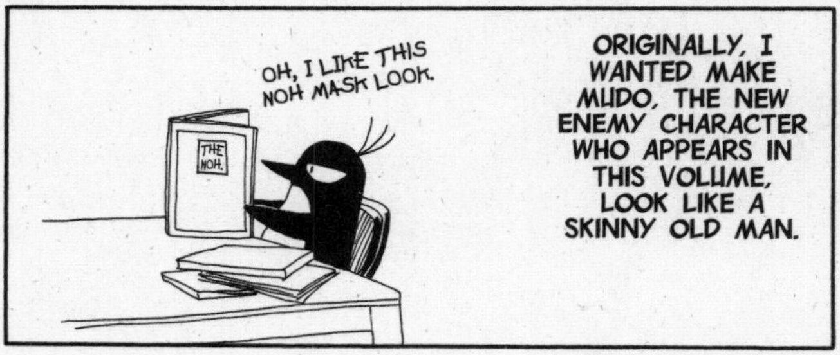
ORIGINALLY, I WANTED MAKE MUDO, THE NEW ENEMY CHARACTER WHO APPEARS IN THIS VOLUME, LOOK LIKE A SKINNY OLD MAN.
OH, I LIKE THIS NOH MASK LOOK.
THE NOH.

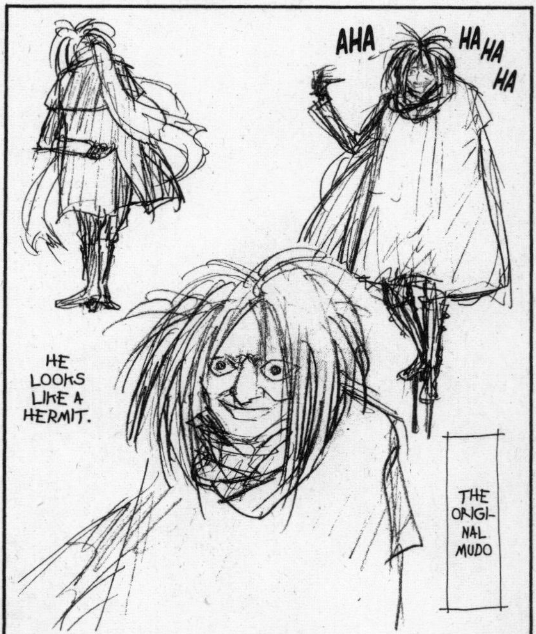
AHA
HA HA HA HA
HE LOOKS LIKE A HERMIT.
THE ORIGI-NAL MUDO

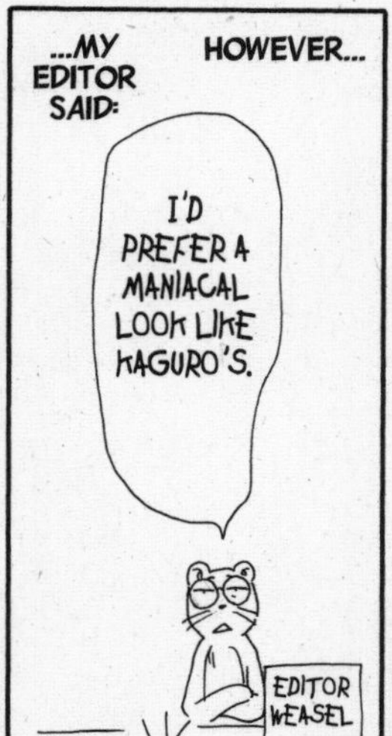
HOWEVER...
...MY EDITOR SAID:
I'D PREFER A MANIACAL LOOK LIKE KAGURO'S.
EDITOR WEASEL
EDITORIAL MEETING UNDERWAY

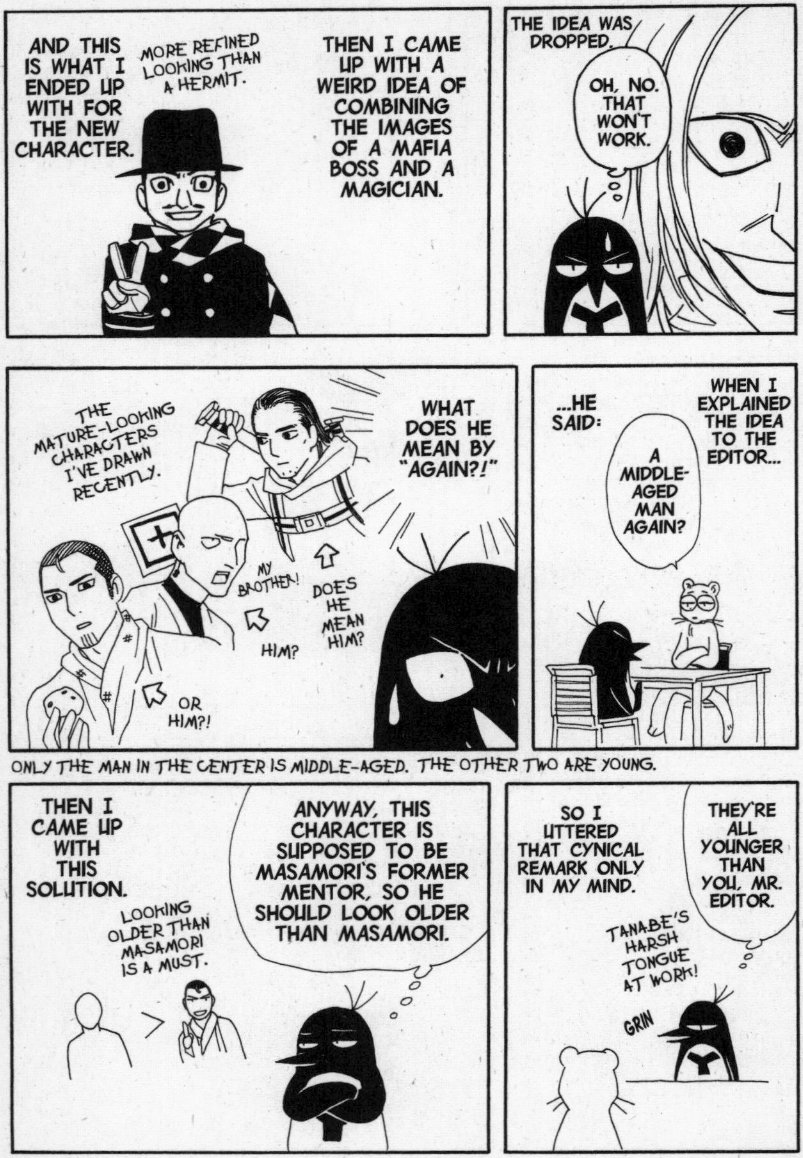
THE IDEA WAS DROPPED.
OH, NO. THAT WON'T WORK.
AND THIS IS WHAT I ENDED UP WITH FOR THE NEW CHARACTER.
MORE REFINED LOOKING THAN A HERMIT.
THEN I CAME UP WITH A WEIRD IDEA OF COMBINING THE IMAGES OF A MAFIA BOSS AND A MAGICIAN.
WHEN I EXPLAINED THE IDEA TO THE EDITOR...
...HE SAID:
A MIDDLE-AGED MAN AGAIN?
WHAT DOES HE MEAN BY "AGAIN?!"
THE MATURE-LOOKING CHARACTERS I'VE DRAWN RECENTLY.
DOES HE MEAN HIM?
MY BROTHER!
HIM?
OR HIM?!
ONLY THE MAN IN THE CENTER IS MIDDLE-AGED. THE OTHER TWO ARE YOUNG.
THEY'RE ALL YOUNGER THAN YOU, MR. EDITOR.
SO I UTTERED THAT CYNICAL REMARK ONLY IN MY MIND.
TANABE'S HARSH TONGUE AT WORK!
GRIN
THEN I CAME UP WITH THIS SOLUTION.
ANYWAY, THIS CHARACTER IS SUPPOSED TO BE MASAMORI'S FORMER MENTOR, SO HE SHOULD LOOK OLDER THAN MASAMORI.
LOOKING OLDER THAN MASAMORI IS A MUST.
>

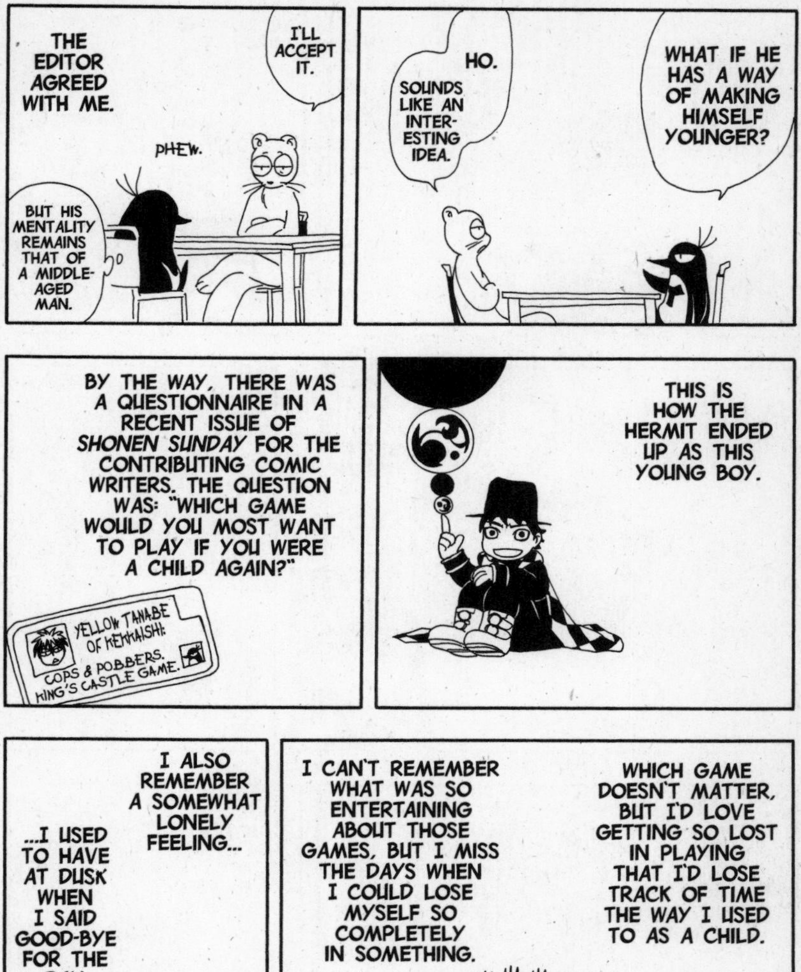
WHAT IF HE HAS A WAY OF MAKING HIMSELF YOUNGER?
HO.
SOUNDS LIKE AN INTERESTING IDEA.
I'LL ACCEPT IT.
THE EDITOR AGREED WITH ME.
PHEW.
BUT HIS MENTALITY REMAINS THAT OF A MIDDLE-AGED MAN.
THIS IS HOW THE HERMIT ENDED UP AS THIS YOUNG BOY.
BY THE WAY, THERE WAS A QUESTIONNAIRE IN A RECENT ISSUE OF *SHONEN SUNDAY* FOR THE CONTRIBUTING COMIC WRITERS. THE QUESTION WAS: "WHICH GAME WOULD YOU MOST WANT TO PLAY IF YOU WERE A CHILD AGAIN?"
YELLOW TANABE OF KEKKAISHI:
COPS & ROBBERS. KING'S CASTLE GAME.
WHICH GAME DOESN'T MATTER, BUT I'D LOVE GETTING SO LOST IN PLAYING THAT I'D LOSE TRACK OF TIME THE WAY I USED TO AS A CHILD.
I CAN'T REMEMBER WHAT WAS SO ENTERTAINING ABOUT THOSE GAMES, BUT I MISS THE DAYS WHEN I COULD LOSE MYSELF SO COMPLETELY IN SOMETHING.
AHA HA HA HA
WAIT!
GOOD AT RUNNING
I ALSO REMEMBER A SOMEWHAT LONELY FEELING...
...I USED TO HAVE AT DUSK WHEN I SAID GOOD-BYE FOR THE DAY.
SEE YOU.

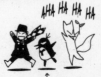

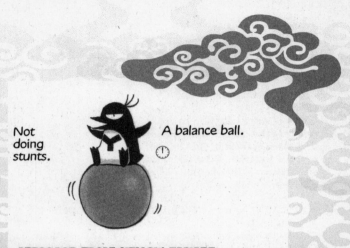

Not doing stunts.

A balance ball.

MESSAGE FROM YELLOW TANABE

To be honest, I'm not interested in fitness at all. But I do own a balance ball. I never get on it, but I kind of like seeing a big, round thing on the floor in my room.

KEKKAISHI

VOLUME 17

VIZ MEDIA EDITION

STORY AND ART BY YELLOW TANABE

Translation/Yuko Sawada
Touch-up Art & Lettering/Stephen Dutro
Cover Design & Graphic Layout/Izumi Evers & Julie Behn
Editor/Ian Robertson

Editor in Chief, Books/Alvin Lu
Editor in Chief, Magazines/Marc Weidenbaum
VP, Publishing Licensing/Rika Inouye
VP, Sales & Product Marketing/Gonzalo Ferreyra
VP, Creative/Linda Espinosa
Publisher/Hyoe Narita

KEKKAISHI 17 by Yellow TANABE © 2007 Yellow TANABE
All rights reserved.
Original Japanese edition published in 2007 by Shogakukan Inc., Tokyo.
The stories, characters and incidents mentioned in this publication are
entirely fictional.

Printed in the U.S.A.

Published by VIZ Media, LLC
P.O. Box 77010
San Francisco, CA 94107

VIZ Media Edition
10 9 8 7 6 5 4 3 2 1
First printing, May 2009

www.viz.com

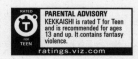

store.viz.com

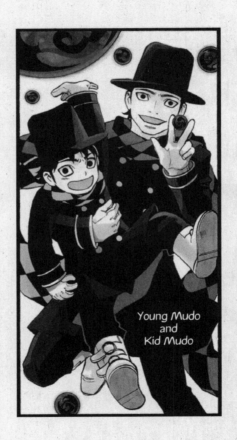

Young Mudo
and
Kid Mudo

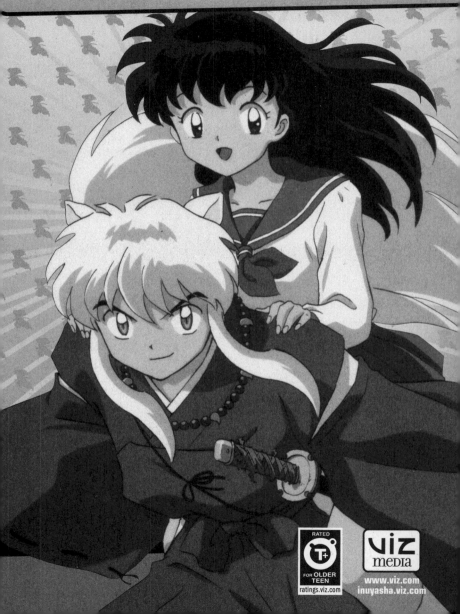

INUYASHA

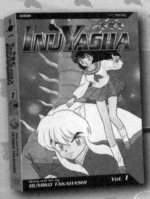

Read the action from the start with the original manga series

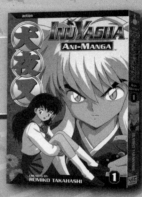

Full color adaptation of the popular TV series

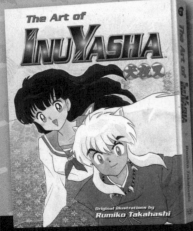

Art book with cel art, paintings, character profiles and more

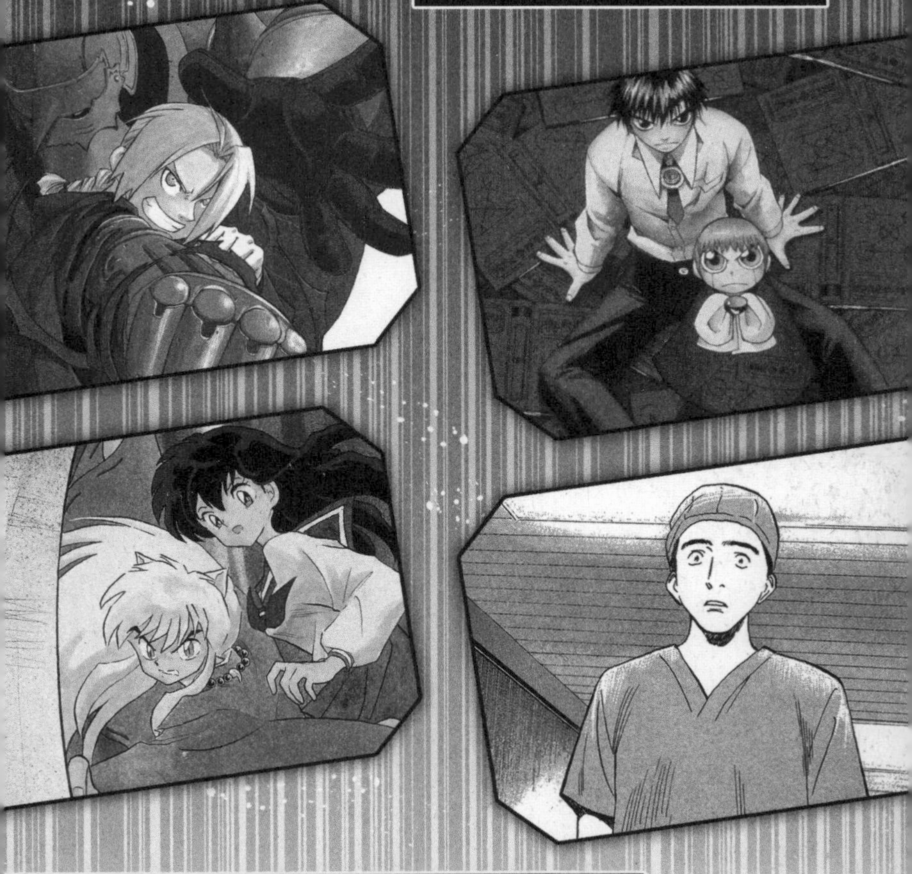